WHOLESALE JUSTICE

Wholesale Justice

CONSTITUTIONAL DEMOCRACY AND THE
PROBLEM OF THE CLASS ACTION LAWSUIT

Martin H. Redish

STANFORD LAW BOOKS
An imprint of Stanford University Press
Stanford, California

Stanford University Press
Stanford, California
© 2009 by the Board of Trustees of the
Leland Stanford Junior University.

Library of Congress Cataloging-in-Publication Data

Redish, Martin H.
    Wholesale justice : constitutional democracy and the problem of
the class action lawsuit / Martin H. Redish.
        p. cm.
    Includes bibliographical references and index.
    ISBN 978-0-8047-5274-9 (cloth : alk. paper)
    ISBN 978-0-8047-5275-6 (pbk. : alk. paper)
    1. Class actions (Civil procedure)—United States.
2. Constitutional law—United States.   I. Title.
KF8896.R438 2009
347.73'53—dc22   2008041874

Typeset by Thompson Type in 10/13 Galliard

For my family: Caren, Jessica, and Elisa

Contents

Acknowledgments

This book is the product of the last five years of scholarship and thought that I have devoted to a reconsideration of the first principles of the modern class action lawsuit. In these pages, I critique the class action procedure from historical, political, and constitutional perspectives. For the reasons I explore in detail, I find it seriously wanting on all counts.

I should emphasize that in no way am I opposed to the existence of a class action procedure. To the contrary, the class action represents an innovative means of resolving major legal problems that might otherwise overwhelm the judicial system. In doing so, however, it should not be permitted to overwhelm our nation's normative and constitutional commitments to democratic accountability, separation of powers, procedural due process, or individual autonomy.

Much of the book grew out of a number of articles I have published over the last five years, many of which were co-authored with former students who deserve substantial credit for their work. Chapter 2 is taken from Martin H. Redish, *Class Actions and the Democratic Difficulty: Rethinking the Intersection of Private Litigation and Public Goals,* 2003 U. Chi. L. Forum 71. Chapter 3 derives from Martin H. Redish & Uma Amuluru, *The Supreme Court and the Politization of the Federal Rules: Constitutional and Statutory Implications,* 90 Minn. L. Rev. 1303 (2006). Chapter 4 is based on Martin H. Redish & Clifford W. Berlow, *The Class Action as Political Theory,* 85 Wash. U. L. Rev. 753 (2007). Chapter 5 is a modified version of Martin H. Redish & Nathan D. Larsen, *Class Actions, Litigant Autonomy, and the Foundations of Procedural Due Process,* 95 Cal. L. Rev. 1573 (2007). Chapter 6 derives from Martin H. Redish & Andrianna D. Kastanek, *Settlement Class Actions, the Case-or-Controversy Requirement, and the Nature of the Adjudicatory Process,* 73 U. Chi. L. Rev. 545 (2006). To the extent the book reproduces all or portions of those articles, it does so with the permission on the reviews in question.

In addition to my co-authors, I owe a debt of gratitude to current or former students who provided extremely valuable research assistance. These include Matt Arnould, Sarah Davis, Alexis Garmey, Abby Mollen, and Dennis Murashko. David Van Zandt, Dean of Northwestern Law School, has made this book possible by his strong financial and moral support; I cannot thank him enough. Finally, my faculty assistant, Dan Truesdell, has been indispensable in the preparation of the manuscript. I owe him a great deal.

As always, however, no one has been more instrumental in helping me to accomplish anything more than my family: my wife, Caren, and my daughters, Jessica and Elisa. I cannot imagine life without the joy they have brought to me.

CHAPTER ONE

Introduction: Class Actions, Legal History, and Liberal Democracy

THE NATURE OF THE CLASS ACTION

The modern class action may appropriately be analogized to an iceberg. Just as only a small percentage of an iceberg appears above sea level, so too are most of those whose legal rights are determined in a class action proceeding largely invisible to the naked eye. A small number of active class representatives may litigate on behalf of hundreds, thousands, or even millions of absent class members. Though those absent class members for the most part remain passive throughout much of the legal proceeding, their rights will be determined as much as if they had themselves actively pursued their legal arguments in open court. If the class representatives succeed, absent class members—even if, on occasion, only as a theoretical matter—will share in the spoils of victory. If, however, those representatives fail, the claims of the absent class members will be legally obliterated by the doctrine of res judicata, just as are those of their class representatives.

The potential benefits of the class action, to both litigants and the legal system as a whole, are substantial. By simultaneously adjudicating the claims of large numbers of litigants, the class proceeding may achieve justice without overwhelming the judicial system. By obtaining relief for many plaintiffs whose claims are insufficiently large to economically justify individual litigation, the class proceeding may simultaneously achieve compensation for injured victims and help police widespread governmental or corporate misconduct that could otherwise escape effective legal regulation. But while ice provides a strong metaphor for the class action, in a different way so does fire. Like fire, the modern class action may give rise to as much harm as good; if not properly controlled it may wreak havoc on the legal system and the values that underlie it. Some have charged that the class proceeding has often been employed as a form of legalized blackmail, by which an unscrupulous group of plaintiffs' attorneys effectively extort money from large companies by threatening their very existence with business-crushing class awards. Others have pointed to the danger of a perverse kind of "race to the bottom," potentially associated with the modern class action, where potential defendants have "sold" their cooperation to the lowest bidding plaintiffs' attorney in the shaping of a class-wide settlement.

For the most part, this debate has taken the form of legal argumentation—that is, by reference to the text of the governing procedural rule and the comparative costs and benefits for both the adjudication of claims and the legal system as a whole. The subject of class actions is taught in civil procedure courses, not in courses in constitutional law or political theory. Law students generally learn that the class action is a complex joinder device that can serve as a powerful check on governmental or corporate excess or illegality. It is unlikely, however, that they are often asked to view the class action device from the broader perspectives of constitutional or political theory.[1] The purpose of this book is to undertake just such an inquiry, and to draw a number of valuable lessons for the structure and viability of the modern class action.

CLASS ACTIONS, DEMOCRATIC THEORY, AND THE COLLECTIVIST-INDIVIDUALIST TENSION

Class action scholars have themselves only rarely acknowledged the political and constitutional implications of the procedure, and when they have done so they have generally either misused, misunderstood, or improperly manipulated the theoretical impact of the process.[2] Yet in important ways the class action implicates many of the most foundational aspects of the nation's constitutional and political structure. This is true when viewed from the perspectives of both the participants in the process (what I call the "micro" perspective) and society as a whole (the "macro" perspective).

From the micro perspective, if misused the class action gives rise to an inherent collectivist-individualist tension. It is important to keep in mind that a lawsuit does not "arise" under Rule 23 of the Federal Rules of Civil Procedure, which governs class actions in the federal courts. The legal rights to be adjudicated, rather, are substantively created by some recognized lawmaking authority—a legislative body, a court, or the Constitution. For the most part, these rights, in their pristine form, are vested by the appropriate lawmaking authority in the individual. The class action collectivizes adjudication of those substantive rights, often revoking—either legally or practically—the individual right holder's ability to control the protection or vindication of his rights through resort to the legal process. Thus, the more freely available the collectivizing impact of the class action, the less opportunity the individual litigant will have to control the vindication of his substantive rights.[3] Though rarely either acknowledged or explored by court or scholar, this inherent tension threatens to undermine both political and constitutional values that place significant weight on preservation and protection of the individual's integrity and autonomy—particularly the autonomy of participation in the democratic processes as a means of protecting his own interests.

From the macro perspective, the class action device could substantially undermine basic notions of democratic accountability by indirectly (and, often, furtively) transforming the essential nature of the substantive rights being enforced. Under the guise of procedure, class actions often effect dramatic alterations in the DNA of the underlying substantive law. The result—whether intended or not—is a form of confusion or even deception of the electorate, which is likely unaware that the essence of the governing substantive law has been altered because the alteration has occurred under the guise of procedural modification. Substantive law is altered, not through resort to traditionally recognized democratic procedures but rather by what is effectively a procedural shell game.[4] Moreover, in certain of its modern manifestations the class action may undermine the traditional restraints that the Constitution imposes on the judicial process, by threatening core elements of the adversary system that are central to the adjudicatory process.[5]

My examination focuses on the distinction between micro and macro theories. On the micro level, the democratic theory perspective considers the extent to which the focus of liberal democratic thought should be the autonomy and integrity of the individual as a free-willed participant in the governing process. Not all versions of democratic theory are grounded in a belief in the value of the individual. The fact remains, however, that a democratic society is ultimately made up of individuals, and the theory of liberal individualism finds implicit in the commitment to government by the people a fundamental level of respect for and belief in the worth of the individual as an integral whole. The liberal model of democracy, as I perceive it, is premised on a synthesis of the instrumental value of developing the individual's intellectual and moral capacities to their fullest,[6] and a foundational commitment to the worth of the individual. It values the self-realization of the individual, not just the ability of the community, to self-determine.[7] Our nation's combined constitutional commitment to representative government and a Bill of Rights that preserves a sphere of behavioral autonomy for the individual demonstrates how the two elements of liberal democracy complement each other as a matter of political theory.

To believe in the value of individual autonomy, it must be emphasized, is not necessarily to imply an unbending commitment to individualist libertarianism in all of its conceivable applications. One can quite reasonably draw a dichotomy between *process-based* autonomy and *substantive* autonomy. The former focuses exclusively on the ability of the individual to control her participation in the governing process, while the latter concerns an individual's ability to control most aspects of one's life. It is the former, not the latter, that is central to liberal democratic thought.[8] The democratic process cannot function effectively unless the individual participants in the process have autonomy in making most choices about the nature of their participation in the process—or *meta* decision making, as it might be called. The individual does not necessarily possess complete insulation from the *results* of the democratic process—that is, substantive laws, enacted through the democratic process, that regulate or proscribe specified private behavior. Except in the most compelling circumstances, however, the individual must be able to decide how he will seek to influence the governing process for the purpose of either protecting or fostering his own personal interests or advancing ideological goals he deems important.[9] Resort to the judicial process for the purpose of protecting private interests is appropriately included within the broader category of governmental processes open, in a democracy, to individual participation. No one can doubt that the adjudication in the courts is as much a part of the governing process as are the actions of the legislative or executive branches. When a private individual resorts to the courts as a means of vindicating his legal rights, his meta-autonomy is triggered in much the same manner as when the individual seeks to influence the governing process through exercise of his First Amendment right of free expression. By collectivizing—often forcibly—the litigation process, the class action procedure threatens core notions of the process-based autonomy that is central to liberal democratic thought. The class action, then, gives rise to at least a prima facie tension between legally imposed collectivization and democratic meta decision making autonomy on the part of the individual.

On occasion, the Supreme Court has recognized that the due process clauses of the Fifth Amendment and Fourteenth Amendment[10] impose restrictions on government's ability to employ the class action procedure. However, this concern has focused exclusively on the *paternalistic* concern that those representing absent class members do so fairly and fully.[11] At no point has the Supreme Court provided any meaningful exploration of the autonomy interests of absent class members that are threatened by use of class procedures.

A number of respected commentators appear to have implicitly anticipated the collectivist-individualist tension and attempted to circumvent it by ignoring or transforming the inherently individualist nature of the substantive claims adjudicated in a class proceeding. They have sought to view the class, in most situations, not as an aggregation of distinct, individually held claims but rather as something that, for the most part, it clearly is not: an "entity," which exists as an organism conceptually distinct from the individual claims of the class members.[12] Were this mythical transformation actually to be accomplished, any concern for individual autonomy would be rendered all but non-existent. The individual's interest, after all, would then exist solely as one element within a larger organic and indivisible entity. But in legal reality, the class is generally not an entity at all. It is, rather, a litigation-based amalgamation of numerous individually held claims that procedurally lend themselves to a process of collective adjudication. In their pristine substantive form, the rights being amalgamated are individually held. Indeed, where class member claims exist solely as part of a pre-existing entity, they already receive special procedural treatment under separate provisions of the Federal Rules of Civil Procedure.[13]

THE ORIGINS OF THE CLASS ACTION

A significant part of the problem may derive from confusion over the historical grounding of group litigation practice in general. Even a brief examination of this history reveals that while as a historical matter representative litigation was confined to what are, as a pre-litigation matter, substantively cohesive and interconnected groups, the modern class action did not take on its current structure, in which separately held individual claims are aggregated and simultaneously adjudicated in a representative manner, until the 1966 amendments to Rule 23 of the Federal Rules of Civil Procedure. Prior to that dramatic modern alteration in representative litigation, the only representative litigations in which passive and absent class members could be legally bound by the result were those involving cohesively tied group rights pre-litigation. This dramatic shift can be established by describing three stages in group adjudication prior to the 1966 amendments: (1) medieval and post-medieval English practice; (2) early American practice as evidenced by the writings of Justice Joseph Story and the early Equity Rules, and (3) the 1938 version of Rule 23 of the Federal Rules of Civil Procedure.

Group Litigation and Early English Practice

While the origins of group litigation are to be found in the legal practice in medieval England, the only form of *passive*-collective litigation (i.e., litigation in which wholly passive non-participants are treated as parties) recognized during that period or the period immediately following involved situations in which the substantive rights in question were group held. In other words, in the only situations in which non-participating individual litigants could be bound, the individuals whose rights were at stake in the litigation were those whose rights and interests were intertwined in the form of a recognized group *that existed pre-litigation.* It is important to understand the fundamental differences between litigation involving cohesive and legally recognized groups that exist, in legally recognized form, pre-litigation, and group litigation involving the aggregation of pre-existing individual claims. In the former situation, the substantive rights are vested by the appropriate lawmaking authority in recognized groups at the outset. In the latter situation, in contrast, the lawgiver has created individually held rights, and the collectivization of those rights occurs entirely at the stage of litigation.

Acceptance of representative litigation in medieval England is understandable when placed in the context of the social and political landscape at the time. English society was grounded in notions of collective action.[14] Whether by necessity in agrarian villages or voluntarily in the towns, individuals generally functioned as parts of established groups. In villages, collective organization was a natural consequence of the realities of the culture and obligations of "villeinage."[15] "Villeins" were the primary occupants in villages. They were bound to a manor and its lord. Their work on the manorial farms inured, for the most part, to the lord's benefit, so villeins were forced to labor on the common farmland for their sustenance. To ensure productivity and allocate the work fairly, villages developed complex systems of localized laws, specifying the villeins' duties both to their lord and to each other. They formed a type of local government to administer the laws. As a result, a form of entity rule emerged. The structure was reinforced by other commonly held obligations, such as membership in a frankpledge group. Members of the group assumed responsibility for each others' behavior.[16] When the interests and obligations of individuals in relation to outside parties flowed exclusively from their membership in a specific group, group members logically stood in identical legal posture with the outside party. Not surprisingly, groups were natural litigation entities. By the seventeenth century, class group litigation was largely confined to rural agrarian settings. Roughly at that point, two new types of litigating groups emerged: joint stock companies and friendly societies. Again, both were defined, legally and socially, outside the litigation process.

Early American Practice

Justice Joseph Story's conception of representative litigation guided American use of the practice roughly until the 1966 amendment to Rule 23 of the Federal Rules of Civil Procedure. He noted several instances in which class adjudication was appropriate, including suits by members of a voluntary society or unincorporated body of proprietors on behalf of the entire organization.[17] While he also included several other categories, such as individual rights claimed in commonly held property, all of his categories shared a common theme: a substantive connection, *independent of the litigation,* between the representative party and those represented.

In 1833, the Supreme Court adopted Equity Rule 48. That provision stated:

> Where the parties on either side are very numerous and can not, without manifest inconvenience and oppressive delays in the suit, be all brought before it, the Court in its discretion may dispense with making all of them parties, and may proceed in the suit, having sufficient parties before it to represent all of the adverse interest of the plaintiffs and the defendants in the suit properly before it. But, in such cases, the decree shall be without prejudice to the rights and claims of all the absent parties.[18]

While by its terms the rule was not confined to pre-existing group settings, it effectively defeated the purpose of group litigation by prohibiting any res judicata impact of the decision on absent and passive class members. The only "true" form of representative litigation, then, continued to involve those suits involving group-held rights that had been recognized at the pre-litigation stage. Thus, through the early part of the twentieth century the courts confined representative litigation almost exclusively to the situations identified by Justice Story in 1820: cases involving pre-litigation groups and cases involving separate claims into a common fund.

The Original Rule 23

The original version of Rule 23 recognized three categories of class actions: true, hybrid, and spurious. "True" class actions were those in which the substantive rights of the class members were held jointly or *commonly,* as opposed to *severally.* "Hybrid" class actions were those in which the class members held rights severally but adjudication concerned rights in the same property. "Spurious" class proceedings were those in which the rights were held severally where there also existed a common question of law or fact and common relief was sought. In the case of spurious class actions, however, a judgment would have no res judicata effect on the rights of the absent class members. The only legal consequence of an aptly named spurious class action was that absent class members could freely intervene as active parties in the adjudication.[19]

Scholars and jurists readily acknowledged that the supposed distinctions between joint and several rights—the basis on which the class action categories were distinguished—"proved obscure and uncertain."[20] The distinction focused upon "the technical or abstract character of the rights or obligations."[21] Whatever confusion may have plagued the joint-several dichotomy, however, the fact remains that the standard employed by the original Rule 23 to determine the viability of the federal class action referenced a distinction that concerned the nature of the rights in their pre-litigation form, untied to the class action procedure.[22] In other words, the conceptual dichotomy between rights that were joint and those that were several had not been developed originally for the purpose of shaping class adjudication. It had developed, instead, in the context of tort-based and property rights—both concepts that concerned the shaping and regulation of pre-litigation primary behavior, rather than the structure of litigation practice. While hybrid classes, like their predecessors in equity practice, did not turn exclusively on the joint-several dichotomy, they, too, were classified on the basis of the pre-litigation substantive nature of the rights—individually held in rem claims in the same property.

One form of what could be described as "group" litigation that differed fundamentally from the bulk of class litigation did exist: the so-called "bill of peace," in which numerous individually held in personam claims of disparate claimants were resolved collectively. However, the process employed in the bill of peace differed dramatically from the classic form of group litigation. Unlike traditional group litigation, which was *representative* in nature, in the bill of peace each claimant's legal interests were represented individually before the court. Thus, while the adjudicatory process was conducted simultaneously for all participants, the interests of passive claimants were not represented by active and participating claimants. Rather, each claimant whose rights were bound by the process was actively and independently involved in the adjudication.[23]

The inherently collective nature of the substantive rights adjudicated in traditional class litigation is far more than a mere historical oddity. Indeed, it has enormous implications for the political and constitutional theory of the modern class action. When the nature of the individual claimant's substantive right that is the subject of group litigation is inherently collective, there can be no legitimate moral or constitutional claim of process-based individual autonomy in choosing how to protect or legally vindicate those rights. The most that either the political guarantee of liberal democracy or the constitutional guarantee of due process can assure in such contexts is that those group members represent the group's interests fully and fairly protect the rights of the absent group members.

When the substantive rights at stake are vested by the appropriate law-making authority—legislature, court, or Constitution—in the individual, the political dictates of liberal theory and the constitutional dictates of procedural due process require considerably more than a paternalistic assurance of adequate representation. In a liberal constitutional democracy, the individual is guaranteed the right to protect his or her property from governmental processes designed to abrogate those interests. This is true as a matter of abstract political and constitutional theory, even where the actual value of the property interest involved is relatively minimal.[24] A commitment to process-based individualism requires at least a prima facie assumption of individual autonomy in deciding how and whether to protect the individual's rights by resort to the judicial process. The constitutionally dictated notion of a litigant's "day in court" as a prerequisite to the legal extinction of individual rights has long served as a corollary to the law of res judicata and collateral estoppel.[25] No other result would be consistent with recognition of the individual's autonomy and integrity that is central to the notion of liberal democracy.[26] Once the class action procedure was altered to permit—indeed, on occasion even require—the group adjudication of purely individually held rights, the stakes for both the political theory of liberal democracy and the constitutional theory of procedural due process were correspondingly altered in fundamental ways.

The 1966 Amendment to Rule 23

In 1966, the Federal Rules Advisory Committee dramatically altered the structure, purpose, and rationale of the class action rule. As part of a major revision of many of the multiparty devices, the Committee rejected the formalistic abstractions that had plagued the earlier version of Rule 23 in favor of a far more pragmatically based set of distinctions.[27] While those who amended the rule appeared not to have focused on the point, in rejecting the joint-several dichotomy the Committee effected a dramatic change in the substantive-procedural intersection central to the class action procedure. No longer would the availability of class action treatment turn on a reference to pre-litigation characteristics of the legal relationship among class members. After the amendment, that determination would be grounded purely in considerations affecting either the nature of the relief sought or the fairness or efficiency of the litigation process. Under revised Rule 23, in addition to satisfying requirements concerning the numerosity of the class and the adequacy and representativeness of the named class members,[28] the class must fall within one of four categories of cases. Under Rule 23(b)(1)(A), a class may be certified if individual actions could result in conflicting obligations on the part of the party opposing the class. Under Rule 23(b)(1)(B), a class may be certified if absent class members' interests could be undermined by separate actions. Rule 23(b)(2) authorizes a class action when the party opposing the class has acted in a manner generally applicable to the class as a whole, thereby justifying predominantly injunctive relief. Under Rule 23(b)(3), a class may be certified if common issues predominate and the class is found to be manageable and a superior method of resolution.

Unlike the group litigation of medieval English practice, early American practice, or even the joint-several dichotomy employed in the original Rule 23, none of these alternatives turns in any way on the nature of the pre-litigation intersection of the substantive rights of the individual class members. Rather, the substantive rights asserted in a modern class proceeding are, for the most part, individually held rights that, for reasons of fairness or procedural convenience, have been grouped supposedly for procedural reasons, at the stage of litigation. Most forms of modern group litigation that could be considered analogous to earlier group practice, where the groups existed in substantive, pre-litigation form, are now governed by Federal Rules 23.1 and 23.2. The former concerns derivative actions brought by shareholders, and the latter actions relate to claims brought by unincorporated associations.

It has been suggested that the interests of claimants in (b)(1)(A), (b)(1)(B), and (b)(2) classes are, in fact, substantively intertwined, presumably much like those of participants in classic group litigation practice.[29] But while situations could be imagined where this could be the case, surely none of the Rule 23(b) provisions *requires* such a pre-litigation connection among substantive rights, and more than likely there will be none. The only necessary connection among the rights of (b)(1)(A) claimants, for example, is that the relief they demand from the party opposing the class is effectively indivisible: either the defendant is forced to provide the relief, or he is not; there is, as both a physical and legal matter, no alternative. In some of these instances, it is true, the rights of the absent claimants will be substantively tied in some way. In others, however, they will not. And even when those rights have some pre-litigation connection, it does not necessarily follow that they are held in common or substantively shared, rather than individually held.

Much the same is true of the claims of members of (b)(1)(B) classes. It is important to emphasize that these classes are by no means identical to the old "hybrid" classes described in the original version of Rule 23, where the rights, though individually held, were asserted into a common fund or piece of property. In a (b)(1)(B) class action, the substantive rights asserted by class members may well be individually held in personam claims against a defendant for tortious behavior aimed at all of them, when a limited insurance fund is available for compensation purposes. In such situations, individual suits may well threaten the interests of individual plaintiffs, for the simple reason that the earliest suits are likely to exhaust the limited fund, leaving the later plaintiffs effectively remediless. Because these individual suits need not be substantively held in common, the (b)(1)(B) category is in no sense confined to the assertion of commonly held in rem claims in property.

More importantly, there exists absolutely no basis on which to assume some special pre-litigation fiduciary-like relationship among the class members in either of these modern categories. Instead, class members will usually be linked by nothing more than substantive parallelism or procedural fortuity. Indeed, on occasion—as where claims exceed the limited funds available—antagonism among claimants, who are competing for resources that cannot possibly satisfy all of them, may well exist. The key point, for present purposes, is that the categorizations adopted in the revised Rule 23, unlike the prior forms of group litigation existing throughout Anglo American history,[30] were grounded not in some form of substantively shaped intertwining of rights, but rather on the basis of purely procedural concerns of fairness, efficiency, and convenience.

When Rule 23 was restructured in 1966, it appears that the drafters never fully considered or recognized the political and constitutional implications of their fundamental transformation in the nature of group litigation. While they did seek to satisfy the paternalistic dictates of due process traditionally associated with classic group litigation by inserting the typicality and adequacy of representation requirements of Rule 23(a),[31] and did require notice to absent class members and provide the option to individual class members of removal from the class in (b)(3) classes,[32] they failed to acknowledge even the prima facie compelling interest of individual litigant autonomy in controlling the course of litigation when individually held rights are at stake in the course of the adjudicatory process.

Recognition of the inherent tensions between the collectivist adjudicatory process of the class action and the values of individualism and autonomy that are central to both liberal political theory and procedural due process requires a substantial restructuring—though by no means abandonment—of the modern class action. Except in the relatively rare presence of truly compelling competing interests of procedural fairness, mandatory class actions (which currently include those authorized under (b)(1)(A), (b)(1)(B), and (b)(2)) should be held unconstitutional.[33] Moreover, class action procedure should generally be characterized by a requirement that class members who wish to waive their constitutional right to individualized control of the adjudication of their claims affirmatively *opt into* the class proceeding. In this sense, the class proceeding becomes analogous to a voluntary political association, where free-willed individuals join together to maximize the effectiveness of their individual rights to influence the results of governmental processes.[34] If there are any situations in which a considerably more passive opt-out procedure should be employed, it must be only in those cases in which the individual claims are so small as to make it reasonable to presume, ex ante, that the class members would deem individual pursuit of their claims impractical.[35]

MACRO DEMOCRATIC THEORY
AND THE MODERN CLASS ACTION

To this point, I have considered the implications of the modern class action for foundational notions of liberal individualism that are essential to modern liberal democratic thought. This aspect of democratic theory, as I have noted, may appropriately be referred to as micro democratic theory because it focuses on the importance of the individual and a system of individual rights to the viability of a liberal democratic society. But the class action has also on occasion been employed in a manner that threatens broader based notions of democratic thought, concerning the implicit but essential social contract of accountability that exists in a democratic society between the populace and its government.

While one could conceivably (albeit unwisely and in an important sense illogically, I believe) adopt a form of democracy that lacked foundational respect for the individual's worth, integrity, and autonomy, as a definitional matter a democratic society must possess a commitment to certain governmental forms and processes. Those who make basic normative choices of social and moral policy (at least those choices that have not been preempted by a form of counter-majoritarian constitutionalism) must at some level be representative of and accountable to those whom they govern. Absent compliance with this basic dictate, it is difficult to understand how a governing system could be labeled democratic at all.

If democracy means anything, those who are represented must have some basic notion of what it is that those who represent them are or are not doing as their governors. Otherwise, the ability of the populace to hold its elected representatives accountable at the next election will be rendered hollow indeed. Thus, were government to be able to enact laws in secret, or if legislators' votes on proposed legislation were kept confidential, the ability of the electorate to judge those whom it has elected would be significantly undermined. Probably even more harmful, however, would be governors' ability to adopt deceptive laws—that is, laws that purport to accomplish one result but in reality achieve a result very different from, or even the exact opposite of, what those laws purported to accomplish. Such legislative deception or manipulation surely contravenes core notions of democratic theory, whatever one thinks about the role of individualism as an element of democracy.[36]

There is, of course, nothing *inherently* deceptive about the use of class adjudication as a means of enforcing legislatively created substantive rights. However, in its modern form the procedure is dangerously susceptible to abusive practices that may well obfuscate under a procedural smokescreen a fundamental alteration in the nature of the substantive law sought to be enforced in a class proceeding. All substantive law that restricts citizen behavior necessarily contains two elements: (1) a behavioral proscription and (2) a remedy and/or punishment for violations of that proscription. The remedial element usually takes the form of criminal penalties (fines or imprisonment), civil or administrative penalties, or private victim compensation. Where the latter is invoked, the remedial element seeks simultaneously to achieve two distinct but mutually reinforcing goals: (1) making the victims whole and (2) punishing and deterring the violators. Where a class proceeding seeks damages for the purpose of enforcing a substantive legislative proscription against an alleged violator, the substantive remedial element being invoked necessarily takes the form of private compensation. However, when a class proceeding *purports* to be brought on behalf of a class of victims seeking compensation, but as a practical matter the individual damages are so small that absent class members are highly unlikely even to participate in a settlement or file a claim to a damage fund once the suit is finally resolved, the nature of the substantive law's remedial element has been fundamentally altered. Instead of compensating victims as dictated by controlling substantive law, the class proceeding effectively imposes an entirely different—and often far more politically controversial—remedial structure, what can best be labeled a "bounty hunter" remedial model. Here private class action plaintiffs' attorneys—individuals who themselves are not victims seeking to be made whole—sue as a type of legal vigilante to enforce substantive behavioral proscriptions against wrongdoers. In such situations the class exists, as a practical matter, solely for purposes of display. In reality, the plaintiffs' attorneys are the real parties in interest; they are the ones who institute and pursue the action and effectively are the only ones who benefit. The so-called class itself is all but comatose. Many class members are likely not even aware that they are plaintiffs in a major legal action, and the overwhelming majority will never even benefit directly from a successful prosecution.

When this situation is viewed from the perspective of macro democratic theory, the traditional response, made by many, that in any event the class action proceeding will have the beneficial effect of enforcing substantive laws and policing illegal behaviors largely misses the point. As already noted, the prohibitory element of substantive law is only one aspect of the underlying law that is being enforced. Often, the remedial element of the substantive law will be equally controversial. Under the guise of a procedural rule, these "faux" class actions have the inescapable, albeit indirect, impact of transforming substantive law containing a private compensatory remedy into a law that contains a bounty hunter enforcement mechanism. This is a potentially controversial result politically that has presumably never even been considered, much less formally adopted, by the lawmaking organ that promulgated the applicable substantive law in the first place.

Many today are uneasy about the ethics and legitimacy of class action plaintiff lawyers. Indeed, they have long been one of the focuses of the so-called "tort reform" movement.[37] Were the electorate to comprehend that these attorneys were effectively the *sole* beneficiaries of large damage law suits, and that the victims supposedly protected by the law in reality are often even unaware of the suits and benefit from them virtually not at all, at the very least it is difficult to predict whether a statute formally transforming controlling substantive law in such a manner would succeed politically. Yet faux class actions achieve exactly this result—albeit without any formal alteration in governing law and under the cloak of superficially neutral procedural implementation.

Will the electorate *always* be deceived in such situations? That is a complex empirical question that will be difficult to answer in every context. But surely the threat to the rule of law in such cases is sufficiently great that a democratic system cannot reasonably take such a chance. When the basis of the federal court's subject matter jurisdiction is diversity of citizenship,[38] added problems of judicial and political federalism arise. In such cases, the underlying substantive law is state created, and that law—whether in the form of statute or common law—universally includes a private compensatory remedial model. Were the federal court to authorize a faux class action, where the only participants with any private economic incentive to sue are the plaintiffs' attorneys themselves, the dictates of the famed Supreme Court decision in *Erie R.R. Co. v. Tompkins,*[39] as well as the Rules Enabling Act from which Rule 23 springs,[40] that state substantive law must control in diversity actions would be ignored. It is, then, incorrect to focus exclusively on substantive law's prohibitionary element in determining whether procedure has been faithful to underlying substantive law. Equally as important, for narrow political purposes and as a matter of abstract democratic theory, is the extent to which the remedial element of the substantive law has been fundamentally altered.

It is important to emphasize that acceptance of my democratic critique would in no way signal the end of the compensatory class action. All that I seek is a prophylactic addendum to the certification process to deter the growth of faux class actions. Under my proposal, a certifying court would be directed to inquire whether, on the basis of what is known at the time, it is reasonable to predict that meaningful compensatory relief to individual class members would result from successful prosecution of the class proceeding.[41]

CLASS ACTIONS, DEMOCRATIC THEORY,
AND THE RULE-MAKING PROCESS:
CONSTITUTIONAL IMPLICATIONS

The problems of macro democratic theory to which the modern class action gives rise extend well beyond the political difficulty caused by faux class actions. Even where class actions do not amount effectively to a fraud on the electorate, no one could reasonably doubt that how the Federal Rules shape the class action rule will inevitably have enormous social, political, moral, and economic consequences for the viability of underlying substantive law, resource redistribution, social compensation, and industrial growth. The economic stakes of the modern class action are often so large that the whole future of a company, if not an entire industry, may be at stake.[42] Yet it is equally true that a revision of Rule 23 significantly restricting the scope and reach of the modern class action would have a correspondingly dramatic impact on the balance of economic and social power in society as a whole. This is true, even though by its terms Rule 23 is "transsubstantive," meaning that it is not tied to adjudication of specific substantive claims, nor designed to alter the impact of substantive law. In short, it is beyond dispute that the substantive stakes in the shaping of the seemingly procedural class action rule are enormous.

Of course, there is nothing especially earth shattering in this revelation. Since relatively early in the Supreme Court's development of the *Erie* doctrine, it has been understood that procedural rules may often have substantial impact on society beyond the four walls of the courtroom.[43] In fact, procedural rules are often promulgated *because of* their impact on society as a whole. While this may be true of many procedural rules, the class action rule presents the most stark illustration. But while there is nothing particularly surprising about recognition of this often inescapable substantive-procedural intersection, it *is* quite surprising that virtually no court or commentator has expressed significant concern over the implications of this intersection for the political and constitutional legitimacy of the rule-making process. The Rules Enabling Act vests in the Supreme Court—the one branch of the federal government whose members are explicitly insulated from any meaningful democratic check[44]—authority to promulgate the Federal Rules of Civil Procedure. Though Congress possesses a potential trumping power through a process of legislative revocation, absent a reversal in legislative inertia the Rules promulgated by the Court stay in force and have full legal effect. When the dust settles, choices of fundamental social policy that are reflected in the shaping of certain procedural rules are being made legislatively by an unaccountable and unrepresentative governmental body.

Conceivable responses to this democratic critique of the rule-making process are many. It could be argued, for example, that the Court often makes fundamental policy choices in its decisions, and in any event as long as Congress retains ultimate authority to reverse the rules promulgated by the Court, democratic interests should be deemed to be satisfied. But when the Court makes policy choices, it is always in the context of its adjudications of adversary cases or controversies, as dictated by Article III of the Constitution. In no other context does the Court sit as the structural equivalent of a legislature, promulgating freestanding, generally framed legislative choices. Because the Framers chose to shape the judiciary as an unaccountable governmental body, largely insulated from political pressures, its operations were confined to performance of the traditional judicial function of case adjudication.[45]

Although Congress may of course overturn particular rule-making choices of the Court, that fact hardly provides a satisfactory answer to the critique from democracy. The same could be said, for example, of the Court's hypothetical exercise of a power to promulgate "rules of antitrust law," untied to performance of its adjudicatory function: Congress would always retain the legislative power to overturn any or all of those rules. Yet I seriously doubt Congress could constitutionally vest such legislative power in the federal judiciary. The reasons, both formalist and functionalist, are simple: As a formalistic matter, the failure to legislate does not have the legal impact of the affirmative enactment of legislation. Congress must exercise the legislative power in order to formally alter the legal topography, and its failure to overturn a legislative choice made by an unaccountable judiciary does not qualify as compliance with the bicameralism and presentment requirements that the Constitution imposes on legislative enactments.[46] From a more functionalist perspective, the difference in political inertia between the enactment of legislation and a failure to legislate is enormous. The fact that Congress is unable or unwilling to reverse the transformation in the legal topography implemented by a judicially promulgated Federal Rule does not qualify the rule as the equivalent of a legislative enactment, for either formalist or functionalist purposes.

It is true that the Supreme Court may appropriately be presumed to possess a fair amount of expertise in the operation of the judicial process—though one may reasonably wonder whether justices who themselves do not sit as trial court judges and who may well never have done so qualify as "experts" on the shaping of pre- and post-trial procedure. But the Court's expertise is not the point. Rather, the issue concerns the question of which branch of the federal government, in a constitutional democracy, should be deemed to possess the opportunity to make legislative choices of social policy. Once again, the class action rule serves as the paradigmatic illustration of the constitutionally and politically problematic nature of the current rule-making process. How aggressively one chooses to arm the class action procedure as a weapon for private enforcement of regulatory laws will have potentially dramatic consequences for competing social, political, and economic interests. Who gets to make that choice, in the first instance, should turn not on considerations of expertise (in the case of the federal rule-making process, held far more by the Rules Advisory Committee that shapes the proposals than by the Supreme Court that ultimately promulgates them) but rather on considerations of accountability and compliance with the constitutionally dictated lawmaking process. As currently structured, the rule-making process fails to satisfy those concerns.

To deem the current rule-making process to be inconsistent with both the Constitution and governing American political theory, however, need not significantly alter the nature of the procedural rules that govern federal court litigation. It would mean, simply, that Congress, rather than the Court, would be deemed to possess the exclusive power to promulgate the Federal Rules, in the form of legislation. Indeed, there is no reason that Congress, in making these legislative decisions, could not rely for valuable input and recommendations on the very same Advisory Committee currently relied upon by the Court in promulgating the Federal Rules. The difference, however, would be that citizens who, for whatever reason, wish to influence the shaping of those rules would, in the first instance, seek to influence their elected lawmakers, rather than an unelected, unaccountable Advisory Committee making recommendations to an unelected, unaccountable Supreme Court. Basic dictates of democratic theory, as well as the case-or-controversy requirement of Article III of the Constitution, demand as much.

THE SETTLEMENT CLASS ACTION AND THE
CONSTITUTIONAL LIMITS ON ADJUDICATION

To this point, we have seen that in some instances the dictates of constitutional or democratic theory call for alterations in the fundamental structure of the process of class adjudication. In others—for example, the faux class action[47]—it is only a specific pathological aberration that needs to be extinguished to satisfy the demands of constitutional democracy. Another such pathological aberration is the so-called settlement class action, a device that has, in recent years, become quite popular among plaintiffs' attorneys, defendants, and judges alike as a means of disposing of potentially complex adjudications in a relatively painless manner.

All class actions, like all litigations, may settle prior to final legal resolution. Because representative parties act in a fiduciary capacity on behalf of a class, however, Rule 23 wisely requires court approval of any settlement before it extinguishes the rights of absent class members to sue.[48] But the settlement class action differs fundamentally from a litigated class action that settles prior to final resolution. In the case of a settlement class action, prior to seeking certification or even formally instituting an adversary proceeding, attorneys purporting to represent the class must agree with the defendants to a settlement that will bind the entire class. Once such an agreement has been reached, the parties jointly request certification of the class proceeding from the court, *if and only if the court simultaneously approves the proposed settlement*. The settlement class action, then, is not litigation in the true sense of the word, but simply the *circumvention* of litigation.

There is, in the abstract, nothing inherently harmful about the desire to resolve disputes without the burdens and expense of enduring the litigating process. This is especially true in the case of a complex class action. But when the federal courts, bound by the Constitution to operate only through the adjudication of active, adversary cases or controversies, issue binding legal decrees in proceedings where all sides are in total agreement from the very initiation of the proceeding, serious questions may be raised about the constitutionality of the entire process. The settlement class action undermines both the formalistic dictates of Article III and the important constitutional values underlying the requirement of adversary adjudication.[49] As I will demonstrate in far more detail in a subsequent chapter,[50] the requirement of true adverseness between the parties protects all those who will seek to make similar arguments in future litigation. It simultaneously assures that the federal judiciary will politically be confined to its intended role of dispute resolution.

SUMMARY: VIEWING THE CLASS ACTION
FROM THE PERSPECTIVES OF CONSTITUTIONAL
AND POLITICAL THEORIES

In this book, I undertake an examination of the modern class action from an intellectual perspective that no scholar has, to date, attempted. I consider the class action from the perspectives of constitutional and democratic theories, and find it seriously wanting on both levels. From a constitutional perspective, the class action—as it is structured in Rule 23 of the Federal Rules of Civil Procedure, as it has been interpreted judicially, and as it has been characterized and rationalized by legal scholars—threatens core constitutional and democratic values.

The two levels of analysis that I employ are by no means identical. The constitutional attacks, if accepted, must of course trump all competing considerations. The arguments grounded purely in political theory, on the other hand, can have only persuasive, rather than legally enforceable, effect. Yet on a number of occasions, the constitutional arguments find a corresponding parallel in the separate universe of political theory. On these occasions, the two levels of analysis complement and strengthen each other. Once one critically examines the modern class action from either perspective, however, one is forced to recognize the substantial need for dramatic alteration in the procedure's underlying theory, modern format, and current doctrinal structure.

CHAPTER TWO

Class Actions and the Democratic Difficulty

INTRODUCTION

Though on its face the class action appears to be nothing more than an elaborate procedural joinder device, in recent years it has become the focal point of much political and legal debate. Courts have noted "the intense pressure to settle"[1] caused by the very filing of a class action, while others believe the procedure amounts to "judicial blackmail."[2] Those who take a more positive view of the class action consider it to provide an effective means of policing corporate behavior and an assurance that injured victims will be compensated in the most efficient manner.[3]

Much of the scholarly commentary has been highly critical of the modern class action.[4] Despite this widespread judicial and scholarly attention, however, neither courts nor scholars appear to have recognized a central problem with the modern class action: In all too many cases, the modern class action has undermined the foundational precepts of American democracy. It has done so by effectively transforming the essence of the governing substantive law that the class action has been created to enforce. This transformation has come about, even though the class action device is not designed for the purpose of altering the underlying substantive law. Pursuant to this process, then, controlling substantive law is not transformed through use of the democratic process of legislative amendment, where the electorate may measure its chosen representatives by how they voted on the proposed revisions of existing law. Rather, this dramatic alteration in governing substantive law arises from, essentially, a form of indirection and subterfuge, by use of a procedural device whose sole legitimate function is the considerably more modest one of implementing and facilitating the enforcement of existing substantive law.

In the American political system, certain counter-majoritarian constitutional principles limit policy making by representative and accountable governmental bodies. For present purposes, however, I proceed on the assumption that the legislative action in question does not violate any constitutional constraint. It is also true, of course, that in our post–New Deal society, many policy choices are made by administrative agencies, which are neither representative nor accountable, at least directly. As a theoretical matter, this fact arguably gives rise to serious constitutional problems for the operation of such agencies.[5] However, as a practical matter, a certain level of administrative discretion is required in implementing general statutes, because enforcement requires that the statutes be applied to specific circumstances. Moreover, such agency action may usually be attributed to the executive, who is both representative of and accountable to the electorate.[6] In any event, as explained more fully in subsequent discussion, the class action device neither interprets nor amends specific substantive laws, while administrative agencies at least purport to be interpreting and enforcing specific legislative directives. Thus, modification of the underlying substantive law by use of the supposedly neutral class action device is completely indefensible as a matter of democratic theory.[7]

In considering the modern class action's problematic impact on American democracy, it is important to keep in mind a central fact often ignored in modern procedural scholarship: the class action was never designed to serve as a freestanding legal device for the purpose of "doing justice," nor is it a mechanism intended to serve as a roving policeman of corporate misdeeds or as a mechanism by which to redistribute wealth.[8] To the contrary, both its structure and description make clear that it is nothing more than an elaborate procedural device designed to facilitate the enforcement of pre-existing substantive law. A class action suit, after all, does not "arise under" Rule 23 of the Federal Rules of Civil Procedure. If no pre-existing substantive law vests a cause of action in plaintiff class members, they cannot bring a valid class action suit. Moreover, because, like virtually all of the Federal Rules of Civil Procedure, Rule 23's class action device is inherently "transsubstantive,"[9] its use should not vary based upon differences in the nature of the substantive claim. Thus, unlike administrative interpretation and application of a particular statute, invocation of the class action device in no way authorizes creative interpretation or application of the particular substantive law in a case.

The substantive laws enforced by use of the class action device—for example, the federal antitrust laws,[10] federal consumer protection laws,[11] federal securities laws,[12] or, in cases falling within the federal courts' diversity jurisdiction,[13] state tort laws—all contain two fundamental elements: the proscription or regulation of an actor's "primary behavior"[14] and the provision of a remedy or remedies by which these behavioral regulations are to be enforced. For the most part, these laws enforce their behavioral proscriptions by establishing claims for damages for private victims of the proscribed behavior.[15] These provisions are designed to make the private victim whole by obtaining compensation from those who have caused them harm. Moreover, as the statutory provision for treble damages in the antitrust laws illustrates,[16] such damage remedies may also include punitive, as well as compensatory awards. In each of these cases, the assertion of private rights to compensation through the mechanism of litigation may well have the incidental effect of advancing the public interest by punishing, deterring, and halting law violations on the part of defendants. In this sense, the private plaintiffs may be viewed as a type of "private attorney general." This is so, even if we presume that the motivation of the private litigants who bring suit to enforce their compensatory rights under the relevant substantive law is solely the desire to improve their own personal economic position. But under that law no plaintiff is ever *required* to enforce his private compensatory right. To the contrary, the substantive law vests that choice exclusively in the individual victim. Thus, in such situations, any incidental benefit to the public interest is wholly contingent upon the private victim's personal decision to seek to judicially enforce her substantively created legal remedy.

Where the government wishes to deter or punish unlawful behavior in a more direct and reliable manner, it has several options available to it. Instead of, or in addition to, the private compensatory remedy, a legislature may utilize any permutation or combination of a variety of conceivable remedial models, including criminal enforcement, civil penalties, and administrative regulation. For purposes of democratic theory, there are several key points to note about the substantive law's choice of remedial model. To be sure, a legislative choice of behavioral proscription may be of enormous political import. Normative issues of social policy often turn on the legislative selection of specific acts to be prohibited or restricted. But also of potentially great social and political significance is the legislative choice of how to implement and enforce those directives—for example, whether a judicially enforceable compensatory remedy will be created, whether relief will be confined to the imposition of criminal penalties, or whether civil fines or administratively imposed penalties will also be authorized. Unless a particular substantive law authorizes enforcement through private victim compensation, the entire structure of private rights compensatory adjudication is generally rendered irrelevant.[17] On the other hand, where a statute provides for enforcement exclusively through victim compensation, enforcement of the statute's behavioral norms by any other method inevitably and profoundly alters the statute's substantive directives.

Careful examination of both the structure of and practice under Rule 23 demonstrates that all too often the device permits the transformation of the remedial enforcement model expressly adopted in the underlying substantive law from a victims' damage award structure into an entirely distinct form not contemplated in the underlying substantive law.[18] In such cases, the suits are not, in any realistic sense, brought either by or on behalf of the class members. The class members neither make the decision to sue at the outset nor receive meaningful compensation at the end of a successful suit. Instead, in these suits, as a practical matter, it is the private attorneys who initiate suit and who are the only ones rewarded for exposing the defendants' law violations. In effect, the promise of substantial attorneys' fees provides the class lawyers with a private economic incentive to discover violations of existing legal restrictions on corporate behavior. Thus, what purports to be a class action, brought primarily to enforce private individuals' substantive rights to compensatory relief, in reality amounts to little more than private attorneys acting as bounty hunters, protecting the public interest by enforcing the public policies embodied in controlling statutes.

In these "faux" class actions, most members of the class never make a conscious choice to seek judicial enforcement of their substantive right to pursue private damages.[19] Indeed, because membership in a Rule 23(b)(3) class is established merely by the class member's failure to opt out of the class (rather than her decision to affirmatively opt in),[20] many members of the class quite probably never focus upon, recognize, or understand the notification of the class suit. At the very least, it is impossible to be certain of the contrary assumption. Thus, it is quite conceivable that many class members are even unaware that they are parties to a lawsuit.

In many (though concededly not all) of these cases individual class members cannot receive compensation without a class member's affirmative filing of a complex claim form. This is so despite the fact that, under the opt-out procedure established in Rule 23, the absent plaintiff becomes a class member by the failure to take any affirmative act. One cannot readily assume that a class member who entered the class passively is likely to exercise his right to relief by now affirmatively filing a claim.[21] When the dust settles, then, the only individuals receiving significant financial awards in these faux class actions are the class's lawyers.[22] For all practical purposes the classes in these suits are reminiscent of the life-sized celebrity cardboard cutouts that occasionally appear on large city street corners, accompanied by a photographer anxious to snap a tourist's picture standing alongside. Much like the cutout's appearance in the photograph, at first glance the class appears to be real, but closer scrutiny reveals that it is little more than a two-dimensional, cardboard version of a real class of plaintiffs.

Of course, one might ask, if the absent class members have so little interest in the outcome of the class action, why should the fact that they receive no meaningful compensation really matter? The answer is not that we should be concerned about the individual class members' failing to receive the minimal compensation owed them as much as we should be concerned about the fundamental transformation of the underlying substantive law through the purely procedural device of the class action. As a result of the class action procedure, what purports to be a substantive compensatory framework has been furtively transformed into a structure in which it is quite possible that virtually no victim receives compensation through enforcement of the underlying substantive law. Instead, it is only the attorneys bringing the class action suit who benefit financially. We can never know whether the public would approve such a transformation in the remedial structure of the underlying substantive law, because it is never informed that such a transformation has been made. Instead, the transformation in the essential nature of the substantive law's remedial model has come furtively and indirectly, under the guise of procedural implementation. It is, then, the impact on the democratic process, rather than the impact on individual class members, that gives rise to concern.

It does not automatically follow that such actions are inherently invidious, immoral, or illegal. Nor does it automatically follow that such actions would necessarily fail to advance the public interest by effectively enforcing the substantive law's proscriptions on defendant's primary behavior.[23] To the contrary, it is not unreasonable to predict that the public interest in assuring corporations' compliance with legislatively imposed restrictions on their primary behavior might be significantly advanced by the creation of economic inducements to private individuals to ferret out and seek judicial relief for violations of those proscriptions. The point, rather, is that these faux class actions seek to advance and protect the substantive law's behavioral norms by resort to a bounty hunter remedial model that is very different from the remedial model established in the substantive law enforced in the class action—one that it is by no means clear would have been deemed politically acceptable had it been proposed directly.[24]

The concept of the bounty hunter holds a venerable position in our nation's history. In the Old West of the second half of the nineteenth century, law enforcement agencies were generally understaffed, especially relative to the high level of criminal activity. One means of augmenting public authorities' resources was resort to partial reliance on private bounty hunters.[25] Rewards were offered for the apprehension—often, dead or alive—of wanted criminals. Motivated as much or more by considerations of personal greed than civic responsibility, bounty hunters made a career out of apprehending these criminals, thereby qualifying for the rewards.[26] In this manner, the bounty hunters effectively furthered the public interest by seeking to promote their own personal economic interests.

In faux class actions, the class attorneys function in a manner strikingly parallel to the Old West's bounty hunters: as a reward for their efforts in ferreting out illegal corporate behavior, these private advocates receive substantial attorneys' fees, either negotiated as part of a settlement or awarded by a court after judgment. Thus, as was the case with the Old West's bounty hunters, the pursuit of private gain motivates private individuals to expose illegal activity, thereby supposedly furthering the broader public interest in having the corporate world adhere to the broad behavioral proscriptions set by governmental authorities.[27] But the bounty hunters of the Old West furthered the public interest not by redistributing illegally held wealth to the poor—one should not anachronistically confuse the bounty hunters of the Old West with Robin Hood—but rather by apprehending those who threatened the public peace. Even when a class's attorneys bring an action that lacks any real plaintiffs, the suit may nevertheless further the public interest, if in so doing it exposes, punishes, and deters illegal corporate behavior. The problem, however, is that these suits are not structured to be bounty hunter suits, but rather private compensatory damage suits, which they often are not. The two forms of enforcement are by no means identical from legal, social, or political perspectives.[28]

The closest legal analogy to the bounty hunters of the Old West has traditionally been the venerable qui tam action,[29] in which private individuals, not claiming to have suffered personal injury as a result of specified illegal behavior against the government, may nevertheless bring suit to remedy that behavior. Though the bulk of the damage award obtained as a result of a successful qui tam action goes to the government in order to compensate it for loss suffered as a result of the defendant's illegal activity, the private litigant is rewarded with a specified percentage of the total damage award. In this manner, government creates private incentives in unharmed individuals to discover and expose behavior that illegally harms the government. The problem with reliance on qui tam actions, however, is that in their current form they have been explicitly authorized by congressional statute; class action bounty actions have not.

In its present state, the faux class action constitutes a wholly improper and unacceptable departure from the fundamental precepts of American democracy, and thus gives rise to what can be appropriately described as "the democratic difficulty." The sources of the serious (and ultimately fatal) problems of democratic theory to which the faux class action gives rise are twofold: (1) Such actions are not what they purport to be—namely, compensatory damage suits—and (2) in any event these disguised bounty hunter actions have never been authorized by the underlying substantive law that such actions purport to enforce. In effect, then, these actions constitute a form of procedural shell game, in which a procedural device that has been designed to do nothing more than facilitate the enforcement of the substantive law's authorization of private damage suits transforms that private remedial model into a qualitatively different form of remedy that was never part of that substantive law. If the substantive law is to authorize a bounty hunter remedial model as a supplement to or replacement for the pre-existing private damage remedy, the change may not properly be effected through the operation of a procedural device such as Rule 23.[30] Such a dramatic modification of the substantive law through resort to an avowedly procedural device contravenes the fundamental democratic notions of representation and accountability, because the process effectively deceives the electorate. As a result of this deception, the electorate is unable to judge its elected representatives by examining how they voted on these important modifications of enforcement models, because those representatives have never been asked to vote on the issue. The democratic process is substantially undermined as a result.

In light of the insights of this democratic critique of the modern class action, one might be tempted to conclude that, as presently structured, Rule 23 violates the separation of powers protections of the United States Constitution, or at the very least the statutory directive of the Rules Enabling Act that a procedural rule may not abridge, enlarge, or modify a substantive right.[31] Ultimately, these attacks are likely to fail; it is not Rule

23 itself that undermines substantive law, but rather its misuse. It does not follow, however, that there exists no recourse. The implications of the democratic critique of Rule 23 make clear that the present situation is intolerable as a matter of normative precepts of American democracy. It is therefore both necessary and appropriate for the Advisory Committee and the Supreme Court to reconsider and substantially modify Rule 23 in order to remedy this troubling situation.

I should emphasize that my argument does not represent an attack on class actions in the abstract. Nor am I suggesting that, as an empirical matter, every class action currently filed should necessarily be viewed as an invocation of a pure bounty hunter remedial model, rather than merely as the procedural collectivization of private compensatory rights. The problem is that, as currently structured, Rule 23 at the very least may be misused by permitting what are pure bounty hunter actions in everything but name. The question then becomes how to modify the adjudicatory structure established by the Rule in order to permit the legitimate class action without simultaneously authorizing the faux class action. This chapter will argue that substantial amendment to Rule 23 is necessary in order to assure that the class action device does nothing more than achieve its stated purpose of facilitating the adjudication of claims authorized by preexisting substantive law. Toward that end, the chapter seeks to fashion specific proposals for revision of the rule that would, under certain circumstances, replace the existing opt-out procedure with an opt-in structure and that would substantially restrict the certification of class actions where there exists doubt that truly compensatory relief to absent class members could ever be fashioned.

Proponents of the modern class action would likely respond that such amendments to Rule 23 would inevitably gut the effectiveness of class actions as a means of policing corporate misdeeds. It is true that many of the class actions currently in existence would be rendered invalid under the amended Rule 23 proposed here. However, the simple fact is that the affected actions do not fit within the private rights adjudicatory model in which Rule 23 is designed to operate.[32] It is true that in some cases private rights adjudication would no longer function as an effective means of furthering the public interest by policing illegal corporate behavior, because the individual claims are so small that maintenance of a true class action and the effective distribution of compensatory relief are rendered infeasible. In such an event, however, it is the legislature's responsibility to consider alternative options by which private activity may be tapped as a means of protecting the public interest. Certainly, express legislative adoption of a bounty hunter model or other qui tam-like actions might provide such an alternative, though consideration of the constitutionality of such alternatives exceeds the scope of my inquiry. In a democratic society it is the legislature's responsibility to take such action overtly through the enactment of substantive legislation, rather than covertly, through use of the disguise of a procedural rule that purports to do nothing more than implement the existing substantive law's private compensatory rights structure. It is only then that the electorate may meaningfully perform its essential function of making informed choices about those who seek to represent it.

In exploring the interaction between modern class actions and democratic theory, the first section of this chapter initially considers the more general question of how the pursuit of private goals and the advancement of the public interest intersect. It also examines this intersection in the specific context of class actions, by exploring how the modern class action is thought to further the public interest as a type of private attorney general action. I next detail the manner in which the current version of Rule 23 effectively transforms the essential nature of the underlying substantive law that the class action procedure is designed to implement. In the following section I explore the problematic impact of this transformation on fundamental principles of democratic theory. The final section describes a series of amendments to Rule 23 that, I suggest, would go a long way toward remedying the problematic intersection of the modern class action and American democracy.[33]

DEMOCRATIC THEORY, PRIVATE LITIGATION, AND PUBLIC GOALS

The modern class action impacts foundational precepts of democratic theory in two ways. One way, raised traditionally in the debates between advocates of communitarianism or civic republicanism on the one hand and pluralism or individualism on the other,[34] concerns the manner in which the pursuit of narrow self-interest impacts the advancement of the broader public interest in a democratic society. In the litigation context, this issue presents itself primarily in the shaping of the so-called "private attorney general" concept. The other way in which democratic theory and class actions intersect concerns the manner in which the modern class action subverts the fundamental democratic precepts of representation and accountability by bringing about a disguised transformation of the underlying substantive law. In order to fully understand the nature of the latter intersection's impact, however, one must initially grasp the essence of the first intersection. For it is only when one comprehends the subtle but significant distinctions, for purposes of democratic theory, in the applications of the private attorney general theory that one can fully understand how the modern class action improperly transforms the essential structure of pre-existing substantive law.

Much of the modern scholarly debate about the scope of democratic theory has focused upon the extent to which the concept of the public interest represents something apart from the mere summing of the citizens' individual private interests. At the extremes of this theoretical debate are the modern version of the theory of civic republicanism, which advocates "the subordination of private interests to the public good,"[35] and the theory of "possessive individualism," in which "society is presumed to consist of relations among independent owners, and the primary task of government is to protect owners against illegitimate incursions upon their property and to maintain conditions of orderly exchange."[36] While these two theoretical extremes are surely oversimplifications of what is a considerably more complex issue,[37] they underscore the fundamental tension between the primacy of the individual's interest in advancing her narrowly focused private interests and the need to have citizens "escape private interests and engage in pursuit of the public good."[38]

For present purposes, one need not attempt to resolve this long-standing debate. The key point to note, rather, is that at some level, most in our society have placed value simultaneously (and not necessarily inconsistently) on both individual autonomy and civic-mindedness. Indeed, in a number of ways, society has sought to harness the drive for personal advancement in order to advance the public interest. By providing personal incentives to those who are in a position to better the community as a whole, our system has been able to advance the public interest. For example, drug companies develop new medicines, presumably not for altruistic purposes, but rather out of the traditional capitalist-based motivation of profit maximization. Yet the development of those drugs substantially advances the community's interests.

In a number of ways, our legal system has even asserted a preference for the pursuit of private gain, rather than communitarianism or altruism. For example, Article III's so-called "injury-in-fact" requirement is clearly premised on the notion that individual litigants may resort to the federal judicial system only when seeking to advance their personal interests.[39] Would-be plaintiffs who are motivated exclusively by altruistic or ideological concerns may not, as a constitutional matter, invoke the federal judicial process.[40] Unless the plaintiff has suffered some form of personal injury traceable to the defendant's violation of law and remediable by judicial action, she constitutionally lacks the standing necessary to invoke the federal courts' jurisdiction.[41] It surely does not follow, however, that federal adjudication is incapable of advancing social, economic, or political interests that extend well beyond the personal interest of the individual litigant. It means, simply, that whatever impact federal adjudication may have on the public interest must come as an incident to the assertion and adjudication of narrower, personal interests.

On occasion, the legislature may create a private statutory right to damages, at least in part for the express purpose of advancing the public interest. Private litigation may often do the government's work for it, by deterring and punishing violations of law. By seeking to benefit the individual litigants, then, adjudication may have the incidental impact of advancing the public interest. As Professor Coffee has written, "[p]robably to a unique degree, American law relies upon private litigants to enforce substantive provisions of law that in other legal systems are left largely to the discretion of public enforcement agencies."[42] Coffee further notes that "[t]his system of enforcement . . . is most closely associated with the federal antitrust and securities laws and the common law's derivative action, but similar institutional arrangements have developed recently in the environmental, 'mass tort,' and employment discrimination fields."[43] This, in short, describes the concept of the "private attorney general."[44]

If a suit brought to vindicate a single individual's private right can be thought to foster the public interest by deterring and punishing violations of law, it would seem to follow logically that a class action brought on behalf of numerous victims could exponentially increase the litigation's beneficial impact on the public interest. Thus, it is not surprising that respected commentators have recognized that "[p]rivate class actions for money damages can yield significant social benefits."[45] According to Professor Yeazell, the modern view of the private class action as a type of private attorney general finds its origins in the 1941 scholarship of Professors Kalven and Rosenfeld, who saw class litigation as:

[A] supplement to governmental regulation of large, diffuse markets . . . reflect(ing) a consensus that the old, ordinary forms of liability were not functioning to discipline their operations. . . . In [Kalven's and Rosenfeld's] view the representative suit would serve to supplement regulatory agencies both by requiring wrongdoers to give up their ill-gotten gains and by ferreting out instances of wrong that might have escaped the regulators' observance.[46]

Yeazell notes that "[t]his concept . . . has become a leading justification for the modern class action" and that "it links [the] concept of the interest class . . . to the general task of law enforcement."[47]

Though at first glance the intersection of private litigation and public goals appears to be both simple and straightforward, closer examination of the role of the modern private class action in the service of the public interest reveals that both empirical and conceptual ambiguities exist about the nature of the public-private interaction. The former have already been noted by others, while the latter appear to have been completely overlooked. On an empirical level, questions have been raised concerning the extent to which the private class action effectively fosters the public interest as a supplement to out-manned and out-gunned governmental agencies. Many class actions come in the form of what have been called "coattail" classes—in other words, class actions that follow successful governmental litigation on either the civil or criminal fronts, and feed off the fruits of the governmental agency's efforts.[48] In such situations, the class action does not itself ferret out illegal corporate behavior, spurred by the private economic incentive provided by the creation of damage remedies. To the contrary, the government has already brought such illegality to light and successfully imposed punishment. The private action simply basks in the light of the government agency's efforts.[49] While some have criticized the coattail class action,[50] it does not necessarily follow that class actions are pointless in coattail situations. The class action may well justify its existence, merely by performing the extremely valuable function of compensating large numbers of victims in a relatively efficient manner.[51] Moreover, even coattail classes may advance the public interest by adding to the deterrence of corporate wrongdoing.[52] The fact remains, however, that coattail class actions obviously fail to perform the classic function of privately generated exposure of unlawful behavior traditionally facilitated by the private attorney general concept.

It is not entirely clear whether the majority of private class actions are of the coattail variety.[53] For present purposes, however, one need not resolve that empirical question. We may assume, solely for purposes of argument, that most modern class actions actually perform the private attorney general function as it has been traditionally understood, by reinforcing otherwise overwhelmed governmental policing agencies in the pursuit of corporate illegality. Serious analytical problems nevertheless continue to exist, because significant conceptual ambiguities exist in the private attorney general concept that both courts and scholars have failed to recognize, much less resolve. Close scrutiny of these ambiguities highlights the manner in which the modern class action has largely transformed the remedial model that plays a central role in the design of the underlying substantive law.

Scholars have already recognized one dichotomy within the broader concept of the private attorney general. Commentators have contrasted what they describe as the "Lone Ranger" and "bounty hunter" forms of private attorney general.[54] The Lone Ranger refers to the private litigant who is motivated in his attempt to serve the public interest primarily, if not exclusively, by idealistic or communitarian concerns. Of course, in light of the constitutional requirement of injury in fact,[55] even these plaintiffs must be able to assert some form of personal injury and private right which they seek to vindicate by the pursuit of judicial action. But for these plaintiffs, such injury serves for the most part as a means to a broader, idealistic end. The bounty hunter, on the other hand, refers to the private litigants who care little for broader concerns of public interest but are instead focused exclusively upon the pursuit of their own private interest. As already noted, however, even litigants falling within this latter category may serve the public interest as an incident to their pursuit of their own private rights.[56] For this reason, recognition of this dichotomy within the category of private attorney general actions may have more sociological than legal import.

What no one appears to have recognized, however, is the legally and theoretically significant dichotomy that exists within the concept of what have been described, somewhat overinclusively, as "bounty hunter" class actions.[57] As already noted, this category is thought to include those actions brought exclusively for the purpose of personal gain, rather than for broader public interest concerns. But two very different subcategories of such "personal interest" litigation exist. One is properly described as "compensatory" litigation. In these cases, one can readily presume that those bringing suit—both plaintiffs and their attorneys—are motivated exclusively by considerations of narrow self-interest: the plaintiffs seek to make themselves economically whole by obtaining compensation for their injuries caused by the defendants, and the attorneys serve as "hired guns," doing nothing more than receiving compensation for performing a service on behalf of a client. Such suits may nevertheless be categorized as private attorney general actions, because they may well have the incidental impact—perhaps even intended by the legislative creation of the private right—of exposing and punishing law violations. In this sense, private litigation serves the public interest, regardless of the motivation of those bringing suit.

The "self-interest" litigation category of private attorney general actions includes an additional subcategory, also appropriately described as "bounty hunter" litigation. But it is important to distinguish this narrow subcategory from the primary category of "personal interest" litigation itself. Neither in the Old West nor in more recent times has a bounty hunter acted on behalf of the interests of specific private individuals, nor have they sought compensation for injury caused to themselves by others.[58] Bounty hunters, instead, have sought to serve the interests of the community by apprehending (and sometimes punishing) those who disturb or threaten the public peace. In exchange, the community has rewarded them. It is reasonable to assume that invariably it was the reward, rather than a sense of civic-mindedness, that has traditionally driven the bounty hunters (though of course the two motivations are by no means mutually exclusive). It is therefore probably fair to say that the work of the bounty hunters effectively illustrates the intersection of self-interest and public interest. But this intersection does not involve the additional purpose of simultaneously compensating the victims of the apprehended wrongdoer. Thus, the appropriate litigation analogy to the bounty hunters is not the private compensatory action, for the simple reason that the work of bounty hunters has never been thought to include efforts to obtain compensation for private victims.

A more appropriate legal analogy to the bounty hunter is the qui tam action. In its modern form, the qui tam action is embodied in the False Claims Act, which authorizes private citizens (referred to as "relators") to bring suit against defendants who have knowingly defrauded the United States government.[59] In order to induce such private action, the Act authorizes the private plaintiff to recover a percentage of the proceeds from the action.[60] In this manner, "the qui tam provision works to provide an incentive for private litigants to expose the fraud and benefit from the recovery."[61] Commentators have noted that "the number of qui tam suits filed is accelerating each year and recoveries are steadily trending upward."[62] The qui tam plaintiff has suffered no personal injury at the hands of the defendant that she is seeking to remedy through adjudication. Rather, the plaintiff's apparent motivation is to obtain the reward offered by the government for ferreting out and judicially punishing fraud against the government.[63] In this sense, the qui tam action represents an adjudicatory parallel to the actions and motivations of the Old West's bounty hunter.[64]

Once one understands the subtle but important distinctions among the categories and subcategories of private attorney general actions, it is appropriate to examine the modern class action in light of this background. Such an examination reveals that in its present form, the modern class action includes cases that fall within all three of the relevant categories: idealistic, self-interested, and the latter's two sub-categories, private compensatory and bounty hunter. The problem is that the substantive law that the class action purports to enforce invariably fails to authorize private attorney general actions of the bounty hunter variety.[65] Moreover, at no point does anyone acknowledge the true character of those class actions that properly fall within the bounty hunter category. Rather, such actions are universally described, quite inaccurately, to be of the private compensatory variety. This is so despite the fact that in many such actions the only individuals involved in and financially motivated by the possibility of recovery are the attorneys, who have never suffered a legally cognizable and compensable injury at the hands of the defendants. The following section provides a detailed examination of the modern class action's legal structure, in an effort to explain how what purports to be a private compensatory action and what legally is permitted to be nothing more than a private compensatory action in reality transforms itself into a disguised bounty hunter action.

THE MODERN CLASS ACTION
AS A BOUNTY HUNTER SUIT

If one seeks to determine exactly how the modern class action fits within the framework of private attorney general actions, it is first appropriate to distinguish between the civil rights class action, in which the class seeks primarily injunctive relief, authorized by Rule 23(b)(2),[66] and those class actions brought primarily in order to compensate a class of victims.[67] The former largely fall under the " idealistic" heading,[68] while the latter generally fall within the "self-interested" category. Of course, even a damages class action may be motivated in part by ideological concerns on the part of both class members and class attorneys. For example, individuals who firmly believe that big business must be curbed for the betterment of the community may eagerly pursue an action for damages as much to bring their political principles into reality as to acquire compensation. Moreover, even a (b)(2) class is designed to benefit both the named and absent class plaintiffs. One nevertheless may draw this dichotomy because the distinction will be accurate more often than not and, in any event, at this level the implications of the distinction are purely sociological, rather than legal. What may well have significant legal consequences, however, is the distinction between the two different subcategories of self-interested litigation: private compensatory and bounty hunter. Yet as presently structured, Rule 23 effectively authorizes both forms.

The Effect of Opt-Out on the Modern Class Action

By establishing membership in the class through the inherently passive procedure of opt-out,[69] Rule 23 creates a framework for litigation that threatens to undermine the essential premises of the private compensatory model of adjudication. Pursuant to the private compensatory model, the substantive law simultaneously proscribes specified behavior on the part of a category of actors and vests in the victims of that behavior the individual right to sue the wrongdoer in order to be made whole. None of the laws in question draws any distinction between individual and class injuries. To the contrary, they do nothing more than vest compensatory rights in individual victims. Thus, in its pre-litigation state, the right to sue belongs solely to the individual victim. Rule 23 permits those individual claims to be aggregated in a single action in a unique manner, in order to bring about litigation convenience and provide a viable procedural means of vindicating the underlying substantive claims. Yet because the rule transforms individual victims into class members solely on the basis of their failure to remove themselves from the class, rather than by manifestation of their affirmative assent to participate, it virtually invites the creation of a class in which, as a practical matter, numerous class members have not only not actually assented to suit, but are completely unaware that they are even suing. The upshot of this process, then, is that quite probably numerous plaintiffs—the individuals in whom the cause of action has been vested in the first place—are made members of the class without the slightest awareness of the suit.[70]

One may fashion several conceivable responses to this attack on opt-out. Initially, scholars have on occasion suggested that the class is more appropriately viewed as an "entity," rather than as an aggregation of single individuals. If one accepts this conceptual characterization, a right of opt-out makes no sense: As a small cog in the entity's wheel, the individual plaintiff logically possesses no individual right to decide for herself whether to bring suit.

David Shapiro is the leading scholarly advocate of the "entity" model of the modern class action.[71] Shapiro first notes that "in the foreground of any discussion of the class action . . . is the continuing debate between advocates of individual autonomy in litigation and the proponents of what has been praised as 'collective' justice."[72] He adds:

> The principal focus of the debate has been the extent to which the class action . . . should be viewed as not involving the claimants as a number of individuals, or even as an "aggregation" of individuals, but rather as an entity in itself for the critical purpose of determining the nature of the lawsuit.[73]

Shapiro concludes that "the 'class as entity' forces should ultimately carry the day."[74] He argues that:

> This conclusion is not quite so radical as it may seem at first, since the idea of the collectivity as an entity is a familiar one in other settings. Thus, a whole range of voluntary private associations—congregations, trade unions, joint stock companies, corporations—and on a less "voluntary" level, municipalities and other governmental entities, have long been recognized as litigants in their own right—entities whose members may have at best only a limited say in what is litigated, in who represents the organization, and on what terms the controversy is ultimately resolved.[75]

Shapiro concedes that:

> The analogy is not perfect of course. Shareholders in a corporation, for example, have chosen to become a part of the corporation for a variety of reasons . . . A member of a class that exists only for the purposes of a litigation may be dragged kicking and screaming into a lawsuit he does not want, or at least would prefer to conduct on his own.[76]

He responds to his own criticism of the entity theory, however, by pointing out that "some of these entities are not so 'voluntary' after all."[77]

In anticipating and responding to criticism of the entity theory, Professor Shapiro effectively underscores the extent to which his entire analysis misses the key point in deciding on the validity of the modern class action. Shapiro, recall, sees the debate as one between individual autonomy and collective justice. He attempts to fight off anticipated attacks on the entity theory that are grounded exclusively in basic autonomy rights of the individual to control his own litigation by pointing to numerous examples of existing entities in which individual members lack autonomy.[78] But the fundamental problem with his analogies is not so much that, unlike the class, membership in these organizations is usually voluntary, but that these organizations are themselves the creations of substantive law that directly regulates private individuals' primary behavior. In contrast, the class action exists as a procedural device designed to implement pre-existing legal regulations of citizens' primary behavior. If the laws establishing these regulations vest compensatory rights not in an entity of plaintiffs but rather in individual victims, then to view the class as an entity effectively transforms the essence of the pre-existing private right.

The most significant problem with the entity theory, then, is not that it undermines some abstract value of individual autonomy, but rather that it allows the class action procedure to transform the "DNA" of the underlying substantive law that it is seeking to enforce. There can be little question that in most current plaintiff class actions, the underlying substantive law does not create a cause of action in an entity, but rather in the individual victims. After all, the substantive law enforced in a class action generally draws no distinction between the compensatory rights asserted by a plaintiff in an individual suit and those asserted by a class of plaintiffs. Thus, to view the debate surrounding the entity model as a conflict of process-based theories, as Shapiro does, overlooks the true political harm to which adoption of an entity model gives rise.

In any event, there is no basis in the text of Rule 23(b)(3) to support the view that the Rule was somehow intended to transform the nature of the substantive rights being enforced from those vested in the individual plaintiff to rights vested in some ethereal entity of plaintiffs. Indeed, while I criticize the Rule for its use of an opt-out procedure,[79] if the Rule's drafters had some form of entity model in mind, they presumably would not have permitted opt-out at all. Instead, the entity of the class would have been permitted to act only as the unitary force that it inherently is.[80] To describe the class as an entity, then, represents nothing more than a convenient, after-the-fact rationalization for what is largely a political effort to facilitate the successful operation of the modern class action. Whatever one concludes about the normative social issues implicated by the modern class action, it is clear that those conclusions should not enable the judiciary to contravene the essential nature of the underlying substantive rights.[81] Adoption of an entity view of the class action, however, does just that.

A less abstract response to my attack on the use of opt-out, in preference to opt-in, focuses on the realities of the modern class action. This argument posits that the opt-out procedure provides more than sufficient protection against the inclusion of unwilling class members, because it is predictable, ex ante, that as a general matter class members would have no reason not to include themselves in the class. Scholars have argued that under an opt-out procedure, at least where the individual claims are not sufficiently large to justify the costs of a separate suit, an individual plaintiff notified of the class action:

> has a choice between two courses of action. She can do nothing, in which case she will receive a check in the mail if the suit is successful and will incur no costs if the suit fails. Or she can go to the trouble of opting out of the action, in which case she will receive nothing whether or not the suit is successful. Such a decision is not hard to make. Nearly everyone who understands the nature of this choice will elect to do nothing and thereby remain part of the class action.[82]

Although this argument was not fashioned specifically in the context of the opt-in/opt-out debate,[83] one could reasonably rely on it to support a preference for opt-out. Because of the overwhelming likelihood that a reasonable class member would choose to include herself in the class, one may appropriately proceed on this presumption, unless and until the class member affirmatively tells us otherwise.

Despite its superficially appealing nature, this argument is fundamentally flawed because it ignores the structural context in which the question about class members' intent is asked in the first place. Initially, it is important to point out that under the private rights model of adjudication, associated with the private compensatory remedial model, the question is not whether a plaintiff has any objection to suit, but whether a plaintiff affirmatively desires to sue. A private compensatory damage remedy is qualitatively different from a "guardian" model, under which the state or a specified private individual or entity is vested with legal authority to protect an individual or class of individuals deemed, for one reason or another, incapable of protecting their own interests. When a legislature provides for a private damage remedy, it presumably understands that the remedy is not triggered unless and until the injured victim decides that the injury is of sufficient magnitude to overcome inertia against suit. To be sure, the availability of the class action procedure makes suit for small claims more feasible, by reducing the costs and burdens of suit through the process of the aggregation of similar claims. But it does not follow that because of the class action procedure, the plaintiff who exercises her substantively vested compensatory remedy need no longer make the initial choice to sue.

An advocate of opt-out might respond, however, that the logical implications of the presumption concerning class members' intent are not merely that the individual plaintiffs have no objection to suit, but that they affirmatively desire to sue. In support of this contention, one may reason that a class member presented with the option would choose to sue, for the simple reason that she would have nothing to lose by suing. A class member who sues could never be in a worse position than if she had failed to sue, and may actually be placed in a better position, if only minimally, by ultimately receiving some form of compensation for her injuries, regardless of how small or useless.[84]

At best,[85] this argument works in the context of what Professor Coffee has labeled "Type B" class actions, in other words "those in which no claim would be independently marketable."[86] In Professor Coffee's "Type A" category, which includes those classes "in which each claim would be independently marketable even in the absence of the class action device,"[87] an individual plaintiff may well have a great deal to lose by remaining in the class, because in doing so he waives his due process right to control his own litigation,[88] and the possibility of such an individual suit is substantial. In virtually no other context are constitutional rights deemed waived by nothing more than a litigant's failure to act.[89] Yet that is exactly the result of the use of opt-out in these "Type A" class actions.

In examining Professor Coffee's "Type B" class actions, however, it is probably appropriate to recognize the possibility of further refinements. On the one hand, claims may be too small to justify the costs and burdens of individual suit, but nevertheless sufficiently large to possibly justify a class member's efforts to file a claim into a settlement fund or jury award. In these cases, the presumption of participation embodied in an opt-out procedure is arguably appropriate. On the other hand, often claims will be so small that even this effort would be unwarranted. Such "Type C" classes[90] represent the paradigmatic faux class action, and do not even warrant certification, much less the benefit of opt-out treatment.

Opponents of opt-in have argued that its use would have a negative impact on minority and low-income individuals, who "might be disproportionately affected by an opt-in requirement."[91] Evidently, the reasoning is that minority and low-income individuals are less likely to be able either to understand a class action notice or to make a sound decision about the suit if they do understand it. Such paternalism, however, is inconsistent with the basic premises of a democratic system because it proves too much. The same reasoning would seem to lead to the conclusion that those who "know better" should be able to exercise the vote for those citizens who are unable to perceive their own interests. Obviously, such logic flies in the face of foundational normative premises of democratic theory, grounded in respect for the individual's ability to decide for herself what her best interests are. Selective paternalism for minority individuals is even more offensive to the premises of democracy, which are grounded in assumptions of equality.

On occasion, government, acting as parens patriae, may choose to intercede in order to protect the interests of its citizens.[92] Such situations occur when, due to high informational or transaction costs, individuals are unlikely to be unable to perceive or protect their own legal interests. It is conceivable that in particular areas Congress could choose to create a semi-parens patriae action, allowing individual plaintiffs to opt out under specified circumstances. But these situations clearly involve substantive policy choices, well beyond the scope of the class action certification process, that generally have not been made in the governing substantive law enforced in modern class actions. Those laws, instead, do nothing more than create a compensatory right in individual victims, to be asserted by those victims in their discretion. To allow a rule that purports to do nothing more than create a procedural mechanism to transform pre-existing private compensatory rights into a crude form of parens patriae action is to abuse the rules of procedure.[93]

Close examination of the 1966 Advisory Committee's rationale for adopting an opt-out procedure demonstrates the manner in which the Committee's choice was designed to subvert the essential remedial structure of the governing substantive law. According to David Levi, the Committee apparently had in mind small-claim, consumer class actions in which no one class member would have a sufficient interest to litigate an individual claim and in which the forces of inertia might be greater than a potential class member's desire to participate, given the small stakes involved.[94] Benjamin Kaplan, who served as reporter for the 1966 Committee, wrote that for the "small people" who may be prevented from affirmatively opting in due to "ignorance, timidity, [or] unfamiliarity with business or legal matters," the class action "serves something like the function of an administrative proceeding where scattered individuals are represented by the Government."[95] But no matter how small the individual claims, their very existence derives from the substantive law's vesting of those rights in the individual victim. According to governing substantive laws, those rights may be judicially enforced only if individual victims choose to exercise them. If the individual injuries recognized by the substantive law are so small as not to justify the individual victim's decision to enforce them, then the rights will not be enforced.

Procedural rules may have the effect of making suit more attractive by reducing adjudicatory transaction costs through an increase in the fairness or efficiency of the litigation process. However, unless the substantive law establishes some form of public guardian empowered to sue on behalf of injured victims the choice to sue remains in the victim. Indeed, Professor Kaplan's analogy of the class action to an administrative proceeding reveals his understanding that the small-claim class action is designed to transform the private compensatory remedy provided for in the governing substantive law into a wholly different concept.

The Effect of Meaningless Relief on the Modern Class Action

The second element in the ominous "bookends" of Rule 23(b)(3) class actions is the relief ultimately provided by the litigation. While in theory a small-claim 23(b)(3) class action may ultimately give rise to the award of compensatory relief to absent class members, as a practical matter in many instances this result is highly unlikely, if not virtually impossible. The practical problems are twofold. First, even if monetary damages have been awarded to the class, in many situations individual plaintiffs are able to recover their awards only upon the filing of complex claim forms.[96] Where those claims are sufficiently small, for reasons already discussed it is unrealistic to expect that absent plaintiffs, made members of the class purely by their passivity, will have the incentive to overcome the severe transaction costs of filing a claim in order to obtain an award.[97] Under the theory of the faux class action that fact does not matter, however, because no one realistically understands the purpose of this form of class action to be the compensation of class members in the first place.

This is not necessarily to imply that in all small claim class actions, absent class members are incapable of receiving meaningful relief. For purposes of argument, I will presume that in a number of modern small claim class actions class members actually receive the relief to which they are legally entitled, or at least meaningful compensatory relief.[98] The fact remains, however, that a not insignificant number of modern class actions are resolved without class members receiving what could rationally be deemed real compensation. As presently structured, Rule 23 allows such a result to take place.

In understanding these points about the structure of Rule 23 and the troubling trend to which it has given rise, it is important to recall the theoretical context in which these issues are raised. The goal of this discussion has not been to make a point about plaintiff class action lawyers' failure to satisfy their obligations to their clients. Nor has it been to criticize the economic inefficiency of the class action device. The point, rather, is that, in all too many class action suits, there is, for all practical purposes, no class being represented. Instead, in these situations as a practical matter the attorneys themselves are the real parties in interest.

One possible response to this argument is that the *constructive* non-existence of a class is far different from the class's *technical* non-existence. In suits here described as constructively non-existent, it might be argued that at least certain class members do, in fact, know they are plaintiffs in a class action, and at least certain class members actually receive a compensatory benefit from the class action's resolution. This differs significantly, the argument would proceed, from a case being described as a class action where literally no class exists at all. From this perspective, the existence of something resembling a class, no matter how feeble, might suffice to satisfy the dictates of the compensatory remedial model provided for by the substantive law. But rarely is modern legal analysis satisfied by reliance on technicalities. Where an examination of practical reality demonstrates that plaintiff class members neither chose to sue nor are likely to receive meaningful compensation as a result of suit, the problems of democratic theory that I raise are triggered. My argument thus turns on the assumption that where the relief awarded to a class as a whole will rarely be acquired by individual class members or is of little practical use to the overwhelming majority of class members, it is reasonable, for purposes of both legal and political analysis, to characterize the plaintiff class in such a suit as faux.

A second response to my criticism of modern class action structure and practice is that, as Professor Hensler has argued, "if the primary goal is regulatory enforcement, carefully matching damages to losses is not a great concern. As long as defendants pay enough to deter bad behavior, economic theorists tell us, it does not matter how their payment is distributed."[99] But an economic response to a critique grounded in democratic theory amounts to an analytical non sequitur. An exclusive focus on achieving the goal of deterrence ignores the often fundamental political differences in the means chosen to accomplish that goal. Attaining deterrence by resort to one remedial model may give rise to socio-political consequences or concerns that differ significantly from those caused by another remedial model. It is just that transformation that modern class action procedure has brought about, or at least permitted to develop. Examination of the nature of remedial models and the manner in which the political selection among them implicates the concerns of democratic theory establishes that the mere fact that a class action may bring about deterrence does not automatically resolve the problems of democracy raised by the modern class action.

REMEDIAL MODELS, BOUNTY HUNTER SUITS, AND THE DEMOCRATIC DIFFICULTY

The Political Consequences of the Choice of Remedial Model

The legislative decision as to what behavior on the part of the citizenry is to be proscribed or restricted quite naturally answers only some of the normative issues of social policy implicated by legislative action. The abstract prohibition of behavior, even if it comes from government, will be nothing more than hortatory unless the legislation imposing that prohibition enforces it in some meaningful way. This choice, too, may implicate serious issues of political and social policy.

As already explained, in many instances the governmental choice to prohibit behavior is legislatively implemented by means of a private compensatory remedial model, which seeks simultaneously to compensate those who have been harmed by that behavior and to deter the behavior by those who have previously engaged in it or are considering doing so.[100] Government, however, has available to it alternative means of enforcing its prohibitions, especially when the effectiveness of the compensatory remedy as a punishment or deterrent is in doubt. This situation will arise where the transaction costs in judicially enforcing compensation remedies are likely to be high, where injured victims may lack the sophistication to bring suit, where either the existence or determination of damage is in doubt, or where the prohibited behavior is deemed sufficiently culpable as to justify punishment, untied to compensation. When this occurs, government may: (1) replace actual damages with a statutorily determined measure of damages; (2) supplement actual damages with either statutorily determined penalties or an authorization of the judicial award of punitive damages; (3) punish the behavior criminally; (4) authorize the imposition of civil fines; (5) create a system of administrative enforcement; or (6) establish a public guardian to act on behalf of the victims. Also, as the discussion of qui tam actions shows, in rare cases government has employed a bounty hunter model, by providing a non-compensatory reward to private individuals to encourage them to assist in enforcing legal regulation of behavior deemed harmful to the public interest.

It is quite conceivable that different methods of enforcement would give rise to different reactions from the electorate. A private compensatory remedy may have the greatest appeal because it has a twofold purpose: to compensate injured victims and to deter unlawful behavior. At the other end of the scale, the electorate may be more suspicious of a bounty hunter remedy, because it places the enforcement of public policy in the hands of individuals who are neither representative of nor accountable to the electorate and who are likely motivated primarily, if not exclusively, by considerations of personal gain. Thus, the legislative selection of a remedial model is potentially of great political significance.

The Foundations of Democracy

My argument, it should be recalled, is that class action suits brought on behalf of what is, for all practical purposes, a non-existent class amount to the use of a bounty hunter model, rather than the private compensatory remedial scheme provided for in the substantive law being enforced in the class action. In this sense, the argument proceeds, the procedure has transformed the essence of that law. To this point, however, a key question about the nature and force of this argument remains largely unanswered: Exactly how does this process of transformation undermine fundamental notions of democratic theory? To answer that question, I need first to posit a basic structural framework of democratic theory. To be sure, political theorists have argued endlessly about the structural and normative contours of democratic theory. Hence in shaping abstract precepts of democratic theory it will be necessary to bring democracy down to its lowest common denominators—elements that without which, virtually all would agree, the concept of democracy is rendered meaningless at best and Orwellian at worst. I must then explain how the modern class action's transformation of the pre-existing remedial model contravenes those precepts. In addition, it is appropriate to explore whether the problems to which I point do nothing more than raise normative issues of political theory, or whether they also give rise to statutory and/or constitutional violations.

Democracy as Representation and Accountability

Any attempt to discern foundational precepts of democracy should start with the concession that democratic theorists have generally agreed on relatively little. Debates between individual autonomy theorists on the one hand and civic republicans and communitarians on the other continue to rage.[101] The views of theorists who believe that democracy flourishes when members of the community are encouraged to participate as much as possible in governmental decision making differ substantially from those of scholars who believe the electorate's role in the political process should be severely restricted.[102]

All scholars who express a foundational belief in democracy, however, must agree on at least one key point. In the words of constitutional and political theorist Alexander Meiklejohn, the ultimate normative premise of democratic theory is that "[g]overnments . . . derive their just powers from the consent of the governed. If that consent be lacking, governments have no just powers."[103] It is certainly true that the American governmental system is far from a pure democracy, grounded exclusively on the value of popular sovereignty. Our society also has a counter-majoritarian constitutional system, which imposes significant limitations on popular sovereignty, both procedurally and substantively. Concern about the unpredictability and danger of decision making by uncontrolled masses played an important role in the minds of those who shaped the American Constitution.[104] Thus, the president is elected, not directly by the people but by an intermediary body.[105] For many years, United States Senators were elected, not by the people but by the state legislatures.[106] Federal legislation is promulgated by means of a complex process that requires the assent of both houses of Congress and, usually, acceptance by the president.[107] It is thus possible, if not likely, that much legislation favored by a majority of the electorate will not be enacted.[108] But all that these facts demonstrate is that majoritarianism, in a technical sense, is not the focal point of American constitutional democracy. It surely does not follow that the normative foundations of the nation's political structure are free of any commitment to the notion of vesting ultimate sovereignty in the people. Indeed, a system lacking such a foundational commitment would, as a definitional matter, amount to an authoritarian state, which is anathema to a society that from its inception rejected the notion of taxation without representation.[109] Even democratic theorists who lack general respect for the intelligence or abilities of the electorate, such as Joseph Schumpeter, believe that, in a democracy, "the people have the opportunity of accepting or refusing the men who are to rule them."[110]

The keys to the form of democracy adopted in the United States, then, are not principles of majoritarianism, but rather—at least for policy choices not controlled by the counter-majoritarian Constitution[111]—the axioms of representation and accountability. In other words, those who make basic, sub-constitutional choices of social policy must (1) have been chosen by the electorate, and (2) be accountable to the electorate if they wish to continue in office. Focus upon commitment to these basic principles of democratic theory at some level moots one of the primary dilemmas of democracy. Both historically and politically, democratic theorists have wavered between the urge to value widespread participatory democracy—what political scientist James Morone refers to as "the democratic wish"[112]—and the simultaneous "dread of government."[113] By selecting those who govern, the electorate contributes to its own governing.[114] At the same time, representative government protects liberty by serving as a check on potentially despotic leadership that has been freed from any accountability to the people.[115]

Attacks on the Representation-Accountability Rationale

This does not mean that modern commentators, particularly in the legal field, have universally adopted an unquestioning commitment to these foundational precepts of democracy, on either normative or empirical levels.[116] My colleague Robert Bennett, for example, has argued that, as a practical matter, the individual's vote is invariably meaningless in choosing elected officials.[117] Therefore the primary value of democracy is neither "representativeness" nor accountability of elected officials. It is, instead, the incidental benefits to be derived from the democratic conversation to which the governing process gives rise.[118] But while Professor Bennett's point about the meaninglessness of the individual vote is no doubt accurate, the generalization of this insight to the entire electoral process is fundamentally flawed, because it effectively renders a benevolent dictatorship morally indistinguishable from a democracy. Moreover, if the electoral process itself is largely meaningless, what is the point of encouraging conversations about that process among members of the electorate? Thus, it is both logically and practically impossible to separate the developmental values of democracy from commitment to the foundational principles of representation and accountability.

Another attack on the representation/accountability version of democratic theory might be that those goals cannot realistically ever be reached, because legislators vote on a multitude of bills, not just one. Thus, it is quite possible that a citizen will agree with her legislator's vote on one bill, but disagree on another. Yet that citizen will be called upon to vote yea or nay on that legislator's retention. Whichever way she votes on that issue, her choice will not fully reflect her views on all of the issues that come before the legislature. To a certain extent, the criticism is of course accurate. It does not automatically follow, however, that providing citizens with a vote on retention fails to achieve any of the representational goals of democratic theory. This point is best comprehended by contrasting the representative system, with all of its imperfections, to an authoritarian state. In an authoritarian state, the citizens have absolutely no say in the choice of governmental decision makers. In contrast, under a representative system at least the citizens may make their choices by consideration of the candidates' positions or votes on the issue or issues he deems of primary importance.

Modern civic republican theorists, such as Cass Sunstein, have urged acceptance of a political theory that seems at odds, on fundamental levels, with the basic tenets of democracy.[119] Sunstein has suggested that, in the pursuit of "the common good," society should be guided, at least in part, by a principle of "universalism" that posits the possibility of "substantively right answers."[120] But it is unclear who, exactly, gets to determine the content of these "substantively right answers." In any event, such reasoning is fundamentally inconsistent with the substantive epistemological humility inherent in any commitment to a democratic system: a society that values democracy only to the extent that it reaches externally derived, predetermined normative conclusions is no more a democracy than Iran was under the Ayatollah Khomeini or the Eastern European Communist states were during the Cold War period. Thus, to the extent modern civic republicans posit the existence of a "good," derived by means external to the will of the populace, that is to legally bind society, they are rejecting democracy, rather than defining it.

Certainly, there exist almost countless permutations and combinations of democratic systems from which a society could choose in deciding how to govern itself. It is appropriate to conclude, however, that if history and language are to mean anything, a society cannot be considered "democratic" in any meaningful sense unless the bulk of sub-constitutional policy choices are made, directly or indirectly, by those who are representative of and accountable to the electorate.

The Political Commitment Principle as a Logical Outgrowth of Democracy

If one accepts the principles of representation and accountability as the foundations of democracy, it logically follows that laws enacted by the electorate's representatives ought not be kept secret. Nor would it logically be possible for legislators to vote by secret ballot. There is little point in allowing the public both to choose and retain its governing representatives, if the public is unaware of how those representatives voted on legislation, both proposed and enacted. Moreover, it would be even more harmful to democratic interests were government to purport to adopt "Law A" while secretly enacting "Law B" or "Law Not A." At least when legislators' votes on legislation are kept secret, the public is on notice to pursue alternative avenues of assuring itself of the political views of its chosen representatives. When legislators publicly proclaim their support (or opposition) to "Law A," but in reality the legislature has enacted a different or contrary law, the public has been effectively defrauded. Indeed, it is difficult to distinguish such political fraud from a candidate's obtaining money from union workers on the basis of the false assertion that he has actively participated in union activities. Such deceptive lawmaking is far more harmful to democracy than secretive legislation—as problematic as such legislation is—because in such a situation the public is deceived into believing that democracy is actually working.

It is true that as a practical matter, much modern law is made by government officials not directly accountable to the populace. Courts, whose judges—at least at the federal level—do not stand for election, on occasion fashion common-law principles, and administrative agencies, in applying and interpreting legislation, have traditionally exercised enormous discretionary power. To a certain extent, from the perspective of democratic theory, both assertions of power may well be deemed problematic, for the very reason that those making the decisions do not satisfy the requirements of representation and accountability.[121] Neither situation, however, is as systemically invidious as the process whereby governing law is surreptitiously transformed into a different or contrary law. In the context of judicial lawmaking, presumably the representative agencies of government have either failed or refused to act on the issue at hand, and a court must fill that vacuum, if only to perform its function within the private rights adjudicatory model: the court must determine governing law, simply to determine who wins. The existence of administrative decision making, in contrast, effectively concedes that generally framed legislation cannot possibly anticipate every conceivable application. Therefore, someone must intercede to perform that function. Moreover, administrative agencies can be considered indirectly accountable, at least to the extent they are considered part of the executive branch. Finally, to the extent legislators cede to administrative agencies fundamental lawmaking power, it is arguable that an electorate unhappy with such open-ended delegation may hold those legislators accountable at the next election.[122] None of these arguably ameliorating factors exists in the context of the surreptitious transformation of governing legislation.

The response might be fashioned that as a general matter, the public is likely to be unaware of and uninterested in either the content or structure of substantive law or the lawmaking process. A majority of the public, the argument proceeds, generally cannot tell the difference between "Law A" and "Law Not A," and therefore little of practical import turns on the openness and candor of the legislative process. In many instances, this assertion would no doubt be accurate. But it most certainly will not be true in all instances. Many segments of the public become energized by one type of law or another, from abortion regulation to welfare standards to international trade policy, to name only a few.[123] Once this point is conceded, however, it becomes impossible to determine, ex ante, which laws will, in fact, engender public interest and concern, and which will not. Therefore, it is necessary to proceed on a general assumption that in order for democracy to function properly, we should presume that all laws stimulate public interest.

One might further argue that it is common knowledge that most laws do not actually mean what they purport to say, because in reality most laws are the outgrowth of a cynical process of bartering among competing special interests—a fact that no legislator is likely to want to make public. This argument basically encapsulates the essence of the argument fashioned by "public choice" theorists.[124] But whatever the truth of this assertion as a matter of legislative process, it is misplaced in the present context. The laws to which public choice theorists refer accomplish just what they claim to. At most, what is kept secret is the true motivation for enactment of the law and how specific special interests will benefit as a result of its adoption. This is by no means the same thing as enacting a law that in reality effects changes diametrically opposed to the results that that law purports to bring about.

Applying the Political Commitment
Principle to the Modern Class Action

All too often, the class action device has been viewed as something other than what it was created to be—"a practical rule of joinder where joinder was otherwise impractical."[125] For example, George Priest suggests that "there has been little effort to explain why class litigation should be made to resemble individual litigation beyond the fact that individual litigation is regarded as the norm and class litigation, the exception."[126] The individual litigation ideal, then, appears to be "little more than preference for the known and accepted status quo."[127] Professor Priest's argument, however, effectively views the class action in a political and constitutional vacuum. He thereby completely ignores the political framework within which the class action device is intended to operate. Priest totally disregards the vitally important fact that the class action was created as—and to this day, purports to be—nothing more than a procedural mechanism by which to enforce pre-existing substantive rights. Yet substantive law generally establishes only individual compensatory rights. None of the statutes enforced by the class action rule distinguishes between individual and class rights. Indeed, all that they create are individual rights—the very rights that are aggregated for purposes of a class action. The class action rule, of course, gives rise to no substantive rights of its own. To view class litigation as something fundamentally different from the aggregation of the individual rights created by substantive law, then, would allow the procedural rule to transform the essence of the substantive law it was designed to enforce. The reason that the class action is modeled on the basis of the individual litigation model is not, as Professor Priest suggests, simply adherence to the "status quo."[128] The basis for the intertwining of the class action and the individual litigation model is, rather, the democratic need to prevent avowedly procedural devices from surreptitiously altering the essence of substantive law that has been enacted by those selected by and accountable to the electorate. So furtive an amendment process undermines the electorate's ability to exercise the fundamental democratic function of selecting its governmental representatives on the basis of their legislative choices.

It might be suggested that even if my view of the modern class action is assumed to be correct, the foundational precepts of democracy are not significantly impacted by the subtle shift from private compensatory remedial model to bounty hunter remedial model. The public has neither the sophistication nor interest to comprehend this shift, and therefore could not reasonably be expected to judge its elected representatives on the basis of their views or votes on the question. I seriously doubt the accuracy of this perception of the public's attitude. For example, the lack of public understanding of all of the nuances of the Enron corporate accounting scandals did not prevent a public outcry over the matter and the scurrying of politicians to curry favor with the electorate on the issue. Similarly, it would defy reality to suggest that issues of tort reform have not appeared high on the nation's political agenda in recent years.[129] Moreover, public attitudes about plaintiffs' class action lawyers have often been strongly negative over that same period.[130] Indeed, at times attitudes among some sectors of the populace toward trial lawyers have been so negative that candidates vying for political office have sought to benefit from an opponent's affiliation with plaintiffs' lawyers.[131] Additionally, the judiciary itself has, on more than one occasion, expressed disdain for plaintiff class action attorneys.[132]

It should be kept in mind that all of these criticisms have been made while plaintiffs' attorneys were operating under the rubric of what purports to be a private compensatory damage class action framework. While many have pointed critically to the willingness of plaintiff class attorneys "to subordinate the interests of class members to the attorney's own economic self-interest,"[133] the public may temper this negative view with its assumption that at the very least, these individuals are serving a valuable public function by facilitating the compensation of victims injured by corporate wrongdoing. Full public recognition of the facts that, in numerous class actions today, (1) injured victims are often unaware that suit has been brought on their behalf; (2) plaintiffs generally receive no meaningful compensation as a result of the suit; and (3) the only ones meaningfully rewarded for the judicial punishment of corporate misdeeds are those very same plaintiffs' attorneys who are so widely disdained and mistrusted, may lead to widespread public outrage.

The response might be made that the public is, in fact, already aware of this information. After all, criticism of modern class actions on the grounds that "class action attorneys are the prime beneficiaries" of damage class actions[134] is already widespread. Thus, public outrage should not be expected to increase were the legal reality to be transformed into formal legal rule.[135] But it is dangerous to assume general public understanding of this issue. The class actions in question are, at least superficially, brought to enforce private compensatory rights established by pre-existing substantive law, and injured victims are often paraded as part of the suits. At the very least, then, the existing legal framework likely gives rise to substantial public confusion on the matter. One might further respond that reliance on democratic principles as a basis for criticizing modern class actions makes little sense when many of the substantive laws being transformed, such as the antitrust laws, were enacted long before any current citizens were even alive and by legislators who have long passed from the scene. But many of the substantive laws invoked in modern class actions, such as consumer protection or environmental protection, are of much more recent vintage.

In any event, such a response misses the fundamental point because it ignores the manner in which Rule 23 shifts the substantive inertia. Imagine, for example, proposed federal legislation expressly authorizing qui tam-like suits by plaintiff class action attorneys that reward them for bringing corporate wrongdoers to justice, sans victims or compensatory damages. It is difficult to believe that, given the already skeptical attitude that pervades the public view of plaintiff class action attorneys, the proposal of such legislation would fail to engender widespread public debate, if not outrage. At the very least, no one could reasonably predict that this would *not* be the result. Yet, if my description of current class action structure and practice is largely accurate, that description is very close to the current situation—although the public may not be aware of it, due to the superficial adherence to the traditional framework. Thus, it is reasonable to conclude that the current class action framework has serious implications for the foundational democratic principles of representation and accountability.

PRAGMATISM, CLASS ACTIONS, AND THE DEMOCRATIC DIFFICULTY

In criticizing the modern class action as a circumvention of the democratic process, I have attempted to link a hard dose of pragmatism to a considerably more abstract analysis, grounded in political theory. I have focused on pragmatic considerations, looking behind technicalities and appearances to determine whether a real class exists by assessing practical realities. I have also focused on issues of abstract political theory, by condemning class actions on the grounds that they often circumvent the democratic process. I have developed this theoretical critique, however, without regard either to the impact of my analysis on the viability of the modern class action or to the arguably positive social benefits performed by the modern class action. Both aspects of my approach arguably leave me vulnerable to attack.

Class Actions, Political Theory, and Social Consequences

If one accepts my argument that all too often the modern class action contravenes fundamental precepts of democracy and therefore needs to be restructured in order to prevent that result, there can be little question that the class action as we have come to know it in recent years could not survive. To be sure, the class action procedure, properly structured, could remain an extremely important joinder device. But it would be disingenuous to suggest that, under this revised structure, class action lawyers would have nearly the same incentives to act that they presently have. Those who favor class actions as they currently exist would no doubt argue that this result is socially and politically unacceptable. Injured victims would be denied an effective procedural means of gaining compensation, and an important deterrent to corporate wrongdoing would be lost.

Such an argument is seriously flawed, on both empirical and conceptual grounds. Initially, it ignores much of the point of my critique: with its current structure, the class action too often fails to provide meaningful compensation to injured victims. It is true that this failure does not alter the use of class actions as a deterrent to illegal corporate behavior. But the exclusive focus of class action defenders on the procedure's deterrence value is itself misguided. Initially, it suffers from what I describe as "the fallacy of the free-standing class action." Scholars who would make such an argument operate under the fallacious assumption that the class action procedure itself provides a freestanding check on corporate illegality. As already noted, however, it is the underlying substantive law, rather than a procedural rule, that establishes both the standards of corporate illegality and the means of enforcing those standards.[136] If the class action enforces those standards by resort to a remedial model, that differs from the remedial model adopted in the substantive law. It is no defense of the class action to suggest that it deters illegal corporate behavior.

It may well be that in the case of many substantive restrictions on corporate behavior, the private compensatory remedial model provides an ineffective means of enforcement and deterrence, for the simple reason that individualized damages are too small to justify the transaction costs of even the class action procedure. An individual plaintiff's damages may be so small that she is unwilling even to take the relatively minimal effort required either to opt into a class at its start or to file a claim at its close. In such cases, it is incumbent on the governing legislative body to find alternative methods of deterring corporate illegality. If criminal, civil, and administrative enforcement mechanisms are deemed insufficient, the legislature may wish to consider creation of a form of bounty hunter-private attorney general action, despite its potential constitutional problems. But surely, a Federal Rule of Civil Procedure may not implement such a change, if the protections inherent in the democratic process are to function properly.

Pragmatism and Class Actions: The Problem of Categorization

It could be suggested that my pragmatic analysis simultaneously ignores class actions' compliance with the technical requirements of the procedural rule and the reality that at least some class members are both aware of and in agreement with the suit and some class members actually benefit, on an individual basis, from the award. In some cases, perhaps the number will not be all that small. In other cases, a significant number of class members may well file claim forms, despite either the limited amount of individual damage suffered or the burdens incurred in completing the form. In yet other cases class members' individual claims may be satisfied without the filing of a claim form, because individual damages are easily determinable and the defendant possesses business records listing all class members. Hence, it could be argued that my critique paints with far too broad an empirical brush, thereby effectively destroying real class actions in an effort to ferret out the occasional faux class action.

The anticipated argument brings to light what could be called the problem of categorization. Closer examination reveals that it is in reality a combination of two distinct yet related issues: the problems of both inter-class categorization and intra-class categorization. Inter-class categorization refers to the overbroad nature of any of the remedies I might suggest, because those remedies are likely to sweep both real and faux class actions within their reach. Intra-class categorization, in contrast, describes the problems caused by my willingness to classify an entire class as faux, even where some minimal number of class members will likely be aware of the suit and/or receive meaningful compensation. The two concerns are linked by their emphasis on the practical difficulty inherent in any attempt to categorize conceptually class actions that in practice defy such categorization. While it is certainly reasonable to raise these concerns about my critique, ultimately they should not present serious difficulties for remedying the problem I have perceived in the modern class action.

The intra-class concern is not persuasive. At least since the legal realist revolution of the early twentieth century, rarely are legal decisions grounded in technicalities that do not reflect social reality. At a certain point, so few class members actually benefit from a class settlement, relative to the number that do not so benefit, that the number benefiting should be deemed de minimis. In these cases, especially when the passivity inherent in use of opt-out is added to the mix, these class suits are constructively transformed from the private compensatory remedial model to the bounty hunter remedial model. One could nevertheless ask how we are to determine, ex ante, which classes deserve this description. The answer, I believe, is that one need never make that determination in an individual case. Rather, the goal should be to deal with the problem in a prophylactic manner, by establishing certification standards that will reduce the likelihood of the problem ever arising.

The pragmatic questions raised in the preceding discussion, concerning the most effective means of avoiding the problems of democratic theory to which the modern class action gives rise, sets the stage for a thorough examination of specific proposals for reform. The fact that, despite these difficulties, a realistic constitutional or statutory challenge to Rule 23 is highly unlikely renders the need for revision that much more compelling.

RESPONDING TO THE DEMOCRATIC DIFFICULTY: RECOMMENDATIONS FOR THE REVISION OF RULE 23

The Permutations of Reform

As already noted, the democratic difficulty is created by a synthesis of the ominous bookends of the 23(b)(3) class action—its start and its close. At its start, the inherent passivity brought about by the use of opt-out sets the groundwork for an entirely comatose class of plaintiffs, who have never chosen to enforce their private rights and are even unaware that a suit has been brought on their behalf. At its close, even a successful class action may fail to vindicate class members' private rights by providing meaningful compensation—a result easily predictable at the outset of the suit, because of the inherent impossibility of translating a class-based award into concrete, individualized damage awards to class members. In one sense or another, both of the bookends contribute to the ultimate transformation of the class action from an aggregative private compensatory action into what amounts to a pure bounty hunter action. Before one can properly consider specific reform proposals, then, it is appropriate to examine the way to combine the reform of the two problem areas.

There appear to be four such conceivable permutations: (1) revise neither one; (2) revise both; (3) revise only the method of initiation; or (4) revise only the method of resolution. I have already rejected option one, for reasons that should by now be obvious. Thus, we are left to choose among the final three options. While revising opt-out would undoubt-edly do much to bring the class action back to the private compensatory rights remedial model expressly adopted in the governing substantive law, it would be unwise to rely exclusively on such a mode of revision. To alter the problematic aspects of initiation while leaving the constructive non-compensatory/bounty hunter remedial phase that pervades modern damage class actions unchanged would be to leave much of the problem unaffected. Indeed, it is the transformation at the remedial stage from pri-vate compensatory to the bounty hunter model that gives rise to the most significant difficulties of democratic theory. Thus, if one were forced to choose between the two stages as the focus of reform, it would seem to make sense to center attention exclusively on the resolution phase, which I have labeled option four. Since there is no logical reason why both ends of the litigation process could not be reformed, however, perhaps the best solution would be to reform both the initiation and the resolution stages—what I have labeled option two.

Initiation Reform

If one decides to protect against the democratic difficulty at the ini-tiation stage of a 23(b)(3) class action, one possible strategy would be sig-nificant reduction in the situations in which opt-out, rather than opt-in, is to be employed as the measure of inclusion in the class.[137] It is true, of course, that such an amendment would not resolve the question of exactly at what point in the litigation process notice must be sent to class mem-bers, but neither would it appear to make that issue any more difficult than it already is. Arguably more troubling are the possible implications of the democratic critique for 23(b)(1) and 23(b)(2) class actions. After all, one could reasonably argue that the very same democratic considerations that render suspect the use of opt-out, rather than opt-in, raise questions, a fortiori, about class actions in which class members may not even opt out. In both situations, rights vested in the individual victim under governing substantive law are being exercised, even when the individual has not made the decision to exercise them. Because of this fact, it might make sense to abandon the mandatory nature of at least some form of mandatory class actions, though that is an issue explored in detail at later points in this book.[138] If particular substantive actions are to be deemed mandatory (subject, of course to procedural due process limitations), it is appropriate for that choice to be made by Congress.

Class actions brought pursuant to Rule 23(b)(2) present somewhat more complex issues, since these actions are brought predominantly for the purpose of acquiring injunctive relief, rather than damages.[139] Moreover, such classes are often brought on behalf of racially or ethnically defined groups, and the idea of individual notice and opt-in would render such classes practical impossibilities. Perhaps a persuasive argument could be made that such actions are therefore distinguishable from other categories of class actions. True, even injunctions may flow out of the violation of individually held rights. However, at least in civil rights class actions brought primarily for injunctive relief, it might be contended that the rights are actually held by the group, rather than the individual. For unrelated reasons to be explored in later chapters, however, I ultimately reject this notion.

Resolution Reform

Reform at the resolution stage would likely be considerably more difficult to implement than initiation reform. This is so even though the need for resolution reform is more compelling. The difficulty is that, unlike in the initiation context, the text of Rule 23 does not directly give rise to the democratic difficulty. The problem, rather, is that the Rule allows particular class actions to be resolved in a manner that gives rise to democratic concerns. The goal in reforming the Rule, then, should be to determine an effective means to prevent that result.

The response could be made that there is no need for reform of Rule 23 in order to ensure against the furtive transformation of the case into a pure bounty hunter action, because courts have more than sufficient power under the current version of Rule 23 to prevent class actions in which the only real parties in interest (other than the defendants) are the class attorneys. Under Rule 23(e), no settlement of a class action may be made absent a judicial determination that the settlement is fair.[140] This mechanism clearly empowers the court to prevent any settlement where it finds that no meaningful relief is to be awarded to individual class members. The problem, however, is not that the current version of Rule 23 prevents courts from avoiding transforming a class action into a bounty hunter action, but that it does not require courts to prohibit such a transformation. Controlled only by the hopelessly vague directive to assure that a settlement is "fair," it is all too easy for class action courts to approve settlements that amount to virtually pure bounty hunter actions in everything but name. The task, then, is to insert language into Rule 23 that will prevent such a result.

In approaching this task, there are two conceivable structural approaches to reform: insertion of categorical directives and insertion of situation-specific directives. Categorical directives are those that concededly sweep within their reach situations that do not present the danger to be prevented, as well as those that do. They do so because of the expected high transaction costs involved in attempting to distinguish between the two situations, and the serious risks that would flow from making an incorrect assessment in a particular case. Situation-specific directives, in contrast, provide a generalized directive that is designed to separate the two types of situations on a case-by-case basis, and it is expected that a court charged with implementation will apply them correctly to specific fact situations. In order to prevent the serious danger of bounty hunter actions within the rubric of class actions, I recommend inclusion of both forms of restrictions, with situation-specific limitations to be added at the outset of the case and categorical limitations to be inserted at the settlement approval stage.

Initially, at the certification stage, the certifying court should be directed to take into account as an important element of its decision the reasonable likelihood that individual members of the class will actually receive meaningful compensation as the result of a successful verdict or a settlement. This inquiry would not focus on the likelihood of success on the merits, but rather on the eventual feasibility of getting damage or settlement awards transmitted to individual class members, assuming such success. Thus, where individual claims are small and the award of payments to individual class members depends on the filing of complex claim forms, a certifying court should be reluctant to certify the class. Even if ultimately successful, such a case is highly likely to turn out to be a bounty hunter action, rather than the private compensatory action that the governing substantive law has made it.[141]

Perhaps one could respond that insertion of such a textual requirement is unnecessary, because certification of a (b)(3) class already takes into account considerations of manageability.[142] But the ease of conducting a case is not necessarily the same thing as certainty of payment to individual class members. Indeed, it is likely that the ability to resolve a case through a method that contemplates payment to relatively few class members makes a case appear to be more manageable to many federal judges. Without insertion of this express directive, there is little reason to hope that a majority of federal judges would concern themselves with this question in making a certification decision. Because this directive asks a reviewing court to apply its general standard to specific fact situations, this recommended reform constitutes a situation-specific rule. In this sense, it would leave room for judicial mistake and manipulation. But there would appear to exist no practical alternative, and express emphasis in the Rule's text on the need to assure feasibility of individualized awards to class members would undoubtedly go far toward restoring the class action as the aggregative compensatory action it must be, under the terms of the substantive laws that it purports to enforce.

At the close of the action,[143] when the court is asked to review the fairness of a proposed settlement, adoption of a more categorical approach is required, for the simple reason that such categorical rules appear to be readily available and can effectively ensure against the practices most likely to bring about the improper transformation of a class action into a bounty hunter action. In this vein, an amendment to Rule 23 dictating that attorneys' fees be measured by reference to the value of the total number of class member claims actually filed, rather than by the total amount of settlement or potential claims, would go far toward deterring pure bounty hunter class actions.[144]

CONCLUSION: DEMOCRATIC THEORY AND LEGAL APATHY

In one sense, given the intense scholarly controversy over and substantial judicial attention to questions about class actions in recent years, the virtually total silence about the ways in which the modern class action impacts the essential democratic precepts of accountability and representation is surprising. In another sense, however, such apathy in the legal world toward the relevance of even foundational issues of democratic theory is not all that unexpected. Numerous commentators, focused primarily on their own normative policy goals, have been willing to cast aside values of self-determination—at least where that process is likely to produce conclusions that differ from their own normative goals.[145] But engaging in legal analysis divorced from its grounding in foundational precepts of American democracy—even when those precepts may not be directly derived from the Constitution—becomes theoretically incoherent at best and invidiously manipulative at worst. And if there are any such precepts, they necessarily embody the value of popular sovereignty, implemented and protected by the principles of representation and accountability for sub-constitutional decisions of public policy.[146]

All too often, the modern (b)(3) class action has surreptitiously transformed the governing substantive law, which unambiguously embodies a private compensatory remedial model as the exclusive, primary, or secondary means of enforcing legislative restrictions on primary behavior, into an entirely distinct "bounty hunter" remedial model—one that has not been enacted as part of the substantive law. Pursuant to this approach, uninjured private individuals are rewarded for ferreting out and judicially punishing corporate illegality, much in the manner that classic qui tam actions historically have.[147] It has done so, even though the class action exists solely as a procedural device designed to facilitate implementation of existing substantive law. Such a furtive transformation of governing law undermines the principles of accountability and representation that are so essential to any political system that views popular sovereignty as an important element.

The class action achieves this result through the initiation process of opt-out and the resolution process of settlements in which no meaningful compensation is received by an overwhelming portion of the class. When combined, these two elements render the class little more than a figment of the class lawyers' imaginations, leaving those attorneys as the only real parties in interest and virtually the only private individuals who stand to benefit financially from successful prosecution of the action. This situation arises even though those attorneys need not be (and generally are not) themselves injured victims.

It is both appropriate and necessary for the Advisory Committee to reform modern class action practice, if only on normative grounds of social policy and political theory. The proposals for reform that I have suggested,[148] for the most part, do not represent dramatically new suggestions. For example, the argument that opt-out should, at least in a portion of class actions,[149] be replaced by opt-in has been made at least since the time I was a law student. The contribution I hope to have made in this chapter, however, is the development of an entirely different theoretical perspective on the modern class action and the provision of an entirely new set of justifications, grounded in fundamental notions of democratic theory, for those proposed revisions.

Perhaps it is proper to include within my goals in writing this chapter the desire to shift the focus of at least a portion of the scholarly debate on the class action issue. All too often, scholars have approached the class action issue as if it were a self-contained device to control illegal corporate behavior.[150] As I have shown, however, it is essential to understand the class action within the broader framework of American democracy.

CHAPTER THREE

The Supreme Court, the Rules Enabling Act, and the Politicization of the Class Action

To a certain portion of the populace, the Federal Rules of Civil Procedure probably represent little more than highly technical and esoteric directives for the day-to-day operation of the federal litigation process—if, indeed, they represent anything at all. Even the average federal litigator may well think of the Rules primarily as either technical requirements that must be complied with or strategic devices employable to facilitate victory. In reality, however, many of the Federal Rules have a dramatic impact on fundamental socio-political and economic concerns: the allocation of governmental resources, the redistribution of private wealth, the effectiveness of legislatively imposed behavioral proscriptions, and concerns of fairness and equality. This is probably not what either the Congress that originally authorized them, the Advisory Committee that originally prepared them, or the Supreme Court justices who originally promulgated them expected the Rules to do. Recognized at the time or not, however, the choices made by the drafters of the Rules have often had a significant impact on foundational moral, economic, and social choices made by society as a whole.

Nowhere is this more evident than in the context of the modern class action. Because the class action procedure makes possible the litigation of countless claims arising under federal and state law, it dramatically alters the real world impact of those substantive laws. But the class action's substantive impact extends well beyond the mere procedural implementation of pre-existing substantive law. Because the very threat of class action liability is often overwhelming, defendants who are averse to "betting the company" will generally seek to settle the moment a class action is certified.[1] Moreover, as demonstrated in an earlier chapter, what are as a matter of controlling substantive law intended to function as compensatory claims may often be transformed by the class action device into what effectively amount to "bounty-hunter" suits, wholly unauthorized by the applicable law.[2] More fundamentally, by so dramatically altering the manner in which individually held substantive claims are adjudicated, the modern class action inevitably impacts—if only indirectly—foundational substantive values concerning wealth redistribution and the policing of corporate behavior. Over the last twenty-five years or so, the political stakes involved in shaping the Federal Rules of Civil Procedure have gradually risen to the surface, and those interest groups most affected have responded accordingly. During that time, the process by which the Rules are revised has been made considerably more open, and affected organizations and entities have significantly increased their efforts to influence the direction those revisions take.

It is all but inconceivable that it could have been any other way. With the benefit of 20/20 hindsight, at least, we can say with some assurance that it is impossible in most cases to completely separate the procedural from the substantive. Viewed from today's perspective, the notion that by confining the Rules to matters of "procedure," as the Rules Enabling Act of 1934 directed,[3] one could somehow prevent them from having important and controversial socio-economic and political consequences outside the courtroom is absurd. But explicit recognition of the often-overlapping nature of the substantive-procedural interaction on a political level did not come until the Supreme Court's 1958 decision in *Byrd v. Blue Ridge Rural Electric Cooperative*,[4] a relatively late point in the development of the doctrine growing out of the Court's momentous decision in *Erie Railroad Co. v. Tompkins*.[5] Even then, the recognition did not come in a case concerning the scope of the Federal Rules. Because *Erie* had not even been decided at the time of the Enabling Act's passage in 1934, it is perhaps unreasonably anachronistic to superimpose on the congressional drafters a sophisticated understanding of how procedural choices may impact substantive policies. Be that as it may, the political realties of today are clear; the impact of many of the rules extends far beyond the four walls of the federal courthouse, inevitably implicating a number of the most controversial modern political debates. On occasion, respected commentators have acknowledged the potentially broad political impact of the Rules.[6] What is so puzzling, however, is that despite widespread recognition of these political realities, no scholar has provided a thoughtful analysis of what implications, if any, this recognition should have on how we are to view the Rules Enabling Act's interpretation or constitutionality.

Recognition of the inherently political nature of such rules as Rule 23, governing class actions, raises fundamental questions concerning the scope of our nation's constitutional democracy. The Supreme Court sits at the pinnacle of the one branch of the federal government formally insulated by the Constitution's Framers from majoritarian pressures.[7] While there were obvious and valid reasons for establishing such insulation, those protections necessarily give rise to recognized risks to a democratic system. To prevent the insulated judiciary from co-opting the power of the representative and accountable branches, the Framers imposed significant restrictions on the scope of the judicial power. The Constitution grants to the judiciary no purely legislative authority. To the extent the Supreme Court may promulgate sub-constitutional federal law, it must do so as an incident to the performance of the inherently judicial function of case resolution.[8] Yet the Rules Enabling Act invests in the Supreme Court lawmaking power untied to the judicial process. It was the statute's express insulation of the authority to abridge or modify a "substantive right" that was generally assumed to preserve Congress's legislative power.[9] Congress appears to have reasoned that where the Court merely promulgates rules of "procedure," it is not overstepping its constitutionally limited bounds because procedure is, by definition, internal to the operation of the judiciary; it has no impact outside the four walls of the courthouse. We now know—and probably should have known at the time of the Act's passage—that this is political nonsense. In numerous instances (especially the context of class actions), procedural choices inevitably—and often intentionally—impact the scope of substantive political choices. This recognition should logically raise a concern that the Act unconstitutionally vests in the Supreme Court power that is reserved, in a constitutional democracy, for those who are representative of and accountable to the electorate.

This is not to suggest that the constitutionality of the Rules Enabling Act—at least as a practical matter—is today in serious doubt. The Supreme Court has confidently asserted the Act's constitutionality on more than one occasion,[10] and there is absolutely no reason to imagine that this attitude will change in the foreseeable future. Nevertheless, engaging in a constitutional inquiry at this point serves two important functions. First, purely as a matter of constitutional theory, there is legitimate intellectual interest in examining where the Court's rule-making power fits within the framework of the nation's commitment to constitutional democracy. Second, and of more immediate pragmatic concern, recognition of the serious constitutional difficulties to which the Rules Enabling Act inherently gives rise can and should have an important impact on construction of the

Act's directives. As already noted, by its express terms the Act insulates authority to abridge, enlarge, or modify a "substantive right" from the Court's rule-making power.[11] Considerable judicial effort has gone into determination of the appropriate interpretation of this phrase, without anything approaching total satisfaction.[12] Scholars have had similar difficulty coming to a consensus on the subject.[13] With specific reference to the class action, this inquiry should illuminate not what the controlling class action standards should be, but rather which governmental body, within the framework of our nation's constitutional democracy, should bear political and legal responsibility for making those normative choices.

All concerned appear to have ignored that the Congress that drafted and passed the Act proceeded on a misguided assumption about the completeness and mutual exclusivity of the substance-procedure dichotomy when it imposed the "substantive right" restriction on the Court's rule-making power.[14] Its obvious goal was to preserve for the accountable and representative Congress fundamental normative choices of social policy, and Congress mistakenly believed it had achieved this goal by vesting in the Court solely the power to regulate "practice and procedure."[15] The question now arises, how do we enforce the language the Act's framers employed to restrict the Court's policy-making function (consistent with the Constitution's democratic assumptions and directives), when they proceeded on wholly fallacious practical and conceptual understandings of the simplicity and totality of the substance-procedure dichotomy? The driving force behind recognition of this interpretive tension is the very democratic directive that underlies the constitutional difficulty already described. In this sense, then, the issues of constitutional and statutory interpretation that surround the Rules Enabling Act are inextricably intertwined. This is so, even if one begins analysis with the recognition that the constitutional issue is today far more theoretical than real.

I reach several conclusions on the basis of my recognition of the serious democratic difficulty inherent in the Rules Enabling Act's vesting of rule-making power in the Supreme Court's hands. First, while the constitutionality of the Act, in whole or in part, is beyond question purely as a matter of controlling precedent, careful examination of the Court's decisions so holding reveals the complete absence of supporting logic or reasoning. Second, if one were to constitutionally analyze the Act's insulation of important policy choices from any organ of government that is even remotely responsive to the electorate, at least in the first instance,[16] it is highly likely that the Act would fail. Finally, even if one were to take the Act's constitutionality as a doctrinal given, it is appropriate to employ parallel reasoning, grounded in concerns of democratic accountability, in construing the cryptic but nevertheless vital statutory insulation of substantive rights from the scope of the Court's rule-making power. It is clear, after all, that the Act's drafters were attempting (albeit crudely) to achieve the same result: the preservation of important policy choices for the elected representatives of the people.

Acceptance of the analysis proposed here would substantially alter the manner in which the class action rule is promulgated. Because, for reasons already explained both in this chapter and prior ones,[17] the choice of class action procedure so significantly and inevitably implicates substantive moral, economic, political, and social policies, in a constitutionally ideal world that choice would be made by those branches most accountable to and representative of the electorate—Congress and the executive, through the traditional process of legislative enactment.[18] Assuming that what I posit to be the constitutionally ideal world is never attained, the goal of representative fashioning of class action procedure should be achieved by resort to principled construction of the text of the Rules Enabling Act.

As the inquiry begins, two overarching points need to be kept in mind. First, to suggest that the rule-making process has become "politicized" is by no means to suggest that the process has become corrupted. To the contrary, those interest groups who have sought to contribute to the rule-making process appear to have done so in a thoughtful, persuasive, and wholly above-board manner. Nor is it to suggest that those involved in the rule-making process—the Advisory Committee, the Standing Committee, or the Supreme Court—have in any way performed their tasks improperly, unethically, or incompletely. In fact, the exact opposite appears to be true. The "corruption" of the system, if indeed that is the correct word, comes purely on the level of political process. In a democratic system, one does not judge political choices by the wisdom or good faith of the decision maker. Any individual or entity lacking the legitimacy of accountability and making sub-constitutional policy choices is, at some level, inherently defective.[19]

THE RULES ENABLING ACT: STRUCTURE AND HISTORY

The Role of the Substance-Procedure Dichotomy in the Rules Enabling Act

The Rules Enabling Act arose out of a period of dissatisfaction with an American civil procedure system that had become overly complicated and cumbersome. Reformers such as Roscoe Pound and Charles Clark believed that the judiciary needed to be more empowered and that judges should be afforded more discretion in shaping judicial procedure.[20] The Act was finally passed during the New Deal era and embodied the anti-formalistic, expertise-oriented spirit of the time.[21] As such, it is unsurprising that neither Congress nor subsequent rule makers clearly elucidated the limitations on the Supreme Court's rule-making power.

By the end of the nineteenth century, lawyers had become increasingly frustrated with the common law pleading system. Because the technical pleading requirements attempted to reduce cases to a single issue, the "system became rigid and rarefied."[22] Parties often lost their suits on procedural grounds rather than on the merits of their claims.[23] The reformers behind the Rules Enabling Act identified this as the primary problem with the legal system.[24]

It was within this legal climate at the dawn of the twentieth century that legal reformers began to advocate dramatic change. They called for a uniform, simplified system and the merger of law and equity courts. Charles Clark bemoaned the complexity of common law procedure, famously writing, "procedure should be the hand-maid and not the mistress of justice . . . [a]nd therefore rules of pleading or practice should at all times be but an aid to an end and not an end in themselves."[25] Clark looked to the equity system for guidance, embracing its simplicity and flexibility.[26] Thus began the twenty-five year battle to pass the Rules Enabling Act, legislation that would revolutionize federal procedure.[27]

The key to the movement was support for the adoption of simple procedural rules that would enable litigants to reach the merits of their claims with relative ease. Pound sought to give judges the power to make their own procedural rules because the task called for the exercise of professional expertise.[28] Flexible and uniform rules would provide judges with "discretion to overlook procedural mistakes and . . . a broader and more pliable litigation package."[29] The language of the Act, in relevant part, provided:

> The Supreme Court of the United States shall have the power to prescribe, by general rules, for the district courts of the United States and for the courts of the District of Columbia, the forms of process, writs, pleadings, and motions, and the practice and procedure in civil actions at law. Said rules shall neither abridge, enlarge, nor modify the substantive rights of any litigant.[30]

Pursuant to the Act, the Supreme Court appointed an Advisory Committee, which was to draft the Rules and revise them as needed over time.[31] After review by the Standing Committee of the Judicial Conference, the

Rules were to be reviewed by the Supreme Court and then submitted by the Court to Congress for review. Unless rejected by congressional act prior to a specified date, the Rules were to go into effect.[32] The first Advisory Committee was appointed and met shortly after the passage of the Act.[33] Charles Clark served as reporter and drafted the bulk of what were to become the Federal Rules of Civil Procedure.[34]

REACTIONS TO JUDICIAL RULE MAKING: THE EARLY MISCONCEPTIONS ABOUT THE SUBSTANCE-PROCEDURE DICHOTOMY

Given the breathtaking scope of power that the Rules Enabling Act allocated to the Supreme Court, it is surprising how few questions were raised as to its constitutionality at the time of its passage. Despite the presence of a few staunch resisters, neither the early reformers nor the first Advisory Committee ever articulated a detailed defense of the Act's constitutionality.[35] This was probably due to the widespread, albeit fallacious, assumption about the mutual exclusivity between matters of procedure and matters of substance. History clearly shows that the drafters of the Act and the early Supreme Court opinions interpreting the Act operated under an unduly simplistic understanding of the substantive implications of procedure.[36] They seemed to have proceeded on the assumption that procedural and substantive law were mutually exclusive—a notion now universally recognized to be woefully unrealistic. The drafters did seem to intuit some of the potential problems of democratic theory to which the Act gave rise, though perhaps more as a strategic protection of congressional domain. Their problem, however, was their failure to recognize how the rulemaking authority affected matters of social policy.

The idea for a uniform federal procedure bill was not well received by everyone. Senator Walsh of Montana, for example, stood fast as an opponent of the bill for over fifteen years.[37] Drawing on Walsh's objections to the reform movement,[38] in 1917 a majority of the Senate Judiciary Committee endorsed a report titled "Views of the Minority" suggesting that Congress may not have constitutional authority to delegate the power to make supervisory rules of procedure.[39] However, due to the "long history of Congress's acquiescence in the Supreme Court's promulgation of Equity Rules,"[40] Walsh did not yet embrace the delegation controversy, but instead focused on the pragmatic interpretive problems and inconveniences the new system would create.[41] By 1926, Walsh expanded his criticisms and openly protested that the judiciary's rule-making authority would usurp legislative power.[42]

In response to these protests, Senator Cummins redrafted the bill to add the somewhat cryptic sentence, "Said rules shall neither abridge, enlarge, nor modify the substantive rights of any litigant."[43] Professor Burbank's historical research suggests that Cummins intended to quell the delegation objections with this addition.[44] In a letter to Chief Justice Taft regarding the addition, Cummins wrote, "Congress could not if it wanted to, confer upon the Supreme Court, legislative power," and therefore the additional sentence should "quiet the apprehensions of those who may be opposed to any measure of this sort."[45] Thus the language of the Rules Enabling Act codified the reformers' belief that as long as the judiciary limited its scope to "procedural" matters and not "substantive" ones, it would not encroach on legislative functions.

The substance-procedure dichotomy soon became the accepted response to separation of powers arguments asserted against the uniform procedure bill. Professor Burbank documents that in the face of numerous criticisms alleging that the bill was a judicial usurpation, the Senate Judiciary Committee simply reiterated that the judiciary would not have the power to affect substantive rights.[46] Puzzlingly, the committee also drew on the history of judicial rule making in England and the several states,[47] despite the quite obvious fact that constitutional restrictions do not bind those entities to the same extent that they restrain the United States Supreme Court.

Thus, the drafters of the Rules Enabling Act believed that historical practice and the enigmatic substance-procedure dichotomy immunized the Act from constitutional scrutiny as an improper delegation of congressional legislative power. However, it soon became clear that neither the drafters nor the first Advisory Committee had much sense of what the terms *substance* and *procedure* meant in the context of the Rules Enabling Act. The Senate Committee, for its part, trusted the Supreme Court to check itself.[48] After the passage of the Rules Enabling Act, the Advisory Committee commissioned to draft the Rules of Civil Procedure in 1935 did not articulate any clear standard for differentiating between substance and procedure.[49] In fact, Professor Burbank's extensive historical research reveals that the Advisory Committee "had no coherent or consistent view of the limitations imposed by the Act's procedure/substance dichotomy."[50] He further notes that although members of the committee occasionally referred to the history of the passage of the Rules Enabling Act, "one leaves the published and unpublished sources with the impression that, although the committee may have recognized the basic purpose of the procedure/ substance dichotomy, in formulating and applying the Act's limitations normative considerations took a back seat to practical possibilities."[51] Burbank's sources also reveal that the committee was satisfied "to rely largely on judgments informed by a sense of the professional and political climate and by the hope that the Supreme Court would preserve it from error."[52]

THE CONFLATION OF SUBSTANCE AND PROCEDURE: THE POLITICIZATION OF THE CLASS ACTION AND THE FEDERAL RULES

It is beyond controversy today that many Federal Rules of Civil Procedure implicate substantial policy issues, often going to the core of modern political and ideological debates. Indeed, the Court itself has noted that "rulemaking under the enabling Acts has been substantive and political in the sense that the rules of procedure have important effects on the substantive rights of litigants."[53] Recognition of this fact should not be earthshaking. Rules 11 (dealing with sanctions)[54] and 26 (concerning discovery)[55] are merely illustrative of the Rules that directly implicate highly controversial tort-reform issues and have therefore become the subject of debate and the object of lobbying efforts by interest groups such as consumer-advocacy organizations, large corporations, and trial lawyers associations.[56] Growing out of the heavily disputed belief that the United States judicial system is overburdened with frivolous civil lawsuits that harass corporate defendants and lead inexorably to higher prices for goods and services, the modern tort-reform movement includes proposals to impose damage caps, rewrite contributory negligence laws, and impose heavier sanctions on people bringing frivolous suits.[57] Underlying the tort-reform debate are more foundational disputes over ideology and normative political theory.[58] These issues implicate the value placed on such substantive policy concerns as civil rights and consumer protection, as well as fundamental questions about societal resource allocation, wealth transfer, and economic efficiency.[59] The inescapable implication is that how society structures its system of adjudication inevitably has a substantial impact on the protection of substantive rights and the foundations of substantive social policy.

The recent political focus on issues of tort reform has underscored the politicization of many of the Federal Rules, of which the class action rule is arguably the most striking example.[60] The political nature of the Rules, however, is by no means a recent development, despite the failure of both the Enabling Act's drafters and the postenactment Supreme Court either to recognize or acknowledge this fact. To the contrary, from the outset many of the Rules possessed a distinctly political nature because the manner in which they are shaped inherently impacts the enforcement of society's substantive policy choices. While the class action rule may be the most prominent example, it is by no means the only one.

One of the most visible illustrations of this phenomenon is Rule 11, which enables judges to sanction lawyers for filing pleadings or motions for dilatory or other improper purposes.[61] As revised in 1983, Rule 11 required certification that, among other things, the pleading or motion was "well grounded in fact."[62] This alteration was quite obviously (albeit indirectly) intended to constrain the sweeping scope of Rule 8(a),[63] which established the so-called "notice pleading" system. Under the framework of the system created by Judge Clark and the original Advisory Committee, all a litigant need do in a pleading is provide "a short and plain statement" of the claim[64]—an intentionally low burden.[65] The underlying goal of the system was to enable litigants to initiate use of the Rules' elaborate discovery process to facilitate the enforcement of substantive claims.[66] By effectively expanding the scope of the parties' burdens at the pleading stage, the 1983 version of Rule 11 dramatically impacted the ability of plaintiffs to enforce their substantive rights[67] and, not surprisingly, gave rise to significant political debate.

In contrast, the next revision of Rule 11 ten years later facilitated plaintiffs' enforcement of substantive claims by removing the requirement that the litigant certify that the assertions contained in her pleading are "well grounded in fact."[68] A central element of the tort-reform movement has therefore been an attempt to strengthen Rule 11 through congressional enactment.[69] In September 2004, the House of Representatives approved a measure amending the current (1993) version of Rule 11 to require sanctions on lawyers who file "frivolous" lawsuits.[70] Not surprisingly, the bill had a politically polarizing effect; Republicans touted it as necessary "to end nuisance lawsuits that . . . were driving companies out of business and costing consumers," while Democrats said it "could make it harder for less-affluent Americans to retain legal counsel if lawyers were nervous about facing sanctions."[71]

More recently, we have witnessed evidence of the dramatic substantive-procedural intersection in the Supreme Court's construction of the pleading requirements imposed by the Federal Rules. In *Bell Atlantic v. Twombly*,[72] the Court construed the language of Rule 8(a)[73] to require more than merely a conclusory allegation of liability, even though prior decisions of the Court appeared to require no more.[74] As a result, it is likely that numerous plaintiffs who otherwise would have been in a position to litigate and possibly vindicate their claims will no longer be able to get to the discovery stage of the litigation process.

Also illustrative of the extent to which the Rules may become intertwined with matters of important social policy is the recent amendment concerning electronic discovery.[75] The Advisory Committee hearings on the issue are replete with testimony by trial lawyers associations, representatives of large global companies, and spokespersons for consumer groups.[76] Naturally, regulations of electronic discovery will have important and inescapable implications both for litigants' ability to enforce existing substantive law and for businesses of all sizes seeking to operate in an economically efficient manner.[77] Plaintiffs' lawyers and consumer advocacy groups favored rules that require litigants to preserve as much material as possible for as long as possible.[78] Large corporations and the defense bar, on the other hand, stressed the great expense of electronic-document storage and favored more lenient provisions on mandatory disclosure and record preservation.[79] Such proposals could readily implicate fundamental policy debates. Plaintiffs often depend on electronic discovery to support their efforts to compel wealth transfer and enforce substantive restrictions on corporate behavior,[80] while the Rules' dictates may force corporate defendants to incur enormous expense in altering their record-keeping systems. The impact of electronic discovery on social and economic policy is thus significant.

As already noted, the rule that has generated the most intense political controversy in recent years is Rule 23, governing the procedures for class action suits. Although Rule 23 was part of the original Federal Rules of Civil Procedure, it was not until 1966 that sweeping revisions transformed class actions into a powerful tool for implementing socio-political change.[81] The modern class action arose out of a period of social and political revolution; in the wake of the civil rights movement and the social revolution of President Johnson's Great Society programs, the rulemakers saw a need for procedural devices that would legally empower otherwise unempowered groups.[82] Thus, in 1966, they transformed Rule 23,[83] and it has since become an important instrument for enforcement of legislative and common law proscriptions of business behavior.[84] On the other hand, because class actions may well threaten a company's very existence, class action suits may coerce corporate defendants into settling even nonmeritorious claims. Because the costs of these settlements will be passed on to consumers, unduly lax class-certification standards will inevitably lead to undue inflation and economic inefficiency. Regardless of their substantive views, both sides of the class action debate can agree that class action procedure implicates core fundamental political and ideological choices.

RECONSIDERING THE CONSTITUTIONALITY OF THE RULES ENABLING ACT

Constitutional Theory and the Rules Enabling Act

It should by now be clear that the assumption of procedural-substantive mutual exclusivity that apparently underlay the thinking of both Congress and the Supreme Court in the early years is totally misguided. No one today could seriously doubt that procedural rule making involves the weighing of substantial policy interests and dynamically alters the development of the substantive law. Surely it is just such policy choices that our system of constitutional democracy contemplates will be made by those who are at some level responsive to the electorate, at least when those choices are made apart from the adjudication of cases or controversies.

What appears to remain unrecognized by anyone are the logical implications of this insight for the widespread assumption of the Rules Enabling Act's constitutionality. The foundational political and ideological debates that are often triggered by the framing of the Federal Rules are not resolved by any individual or entity even indirectly responsive to the public will. To the contrary, final choices are made by the one organ of the federal government that is constitutionally insulated from electoral pressures.[85] Intuitively, at least, this segregation of key political choices from responsive governmental organs appears highly problematic.

When one attempts to translate this intuitive uneasiness into hard constitutional law, one is naturally drawn to the nondelegation doctrine[86] and to the case-or-controversy requirement of Article III.[87] In relying on the nondelegation doctrine and the case-or-controversy requirement, I readily acknowledge that the instinctive reaction of most constitutional observers will be either a collective yawn or a feeling of constitutional déjà vu. It is true, after all, that the last time the nondelegation doctrine played an important role in constitutional law, Franklin Roosevelt was president.[88] Though the case-or-controversy requirement has continued to play a significant role in the shaping of modern justiciability doctrine,[89] the Court has been something less than rigid in enforcing its dictates where Congress has made clear that it wishes federal judges to perform nonadjudicatory tasks.[90]

Yet one may reasonably begin the constitutional analysis by reference to the following assumption: Were Congress, hypothetically, to enact a law delegating to the Article III judiciary the authority to promulgate prospectively controlling "rules" of federal products liability or consumer protection law, the legislation would be held unconstitutional. No matter how much modern constitutional scholars mock structural doctrines of separation of powers and declare them irrelevant, there is some point at which the Constitution will be found to prohibit the delegation of purely legislative authority to the Supreme Court. The inquiry, then, should concern where that constitutional line should be drawn, and on which side of that line the Rules Enabling Act falls.

The best way to assess the constitutionality of the Rules Enabling Act is to inquire exactly what it is about the hypothetical delegation statute that renders it so unambiguously unconstitutional; why is it that Congress may not constitutionally delegate to the Supreme Court the authority, independent of the adjudicatory function, to promulgate rules of federal consumer protection or products liability law? Textually, there is little doubt that if the Supreme Court could exercise such power, Article III's case-or-controversy limitation would be meaningless; the Court would be doing far more than adjudicating cases or controversies. Moreover, the Court would be exercising purely legislative authority, vested solely in Congress by Article I.[91]

It is important to note that this hypothetical statute would be unconstitutional, despite the fact that the Court has validated sweeping delegations of legislative authority to executive agencies.[92] The differences are twofold, and both derive ultimately from the Court's unique status in the American political system. Unlike any member of Congress or the president, justices are not elected.[93] Unlike any administrator, they sit for life and have special protection of their independence.[94] Professor Mashaw has argued that delegations of legislative authority to executive agencies are constitutional, because members of those agencies are accountable to the president, who is himself representative of and accountable to the electorate.[95] The same cannot be said of Supreme Court justices. Thus, to the extent one key concern about congressional delegations of legislative authority is a dilution of decision-making accountability that is the sine qua non of a democratic system, the constitutional difficulty is significantly exacerbated by delegations to an unrepresentative and unaccountable Court.

One might respond that congressional delegation of lawmaking authority to the federal judiciary is a well-accepted practice. For example, Congress vested in the courts the power to fashion the law of restraint of trade,[96] or shape the federal law of labor contracts.[97] But the obvious difference is that the federal courts are vested with the power to do so only through performance of the adjudicatory function.[98] Courts must possess authority to fill gaps in controlling substantive law in this manner, if only as a means of facilitating the resolution of live disputes.[99] This is far different from the rule making of administrative agencies, which is untied to such dispute resolution.[100]

It is performance of the adjudicatory function that leads to the second constitutional problem with the hypothetical statutory delegation of law making authority to the Supreme Court: The absence of any limitation of the judicial function to the resolution of live disputes. Once again, the concern finds its origins in the nation's foundational democratic commitment to lawmaking by representative and accountable decision makers. The case-or-controversy limitation clearly has the effect of restraining the one branch of government constitutionally insulated from political pressure. There are, of course, many valid reasons for the Framers' decision to include such insulation.[101] But in a nation whose founders fought to end taxation without representation, the establishment of a coordinate branch of government that is representative of, and accountable to, no one naturally gave rise to the concern that said branch might usurp the lawmaking authority vested in the more representative branches. The means for preventing this development, then, was the simultaneous restriction of the judiciary's power to the performance of its traditional function of dispute resolution. If the courts were to make law, it would have to be as an incident to the performance of this function.

The hypothetical authorization of freestanding judicial lawmaking quite clearly undermines this fundamental element of American political theory. The constitutional difficulty, then, goes far deeper than merely some formalist, textual focus on the words, *case* or *controversy*, appearing in Article III.[102] Here, abandonment of the Constitution's case-or-controversy limitation would lead to the very result that the Framers were presumably seeking to avoid by imposing the case-or-controversy limitation in the first place.

Before one can apply this constitutional analysis of the hypothetical legislative delegation of consumer protection or products liability lawmaking power to the Supreme Court in the Rules Enabling Act context, one must consider the opposite end of the constitutional spectrum. While Article III confines the judicial power to the adjudication of cases and controversies, there must be certain commonsense qualifications on such a restriction. For example, the federal judiciary may hire law clerks and secretaries, even though neither activity, in and of itself, constitutes adjudication of a case or controversy. Presumably, the federal judiciary could also hold conferences or plan an annual holiday party, despite the total absence of any adjudicatory element. At least as an intuitive matter, these conclusions seem uncontroversial. As an analytical matter, however, the questions to ask are: (1) How, for constitutional purposes, do these situations differ from the hypothetical delegation of consumer protection lawmaking power? and (2) to which of the two paradigms is the Rules Enabling Act closer?

The constitutional difference between the two extremes should not be difficult to discern. On the one hand, statutorily authorized lawmaking (what can be called "paradigm one") is simply a blatant circumvention of the case-or-controversy requirement and of the democratic purposes that requirement is designed to serve. On the other hand, the hiring, conferences, and party-planning hypotheticals ("paradigm two"), have no readily discernable impact on the lives of private citizens or governmental bodies beyond the four walls of the courthouse.

The drafters of the Rules Enabling Act erred in assuming that, by confining the Court's rule-making authority to matters of "procedure," they were creating a "paradigm two" judicial power when, in reality, they were creating what, in all too many instances, is a "paradigm one" power. The assumption—absurdly simplistic when viewed from today's conceptual and pragmatic perspectives—appears to have been that matters of "procedure" necessarily have no impact on substantive rights. Thus, by only issuing rules of procedure, the Court would be doing nothing more than regulating matters whose impact would largely be confined within the courthouse's four walls.[103] However, many of the rules—the class action rule in particular—either (a) give rise to significant political or ideological controversy; (b) have a significant impact on the enforcement of substantive rights;[104] (c) are intended to affect the substantive reallocation of private societal resources;[105] (d) have a significant impact on private prelitigation behavior;[106] (e) directly impact, if not control, subsequent litigation in other forums;[107] or (f) affect the burdens on, expense of, or delays in the federal courts, thereby affecting citizens well beyond the scope of the individual case.[108] Yet all of these rules are, in some reasonable sense, also capable of being classified as "procedural," because on some level they all concern the nature of the adjudicatory process.

It is certainly true that not all of the Federal Rules give rise to such an impact. A number of them are readily classified among the "housekeeping" variety, at most affecting any interest beyond the confines of the instant case only remotely.[109] Thus, it is conceivable that some number of the rules could properly be deemed closer to paradigm two than to paradigm one for purposes of constitutional analysis. But the nondelegation and case-or-controversy limits are normatively driven by the fundamental goal of preserving basic policy making for those who are in some sense representative of, and accountable to, the populace.[110] Acknowledgment of this fundamental precept of American political and constitutional theory renders the Rules Enabling Act, as implemented by the Advisory Committee and the Court, constitutionally suspect.

One might respond that Congress always possesses the power to trump the rules the Court promulgates pursuant to the Act, simply by enacting a statute doing so. Therefore the accountability value is still satisfied. While in a certain sense this is true, it would be just as true of the Court's authority to promulgate freestanding rules of federal consumer protection law (paradigm one): Congress could always enact legislation voiding a particular rule, just as it can for the Federal Rules of Civil Procedure. Yet, presumably, recognition of this legislative safety valve would not save the constitutionality of such legislative delegation to the Court.[111] This is because by affecting the daily lives of citizens and stimulating political controversy, the judicially promulgated Rules alter the legal and behavioral status quo.[112] When rules have been issued, the inertia of the legal and political systems has been placed squarely in favor of the standards adopted in those rules. Congress must overcome the serious (and intended) inertia against legislative action to alter or supplant the Rules' dictates.[113] Absent the Rules, in contrast, there would be no political inertia in favor of any alternative. With the Rules in place, congressional inaction effectively amounts to legislative action, in contravention of the Constitution's bicameralism and presentment requirements;[114] with no Rules promulgated by the Court, congressional inaction is just that.

To suggest that it might be unconstitutional for Congress to vest procedural rule-making power in the Supreme Court is most certainly not to suggest that there could be no procedural Federal Rules, or even that there could be no Advisory Committee. It would mean, simply, that the Rules (at least those not of the housekeeping variety) would ultimately have to be enacted by Congress and be signed by the president, in accordance with the constitutionally prescribed legislative process. Presumably, the Advisory Committee could still make recommendations, but they would be made to Congress, rather than to the Court. Alternatively, the accountability critique could be applied in a more limited fashion, holding unconstitutional only those rules that are found to implicate significant economic, social, or political dispute. Such an approach would leave a somewhat wider constitutional range of Supreme Court rule-making authority.

The concern of many, no doubt, would be that if the initial power and obligation to promulgate the Rules of Procedure lay in Congress's hands, interest groups of all shapes and sizes would likely consume the legislative process. The concern is that having Congress make the decisions would be too "political." But the point is that many of these rules will be appropriately classified as "political," whichever governmental body gets to shape them, because they inevitably will substantially affect the lives of the citizenry and implicate fundamental ideological choices about loss allocation and resource redistribution. Taking the decision out of the hands of those who are representative of and accountable to the populace will mean, simply, that the one branch of government insulated from the populace will be making important political decisions in a manner never contemplated by the text, structure, or history of the Constitution.

The Constitutionality of the Rules Enabling Act in the Supreme Court

To this point, the analysis has demonstrated that were one to assume the position of a Martian observer, come to our planet to examine the constitutionality of the Rules Enabling Act as applied in the Federal Rules of Civil Procedure,[115] one should at the very least have serious difficulty with the question. Yet, mired in the history and practicalities of our own constitutional doctrine, it is generally understood today that the Act's constitutionality is beyond question. When one engages in more careful analysis of the Supreme Court decisions reaching this conclusion, however, it is striking how flimsy is the judicial house of cards doctrinally supporting the Act's constitutionality.

Sibbach v. Wilson & Co.

No decision appears to have adjudicated a direct, serious constitutional challenge to the Rules Enabling Act, either on its face or applied. The decision in *Sibbach v. Wilson & Co.*, generally assumed to have held the Act constitutional, actually dealt only with the validity of Rules 35 and 37, concerning the use of mental or physical examinations in discovery and discovery sanctions, respectively.[116] It is true that, in the course of upholding those Rules under the Act, the Court indicated in dictum that the Act is constitutional.[117] But it is interesting to note how devoid of supportive reasoning this conclusion was: "Congress has undoubted power to regulate the practice and procedure of federal courts, and may exercise that power by delegating to this or other federal courts authority to make rules not inconsistent with the statutes or constitution of the United States."[118] Decided at the height of the New Deal, *Sibbach*'s conclusory dismissal of structural constitutional concerns such as the non-delegation doctrine and the case-or-controversy requirement is perhaps not surprising. But what may be most telling about the decision is language that reveals—in a manner reminiscent of the flawed assumptions of the Act's drafters[119]—the Court's fatally simplistic understanding of the substance-procedure distinction. Congress, said the Court, "has never essayed to declare the substantive state law, or to abolish or nullify a right recognized by the substantive law of the state where the cause of action arose, save where a right or duty is imposed in a field committed to Congress by the Constitution."[120] Rather, "the Act . . . was purposely restricted in its operation to matters of pleading and court practice and procedure."[121] Noting that "the petitioner admits, and, we think, correctly, that Rules 35 and 37 are rules of procedure,"[122] the Court upheld the rules because "[t]he test must be whether a rule really regulates procedure,—the judicial process for enforcing rights and duties recognized by substantive law and for justly administering remedy and redress for disregard or infraction of them."[123]

Like the Act's drafters who inserted the restriction on the Rules' ability to modify, enlarge, or abridge substantive rights, the Court seems—implicitly, but necessarily—to assume a mutual exclusivity of procedure and substance.[124] A strict construction of the case-or-controversy requirement might still be problematic for the federal courts' power to issue freestanding rules of even pure procedure, since the Court promulgates them in a manner untied to conduct of the adjudicatory process. However, when viewed from the perspective of the democratic rationale for this constitutional requirement,[125] the concern would not be nearly as great were the Supreme Court's rule-making power actually confined to procedural concerns that did not extend beyond the walls of the courthouse. We know today, however, that it is absurd to assume such a mutual exclusivity for all but the most mundane of housekeeping rules. Procedural rules often have dramatic impact on the citizenry's planning of their primary behavior,[126] and often involve issues of significant concern to policy makers and those whom they represent. Rarely, then, does the concept of totally insulated procedural rules, assumed by the Court in *Sibbach*, actually exist.

Mistretta v. United States

While in *Hanna v. Plumer* the Court assumed the constitutionality of the Rules Enabling Act,[127] the only decision other than *Sibbach* in which the Court expended any effort to discuss the Act's constitutionality—albeit purely as dictum—was *Mistretta v. United States*.[128] The issue in *Mistretta* concerned the constitutionality of Congress's location of the Sentencing Commission in the judicial branch and the required inclusion of members of the Article III judiciary on that Commission.[129] A challenge had been made to the Act on the grounds that it violated the case-or-controversy requirement of Article III.[130] In rejecting that challenge, the Court noted that in past decisions it had "recognized the constitutionality of a 'twilight area' in which the activities of the separate [b]ranches merge."[131] Specifically, the Court relied on *Sibbach* for recognition of Congress's "undoubted power" to delegate procedural rule-making power to the Court.[132] This reference, of course, is no less conclusory than was the Court's original statement to the same effect in *Sibbach*.[133] To the extent the Court provided any supporting reasoning at all, it was in its assertion that "consistent with the separation of powers, Congress may delegate to the [j]udicial [b]ranch nonadjudicatory functions that do not trench upon the prerogatives of another [b]ranch and that are appropriate to the central mission of the Judiciary."[134] The point, apparently, is that the case-or-controversy requirement exists solely to protect the authority of the other branches of the federal government.[135] This analysis, of course, ignores the vitally important democratic rationale supporting the constitutional restriction of the authority of the one unrepresentative branch to the adjudication of cases or controversies.[136] Even assuming that the Court's assessment of the Rules Enabling Act was correct, it would still not mean that judicial rule making constitutes adjudication of a case or controversy, which the Constitution's text seems unambiguously to require, though concededly this point is probably of concern only to constitutional formalists.[137] More importantly, the Court's reasoning in no way responds to the fundamental concern over the representativeness or accountability, direct or indirect, of the nation's policy makers.

One might suspect that the underlying, if unstated, assumption of the Court was that because the Federal Rules concern only "the appropriate mission of the Judiciary," they are of purely procedural importance and therefore do not encroach on the authority of the policy-making branches of the federal government.[138] We now know, of course, that such an assumption is nonsense.[139] But the most puzzling aspect of the *Mistretta* Court's discussion of the Rules Enabling Act's constitutionality is that the Court apparently did understand that the Federal Rules are not created in a procedural vacuum. Indeed, the opinion explicitly acknowledged that "this Court's rulemaking under the enabling Acts has been substantive and political in the sense that the rules of procedure have important effects on the substantive rights of litigants."[140] In an accompanying footnote, the Court pointed to Rule 23, providing for the use of class actions, which "has inspired a controversy over the philosophical, social, and economic merits and demerits of class actions."[141] But if this is so, then why does the Rules Enabling Act not do the very thing that the *Mistretta* Court had stated that a delegation to the judicial branch may *not* do: interfere with the authority of the representative branches of the federal government?[142] It appears that the Court, by relying on *Sibbach*, first validates the Rules Enabling Act by implicitly invoking that decision's faulty premise of procedural-substantive mutual exclusivity (if only as a matter of Supreme Court precedent),[143] and, having thus found the Act constitutional,[144] readily acknowledges the faultiness of this essential premise. It is almost as if an acquitted criminal defendant, knowing he is protected by the constitutional prohibition on double jeopardy, openly admits his crime.

The doctrinal support for the Rules Enabling Act's constitutionality, then, is readily exposed as a house of cards. To be sure, legitimate or not, the holding of the Act's constitutionality is not likely to change in the foreseeable future.[145] However, the skeptical constitutional analysis advocated here is valuable for two reasons. First, it is valuable simply as an intellectual study in constitutional theory, an activity in which constitutional scholars readily engage regardless of the likely practical impact. Second, on a more practical level it may have an important spillover effect on determination of the most appropriate construction of the Act's "substantive right" limitation. It is therefore to a discussion of this issue of statutory interpretation that the inquiry now turns.

CONSTRUING THE RULES ENABLING ACT:
IMPLICATIONS OF THE ACCOUNTABILITY CRITIQUE

One highly respected commentator has suggested that the question of whether a Federal Rule is "substantive" or "procedural" for purposes of the Rules Enabling Act is "inherently unresolvable."[146] The Supreme Court has never invalidated a Federal Rule for violation of the Act's "substantive right" limitation. Nevertheless, there has been a good deal of controversy, both within the Court[147] and without, on this issue of statutory interpretation.[148] I have already conceded the pragmatic futility of today seeking to raise serious questions about the Act's constitutionality. It is conceivable, however, that a parallel sub-constitutional concern about the need for accountable policy makers should guide construction of the cryptic substance-procedure distinction imposed by the Act itself.

The greatest problem with any attempt to construe the Act's substance-procedure distinction in a manner designed to consider this democratic concern over the political accountability of the decision maker is that the Act's drafters were driven by two goals that are potentially in tension—a fact of which the drafters appear to have been blissfully unaware, for reasons previously discussed.[149] In addition to the desire to preserve legislative authority over issues extending beyond the courthouse walls, the drafters were simultaneously driven by the seemingly contradictory goal of establishing a uniform system of federal procedure.[150] The more that the statute's interpretation is designed to achieve the first goal, the more it is likely to undermine the second goal: because so many Rules impact important socio-political concerns, many Rules would fail under the accountability critique we have described.

There exist three interpretive options available in construing the Act's substance-procedure distinction in order to take into account the democratic accountability critique. First, the Act could be confined to those few rules that are largely of the housekeeping variety. Under this approach, the Act would authorize only those rules that were likely to have no more than a remote impact beyond the courthouse walls. The obvious problem with this approach—at least as a matter of statutory construction[151]—is that it would seriously undermine attainment of the additional statutory goal of establishing a uniform system of federal procedure.

A second option would be to exclude from the Court's rule-making authority only those rules that undeniably give rise to widespread political concern. This second alternative would leave to the Court a large body of rules, but would likely exclude rules such as those dealing with class actions,[152] as well as rules involving pleading burdens[153] and electronic discovery.[154] The obvious problem with this interpretive alternative is its political fluidity and difficulty in application. However, it at least represents an effort to reconcile the competing goals of the Act, by attempting to leave in the Court's rule-making power the majority of the current rules.

The final alternative is similar to the standard the Court itself seems to have adopted, though without any supporting reasoning grounded in precepts of American political theory.[155] It is to confine the rules to those whose impact is predominantly designed to affect nonprocedural interests.[156] Recognizing that the rules will often have incidental impacts on substantive concerns, the Court has confined the Act's substantive right limitation to exclude from its reach primarily procedural rules whose impact beyond the courthouse walls is merely incidental.[157] This is so, even if that incidental and unintended substantive impact is substantial.

It is difficult to choose among these alternatives, because they all possess significant flaws. However, from the perspective of the concern about truly accountable policy making, the second alternative seems to be the least of three evils.

CONCLUSION: THE CLASS ACTION, THE RULES ENABLING ACT, AND THE CONSTITUTION

One often hears the term *politicization* used in a pejorative sense.[158] To "politicize" something is usually to demean a process by removing it from the lofty heights of dispassionate analysis and thrusting it into the jungle of interest-group struggles. But when one employs the term in the context of a discussion of American political theory, it refers simply to a return of foundational normative choices of social policy to those who are representative of and accountable to the electorate.[159] In a system committed to the values of representative government, then, politicization is by no means an inherently negative development.

Nowhere is the need to return the fundamental social policy choices inherent in the shaping of procedural rules more striking than in the context of class actions. Whether one favors or opposes the procedural framework embodied in the current version of Rule 23,[160] no one could realistically doubt the rule's inevitable social, economic, or political impact.[161] The fatal flaw in the current mode of fashioning the rule is its lack of grounding in representative and accountable decision making. To be sure, there are certain issues that our political structure has sought to insulate from the democratic process. For example, we have wisely deemed questions of constitutional interpretation to be reserved, in the final instance, for the one branch of government purposely insulated from the democratic process—the judiciary. However, the same has never been true for sub-constitutional issues of social policy.

The fact that the Federal Rules of Civil Procedure at least at some level concern processes employed within the federal courts does not automatically imply that they fail to implicate matters of serious concern to the polity. Indeed, it is this fatally simplistic assumption that has historically guided both Congress and the Supreme Court in the drafting and early construction of the Rules Enabling Act of 1934.[162] It was also this flawed assumption that led the Court early on to assume the constitutionality of the Act's delegation of lawmaking power to the Supreme Court. Today, all of those concerned recognize the inherent intersection of substance and procedure.[163] However, none has sought to go back in time to reconsider the modern constitutional and statutory implications of this all too facile assumption.

In this chapter, I have dared to think the unthinkable: The possibility that the Rules Enabling Act—at least as currently implemented—should be found unconstitutional. While delegations of federal legislative power to executive agencies are today commonplace,[164] comparable delegations to a wholly unaccountable coordinate branch of government whose authority to act is explicitly confined by the Constitution to the adjudication of live disputes give rise to an entirely different set of political and constitutional difficulties.[165] Because of its intentional insulation from democratic processes, the federal judiciary's lawmaking authority was constitutionally confined to the traditional adjudicatory process. By delegating important policy-making authority to the Supreme Court outside of the adjudication of cases or controversies, Congress in the Rules Enabling Act has violated the essential dictate of the separation of powers, and in so doing has undermined the essence of the democratic process.

It is true, of course, that Congress always retains authority to legislatively reject or overrule a particular exercise of the Court's rule-making power. But this fact would surely not validate a delegation of power to the Court to promulgate freestanding rules of consumer protection or products liability law, though the point would be equally applicable there; nor should it save the otherwise unconstitutional delegation embodied in the Enabling Act. Once the Court promulgates a rule and the rule goes into effect, that rule becomes law. It has altered the legal status quo and reversed the inertia inherent in the legislative process. Absent the rule's existence, Congress would have to act, in one direction or the other, or choose to let judicial procedure develop incrementally as an incident to the adjudicatory process.[166] In contrast, with the rule in place Congress's failure to act is effectively transformed into legislative action, in direct contravention of the bicameralism and presentment requirements provided for in the Constitution.

Holding that much of the rule-making power must constitutionally rest in congressional hands does not necessarily imply that the Court could have no influence in the process. By making their expertise available to Congress, those presently involved in the rule-making process could still play an important role. However, the ultimate choice would remain where a constitutional democracy intends it to be: in the hands of the representative branches of government.

In the highly likely event that my proposed reconsideration of the Act's constitutionality falls on deaf ears, it is conceivable that the accountability critique fashioned here could still play a role in the interpretation of the Act's cryptic "substantive right" qualification. More than seventy years after the Act's passage, the meaning of that provision remains the subject of vigorous and widespread debate. I have suggested here that the provision be construed in the very manner apparently intended by the Act's drafters: to preserve to the representative branches fundamental choices of social policy. Now that we recognize that many of the rules are inherently intertwined with such policy issues (a key fact the Act's framers appear not to have grasped), it is appropriate to redefine the phrase in a far more aggressive manner than it has been to date. Were either my proposed constitutional or statutory models accepted, the authority to shape the manner in which class actions are to function would lie, in the first and last instance, with the branches of the federal government closest to the electorate. In a fundamentally democratic society, such a proposal should hardly be controversial.

CHAPTER FOUR

The Class Action as Political Theory

INTRODUCTION

In an important sense, class actions give rise to an anomalous situation in the American tradition of civil adjudication by allowing one person to litigate the individual claims of an entire group of people in a single proceeding without their explicit endorsement of or participation in the litigation.[1] Paradoxically, on different levels the absent class members are simultaneously full participants and total non-participants in the litigation. The academic literature examining this form of litigation has portrayed the class action at times as a savior, bringing about justice in an otherwise flawed system of individual adjudication,[2] and other times as a villain, serving to artificially expand defendant liability and create a specialty practice for entrepreneurial plaintiffs' lawyers.[3] At the heart of these tensions lies the awkward existence of a mechanism for collective adjudication of predominantly passively enforced individual claims in a civil justice system largely designed for the purpose of vindicating actively pursued, individually held claims.

Although there is little consensus in class action scholarship as to why this island of collectivism exists in a sea of individualized dispute resolution,[4] there appears to exist near universal agreement that the pressures of modern society necessitate the existence of some tool for the adjudication of mass collective suits. Few doubt that "some litigious situations affecting numerous persons 'naturally' or 'necessarily' call for unitary adjudication."[5] The major issues in the class action debate center on how courts determine precisely when those situations arise and what control the class members retain over the adjudication of their individual claims.

Rule 23 of the Federal Rules of Civil Procedure attempts to provide at least some guidance in this regard. As noted in a prior discussion,[6] Rule 23(a) lists four requirements that a court must find satisfied before certifying a class.[7] The rule then specifies that if a case meets all four of these requirements, it must still fall within one of the three categories of class actions described in Rule 23(b).[8] Only after satisfying this bifurcated examination can a case be certified as appropriate for class treatment. If a class is certified, depending on which of the Rule 23(b) categories the case falls within, the rule at times provides class members with the opportunity to leave the class and go it alone, while at other times withholding that opportunity from absent class members.[9]

Because it is merely a rule of procedure, not surprisingly Rule 23 fails to provide a comprehensive theory of the class action's role and function. In light of the significant practical consequences that flow from class certification for potential litigants, however, scholars have sought to provide guidance on this issue, proposing a range of normative models of the class action aimed at promoting the procedure as a means for attaining broader legal or social ends.

The scholarly debate over these proposed class action models has focused largely on the comparative social and economic costs and benefits associated with the various possible roles for Rule 23.[10] This sort of analysis has perpetuated the view of the class action, implicitly embraced by many scholars, as a legal device that is appropriately subjected, all but exclusively, to either a purely legalistic or economic mode of analysis.[11] Nothing, however, could be further from the truth.

On one level, of course, Rule 23 is nothing more than an elaborate joinder device that facilitates the application of legislatively enacted or common-law created substantive causes of action within a broader system of civil dispute resolution. Viewed in this light, the class action is in reality far *less* than what many scholars have perceived it to be. Commentators have been quick to view the class action as a device to simultaneously achieve social justice, redistribute wealth, and transform the nature of the entire adjudicatory process.[12] They have viewed the class action in this manner, despite the fact that, under the express terms of the Rules Enabling Act, a Federal Rule of Civil Procedure may not alter or modify underlying substantive rights.[13] On another level, however, the class action is considerably *more* than what legal scholars have generally conceived it to be. Because the class action imposes collectivist treatment—often coercively—on the adjudicatory process by which individually held rights are vindicated or protected, it inescapably implicates some of the most important debates of modern normative political theory. Yet only rarely have legal scholars even acknowledged the implications of the modern class action for the foundational issues of normative political theory.[14]

Just as the Truth in Lending Act requires creditors to disclose the terms and costs of a loan to potential borrowers,[15] this chapter seeks to identify the framework of political theory underlying each doctrinal or conceptual model of the modern class action. It does so in order to enable potential adherents of each approach to fully recognize and understand the consequences that inexorably flow from acceptance of one or the other of the proposed legal models. Acceptance of any legal model of the class action requires acceptance of the underlying normative theoretical judgments that inspire its creation. The choice of a legal model of the class action represents, at least implicitly, judgments on important normative controversies of political theory, carrying profound consequences beyond those appearing explicitly within the four corners of the class action rule.

In this chapter, I examine structural legal models of the class action proposed by leading legal scholars from two distinct perspectives. The first perspective can be characterized as analytical and taxonomical. It seeks to categorize each of these proposed models in terms of normative political theories that, I believe, are necessarily implicated by the various models. The second perspective can best be described as normatively critical. On the level of political theory, I reject all of the existing scholarly models because all of them ignore or reject core notions of liberal individualism which, I believe, underlie American liberal democracy in general and our adversary system of litigation in particular. I then fashion my own proposed model of the class action, labeled the "individualist" model, which seeks to develop a legal framework of the class action that fosters the values inherent in a commitment to liberal individualism. Because one must understand the consequences associated with a political theory in order to appreciate its impact, I initially describe the various political theories implicated by the modern class action debate. I take as a baseline traditional liberal political theory, grounded in a foundational commitment to a belief in the worth and integrity of the individual as a core participant in a democratic society, and proceed to compare liberalism with the political theories implicated by the existing class action models advocated by modern procedural scholars.

Of particular significance in the class action debate is the emphasis that liberalism places on an individual's right to personal autonomy.[16] The concept of "personal autonomy," however is ambiguous. In its most extreme manifestation, the concept embodies traditional libertarian precepts of wide-ranging individual choice, free from control or direction by the state. In shaping the liberal individualist model of the class action, however, I need make no commitment on such foundational issues of substantive libertarianism. Because the class action is an adjudicatory device, the only area of individual choice necessarily implicated by my liberal individualist model of the class action is a type of *meta* decision making that focuses exclusively on what I call *process-based autonomy*. This concept refers to the category of decisions an individual is able to make concerning the nature of his participation in the democratic process or his efforts to influence the decisions made by democratic institutions. This form of autonomy is to be distinguished from *substantive* autonomy, which concerns an individual's freedom to make decisions concerning the conduct of his day-to-day existence.

Pursuant to the concept of process-based autonomy, an individual is deemed to possess autonomy over decisions about how to participate in the process of collective decision making concerning such substantive decisions, and not necessarily on the freedom to make those substantive choices. Thus, an individual has autonomy to determine what he will say in an effort to influence the political process or the manner in which he will attempt to petition the government for redress of grievances. Both liberal democratic theory and American constitutional law for the most part insulate these decisions from external control. An individual's resort to the adjudicatory process in order to vindicate or protect his substantive legal rights is appropriately viewed as simply an additional manifestation of the political meta-autonomy that forms a central element of liberal democratic theory. A class action rule that disregards these protective participatory rights dangerously undermines the proper role of autonomous individuals within a liberal democratic civil justice system. After elaborating upon this political theory, I then contrast the emphasis on individual political autonomy in liberal theory with the alternative approaches to political theory that are implicated in the class action debate: utilitarianism,[17] communitarianism,[18] and civic republicanism.[19] In each case, I conclude that the subordination of the individual to external considerations conflicts with the importance placed on process-based individual autonomy by liberal theory. The version of liberal individualism which I adopt, I should emphasize, is tempered by a limited degree of collectivist utilitarianism: In the presence of a truly compelling interest, practical realities dictate that the interests of individual autonomy must give way. But recognition of the great value that liberal democracy places on meta-autonomy must authorize restriction only after full and open debate, and only in the most extreme circumstances.

I then consider the implications for political theory of the class action models proposed by leading legal scholars. I reject all of these models for their failure to recognize the central role of the individual in the political and judicial processes. Absent the presence of the most compelling of practical circumstances, a class action model premised upon liberal theory will permit abandonment of process-based individual autonomy when, and only when, to employ collective treatment would, paradoxically, facilitate the exercise of individual choice. Certainly individuals may always voluntarily elect to act collectively, and in some cases the prohibitive cost of bringing an individual claim would, as a practical matter, preclude individuals from pursuing their claims without pooling their resources as part of a class. While those claims are still retained by the individual class members, it is generally understood that when a small injury is inflicted upon a large number of people, resort to the class action may be the only way for the individual class members to recover for their injuries.[20] The liberal political theory model of the class action proposed here necessarily implies the need for a sliding scale measure by which to determine the validity and acceptability of class action treatment. This scale is tied to considerations related to the size of the individual claims at stake and a rough prediction about the corresponding ability of individuals to vindicate their private rights by individual pursuit of their claims.

I have two goals in this chapter. Initially, I seek to alter the nature of the class action debate, by expressly inserting the perspective of political theory. By recognizing how the modern class action is structured may have significant consequences for the foundations of normative political theory, I hope to remove the theoretical superficiality that has characterized much of the modern scholarly debate concerning class actions. While on occasion that debate has touched on questions of political theory, those references are generally rare, superficial, or misguided. At the very least, then, I hope to establish that acceptance of one or the other of the scholarly models of the class action necessarily brings with it significant political baggage; we cannot get one without the other. Second, I hope to convince the reader that, when viewed from this theoretical perspective, all class action models that have been proposed to this point should be rejected because they ignore, undermine, or dilute fundamental notions of process-based individual autonomy that are essential to the functioning of a civil justice system within a liberal democratic society.

CLASS ACTIONS UNDER RULE 23

Class Certification and the Right to Opt-Out: A Quick Review

Rule 23 requires that the proposed class satisfy a list of requirements. As explained at an earlier point in this book, this involves a two-step inquiry. First, potential class representatives must demonstrate that they meet each of the four 23(a) prerequisites: (1) the number of potential class members must be so large that the use of permissive joinder is impractical ("numerosity"); (2) the class must share common questions of law or fact ("commonality"); (3) the claims of the class representative must be "typical" of the entire class ("typicality"); (4) the class representative must be capable of adequately representing the interests of the entire class ("adequacy").[21] Upon establishing these four conditions, the litigant moving for class certification must show that the suit falls within at least one of the three categories of class actions described in Rule 23(b).[22] The differences among these categories may have great practical significance because the categories afford different levels of protection for and impose different restrictions on absent class members. One category of class actions, those brought pursuant to Rule 23 (b)(3), allows absent class members to opt out of the litigation. For classes in which absent class members possess the right to opt out, potential class representatives are burdened with the obligation to provide notice to as many absent class members as is practicable.[23] Other categories, however, do not automatically require potential class representatives to shoulder this burden, because class members are not permitted to withdraw from the class. These classes are described as "mandatory."[24]

The first of these different categories is the 23(b)(1) class, which is subdivided into two sub-categories: the (b)(1)(A) class and the (b)(1)(B) class. The (b)(1)(A) class includes those instances in which the defendant could potentially face inconsistent obligations if individual claims were to be litigated separately.[25] The (b)(1)(B) class, on the other hand, applies when the interests of the individual claimants could be undermined by separate adjudications.[26] The classic example of this occurs when a defendant has a limited fund from which to pay damages, and the total of the individual claims is likely to exceed the fund.[27] For both (b)(1)(A) and (b)(1)(B) classes, membership in the class is mandatory, with no requirement of notice to absent class members.[28]

The second category of class action is provided for in Rule 23(b)(2), which applies to instances in which the relief sought is primarily or exclusively injunctive or declaratory relief applicable to the class as a whole.[29] The paradigmatic example of a (b)(2) class is a civil rights litigation where a defendant has acted in a manner generally applicable to the class as a whole.[30] As in the case of (b)(1) classes, (b)(2) classes are mandatory with no notice required.[31]

The final category of class suit is the Rule 23(b)(3) class. For these cases, class certification does not follow directly from the interwoven nature of the interests at stake in the litigation, but would "achieve economies of time, effort, and expense, and promote uniformity of decision as to persons similarly situated, without sacrificing procedural fairness or bringing about other undesirable results."[32] Plaintiffs seeking class certification as a (b)(3) class must demonstrate that questions of law and fact "predominate" over the individual issues in the litigation.[33] They must also show that litigation as a class is "superior" to other forms of adjudication.[34] Rule 23 provides judges determining predominance and superiority with a list of four factors to consider in making their evaluation: (1) the interest of absent class members in directing the litigation of their claims in separate actions; (2) the existence of ongoing litigation concerning the class; (3) the desirability of having all litigation adjudicated in one forum; (4) the potential difficulties in managing the class.[35] For class actions falling within Rule 23(b)(3), plaintiffs must provide notice to absent class members, and absent class members must have the opportunity to opt out of the litigation.[36]

An opt-out system differs from an opt-in system in its treatment of absent class members' inertia. Under an opt-out system, absent class members are presumed to be part of the class, while under an opt-in system, they are presumed to have elected not to participate in the class litigation absent their affirmative act to include themselves. The practical difference is that under an opt-in system passive class members retain their individually granted rights to sue while defendants are typically subjected to greater damage awards under an opt-out system due to the larger class size.[37] No category of class action under the current federal rule provides for an opt-in procedure. Classes are either mandatory or, under (b)(3), opt-out in structure.

Positive and Negative Value Class Actions

An important subject discussed in the class action literature concerns the size of the individual claims at stake in the class litigation. Scholars have noted a significant distinction between two types of class actions based on the size of individual class members' claims.[38] Type-A class actions, or "Positive Value" class actions, include those class actions in which individual claims are sufficiently large so that "each claim would be independently marketable even in the absence of the class action device."[39] Type-B class actions, or "Negative Value" class actions, on the other hand, refer to those class actions where the costs in establishing and collecting the individual claims are greater than the potential recovery.[40]

The importance of this distinction lies in the alternative rationales typically offered to justify the claims' inclusion in a class proceeding. The standard argument in favor of negative-value class actions is that absent the class proceeding, these claims would never be brought because it would be economically inefficient to pursue them on an individual basis.[41] By authorizing class treatment of negative value claims, a class action rule is thought to achieve distinct goals. First, it enables individual claimants to obtain compensation when such relief would have been otherwise infeasible. Second (and, to many commentators, far more important),[42] allowing litigation collectivization in these situations effectively enforces existing substantive legal restrictions on private or governmental offenders that would otherwise go unenforced. In the case of positive-value class actions, however, the rationale typically offered in support is that they minimize the expenditure of resources by consolidating all claims into a single proceeding and avoiding duplicative litigation.[43]

POLITICAL THEORIES RELEVANT
TO THE CLASS ACTION DEBATE

While Rule 23 sets out the existing legal framework of the modern class action, surely its contours do not exhaust the scope of potential normative debate over the scope and structure of the class action. There are many ways the class action device may be structured, and Rule 23's dramatic revision in 1966 underscores the fact that the provision is always subject to normatively based reconsideration and modification. The tension among competing normative judgments about the costs and benefits of the class action become clear only through an intensive examination of the underlying political theories implicated by the various proposed normative models of the device. Most class action scholars have ignored the political theory implications of the class action models they advocate. Yet the political theory implicit in the various proposed structures can speak volumes about their merits.

In order to make the consequences of these theoretical ties explicit, it is first necessary to provide a brief description of the various political theories implicated by the class action debate. What becomes immediately obvious is that only liberal theory emphasizes the role of the individual in controlling the legal pursuit and protection of his interests. The other major political theories implicated by modern class action scholarship view individualism either as an irrelevancy, a consideration unworthy of significant emphasis, or even as a morally deleterious consideration. An exhaustive study of the nuances suggested by these political theories is beyond the scope of my inquiry. Yet by examining how the basics of each political theory respond to fundamental questions about the state, government, politics, and justice, we are in a better position to understand how each of these political philosophies has dealt with what should be seen as the central issues implicated by the modern class action debate. In this section, I explore the basic elements of the four political theories I find implicated in the legal scholarship of class action commentators: liberalism, utilitarianism, democratic communitarianism, and civic republicanism.

Liberalism

Although there are many often conflicting variations, liberal political theory generally emphasizes the centrality of the individual's personal growth, integrity, liberty, or all three. The worth of the individual is central to Kantian moral philosophy,[44] and is assumed to be fundamental in John Stuart Mill's more instrumental justification of liberalism.[45] Under these versions of liberal philosophy, the primacy placed on the worth of the individual dictates recognition of the individual's role in the operation of the democratic state.[46]

Autonomy, Liberal Theory, and the Democratic State

While the various sub-categories of liberal theory differ in a number of ways, at some level most recognize the centrality of some form of individual autonomy. John Rawls provides a useful definition of autonomy by asserting that people are autonomous when they "act from principles that they would acknowledge under conditions that best express their nature as free and rational beings."[47] Although this view of autonomy has not been universally accepted,[48] the subtle distinctions in the outer reaches of autonomy are beyond the scope of this chapter.[49] At its foundation, autonomy dictates a significant level of free choice for the individual on issues of some consequence to him, unfettered by coercive external forces, either governmental or private. Of special concern, however, is the fundamental dichotomy between alternative visions of individual autonomy, rather than its generic application. Democratic theory, I believe, recognizes a fundamental distinction between *process-based* autonomy and *substantive* autonomy.

Process-based autonomy refers to the ability of individuals to control the nature of their participation in the processes of collective democratic government.[50] The concept, in other words, refers to the individual's ability to make decisions about her efforts to influence the collective decision-making process—or "meta decisions." Examples of these meta decisions include whether, when, and how to speak publicly on a political issue, to petition the government for a redress of a grievance, to participate in a political campaign, or to vote. The extent of one's process-based autonomy determines how much control an individual has over decisions impacting both how she participates in the democratic process and the ways in which she attempts to influence the decisions made by democratic institutions. By way of contrast, substantive autonomy refers to the more general power of individuals to make decisions directing the course of their lives. This broader category of decision making includes choices that an individual makes as part of her private life, unconnected to direct participation in the democratic process. Examples include such activities as whom to marry, where to work, and whether to have an abortion or use narcotics. Depending upon how broadly one chooses to define the concept of substantive liberty, it may extend beyond such relatively intimate, personal choices to also include individual decisions that simultaneously and directly impact the interests of other members of society, such as whether to sell automatic weapons, pay workers a living wage, or test a new medication before placing it on the market.

Recognizing and understanding the process-based/substantive liberty dichotomy is central to a full understanding of liberal theory. Liberal theory, in the narrow form I employ, is by no means necessarily synonymous with libertarianism. Instead, on most issues of substantive autonomy, liberal theory—again, in the narrow incarnation that I advocate—is wholly agnostic. What it is not agnostic about is the need for commitment to core notions of individual autonomy in deciding how to participate in the processes of democracy.[51] In contrast, the libertarian branch of liberal theory, in its modern form associated primarily with the scholarship of Robert Nozick, calls for nearly limitless protection of substantive individual autonomy. Nozick proposed that the state may only restrain autonomy for the "protection against force, theft, fraud, enforcement of contracts, and so on."[52] Anything beyond those restrictions violates the core right of the individual because individuals properly enjoy virtually total autonomy over their actions.[53] This approach erects individual autonomy as a nearly impenetrable barrier against state intrusion and has been relied upon to support the legalization of all narcotics and prostitution, as well as the abolition of taxation.[54]

Rawls takes a more expansive view of the appropriate role of the state in restricting autonomy, determined by means of a thought experiment he calls the "veil of ignorance."[55] This model assumes that in a state of nature called the "original position" and behind a "veil of ignorance," where an individual is presumed to be unaware of his social status in future organized society, the individual would choose a rule limiting individual autonomy, then the state may legitimately restrain that exercise of autonomy.[56] Rawls believed that this inquiry leads to his so-called First Principle, which requires that individuals be given as much liberty as possible so long as each member of society enjoys the same degree of liberty.[57] The legitimacy of inequalities in liberty among individuals resulting from state intervention is determined on the basis of their conformity to Rawls's Second Principle, which posits that these inequalities must satisfy two conditions: (a) They are to provide the greatest benefit to the least advantaged members of society; and (b), they are to be attached to positions and offices open to all, under conditions of equality of opportunity.[58] He calls this "the difference principle," which serves to allow a limited amount of state interference in individual autonomy where doing so serves the interests of justice.[59]

It is true that Nozick and Rawls failed explicitly to recognize the process-based/substantive dichotomy when crafting their theories. However, both theories are at least consistent with, even if not expressly confined to, a commitment to process-based autonomy. The minimalist state advocated by Nozick, for example, would find little reason for restricting the ability of individuals to control their meta decision making. Arguably more complex in this regard would be Rawls's use of the veil of ignorance construct. It is perhaps conceivable that some restriction on process-based autonomy could be imposed if it would be legitimately selected by those in the original position. But Rawls's First Principle would seem to preclude the possibility of imposing such a restriction from behind the veil, because it suggests that people would select a procedure that takes away their ability to direct the course of their personal interactions with the institutions of democracy. Rawls proceeds on the assumption that individuals behind the veil would be risk-averse about threats to their liberty, preferring procedures that maximize individual autonomy over the sort of authoritarian procedures that allow process-based autonomy to be exercised by someone other than the individual. Thus, the notion that any branch of liberal theory would allow for the legitimate subjugation of an individual's process-based autonomy is highly doubtful.[60] A legitimate liberal-democratic government requires that individuals be autonomous when participating in governmental processes and seeking to influence the decisions of democratic institutions.

Process-Based Autonomy, Adjudication and the Adversary System

To this point, I have established that liberal theory places great value on an individual's autonomy over meta decisions—that is, decisions about the nature, scope and extent of the individual's participation in the processes of collective decision making that characterizes liberal democracy. The most obvious forms of collective decision making affected by process-based autonomy are political in nature: attempts to persuade or influence other private individuals or governmental officials, participation in political campaigns, or voting. An individual's attempt to protect her legal rights and interests by resort to the judicial process, however, is also appropriately characterized as an exercise of process-based autonomy. The adversary system of adjudication is another governmental process that vests meta decision making authority in individuals who seek to influence a governmental institution's ultimate decisions that will impact their lives. Just as democratic theory necessitates the existence of process-based autonomy because it ties the legitimacy of governmental decision making to recognition of individual autonomy of participation, so, too, does the legitimacy of the adversary system rely on a judgment that, within the established procedural framework, individuals must be able to make autonomous choices about how best to pursue and protect their own interests in court.

Fundamental to the adversary system is a party's ability to control fact development and presentation of legal arguments.[61] In the words of Lon Fuller, this "defining characteristic" of the adversary system "confers on the affected party a peculiar form of participation in the decision, that of presenting proofs and reasoned arguments for a decision in his favor."[62] The legitimacy of the outcomes produced by the adversary system rests on the notion that litigants will be able to present their cases to the court in the way they see fit. The selection of the adversary mode of dispute resolution confirms and fosters the American commitment to liberal theory.[63] It recognizes the inevitability of differences of opinion in a pluralistic society on issues "involving both societal and individual needs, interests, and values."[64] As such, it embraces the notion of conflict and its orderly resolution, and legitimizes the outcome of this resolution process by providing litigants with control over the legal pursuit and protection of their interests.[65] The liberal character of American civil adjudication stems from the presumption that in exercising this control, litigants are, in Rawls's words, "acting from principles that they would acknowledge under conditions that best express their nature as free and rational beings."[66] The adversary system harnesses the ability of litigants to make autonomous decisions in legitimizing the outcomes it produces. Individuals are presumed to have no legitimate complaint if they were allowed to present their case in the way they chose to present it—or, to put it another way, had "their day in court."

Beyond a few rare, statutorily created exceptions,[67] our adjudicatory system is largely predicated upon the idea of individualized adjudication for the purpose of vindicating or protecting the individual's legally protected rights and interests. Indeed, Article III's injury-in-fact requirement arguably reflects a belief that litigants should use private adjudication *only* to vindicate harms done directly to them.[68] A litigant's decision to pursue his private right to sue may operate in a way that benefits another party, but doing so must be incidental to the vindication of his own rights. The adversary system recognizes that although many people may share a common interest and wish to advance that interest, they may disagree about how best to advance it. They are therefore granted the authority, on an individual basis, to pursue those interests in the way that they see fit. Litigants are burdened with the bars of collateral estoppel and res judicata for the outcome of the cases they litigate. Justifying the potentially harsh consequences of these bars reflects a presumption that litigants have had the opportunity to present their cases in the way they deem most effective.

It is true, of course, that the discretion to mount one's own case in the manner one sees fit is not absolute. Rules of ethics, laws of evidentiary admissibility, and the potentially competing interests of other litigants, among other restrictions, naturally constrain the scope of individual discretion in certain instances. But the same is true of even the most highly prized forms of process-based autonomy. Felons and those under the age of eighteen are generally denied the right to vote, and few consider the right of even politically focused expression to be absolute. But it does not follow that individual choice in such matters is of less than compelling significance. In the case of adjudication brought to vindicate private rights, a system that bound one litigant by the decision in a case over which another person had total control would run counter to the value placed on process-based autonomy. At a minimum, it would represent a highly paternalistic system, derived from an underlying assumption that someone else knows better how to vindicate an individual's rights than the individual herself, even when the individual would have affirmatively chosen to actively protect her own rights. It would surely be difficult to reconcile such presumptions with the dictates of process-based autonomy inherent in liberal democratic theory.

Utilitarianism

The basic position of utilitarian philosophy is that the state has a duty to make decisions that will maximize happiness—"the surplus of pleasure over pain"[69]—aggregated over all of the members of society. Utilitarian theory views the state's primary function to be the promotion of the broadest possible "utility." In the language of its recognized innovator, Jeremy Bentham:

> By the principle of utility is meant that principle which approves or disapproves of every action whatsoever, according to the tendency which it appears to have to augment or diminish the happiness of the party whose interest is in question . . . if that party be the community in general, then the happiness of the community: If a particular individual, then the happiness of that individual . . . "The interest of the community then is, what?—the sum of the interest of the several members who compose it."[70]

Since Bentham's era, the vast literature dissecting utilitarianism has given rise to a seemingly limitless variety of nuanced approaches to the theory. Scholarship examining Bentham's writing has described him as everything from a totalitarian to an individualist.[71]

Bentham recognized that the interests of individuals would be both selfish and varied. As one scholar has noted, Bentham "offered no hope that a man will act other than in pursuit of his own interests, and little hope that these interests will naturally be associated with the interests of others."[72] In order to counterbalance the inherent selfishness of man, he proposed that legislators attempt to craft laws that would influence the behavior of the public to act in the general interest.[73] But Bentham also states that: "The Legislator is not the master of the dispositions of the human heart: he is only their interpreter and their servant. The goodness of his laws depends upon their conformity to the general *expectation*. It is highly necessary, therefore for him rightly to understand the direction of this expectation, for the purpose of acting in concert with it."[74] An effective lawmaker, then, must attempt both to project the desires of the individual members of society and enact laws reflecting those passions, while also crafting laws that would subordinate these hedonistic desires. This democratic aspect of utilitarianism focuses on the preferences of the individual members of society and recognizes that those preferences may differ. Yet it has been simultaneously recognized that utilitarianism also includes an anti-individualist streak,[75] since it allows for utilitarian justice to be deeply paternalistic by requiring a determination by a lawmaker as to what will make an individual happy.

Despite this confusion, when the dust settles it is apparent that individual autonomy is of no special importance in utilitarian philosophy. Even under a form of "individualist utilitarianism," which does, relatively speaking, provide greater weight to the preservation of individual autonomy than do other forms of the theory,[76] the value placed on self-determination reflects a judgment about the amount of utility derived from liberty, rather than recognition of any inherent value in individual choice and integrity. Again, the sole concern of the utilitarian theorist is whether a policy will maximize the overall happiness present in society.[77] Thus, to a utilitarian the protection or promotion of autonomy "is in itself of no special moral interest. Since as a rule people capable of autonomy want opportunities to live autonomously and find satisfaction in living autonomously, there is on utilitarian grounds abundant reason for increasing people's opportunity to live in that way."[78] John Stuart Mill is perhaps the most well recognized "individual autonomy utilitarian" in the way he justifies the preservation of individual autonomy on pragmatic, self-developmental grounds.[79] Unlike the Kantian approach, which views individual autonomy as a first principle absolutely and unquestioningly shielded from government intrusion, Mill justifies the central role of individual choice solely on the basis of the value it serves in enhancing the happiness of the individual. Whatever one thinks of the Millian defense of autonomy, however, there can be little doubt that the bulk of utilitarian thought focused not at all on the values of individual choice.

More fundamentally, the fact that utilitarian theory regards individualism as simply another factor among many illuminates the broader problem with utilitarianism in a political system premised on the existence of individually held rights. In the words of Judge Posner:

Rights in a utilitarian system are strictly instrumental goods. The only final good is the happiness of the group as a whole. If it is maximized by allowing people to marry as they choose and change jobs and so on, then rights to these things will be given to them, but if happiness could be increased by treating people more like sheep, then rights are out the window.[80]

While this perception may be easily overstated,[81] it is beyond dispute that utilitarianism is a philosophy "which judges actions neither by their motives nor their intrinsic qualities, but by their consequences."[82] The broader point is that "[u]tilitariainism in itself does not make any class of actions categorically wrong; everything depends upon one's guess about the effects of a policy upon the psychic state of millions of individuals."[83] It is this communal aspect of utilitarianism that Rawls criticized in crafting his *Theory of Justice*.[84] To utilitarian theorists, the individual matters only in so far as individuals are deemed units for deriving measurements of utility.[85] Utilitarian theory acknowledges the individual's ability to choose what makes him happy and what does not, and will generally leave those preferences undisturbed. Yet if abridging the happiness of an individual will create greater happiness for others, then the individual's will must give way to the interests of the majority.

Communitarianism

The modern strains of communitarian political theory function primarily as a response to Rawlsian liberalism, rather than as a single unified political philosophy.[86] Perhaps reflecting this responsive character, the common characteristic of modern communitarian theorists is disdain for liberalism's overemphasis on individualism. This shared objection manifests itself in two largely distinct political philosophies with different approaches to the way communal will may constrain the autonomous decision making of the individual. The first of these approaches is appropriately labeled "democratic communitarianism," a theory that vests the power of self-determination in the community as a whole, rather than in the individual, based on its belief in the primacy of social tradition and context in determining the identity and views of an individual. This approach does not predetermine what the substantive normative decisions made by and for the community should be, but instead posits that as a general matter, any attempt to define justice in a way that disregards broader communal interests, whatever those interests are determined to be, is incoherent. The second of these approaches, appropriately described as "objective truth communitarianism," posits that there exist objectively good and bad policy decisions and that the government has a responsibility to enact policies that promote the "good life" for all of society. This approach contends that government should not be neutral toward the views and actions of the public, but rather should steer society toward a predetermined ideal society, even if that requires the constraint of individual preferences.

Each version shares a related disagreement with the normative conclusions associated with liberal theory. Yet their differing approaches to the means of incorporating the communal interests at stake raise distinct concerns. The democratic communitarians effectively subordinate the value of individual autonomy to the social institutions that shape the community as a whole. The objective truth communitarians, in contrast, allow justice to be defined by the purely political preferences of those who, for whatever reason, have been vested with the a priori power to define justice. Because modern class action theory appears to reflect only issues of process-based communitarianism, my theoretical inquiry here is confined to that version of communitarian theory.

Democratic communitarianism, much like liberal theory, places value on a commitment to a foundational premise of societal self-determination. The theory rejects the notion that there exist values external to those determined by the society of self-governing citizens. In this important sense, the theory rejects any form of totalitarianism or authoritarianism. Thus, communitarians believe that society is best served by political decisions— both process based and substantive—that reflect the preferences of the entire community.[87]

In contrast to liberalism, democratic communitarianism views the community, rather than the individual, as the foundational democratic unit. The individual is seen only as a part of broader social institutions to which he is inescapably and organically connected. Democratic communitarians believe that the interests of society are best served by a state that adopts policies designed to promote the communal entities that shape an individual's identity. Individual autonomy is to be protected only to the extent that doing so does not undermine these different communal attachments that play such an important role in shaping the life choices made by individuals.

Democratic communitarianism rejects the value that liberalism places on atomistic individual autonomy. Where liberals like Kant and Rawls argue that individuals have a supreme interest in selecting and pursuing the aims they deem important, democratic communitarians argue that individuals are defined largely by their various communal attachments. The ultimate result of this insight is that the policies selected by the state should not emphasize the protection of an individual's ability to make autonomous choices, but should instead initially seek to sustain and promote the communal attachments that allow for the very sense of well-being and self-respect that lies at the heart of the justification for liberal individualism. Communitarian theory is grounded in the belief that individual autonomy divorced from the communal ties that shape that autonomy is incoherent because the reasons for the actions one selects are derived from the experiences shaped by communal groups that are often involuntarily or passively selected, such as racial, gender, or religious affiliations.[88] They contend that government policies best further the interests of society by seeking to promote the interrelationship between individuals and society as a whole.

At the heart of the communitarian argument lies a metaphysical view of an individual's identity as bound up with each person's various communal attachments. Charles Taylor has perhaps most clearly articulated this view of identity and why it requires a reconceptualization of the liberal view of justice.[89] Taylor advocates an Aristotelian view of the individual as "a social animal, because he is not self-sufficient alone, and in an important sense is not self-sufficient outside a polis . . . [individualism] affirms the self-sufficiency of man alone."[90] He considers liberal individualism flawed because it ignores the fact that "living in society is a necessary condition of the development of rationality . . . or of becoming a fully responsible, autonomous being."[91] The autonomy contemplated by liberal theory "is a freedom by which men are capable of conceiving alternatives and arriving at a definition of what they really want, as well as discerning what commands their adherence or their allegiance."[92] He contends that this sort of autonomy can only be developed by the norms imposed by society as a whole. Further, the very desire to possess this sort of autonomy derives from "the developments of art, philosophy, theology, science, [and] the evolving practices of politics and social organization."[93] He reasons that these institutions, which shape and provide meaning to the individual, "require stability and continuity and frequently also support from society as a whole—almost always the moral support of being commonly recognized as important, but frequently also considerable material support."[94] As a consequence, "the free individual of the West is only what he is by virtue of the whole society which brought him to be and which nourishes him . . . all this creates a significant obligation to belong for whoever would affirm the value of this freedom; this includes all those who want to assert rights either to this freedom or for its sake."[95]

The consequence of this view of the self from a political theory perspective is that it elevates the importance of community to a level far higher than that of the individual alone. In the words of Professor Taylor:

> The crucial point here is this: since the free individual can only maintain his identity within a society/culture of a certain kind, he has to be concerned about the shape of this society/culture as a whole. He cannot . . . be concerned purely with his individual choices and associations formed from such choices to the neglect of the matrix in which such choices can be open or closed, rich or meagre. It is important to him that certain activities and institutions flourish in society. It is even of importance to him what the moral tone of the whole society is—shocking as it may be to libertarians to raise this issue—because freedom and individual diversity can only flourish in a society where there is a general recognition of their worth.[96]

The failure that democratic communitarians like Taylor identify in liberalism lies with its promotion of an atomistic notion of the self that they believe to be metaphysically incoherent and to inspire hedonistic behavior.

There are many flaws in the reasoning underlying democratic communitarianism. Initially, communitarians fallaciously treat the normative and the descriptive perspectives as interchangeable. As purely an empirical matter, it is of course true that individuals rarely, if ever, exist in atomistic isolation. None of us, after all, is Robinson Crusoe—and even he benefited from having his companion, Friday. We all live within a broader society which, to a certain extent, shapes and frames us. It does not follow, however, that society should not be structured by an abstract normative commitment to recognition of the individual as an integral unit, worthy of respect apart from his communitarian associations. Indeed, it is for the very reason that the individual may so easily be overwhelmed by the society as a whole that the need to emphasize the importance of the individual's growth and development is so compelling. A democratic society could not function effectively otherwise. Even modern civic republicans, who generally deplore the selfishness of the individual and instead value communal pursuit of the public interest, acknowledge that absent the opportunity for personal and intellectual growth the individual will be unable to function as an active participant in the governing process.[97] The simple fact is that a community is, ultimately, composed of individual citizens. If society places no value on their worth or growth, we will be left with a community of automatons—hardly the basis of a democratic society, and hardly the appropriate building block for active, flourishing communal institutions.

It is quite conceivable that one could choose to prefer at least a diluted form of communitarianism over the extreme substantive libertarianism of

Nozick. It is quite another thing, however, to choose communitarianism at the expense of the process-based (or "meta") autonomy that, I believe, lies at the heart of liberal theory. Absent a commitment to the individual citizen's ability to make choices about the nature of his participation in the governing process or to protect his own rights and interests within that process legally unfettered by external communal forces, the concept of a viable democracy is rendered incoherent, because the concept of an active, thoughtful citizen will have become incoherent. It would therefore be nonsensical to commit to democracy as one's chosen form of government without accepting, on at least some level of abstraction, the value of individual self-determination.[98] A community is composed of individuals, and it is the free will of those individuals, acting individually or in association with others, that is exercised when policy choices are made. Without some foundational respect for the moral and intellectual integrity of the individual, any notion of democracy is ultimately rendered incoherent.

Civic Republicanism

Related to but in an important sense distinct from communitarianism is the revised theory of civic republicanism that surfaced late in the twentieth century. In its origins generally tied to such morally distasteful precepts as racism, jingoism, and sexism,[99] in its modern and streamlined form civic republican theory has shifted dramatically to the political left. As revived by such leading legal scholars as Cass Sunstein and Frank Michelman,[100] civic republicanism is characterized by its commitment to the deliberative pursuit of the public interest and disdain for the selfish, pluralistic pursuit of narrow personal interests.[101] Individualism, not surprisingly, is for the most part a political casualty of this focus. Because I have previously coauthored an extensive scholarly critique on the modern version of civic republicanism,[102] I decline to mount such an attack here. My present focus, rather, is on a comparison of civic republicanism to the various forms of communitarianism.

In their disdain for the value of individualism and their focus on some sense of community, the two theories are clearly linked. However, communitarian theory does not appear to be as narrowly tied to pursuit of some political form of the public interest. Presumably, communitarian theory could find value even in more narrowly defined communities—even those grounded in notions of self-interest, as long as the "self" in question is defined on a community basis. For example, the National Association of

Manufacturers or the National Chamber of Commerce could presumably qualify for protection under at least some forms of communitarian theory, broadly defined. The same is definitely untrue of modern civic republican theory. Civic republicanism finds selfish pursuit of private profit-making interests to be harmful, rather than beneficial, whether the pursuit is individually or group based.

LEGAL MODELS OF THE CLASS ACTION

To this point, I have described four normative models of political theory: liberalism, utilitarianism, democratic communitarianism, and civic republicanism. My thesis is that (1) the various normative approaches to the class action that have been advocated by prominent legal scholars are best understood largely as manifestations of one or another of these broader political theories, and (2) when viewed from this theoretical perspective, each should be found wanting because of its improper departure from the fundamental norms of liberal theory, which value the process-based autonomy of the individual. Before one can recognize and comprehend these legal-political intersections, however, it is first necessary to understand the structures of the various legal models of the class action. It is therefore to that exploration that I now turn.

One can readily identify three class action models that illustrate the breadth and depth of legal scholarship on the normative rationale and proposed structure of the modern class action. I call the first of these models the "utilitarian justice" model, which is principally linked to the writings of Professor David Rosenberg. It relies on the belief that the common good is best served by a class action device that provides optimal deterrence in mass tort cases. Such deterrence can be achieved, Rosenberg argues, only by means of all-inclusive, mandatory classes. The second approach, which I label the "communitarian process" model, emerges from the writings of David Shapiro and Samuel Issacharoff. This approach seeks to view the class action, in a significant portion of the cases, as the adjudication of claims held by community-like entities, rather than as the aggregation of separately held individual claims. The final model, which I associate with Owen Fiss, I label the "public action" model. This approach views the class action exclusively as a device to vindicate the public interest by enforcing public rights against governmental or private offenders. From the perspective of the public action model, individual claimants are little more than the instrumental vehicle by which the public interest is legally vindicated.

The Utilitarian Justice Model

The "utilitarian justice" model of the class action seeks to utilize the class action as a mechanism for overcoming what are perceived to be the inefficiencies in the adversary system's treatment of mass exposure tort claims by adjudicating all such claims that are individually held in the form of mandatory class actions. By requiring the aggregation of individually held claims in mass torts, this model envisions a class action rule that facilitates the use of substantive tort law as an instrument for ensuring an optimal level of deterrence. Following in a long tradition of utilitarianism,[103] the utilitarian justice model determines the appropriateness of the invocation of the class action procedure entirely on the basis of an estimate of the overall societal utility to be achieved as a result.

This approach was first described by David Rosenberg, and it is in his scholarship that this model has been most clearly detailed and refined (though Professor Rosenberg does not employ the label I have placed on it).[104] Rosenberg's initial treatment of the class action came in an article in which he advocated a reconceptualization of tort law in mass exposure cases.[105] Deeming the class action to be the "keystone" of a reformulated mass exposure tort system,[106] Rosenberg focused his early work on its facilitative value in creating a tort system he believed would "enhance the system's functional productivity considerably."[107]

Rosenberg's approach to the class action sought to deal with the problem that individual plaintiffs face in mass exposure cases in proving causation by a preponderance of the evidence. They are frequently unable to do this for two reasons. First, there exists a "problem of determining the origin of the victim's disease."[108] When the injury in a mass exposure case involves illness, there are typically multiple possible causes of the disease. It is often the case that collectively only a certain percentage of a particular class of injury or harm is caused by exposure to a defendant's product, effectively rendering impossible determination of causation in the individual case. Usually, the most an individual plaintiff bearing the burden of proof is able to establish is a statistically higher rate of disease among those who have come into contact with the defendant's product, and it is at best unclear how successful such a trial strategy would be. The second obstacle possibly facing mass exposure plaintiffs occurs because "it is often unclear which one of several manufacturers of a given toxic agent produced the particular unit of the substance that harmed the plaintiff."[109] Mass exposure cases often involve several manufacturers who make effectively identical products, and potential plaintiffs will come into contact with products produced by more than one of these manufacturers. This makes it nearly impossible for individual plaintiffs to establish, by a preponderance of evidence, which factor actually caused his injury.

The paradigmatic example of these problems of proof occurred in the Agent Orange litigation of the 1980s. In the years following the Vietnam veterans' return, a number of them died prematurely, reported debilitating illnesses, or had children who were born with serious birth defects.[110] When the veterans linked their conditions to their exposure to the chemical agent known as Agent Orange, which had been employed as a defoliant during the war to clear parts of the Vietnam jungle, they faced both of the evidentiary problems Rosenberg identified. It was, as a practical matter, all but impossible for an individual plaintiff to prove that his particular illness had been caused by exposure to Agent Orange.[111] Science was unable to definitively tie the various illnesses to a singular cause. Additionally, Agent Orange had been manufactured by a number of different chemical companies. It would be impossible to keep track of which chemical company's Agent Orange had been used in which parts of Vietnam in order to establish individual causation by a preponderance.[112] Yet despite these evidentiary barriers, it was at least conceivable that Agent Orange had, in fact, caused some of the illnesses suffered by the Vietnam veterans and their families. Judge Jack Weinstein of the United States District Court for the Eastern District of New York addressed this problem by effectively implementing Rosenberg's model through the process of inducing settlement.[113] He cited Rosenberg's 1984 article and chose to certify the class, allowed statistical evidence to be introduced, and imposed damage scheduling once the litigation reached a settlement.[114]

The Agent Orange litigation arguably provides real-world support for Rosenberg's key observation that in the mass tort context, the impact of the causation problem can give rise to potentially significant problems for individual plaintiffs. Yet under the restrictions imposed by an individualized adjudicatory system, where the assessment of damages is preceded by the all-or-nothing assessment of liability on an individualized basis, the total damages assessed against that defendant are likely to be significantly lower than had the adjudication been class-wide in effect.

Rosenberg's attempt to remedy this danger inspired his proposed "public law" reformulation of the tort system in mass exposure cases.[115] A key element of this public law model was the use of the class action as a tool to achieve the broad objective of the tort system of deterring future tortious conduct.[116] Rosenberg proposed a collectively based "proportionality rule" to replace the individualized case-by-case preponderance rule in mass tort cases. He argued that both compensatory and deterrence objectives would be better served by "impos[ing] liability and distribut[ing] compensation in proportion to the probability of causation . . . regardless [of] whether that probability fell above or below the fifty-percent threshold and despite the absence of individualized proof of the causal connection."[117] In practice, this would mean the use of statistical averaging and damage scheduling that would allow a class to recover a statistically determined amount if its members could establish an overall statistical probability that their illnesses were caused by exposure to a product, even if that probability would likely amount to less than a preponderance in an individualized adjudication. Thus, even if certain especially resourceful plaintiffs or plaintiffs with unique circumstances would have been able to take advantage of an individualized system of adjudication, as a collective matter the class of plaintiffs would benefit substantially from a unified form of adjudication.

Rosenberg further noted that the causal connection problem is exacerbated by the institutional advantages defendants enjoy in a one-on-one litigation system that allows them to litigate what is effectively the same case over and over again, while each plaintiff is forced to start from scratch. [118] He argued that a system composed exclusively of individual adjudications allows "[t]he defendant firm, but not the plaintiffs, [to] take advantage of economies of scale in case preparation, enabling it to invest far more cost-effectively in litigation."[119] He believed that this institutional advantage leads to lower recovery for plaintiffs precisely because there are a large number of them.[120] He suggests that as an alternative, the class action "prevents the defendant from using the plaintiffs' numerosity against them by providing plaintiffs with a similar scale economy that defendants enjoy."[121]

Under this utilitarian justice model, then, the class action is made to function as a mechanism for requiring potential individual claimants to act collectively in pooling their resources and subordinating their desire to maximize their personal interests in order to ensure the optimal outcome for the group.[122] According to Rosenberg, this model of the class action has three basic elements:

First, to exploit litigation scale economies fully, courts should automatically and immediately aggregate all potential and actual claims arising from mass tort events into a single mandatory class action, allowing no class member to exit. Second, to achieve optimal deterrence efficiently, courts should statistically estimate total aggregate liability and assess the appropriate level of damages (normally, and for present purposes, assumed to equal total aggregate tortuous harm). Third, to advance the goal of optimal insurance, courts should distribute damages to class members according to the relative severity of their injury rather than the relative strength of their legal claim.[123]

In support of this model, Rosenberg focused on how the underlying philosophy of his class action rule would function in practice under a reformulated tort system. He summarized his foundational theory by noting:

The law should seek to minimize the sum of accident costs—specifically, the total costs of precautions against accident, unavoidable harm, risk-bearing, and administration of the legal system . . . I posit systemic failure of administrative regulation to control risk appropriately and of government and commercial first-party insurance to cover loss adequately. Therefore, the need exists for "optimal tort deterrence" to prevent unreasonable risk of accident and for "optimal tort insurance" to cover residual risk.[124]

He argued that the class action fulfills this need. He thus concluded that his model's effectiveness requires that all class actions in mass tort suits be mandatory.[125]

At the heart of this proposal is Rosenberg's view that the debate over class actions is incorrectly focused on procedure, rather than on its substantive tort law dimension.[126] Process-oriented analysis, Rosenberg believes, distracts from the potential utilitarian virtues of the class action procedure in facilitating tort law's goal of deterring unjustifiably harmful behavior.[127] He charged the "myopic proceduralist" with placing too much stock in the virtues of individualism and procedural formalism, while ignoring the functional benefits of what I here describe as his utilitarian justice model.[128] He noted that "[p]roceduralists" compound their analytical shortcomings with "shoddy cost-benefit analysis, general disregard of presuit, ex ante conditions, and resort to deontological and even ontological claims, usually asserted in the form of vacuous and question-begging moralisms, hackneyed slogans, pseudo-traditions, and other conceptual shell games like 'plaintiff autonomy,' 'day in court,' and 'process values.' "[129] He further argued that a formalistic approach to individual justice causes a net loss to individual plaintiffs and ignores the ex ante preferences they would have from behind a Rawlsian veil of ignorance.[130]

In contrast to the majority of class action scholars, Rosenberg actually does make an effort to ground his class action model in broader precepts of political theory. However, in doing so he inaccurately portrays his approach as effectively all things to all people, satisfying the dictates of virtually every normative model of political theory. In reality, Rosenberg's class action approach, when viewed through the lens of political theory, amounts to a form of stark, Benthamite utilitarianism, with all of that theory's disdain for the values of individualism contemplated by liberal theory. Rosenberg's tort law view of the class action relies on the basic utilitarian principle that the social utility of law is to be determined by reference to the extent that it fosters the greatest good to the greatest number. As is true of all such utilitarian approaches, this model values individualism only up to the point that it is necessary to maximize overall utility.[131] Indeed, in shaping the utilitarian justice model Rosenberg considers arguments focused on individual autonomy to be disingenuous, to the extent they rely on "self-validating assertions that individual participation 'increases self-respect.'"[132] While he does purport to rationalize his model by reference to liberal theoretical perspectives as well, such references are wholly specious. For good or ill, his close and dominating tie to utilitarianism is clear.[133]

The rationale Rosenberg provides for his system makes clear that his sole aim in developing the utilitarian justice model is to provide the greatest good to society as a whole, regardless of its impact on the individual plaintiff's ability to control the protection of his individually held legal rights. His argument in support of this model is divided into two parts: a "utilitarian appraisal" and a "rights-based appraisal."[134] Yet both are, ultimately, forms of utilitarian analysis, with the "rights based-appraisal" simply an extension of his "utilitarian appraisal," which overtly focuses exclusively on considerations of economic efficiency.[135] In later writing, Rosenberg declared that his model "rests on the normative premise that the law should promote individuals' well being, that is, their welfare or utility."[136] While he does use the word, *individuals,* that hardly qualifies his theory as an example of liberal individualism. In fact, but for the largely cosmetic use of the word, *individuals,* Rosenberg's approach roughly parallels Bentham's approach, which was premised on the postulate that "general utility ought to be the foundation of [a legislator's] reasonings. To know the true good of the community is what constitutes the science of legislation; the art consists in finding the means to realize that good."[137] Both Rosenberg and Bentham appear to believe that "society is rightly ordered, and therefore just, when its major institutions are arranged so as to achieve the greatest net balance of satisfaction summed over all the individuals belonging to it."[138] Rosenberg makes this collectivist premise the principal justification for his model.[139] He effectively adopts a "utility as deterrence" rationale, which sees the greatest utility generated by the greatest deterrence. The effect of this benefit can only be maximized by use of a mandatory system of class actions, where there is no possibility of opt-out and plaintiffs do not have to assume the cost of notice to absent class members.[140]

Rosenberg incorrectly believes that his class action model also grows out of a "rights-based appraisal" on the basis of wholly unsupported assumptions about the desires and interests of potential plaintiffs. Because the claims adjudicated in a class action are, in their pristine substantive form, individually held rights on the part of claimants, each of those claims individually carries at least the potential for an award of the maximum damages allowed by the substantive law. Any model of the class action truly grounded in individualism would allow individual claimants to choose to take their chances in individual suits to seek those maximum damages.

Rosenberg nevertheless argues that his model goes beyond utilitarianism, satisfying elements of both the libertarian analysis of Nozick and the liberal theory of Rawls. Yet any claim that his model can be reconciled with liberal theory should be met with a high degree of skepticism. Rosenberg's claim that his model is consistent with Nozick's brand of libertarianism fails adequately to account for the total and unbending role of individual autonomy laid out by Nozick.[141] Rosenberg asserts that rights-based theories "are premised on the concept of individual entitlements to personal security and autonomy—entitlements that may not usually be overridden or compromised for the good of society."[142] He then claims that "[t]ortuous [sic] conduct, whether defined by moral, political, or economic criteria, constitutes a wrongful infringement of those entitlements."[143] He concludes by arguing that "[f]rom a rights-oriented standpoint, then, the role of the tort system is to perform 'corrective justice' in order to preserve entitlements against wrongful infringement."[144] In making this case Rosenberg has two aims. The first is to justify his emphasis on deterrence as the primary goal of his class action model above compensation. He argues that because there can never be total compensation for the invasion of a right,[145] achieving optimal deterrence is a more important goal of the tort system in achieving the aim of "preserv[ing] the value of entitlements."[146] The second is to justify any perceptible invasion on rights of individuals stemming from the use of the class action.

Despite this explanation, Rosenberg fails to satisfy the concerns of libertarian theory. Nozick did suggest that the state is justified in providing "protection against force, theft, fraud, enforcement of contracts, and so on."[147] Certainly, protection from and compensation for the negligent acts of others falls within that framework. But Nozick also noted that "the state may not use its coercive apparatus for the purpose of getting some citizens to aid others, or in order to prohibit activities to people for their *own* good or protection."[148] Rosenberg ascribes to Nozick a balancing approach to individual rights—namely that the law should provide the greatest degree of autonomy and personal security to as large a segment of society as reasonably possible. But there is little to suggest Nozick would endorse such an approach to individually held rights. In their pristine form, both common law and statutory tort rights are individually possessed. Even accepting Rosenberg's functional evaluation that one's rights would be best served by group treatment under a class action, he still fails to account for the individual's autonomy interest in determining how to enforce rights that are, as a matter of controlling substantive law, individually possessed. Thus, while Nozick would presumably allow the state to create a system of redress for personal wrongs, the suggestion that he would concur in anything approaching Rosenberg's collectivist utilitarian approach to the adjudication and enforcement of those rights is highly questionable.

More recently, Rosenberg sought to invoke the veil-of-ignorance thought experiment propounded by Rawls, in an effort to rationalize his approach as a form of liberal theory.[149] Rosenberg argued that an ex ante approach to rule-making demonstrates that his use of his approach to the class action is the most just because any individual unaware of the society to come would prefer his mandatory approach in light of its optimal deterrence effect.[150] From this point of view, he might claim that he actually does respect the role of the individual by valuing individuals up to the point that an unbiased individual would do so, phrasing the individual's choice from behind the veil of ignorance as one between reduced compensation and no compensation. Based on the risk-averseness Rawls associates with decisions made from behind the veil of ignorance, Rosenberg argues that "any rational individual would choose a legal system that minimizes the sum of accident costs and uses mass tort liability to do so."[151] Once again, Rosenberg fails in his effort to be all things to all political theorists.

Rawls described his theory as "an alternative to utilitarian thought generally," finding utilitarianism deficient for reasons that apply equally to Rosenberg's class action model.[152] Utilitarians automatically allow individual interests to be overcome if such action is found to correspond to a sufficient increase in the happiness of other societal members. Rawls notes this by saying "[t]he striking feature of the utilitarian view of justice is that it does not matter, except indirectly, how this sum of satisfactions is distributed among individuals."[153] As a result of this analysis, Rawls ultimately concludes that "[u]tilitarianism does not take seriously the distinction between persons."[154] But clearly, Rosenberg's approach suffers from the identical shortcoming. Rawls might well have objected to the loss of individual choice that necessarily comes with Rosenberg's collectivist approach.[155] Rawls's First Principle, derived from the veil of ignorance thought experiment, seeks to maximize individual autonomy to the greatest extent possible. Rosenberg, in contrast, uses the thought experiment as a method for maximizing the restriction of individual autonomy based on the broader interest of society.

Rosenberg substantially misuses the Rawlsian veil-of-ignorance construct, primarily because he invokes it at the wrong point in the process. When individual class members make the strategic decision whether to opt out of a class proceeding (the point at which he employs the construct), they are *not* behind a veil of ignorance, at least in the sense Rosenberg suggests. Of course, individual plaintiffs do not know with certainty what the outcome of their individual suits would be. But they do know what resources and evidence they will be able to bring to an individual suit. Under any system that values process-based individual autonomy, the choice whether to sue individually or as part of a collective effort is best left to the individual herself. Any externally imposed assessment amounts to a form of paternalism that is anathema to core notions of liberal individualism. Liberal theory would therefore necessarily reject Rosenberg's model because of its reliance on the utilitarian tradition of justifying a heavy sacrifice of individual autonomy—in this case, purely process-based autonomy—when the societal good is sufficiently powerful.[156]

Rosenberg's contravention of the precepts of liberal theory goes much farther than his undermining of process-based individual autonomy. By employing what is openly and unambiguously designed to be purely a rule of *procedure* (the class action rule) as a means of surreptitiously altering the DNA of pre-existing substantive tort law, Rosenberg's model blatantly subverts the foundations of representative democracy on a "macro" level. While substantive libertarianism would probably oppose direct modification of substantive law in order to collectivize previously individually held rights,[157] the process-based branch of individual autonomy would likely be agnostic on the issue.[158] But the fact remains that current substantive mass tort law, whether in the form of legislation or common law, for the most part vests the substantive claim in the victim in an individual capacity. If the liberal presumptions about individually held rights is, in fact, to be transformed due to compelling and overwhelming counter utilitarian interests, such a transformation should be achieved by means of an open and transparent exercise of the democratic process, rather than furtively under the guise of a rule of procedure.[159]

The Communitarian Process Model

An alternative to the utilitarian justice model can be appropriately described as the "communitarian process" model of the class action, which, in most cases, views a class as a stand-alone "entity," rather than an aggregation of separate individual claims. This model, associated principally with the scholarship of highly respected procedural scholars David Shapiro and Samuel Issacharoff,[160] deems the class in most cases to be an organic entity, in which each individual class member is conceptualized as little more than an inherent element of that entity. The individual class members retain little, if any, control over their individual claims as the claim itself becomes the property of the class entity, which is empowered to make decisions about how to act in the best interests of the group as a whole. Though its legal advocates for the most part do not frame the model in terms of abstract political theory, to a large extent it implicitly reflects the normative precepts of democratic communitarianism.[161]

Perhaps the chief scholarly advocate of an "entity" approach to the class action is Shapiro.[162] He characterized the "principal focus" in the debate over the correct perspective on the class action to be whether a class "should be viewed as not involving the claimants as a number of individuals . . . but rather as an entity in itself."[163] In determining that "the 'class as entity' forces should ultimately carry the day,"[164] he argues that the consequence of such an interpretation is that "the individual who is a member of the class, for whatever purpose, is and must remain a member of the class, and as a result must tie his fortunes to those of the group with respect to the litigation, its progress, and its outcome."[165] Shapiro conceptualizes the distinction between an "entity" approach and an aggregation-of-individuals approach as one between "advocates of individual autonomy in litigation and the proponents of what has been praised as 'collective' justice."[166] By contrasting his "entity" model with one favoring individual autonomy, he effectively acknowledges the subordination of individuality inherent in his model. He states that "[t]he conclusion that the entity model is preferable is not an easy one for a person like me, who believes in the virtues of autonomy and individual choice."[167] While conceding the tension this creates with individual notions of autonomy, particularly if individual choice involves the right to have "a personal 'day in court'—of the ability to participate in the fullest sense in the adjudication of a claim of right," he argues that this virtue is "far from evident: if such participation is not cost-effective, and would be seen by the vast majority of those similarly affected (as well as by their adversary) to run counter to their own objective of a fair and effective outcome, then the argument proceeding from the value of autonomy may be flawed."[168] Without squarely arguing that there is a right to a personal day in court, Shapiro does seem to suggest that even if that right does exist, other factors can override its importance.

The rationale Shapiro offers for recognizing the inseparable intertwining of class members into a coherent, organic unit varies based on the nature of the class action. He identifies three general types of class actions and proposes differing rationales for an entity approach to each type. He claims that the strongest case for entity treatment applies to (b)(1) and (b)(2) classes because "the class must in essence stand or fall as a unit because of the truly indivisible interests of the class members."[169] He therefore argues that they "afford less basis for concern about issues of individual autonomy and control."[170] This assumption of class indivisibility, however, in most cases has no basis in reality. In (b)(1)(A) class actions, for example, the only "indivisible" aspect is the behavior of *the party opposing the class.* In no legal sense are the *rights of the class members* necessarily indivisible. Purely as a theoretical matter, each could be pursued in its own proceeding, because each is, as a matter of substantive law, held by the litigant in his individual capacity.

Indivisibility of class member rights is even less evident in (b)(1)(B) classes. For example, where individually held tort claims are aggregated because of the availability of only a limited insurance fund to pay damages, the plaintiff class member claims are legally intertwined in no substantive sense. To the contrary, in the presence of only a limited fund for damages, the strategic antagonism among plaintiff class members is even greater than in (b)(3) classes, where defendant's resources are assumed to be large enough to cover all damages. Finally, in (b)(2) classes, where injunctive relief is necessarily the predominant remedy, there is not even a requirement that the *defendant's* behavior toward class members be indivisible, much less that the claims of plaintiff class members be indivisible. All that is required is that the party opposing the class have acted in a manner generally applicable to the class. It is certainly conceivable that such class-wide behavior could be easily divisible. For example, an employer could conceivably discriminate racially against some employees without doing so against others. For example, a white employer might accept what he deems to be "docile" African Americans as employees, but not one whose behavior could not be characterized in such a manner. Hence individualized injunctive relief against the party opposing the class could easily be confined only to specified employees. Shapiro's description is accurate, then, only in the circular sense that Rule 23 renders it so.

The second type of entity-based class Shapiro calls the "small value" claim or, in the language used earlier,[171] the "Negative Value" or "Type B" class action. He argues that the purpose of a small claim or negative value class action is not "compensating those harmed in any significant sense, or of providing them a sense of personal vindication, but rather, and perhaps entirely, the purpose of allowing a private attorney general to contribute to social welfare by bringing an action whose effect is to internalize to the wrongdoer the cost of the wrong."[172] The context of the small value class action, Shapiro reasons, makes whatever private rights may be sacrificed to the entity a secondary consideration. From this observation, he argues that "notions of individual choice, autonomy, and participation—and their resonance in the constitutional guarantee of due process—are not so rigid that they cannot yield to practical arguments about the nature of the case, the character of the wrong complained of, and the individual interests at stake."[173]

The final category of class actions identified by Shapiro concerns positive value class actions under Rule 23(b)(3). He describes these classes as "the hardest to bring within" an entity model precisely because "the rule-makers in 1966 expressed doubt that such cases were appropriate for class treatment at all."[174] He nevertheless finds persuasive support for the view "that a mass tort is, and should be treated as, substantively different from a one-on-one tort."[175]

Shapiro's conceptualization of the class as an entity has a number of important procedural implications for the operation of the class proceeding. For example, he believes acceptance of the entity approach leads logically to significant restrictions on the availability of both notice and opt-out, even in (b)(3) classes.[176] He unquestioningly accepts the absence of both in the other categories.

Shapiro's description of the entity theory allows for two possible ways to conceptualize the entity itself. The first is as an entity that is conceptually distinguishable from the aggregation of distinct, individualized claims held by each member of the class. Under this theory, the aggregation of rights in a class action is metaphysically transformed into something distinct from the sum of its parts. The other interpretation of the entity is one that conceptualizes the class as a form of aggregation of individual claims, but in which the interests of the individual class members are pragmatically overwhelmed by the needs of the class as a whole. If viewed as the latter, the theory is reminiscent of a form of Benthamite utilitarianism.[177] If viewed as the former, the entity model is more appropriately seen as a type of democratic communitarianism: The substantive rights being enforced are determined by democratic processes, but once created they are deemed to be held in a communitarian form, where each individual's right is defined by and inseparable from the whole.

The very use of the word *entity* to describe the model would seem to imply more of a communitarian rationale. However, Shapiro appears to employ both theories at various points in his analysis, primarily taking an "entity-as-distinct-organism" approach when discussing the so-called impersonal (b)(1) and (b)(2) class actions, where he contends the right is effectively a group right because of the nature of the interests being litigated.[178] In the case of (b)(3) classes, however, Shapiro seems to advocate a more starkly pragmatic form of utilitarianism.

Though he appears to care little about litigant autonomy, Shapiro does acknowledge that the most important concern in class litigation is that the absent class members are adequately protected by the class representative. The fiduciary roles of the class representative and class counsel become particularly significant under a model that views the group as an entity that subsumes its individual members.[179] At some level, at least, Shapiro's class action approach bears similarity to democratic communitarianism and its disregard for the norms of liberal individualism. Whether because of a process of rights reconceptualization or a categorical concession of the superiority of group needs in class action contexts, Shapiro's entity model readily transforms individually held claims into a communitarian framework. As in classic communitarianism, rights of the individual are viewed as inseparable from the needs and interests of the community as a whole. In this sense, the entity model is reminiscent of Charles Taylor's critique of classical liberalism in justifying a definition of individual rights based on group needs. The individual class member is defined, with respect to his injury, by his membership within the larger entity. By conceptualizing the individual class members largely, if not exclusively, as members of a group, the communitarian process model's approach to the individual is the antithesis of the liberal "atomism" attacked by Taylor. The rationale that Shapiro supplies for this approach focuses primarily on the deterrence objectives of class actions.[180]

The value neutrality of democratic communitarianism distinguishes it from a device designed from the outset solely to generate predetermined policy outcomes.[181] In this sense, the approach is distinguishable from the "objective truth" version of the theory, which defines the community in terms of its commitment to some moral "truth" higher than the normative choices reached by democratic processes.[182] Thus, Shapiro's class action model involves no commitment to a particular set of predetermined substantive value choices. Nevertheless, as a matter of the liberal democratic process his model expresses little concern for the autonomy of the individual in determining how he will employ the legal system as a means of protecting his individually held substantive rights. Shapiro's concern for the individual is focused for the most part, instead, on the paternalistic concern that individual plaintiffs will be fairly and adequately represented.[183] While such a concern is no doubt legitimate in those situations in which the individual is, for legal or practical reasons, unable to make such choices for herself,[184] to deem satisfaction of these paternalistic requirements as *sufficient*, rather then merely necessary, is to ignore the foundations of liberal process-based autonomy that are so central to the normative structure of liberal democracy.

Shapiro's class action model achieves its goal by transforming what in every class action category is nothing more than an aggregation of the claims of individual plaintiffs possessing individually granted rights into a new legal animal—an "entity," in which an individual's claim is seen essentially as an element within a broader communitarian whole. That such a transformation is wholly illegitimate and extra-legal can be proven by answering a very simple hypothetical question: Under governing substantive law, could *each* of the plaintiffs who are made members of a class bring a legally valid claim individually against the defendant, had the class proceeding never been instituted? The answer in every situation, of course, must be yes. Rule 23, in *all* of its categories (with the exceptions of Rules 23.1 and 23.2, both of which concern suits by *substantively established* legal entities),[185] does nothing more than aggregate pre-existing individual claims. This distinguishes claims of class members from claims brought by true entities, such as partnerships or trade unions.

To be sure, unless one is a rigid Kantian or a Nozickian libertarian, it is conceivable that, in the presence of compelling circumstances, an individual's ability to control adjudication of his individually held claim may be restricted in the interests of a more broadly defined group of claimants. But there are two fatal flaws in Shapiro's articulation of such a model. First, he is far too willing to sacrifice the individual to broader communitarian interests, never demanding anything approaching a showing of a compelling interest for the subjugation of an individual's process-based autonomy in the litigation context. And from his perspective, the refusal to demand a compelling interest makes perfect sense. After all, why should one be required to justify restriction of individual autonomy, when all that is involved in the first place is an entity, where any claim of the individual is fully shared with others? Second, he seems quite content to allow this alchemy-like transformation of individual right into entity-held right through reliance on a procedural rule that, by statutory origin, is not permitted to modify or abridge substantive rights. If individually held substantive claims are either to be transformed into entity claims, or sacrificed to broader communitarian interests, surely it is only by transparent resort to the representative and accountable branches of government that such results are appropriately achievable. Through reliance on the smokescreen of procedural joinder and fictionalized entities, however, Shapiro is somehow able to avoid both an analysis of the need for the compelling interest standard and the need for acquiring support in the democratic process.

The Public Action Model

The "public action" model of the class action views the private class action exclusively as an instrument to enforce public goals and values, as embodied in governing law. In this sense, the model differs fundamentally from both the liberal and communitarian models.[186] The public action model evaluates the proper role of the class action on the basis of a normative judgment of what is "good" for society in two ways. Public action model adherents claim that while individual litigant participation in a lawsuit is important in certain types of litigation, the class action is justified solely because it aids in the enforcement of laws that implement broader public purposes.[187] Advocates of the public action model view the class action as a means of protecting the public interest, rather than vindicating aggregated legally protected private interests.[188]

The public action model's strongest advocate is Owen Fiss. Fiss asserts that the class action device exists because certain laws are aimed at protecting the public, and private suits brought to enforce those laws will have the beneficial effect of vindicating the public interest.[189] He reasons that class certification increases the value of claims that, standing alone, would have been economically inefficient to pursue, even though socially significant. The goal, then, is to make them viable causes of action that provide sufficient economic incentive for attorneys to pursue them.[190] The public's interest in seeing these cases litigated justifies any restriction that class action procedure may impose on an individual's process-based autonomy.[191] Fiss, along with Professor Bronsteen, advocates a limitation on the use of the class action on the basis of this underlying philosophy, arguing that "[a] court should not permit a plaintiff to bring suit on behalf of unnamed class members unless the class lawsuit is necessary to vindicate important public rights and the named plaintiff satisfies the court that he will adequately represent the interests of the other class members."[192] Fiss never states precisely what makes the subject of a class action "an important public right," limiting his description to those statutes "aimed at protecting the public."[193] He does suggest, however, that some normative judgment about the "importance" of a suit should color the drafting, and possibly the application, of the class action rule.[194]

Fiss makes clear that in his view, the class action supersedes an individual's interest in having his own day in court, because the device is designed principally to advance the public good.[195] He distinguishes the types of litigation in which the individual's right to participate is to be respected by claiming that "the fairness of procedures turns, in part, on the social ends they serve."[196] The distinction rests on the difference between what Fiss calls "interest representation," which he associates with class actions, and representation that he describes as "consistent with individualistic values."[197] Interest representation occurs where an "individual [is] bound by the action of someone purporting to be his or her representative even though that individual had no say whatsoever over the selection of that representative, indeed, might not have even known of the appointment or that he or she was being represented."[198] He believes that while "the value of individual participation has an important role to play in the legal process . . . we must also recognize that we accord that value different weight in different contexts."[199] Fiss concedes that a system in which "[t]he named plaintiff is not the agent of the other class members" is "inherently suspect and grate[s] against even a minimum regard for allowing individuals to be in charge of their own destiny."[200] Yet he justifies the "interest representation" for class actions solely because such proceedings, under the circumstances in which he envisions their use, "enhance private enforcement of public laws."[201]

Fiss determines under what circumstances the value of individual participation is to be deemed sufficiently strong to preclude interest representation based on a determination of whether, in the particular situation, society is best served by abridging an individual's process-based autonomy. He uses the examples of criminal cases and adjudicatory administrative proceedings as instances in which individualized participation "is a value in its own right," because "particular individuals have been singled out."[202] In these instances, he finds "a public commitment to the dignity and worth of the individual, as well as . . . a more instrumental end . . . [in] ensuring that the facts and issues are presented to the court in the sharpest possible terms."[203] Fiss argues that class actions do justify restriction of an individual's right to participate in litigation, however, "for the private enforcement of laws that are aimed at protecting the public."[204] This suggests that the public purposes he attributes to these laws do not single out individuals in a manner that signifies a public commitment to their dignity and worth. Indeed, he criticizes the sort of individualism that is "Kantian in nature and gives each individual total control over his or her rights."[205] His contextual view of rights, based on his own assessment of societal consequences, allows him to draw a line between litigation in which process-based autonomy should be protected and those in which it should not, based on his assessment of the suit's social importance.[206]

From the perspective of liberal individualism, Fiss manages to combine the worst of both worlds. In cases deemed to have been brought in furtherance of the public interest, the individual's autonomy interest in control over his claim means preciously little. The autonomy interest is to be summarily sacrificed to the needs of a broader collectivist process.[207] This is so, even though the triggers for the lawsuits—the vehicle by which the public interest is to be legally enforced—are legal claims vested by lawgiving authority solely in the individual claimants themselves. Their pursuit may well advance the public interest, but that does not alter the fact that the legal rights being enforced are privately held. However, when the claims being enforced are deemed to have been brought predominantly in furtherance of *private* interests, the strategic and efficiency benefits of class treatment are apparently to be largely denied to them, even in cases in which the interests of individual claimants could possibly be furthered by use of class action treatment.

Though Fiss does not expressly employ the characterization and the fit is by no means perfect, the public action model appears to be strongly reminiscent of a form of modern civic republicanism. That political theory, it should be recalled, focuses on pursuit of some vague notion of the public interest that differs qualitatively from the aggregation of individual interests.[208] The theory expresses disdain for individualism, in most contexts, as the morally unacceptable pursuit of selfish personal interests at the expense of the public at large.[209] If one sees the individualism central to liberal theory as necessary for the flourishing of the citizenry and the ultimate success of democracy, as I do,[210] then modern civic republicanism must be deemed a serious threat to the moral and personal pluralism so vital to an active and ever-developing democracy. To the extent the public action model of the class action reflects a normative commitment to some notion of the public interest divorced from and in lieu of the vindication of individual rights—which it appears to do—then, like civic republican political theory, it must be rejected.

It surely does not follow, it should be emphasized, that the class action is to play no role in facilitating enforcement of public regarding law. As Fiss correctly notes, the class action has often been rationalized as a form of "private attorney general." The earliest explanation of the private attorney general rationale for the class action dates back to the seminal article by Professors Harry Kalven and Maurice Rosenfield. Kalven and Rosenfield envisioned the class action as a device for filling gaps in the enforcement of statutes. They argued that the need to effectuate the "deterrent effect of the sanctions which underlie much contemporary law" had been largely addressed by "the contemporary development of administrative law," but that this method of enforcement had alone proven insufficient.[211] Further, they argued that use of traditional joinder devices failed to provide an adequate group remedy because "it presupposes the prospective plaintiffs advancing en masse to the courts."[212] Only class actions, a system in which courts "ignore the various claimants until a decree has been obtained,"[213] would serve as the needed "vehicle for paying lawyers handsomely to be champions of semi-public rights."[214]

The reporter for the rules advisory committee that promulgated the pivotal 1966 amendments to Rule 23 also considered the class action to be consistent with the private attorney general concept. Professor Benjamin Kaplan, while not expressly using the term "private attorney general," clearly recognized the use of class suits as a means of advancing the public interest.[215] But there was certainly nothing in the revised rule that *confined* the benefits of the class action to such "public interest" situations. The 1966 amendments to Rule 23 sought to create a standard that would "sort out the factual situations or patterns that had recurred in class actions and appeared with varying degrees of convincingness to justify treatment of the class *in solido*."[216] The focus of these amendments was on the legal and factual situation at hand, not exclusively on the pursuit of a broader societal interest.

The variation on the private attorney general approach that Fiss employs to rationalize the class action led him to suggest a series of changes to Rule 23, designed to better reflect what he believed to be the procedural device's proper philosophical foundation. He argued that class actions are justified only where they serve to provide for private enforcement of "public laws," and that the current incarnation of Rule 23 should be "revise[d] . . . to make certain that it is used only in those situations where that social purpose is served."[217] The key alteration he proposed was elimination of the class action categories set out in Rule 23(b), making every class action subject to an analysis using both the current 23(a) factors and the two factors listed in 23(b)(3).[218] Fiss also proposed reinterpretation of some of the factors he would preserve from Rule 23(a) and 23(b)(3). In addition to his suggested approach to the (b)(3) requirement of superiority,[219] he argued that the "numerosity" requirement of Rule 23(a) should be read to make sure that class actions are only allowed where "there are many small individual claims" that in the aggregate "constitute a [sufficient] social harm," seemingly implying that the class action should be confined solely to negative value claims.[220] Fiss claims that the considerations that go into creating separate types of class action under 23(b) do not "serve the purpose of directing a court to scrutinize either the adequacy of interest representation or the social value and practical necessity of bringing a lawsuit as a class action."[221] He then called for a uniform standard for individualized notice, with an eye toward minimizing costs to the plaintiffs.[222]

Because Fiss's model, much like the theory of civic republicanism, focuses exclusively on protection of the public interest, rather than on the need to vindicate individuals' private interests, he seems to dismiss the possibility that, under certain circumstances, use of the class action device could effectively facilitate the vindication of private rights. There is no reason, however, why the public and private uses of the class action need be considered mutually exclusive. Contrary to Fiss's suggestion, the class action may produce strategic benefit even to positive value claim holders, whatever its impact on enforcement of public regarding laws.

Where Fiss's model runs into potential difficulty, above and beyond its unnecessary truncation to public law enforcement, is its conceivable use to rationalize "faux" class actions. These are suits that purport to be negative value class suits, but in which the individual claims are so small that no reasonable class member could be expected to expend the time and effort to claim his minimal portion of the ultimate award.[223] Presumably Fiss would have no problem with such a use of the class action, since it is designed solely to further the public interest by enforcing public values and policing governmental and corporate misbehavior. This analysis, however, dangerously ignores the significant alteration in the remedial portion of the underlying substantive law. That law has vested a *compensatory remedy* in the *individual claimant,* not in bounty hunter private plaintiffs' attorneys—the only individuals who benefit directly from a faux class action. Such a fundamental transformation in underlying law requires transparent modification through democratic processes.[224]

FASHIONING AN "INDIVIDUALIST" MODEL OF THE CLASS ACTION

Thus far, I have established that existing scholarly models of the class action necessarily emanate, at least implicitly, from traditions of political theory that either minimize or disregard the significance of process-based individual autonomy. Indeed, one might be tempted to assume that, because of its essentially collectivist nature, the class action is inherently inconsistent with foundational notions of liberal individualism, and that to accept the procedure is necessarily to undermine the values of individualism. There are, to be sure, potential tensions between the class action procedure and the political theory of process-based individualism. In situations where this tension is inescapable, the dominant normative force of process-based individualism requires that the class action procedure be justified by a showing of a truly compelling justification. It is important to understand, however, that the two should not always be seen to be in conflict. To the contrary, numerous instances will arise where authorizing a class action will actually serve as a catalyst to the attainment of individualist goals and the furtherance of individualist values. In this section, I seek to fashion a normative model of the class action that achieves these salutary ends.[225] In so doing I seek to overcome the shortcomings of the three existing models previously identified, by better reflecting the liberal individualist norms that are properly found to inhere in our civil justice system and its foundational commitment to the adversary process.[226]

The "Individualist Difference" Principle

The initial problem in designing a class action framework consistent with liberal theory is the prima facie individualist-collectivist tension that exists between an individual's interest in process-based autonomy (dictating unfettered individual discretion in controlling litigation) on the one hand and the scope of authority vested in class representatives in a class action that effectively supersedes the individual class members' ability to control adjudication of their own claims, on the other. The class action inevitably constrains an individual's ability to direct the course of his interaction with the judicial process because class representatives effectively make all the decisions about how the individually possessed claims will be pursued. While there may be some opportunity to influence selection of class counsel, those class members eventually excluded from that choice will nevertheless be controlled by decisions made by the ones ultimately selected. In mandatory classes, the infringment on an individual's process-based autonomy interest is even greater because individual class members lack even the basic choice whether to participate in the collective and passive litigation of his rights.

In crafting a model of the class action that focuses on the fundamental importance of an individual's process-based autonomy, I draw a loose methodological analogy to the two principles of justice identified by Rawls in his *Theory of Justice*. Rawls's First Principle, it should be recalled, requires that all people enjoy the greatest degree of liberty compatible with like liberty for all.[227] In a parallel manner, my class action model begins with the premise that, at least as a prima facie matter, all individuals are entitled to full control over the process-based choices made while pursuing their individual claims,[228] and that—again, at least as a prima facie matter—control of those choices may not be taken away without the individual's unambiguous expression of consent. Rawls's Second Principle, which he labels "the Difference Principle," requires that social and economic inequalities be attached to positions open to all under fair equality of opportunity, and that these inequalities be arranged to the greatest benefit to the least well-off members of society.[229] The foundation for this perspective is Rawls's belief that it would be unjust to have "inequalities that are not to the benefit of all."[230] The Difference Principle, therefore, applies only where the unequal distribution of social and economic power is justified if, and only if, that inequality acts to benefit society's least well off.

The justification for the Individualist Model of the class action relies on a loose analogy to Rawls's Difference Principle. I therefore label it an "Individualist Difference Principle." Just as Rawls's Difference Principle justifies inequality based on the paradoxical potential for those inequalities to benefit the least well-off members of society, the Individualist Difference Principle justifies the limitations that class certification places on an individual's process-based autonomy rights if, and only if, treating him as part of a collective litigating unit would ultimately advance his individual interests in a manner he is incapable of achieving as an individual litigant. While my First Principle posits that individuals be able to protect their legally recognized interests independently by resort to the litigation system, the Individualist Difference Principle recognizes the occasional value of collectivism in promoting the exercise of an individual's litigating autonomy. The use of the collectivist class action procedural device is thus justified in those instances where, absent such a process, the individual claimants will be effectively unable to vindicate their individual claims if they are required to pursue them on their own.[231] The Individualist Model conceptualizes the class action as a tool for aiding the individual's pursuit of his own interests and as a means of furthering process-based autonomy by providing individuals with the option of an alternative collectivist strategy for maximizing their claims through a process of voluntary collectivism.

While the class action model advocated here selectively authorizes procedural collectivization, it is designed to remain consistent with core values of process-based autonomy. Even when it authorizes collectivization, it views litigants as autonomous beings brought together as an aggregate of individuals, rather than as a stand-alone entity. In this sense, the substantive rights sought to be vindicated remain individually held and are simply brought in one proceeding, with the nuances between individual claims recognized through the use of sub-classes and separate damage hearings, where necessary. In so doing, the model is careful not to transform the underlying substantive law being enforced in the class proceeding.

The Mechanics of the Individualist Class Action

Crafting a model of the class action that flows from the normative value that liberal theory places on individualism requires that any rule providing for the creation of class actions have as its primary focus the ultimate preservation and facilitation of individualist process-based autonomy. In this sense, the class action is appropriately seen as a procedural analogy to the substantive freedom of association that has been recognized under the First Amendment right of free expression.[232] In both contexts, individuals may choose to collectivize in order to more effectively exercise their individually held process-based autonomy. Such a view of the class action is fully consistent with the dictates of the substance-procedure dichotomy embodied in the Rules Enabling Act, pursuant to which the class action rule is promulgated,[233] because it recognizes that the applicable substantive law has, in most cases, created exclusively individually held, rather than group held, claims. In shaping my model, I seek to demonstrate that a class action rule derived from liberal theory provides a powerful alternative to existing class action models premised upon utilitarian, communitarian, or civic republican theory. The primacy afforded the role of individuals and the exercise of their process-based autonomy under liberal theory would appropriately establish a class action rule that maintains the American adversary tradition in which, in most cases, litigants are allowed to voluntarily choose to make use of the judicial process in order to protect or vindicate their individually held rights.

Mandatory Classes

Perhaps the easiest conclusion for one committed to liberal individualism is that mandatory class actions will almost always be deemed invalid because of their negative impact on process-based autonomy.[234] The notion that a class representative could require another individual to resort to the judicial process for redress of a wrong inflicted against the two of them, and limit or remove that individual's ability to control the litigation, serves as an egregious example of an unwarranted restriction of process-based autonomy. Liberal theory contemplates that individuals will possess the opportunity to exercise their autonomy in choosing either to exercise or refuse to exercise the right to initiate litigation, and to control it once instituted.[235]

That is not to say, however, that all mandatory classes are necessarily unjustifiable under all but the most rigid forms of liberal theory. Where the rigid protection of individual autonomy is simply not feasible or would lead to absurd results, any form of liberal theory other than presumably a rigid libertarian version would recognize the need for individualist values to give way. Such circumstances would amount to the showing of a truly compelling justification for abandonment of liberal individualism. This appears to be so in the case of the Rule 23(b)(1)(A) class, where individual suits could give rise to conflicting obligations for a litigant opposing the class. But while Professor Shapiro justifies the mandatory nature of these classes on the basis of the interrelationship of the interests of the litigants,[236] such a view, for reasons already explained, is clearly incorrect.[237] The point, rather, is that there exists a compelling need to avoid anomalous results that would flow from permitting separate actions. The coercive power of the state cannot justly be used to force a party into a no-win situation. Imposing anomalous obligations on individual defendants forces them to exercise their autonomy in a way that compels them to ignore one of the obligations placed upon them. The severe restriction on the defendant's autonomy that results would seem to justify restriction of the autonomy of the various potential plaintiffs in this context.

Currently, Rule 23 also makes the so-called "limited fund" classes under Rule 23(b)(1)(B) mandatory. When considered from the vantage point of liberal theory, this conclusion is difficult to justify. In the case of limited fund class actions, the rationale for treating them as mandatory classes is that it provides for a more egalitarian distribution of compensation in cases where it would be impossible for every member of the class to collect their complete damages if every suit were brought as an individual action.[238] While this is a plausible argument, it does not go so far as to eliminate an individual's interest in process-based autonomy. The decision to opt-in or opt-out of a class represents an individual's decision as to how he can best advance his interests. If a litigant concludes that his interests would be better advanced by not participating in the class and either proceeding on his own with the representation of his choosing or not proceeding at all—perhaps for ideological reasons—there is no reason to prevent him from exercising that choice. Unlike in a (b)(1)(A) class, the act of opting out of a (b)(1)(B) class would not create a scenario where the protection of process-based autonomy would give rise to anomalous or logically untenable results. Rather, it would merely reflect the high value placed on process-based autonomy by the adversary system and the liberal political theory of which it is an outgrowth.

Currently, Rule 23 also makes classes primarily seeking injunctive or declaratory relief under Rule 23(b)(2) mandatory.[239] The argument for treating them as mandatory classes is that the relief will benefit the entire class as a whole, making the act of opting out largely meaningless. Further, should individuals choose not to participate in a class action, the fear is that they could subject a defendant to the cost of litigating the same suit for injunctive or declaratory relief over and over again.

Yet in the special case of the (b)(2) class, recall that the plaintiffs are often civil rights plaintiffs seeking ideologically idealistic ends.[240] It is certainly conceivable that some individuals may not agree with the idealistic ends being sought, and it would be improper to presume their assent to that end. From the perspective of liberal theory, then, individuals should be able to register their dissent from the ideological ends being pursued. Thus, an individual should be able to register that dissent through self-removal from the class. While it is reasonable to operate from a presumption that the individual interests of the class members will be consistent with one another, this alone does not justify the mandatory nature of the (b)(2) class. Class members in a (b)(2) class may disagree with the entire notion of the suit or conclude that their interests are better served by exiting the class. Under liberal theory, they retain this option. These considerations lead to the conclusion that (b)(2) classes should allow for self-exclusion from the class.

It should be recalled that Professor Rosenberg's class action model would dictate the use of mandatory class proceedings in all mass tort exposure cases.[241] While Rosenberg provides interesting and thoughtful rationales for such mandatory treatment, I cannot deem his justifications to be sufficiently compelling to validate abandonment of a litigant's right to pursue his claim individually. In such cases the individual stakes are likely to be quite high. At the very least, if such a drastic modification of our adjudicatory system is to be implemented, it must be through resort to the governing processes by which the substantive rights are created in the first place. If the authoritative organs of government—whether legislative or judicial—wish to transform the DNA of the substantive rights involved by reconceptualizing them as group-held rights, the political process may police such choices. To continue to conceptualize the substantive rights as individually held while simultaneously transforming them under the guise of procedural modification is to divert—and probably pervert—the democratic process. In this sense, the "micro" version of liberal democratic theory, focused on preservation of the right of the individual litigant to enforce his substantive rights, serves also to protect the "macro" version of the theory that assures representative and accountable decision making by preserving basic notions of transparency and accountability.

Class Actions, Opt-Out, and the Sliding Scale

As I have shown, liberal theory authorizes mandatory class actions only in the rarest and most compelling of circumstances. To the extent class participation by individual claimants is purely voluntary, however, one might reason that no tension exists between the collectivist class action proceeding and individualism: under reasonable notions of the freedom of association, individuals may choose to associate with others in pursuing enforcement of their legally protected rights. Viewed in this manner, the class proceeding might be seen as simply another voluntary joinder device, or an analogy to the First Amendment freedom of association. But while such reasoning is correct purely as a matter of theoretical abstraction, the issue tends to become more complicated when placed in the context of litigation reality. There are two conceivable means by which a litigant may exercise her choice not to participate in a class action: (1) failing to include herself in the class ("opt-in") or (2) failing to remove herself from the class ("opt-out"). Because the inertia is so very different in the two situations, the practical and theoretical consequences may differ dramatically, depending on which methodology is chosen. Many who fail to remove themselves from the class may well do so either because of misunderstanding, confusion, or simple forgetfulness. Thus, a failure to opt-out may not always reflect a class member's considered decision to pursue his claims through the class proceeding.

In shaping the individualist model, I seek to establish a sliding scale for determing when, if ever, the more passive opt-out procedure, rather than an affirmative opt-in procedure, should be permitted. As the size of the individual claim increases, the likelihood that an individual will consent to the surrender of his process-based autonomy rights probably decreases. As such, the individualist model of the class action ties the decision between a system that utilizes opt-in or opt-out based on the value of the individually possessed claims. It requires class members to opt in where the class action involves a positive value claim and permits use of an opt-out procedure in cases involving of course negative value claims, under certain circumstances. This reflects the reasonable ex ante presumption that individuals are more likely to choose to participate in the class when their claims are so small that individual suit would not be viable. But because under an opt-out system this presumption is rebuttable, my approach preserves the ability of every individual to make the decision to choose not to participate in the judicial process at all or take his chances by leaving the group and going it alone.

In drawing this distinction, I draw upon Professor Coffee's labels to distinguish positive value claims from negative value claims.[242] Yet while Coffee focused primarily on a difference between positive value "Type-A" class actions and negative value "Type-B" class actions, I propose the recognition of a third type of action, one very different from Professor Coffee's own version of the category: the "Type-C" class action. There are,

I believe, two distinct types of negative value claims. On the one hand, some negative value claims are of sufficient size that a rational person would want to go to the trouble of taking affirmative steps to redeem a favorable award, even though individualized pursuit of the claim by resort to the litigation process would presumably not be viable. The appropriate rationale for use of an opt-out procedure, as currently employed in (b)(3) class actions, is the presumption that an absent class member would generally have no reason not to participate in the class proceeding. In those particular situations in which the individual class member does wish to do so, affirmative action on his part should be required to reverse that presumption. On the other hand, some negative value claims are so low that a rational person would be unlikely even to go to the trouble to put in for the claim once a class-based award has been made or settlement reached, much less pursue individualized litigation. As explained in a prior chapter, this sort of proceeding is appropriately described as the "faux-class action,"[243]—which I here label "Type C" classes—because absent class members are litigants in name only. These Type C classes should never be authorized, because they do not represent the true aggregation of individual claims that is both required and assumed by Rule 23 and the underlying substantive law. Instead, they are effectively nothing more than "bounty hunter" suits, in which the plaintiff attorneys, rather than the class members, are the real parties in interest. These suits are illegitimate, not because they are inherently immoral or illegal but because they are unauthorized by the substantive law being enforced in the class proceeding. As nothing more than a procedural rule, Rule 23 may not transform the underlying substantive law that provides the basis for the suit in the first place.[244] The prohibition on Type-C classes under an opt-in rule does not follow as a result of liberal theory's concern for individualism, but from the concerns of macro democratic theory.[245] The substantive statutes that establish private damage remedies typically create remedies vested in, and to be enforced by, the individual as victim. A class action is, in every legal sense, merely the procedural aggregation of those individual claims. When claims are so miniscule that individuals are unlikely even to take the effort to recover their awarded claims, then the lawsuit effectively becomes a qui tam action—inducing the uninjured plaintiff attorneys to act as private enforcers of substantive legal restraints—that is not created by the substantive law itself.[246] This effectively allows a rule of procedure to amend the substantive statutes enacted by the legislative process, running counter to even the most foundational principles of democratic government.

As this trichotomy of plaintiff's claims underscores, however, predictions about plaintiffs' strategic choices are not always easy to make. Plaintiffs with Type A claims are, it would seem, just as likely to choose to pursue their claims on their own as to effectively forfeit all control to class representatives. The entire basis for the reasonable presumption of absent class members' willingness to be included in the class, then, breaks down in Type A classes. What remains in its wake is liberal theory's presumption of an individual's process-based autonomy—that is, the individual's authority to control pursuit of his individual legal claims. Thus, for Type A claims, where the economic stakes to the individual plaintiff are substantial, an opt-in procedure should be required; there is simply no basis on which to presume the choice to be included in the class. There is nothing to prevent an individual litigant from agreeing to become a member of the class based on his assessment that his interests would be best advanced by collective litigation. But the presumption about class member choice inherent in an opt-out system fails to reflect the value placed on individual autonomy in liberal theory and imposes a higher burden on those who wish not to sue than on those who want to sue. In short, opt-out has the effect of putting words into a litigant's mouth—a practice that contradicts fundamental precepts of liberal theory, absent some strong ex ante basis to assume the contrary.

The presumption that individuals wish to retain their process-based autonomy is far less persuasive in the context of the Type-B class. For negative value claims, the ability of a litigant to control his claim is largely illusory, because by hypothesis his claim is not practically sustainable as a separate, individual suit, even though the formal possibility of pursuing the claim through individualized resort to the litigation process remains. The presumption in favor of an absent class member's consent to sue in this context arguably leads logically to authorization of an opt-out system. Here, for an individual to vindicate his claim, he has few, if any, options beyond consenting to be a part of a class. Should individuals in this position wish to take their chances and attempt to seek a better means of protecting their own interests, then they retain the autonomous decision-making power to do so. This conclusion follows directly from my Individualist Difference Principle: Use of opt-out and opt-in are varied, based on which of the two procedures is more likely to further the individual claimant's interests in vindicating his rights.

CONCLUSION

In this chapter, I have sought to make explicit what to date has been largely implicit: the ramifications for political theory of existing class action models. Further, the chapter has offered a class action model rooted in the individualist concerns that lie at the heart of liberal theory. Once this theoretical centrality is accepted, the class action models proposed by leading legal scholars are revealed for what they basically are: rejections of liberal process-based individualism on basic choices as to how the individual's legal rights are to be exercised.

The class action model advocated in this chapter attempts to reconcile the role of process-based autonomy with the inherent collectivism of the class action device. Our system's traditional commitment to process-based individual autonomy presents inescapable problems and questions for any system of class adjudication. Yet the focus of the class action literature has largely ignored the theoretical "elephant in the room" and as a result has failed to recognize the tension between a collectivist procedural device and an adversarial system premised on notions of process-based individual autonomy.[247] All of this leads to focus on and acceptance of my alternative model of the class action, which seeks to minimize encroachment upon process-based autonomy inherent in existing models while simultaneously protecting the integrity of the democratic process. Only by keeping these twin objectives in mind can we be reasonably certain that the class action will operate to further, rather than retard, the values of process-based individualism that lie at the heart of our civil justice system.

CHAPTER FIVE

Class Actions, Litigant Autonomy, and the Goals of Procedural Due Process

INTRODUCTION

Literally hundreds of scholarly works have been written about the modern class action. While academic and judicial attention to the subject is unending, the controversy over class actions has also worked its way into America's mainstream political discourse.[1] Surprisingly little of this wealth of discussion, however, has concerned the collectivist-individual tension that inheres in much of the class action framework. With the melding of multiple individual claims into a single class proceeding necessarily comes a dramatic reduction in an individual's ability to control her lawsuit—or, indeed, to decide whether to pursue her claim in the first place. Because the Constitution's due process clauses[2] are generally construed to assure that an individual's legally protected rights cannot be adjudicated without providing her with a day in court, there would seem to exist at least a prima facie conflict between the dictates of procedural due process and the collectivist goals of the class action procedure.

To a limited extent, this tension has been recognized. The Supreme Court has long noted the due process clause's relevance as a constitutional limit on class actions.[3] Moreover, on occasion, respected commentators have explored the scope of due process protection in the context of class actions.[4] However, virtually all of this judicial and scholarly attention has focused on the paternalistic concern that the named parties adequately protect the interests of the absent class members. At no point has court or scholar recognized, much less focused upon, what should be acknowledged as the theoretical foundation of the procedural due process guarantee: the individual litigant's autonomy in deciding whether to pursue her claim and if so, how best to conduct that litigation.[5] The individual's autonomy to advance her interests in the manner she deems most advisable through resort to governmental processes—either political or judicial—grows out of the precepts of liberal democratic theory that appropriately underlie our nation's normative commitment to self-determination and individual rights.[6] No one could reasonably doubt this autonomy principle in the political realm: Government may not paternalistically choose a candidate to support on behalf of a citizen; nor may it determine for an individual what she will and will not say on behalf of her political positions. Governmentally imposed paternalism should be no less acceptable when it comes to the individual's ability to resort to the judicial process in order to protect her interests.

This does not mean that litigant autonomy should necessarily be deemed an absolute. It has long been understood that the procedural due process inquiry triggers some form of weighing process that takes into account competing interests and values.[7] It is truly amazing, however, that at no point has the Supreme Court, in either its due process or class action jurisprudence, even fully acknowledged the existence of the litigant autonomy interest, much less attempted either to understand the interest's role as an element and outgrowth of American political theory or to sift it through the filter of the constitutional balancing inquiry that is procedural due process.

This chapter undertakes both inquiries. In accord with the framework of political theory advocated in the prior chapter,[8] it concludes that litigant autonomy should be acknowledged as a logical outgrowth of the nation's commitment to process-based liberal democratic thought, and therefore a foundational element of procedural due process analysis. This is not, it should be emphasized, because of some ideological commitment to a libertarian political philosophy.[9] It is, rather, because of a belief in the centrality of individual autonomy *when—and only when—the individual seeks to advance her interests or protect her rights by participation in the processes of government, either political or judicial.* In other words, the autonomy valued here is autonomy in the resort to democratic processes—what in the prior chapter I called "meta-autonomy." The due process clauses of both the Fifth and Fourteenth Amendments, I believe, represent the mechanism by which the Constitution embodies, implements, and legally enforces and protects the political value of meta-autonomy in the litigation context. In this important sense, the due process version of litigant autonomy grows out of the same constitutional grounding as the First Amendment right of free expression.[10] Surely one may accept the importance of individual autonomy in the exercise of rights to participate in the governmental process without simultaneously committing oneself to libertarianism in every aspect of the individual's existence. The same should be true for the individual's protection or enforcement of her rights in the judicial process. As a result, in conducting the due process calculus the interest in litigant autonomy should be overcome only by a showing of a truly compelling competing interest.[11]

Application of this constitutional analysis to the current class action framework dictates a dramatic alteration in that structure. Except in very limited circumstances, mandatory class actions, currently authorized by the Federal Rules of Civil Procedure in a variety of situations,[12] should be found to be unconstitutional.[13] More importantly, because the right to control one's own litigation possesses significant constitutional status, considerably more than total passivity on the part of the individual class member should, in most cases, be required to waive the right. Thus, the opt-out procedure established for Rule 23(b)(3) class actions, which irrefutably deems such total passivity on the part of absent class members to constitute waiver of the right of litigant autonomy, must—at least under certain circumstances—also be deemed unconstitutional.[14] This chapter will initially explore the Supreme Court's current approach to procedural due process, explain its inadequacies, and describe how it should be reshaped to take into account the foundational interest in litigant autonomy. It will then consider the implications of the autonomy model of procedural due process for the current class action framework.

PROCEDURAL DUE PROCESS AS AMERICAN POLITICAL THEORY: TOWARD AN AUTONOMY MODEL

This chapter, in part, seeks to establish the woeful inadequacy of the Supreme Court's current doctrinal framework for implementing foundational values underlying the constitutional guarantee of procedural due process. Nowhere is this conclusion better illustrated than in the application of the Court's due process framework to the modern class action. First, this section will explore the Court's current doctrinal framework for procedural due process by pointing out its serious flaws, particularly its failure to recognize the vital role that the autonomy valve should play. Next it will explore the autonomy value's foundations in American constitutional and political theory. Finally, it will propose a revised due process calculus, designed to take into account the importance of litigant autonomy.

Procedural Due Process in the Supreme Court

The *Mathews-Doehr* Test

The Court's current procedural due process doctrine in the civil context finds its origins in its 1976 decision in *Mathews v. Eldridge*.[15] The case questioned whether the federal government's denial of a live hearing to a recipient of statutorily created entitlements in an agency proceeding to terminate those benefits violated procedural due process. In holding that this denial was constitutional, the Court fashioned a three-pronged balancing test that considered the private interest that is to be affected by the official action, the risk of an erroneous deprivation of that interest through use of the challenged process and the probable value, if any, of additional or substitute procedural safeguards, and, finally, the government's interest, including the fiscal and administrative burdens that those safeguards would entail.[16] By "private interest," the Court referred to the stakes for the individual—what she ultimately had to gain or lose.[17] In examining the remaining two factors, the Court drew a balance between impact on accuracy and the costs and burdens entailed in implementing the sought-after procedure.

In its subsequent decision in *Connecticut v. Doehr*,[18] the Court expanded the scope and reach of its *Mathews* test, by applying it to suits between private individuals, as well as to suits between a private individual and the government. As a result, the Court added examination of the level of the other private party's interest as a factor to be included in the balance.[19] Reiterating the oft repeated caveat that "[d]ue process, unlike some legal rules, is not a technical conception with a fixed content unrelated to time, place and circumstances,"[20] the Court applied a balancing test adapted from the one initially shaped in *Mathews*. The *Doehr* test balances three potentially conflicting interests: (1) the private interest that will be affected by the prejudgment measure; (2) the risk of erroneous deprivation through the procedures under attack and the probable value of additional or alternative safeguards; and (3) the interest of the party seeking the prejudgment remedy. In addition, as in *Mathews,* the balancing court is to give due regard for any ancillary interest the government may have in providing the procedure or forgoing the added burden of providing greater protections.[21]

In assessing the risk of erroneous deprivation, the Court considered the ultimate goal of securing an award to the plaintiff that the defendant might not otherwise satisfy. In effect, the Court evaluated the statutory considerations of the plaintiff's likelihood of success on the merits to ascertain the increased risks of error in the absence of additional safeguards. Although the statute required probable cause, the Court noted an unresolved ambiguity suggesting a lesser standard. Aggravating the risk of error were the "one-sided, self-serving, and conclusory submissions" in both the affidavit and complaint that provided no basis for judicial review.[22] The risk of mistaken deprivation was high since the underlying claim was a tort action not subject to documentary proof. The Court found few safeguards to alleviate this risk. The statute did provide for post-attachment notice and hearing and for a double damages action for commencement of suit without probable cause.

Finally, the Court considered the plaintiff's interests to be de minimis—nothing more than the plaintiff's desire to ensure availability of sufficient assets to meet the potential tort judgment award.[23] There was no pre-existing interest on the plaintiff's part in the property, and the plaintiff had not alleged exigent circumstances that would render the property unavailable to satisfy the judgment. The Court found no additional state interest, specifically stating that the difference between pre- and post-deprivation hearings could mean little in terms of administrative or financial burdens.[24]

Locating the True Defect in the *Mathews-Doehr* Test

Scholars have often attacked the *Mathews-Doehr* test for its narrowly utilitarian focus.[25] They have argued that by considering exclusively concerns of efficiency, accuracy, and practicality, the test fails to take into account what Professor Mashaw has described as "dignitary" values—values that focus on the preservation of the individual's dignity within the political system.[26] Specifically, Mashaw refers to the individual's interests in participation, equality, predictability, transparency and rationality, which could conceivably be fostered by the use of procedures that will have only minimal impact on decision-making accuracy.[27] By failing to consider such largely non-instrumental factors, it is argued, the test improperly ignores due process's moorings in the values of liberal political theory.[28] These criticisms are, on the whole, well grounded. However, they fail to take their focus on values of liberal democratic theory to its logical conclusion: a foundational belief in the value of allowing individuals to make fundamental choices about the judicial protection of their own legally authorized rights. It is, ultimately, the interest in self-determination and individual control that must stand, at the very least, as the presumptive normative foundation of procedural due process.[29]

It is probably understandable that critics of the Court's due process test would fail to consider the implications of procedural due process for controlling litigation. In the large majority of contexts no external force seeks to grasp decision-making control over litigation choice and strategy from the individual. Situations will arise where the individual prefers use of certain procedures that the government has chosen not to employ. But even where government has denied the individual the benefit of these procedures, the ultimate authority to decide how best to defend the individual's interests, within the procedural framework established by government, rests with the litigant herself. However, by recognizing how procedural due process is implicated in the modern class action, one should be able to see that both the Court in shaping the *Mathews-Doehr* test and the scholarly critics of that test ignored this vitally important aspect of the political theory of procedural due process.

In fashioning the litigant autonomy model of procedural due process, I do not intend to ignore the realities of modern litigation. It would, of course be unrealistic to suggest that—at least in the majority of cases—a litigant makes many litigation decisions beyond the initial choice of her attorney.[30] But that situation differs little from the political process, where the individual chooses the officials who will make day-to-day choices of government, but generally has little, if any, role to play in the actual shaping of those decisions.[31] No one, presumably, would argue that as a result the individual's role in choosing those who make those decisions is anything but central to the precepts of democracy.

Recognizing the Paternalism-Autonomy Dichotomy

Neither the Court nor its critics have focused upon an important tension that illustrates the foundational liberal democratic battleground of procedural due process: what can be called the paternalism-autonomy dichotomy. *Paternalism* refers to the interest in having others protect the property interests of individuals who could conceivably be affected by the outcome of litigation.[32] *Autonomy,* in contrast, refers to the individual's interest in having power to make choices about the protection of her own legally authorized or protected rights through resort to the litigation process. The two, it should be noted, are not necessarily in conflict. Our legal structure could conceivably begin with recognition of the presumptive value of litigant autonomy, but nevertheless supplement that value with an infusion of paternalistic concern when it is simply infeasible to permit the effective exercise of individual autonomy. For example, it is conceivable that countless non-litigants could be affected by the stare decisis impact of a litigation's outcome in parallel situations, as a practical matter undermining their ability to control their own litigations. However, it would often be infeasible to permit all of those non-litigants to protect their individual interests by intervening in the litigation itself. Even if such a course of action were feasible, many of the non-litigants would be unaware of or uninterested in the litigation and therefore unlikely to exercise their intervention right. Thus, Professor Brilmayer has argued that we construe the case-or-controversy requirement of Article III to require those who litigate on behalf of the same or similar interests to have suffered injury in fact, largely as a means of ensuring that they possess sufficient incentive to pursue those interests effectively on behalf of all future litigants who are likely to be practically impacted by the litigation's resolution.[33]

Another example of litigation-based paternalism is a state's ability to assert parens patriae standing, under certain circumstances, on behalf of its citizens.[34] Moreover, governmental consumer protection or anti-fraud programs that authorize government to seek judicial redress in order to protect its citizens can be appropriately viewed as a form of paternalistic litigation. In certain contexts, a court may appoint a guardian to represent the interests of outsiders who are unable to protect those interests themselves in the course of litigation.[35] In all of these situations, the litigation system authorizes or commands individuals or entities, either in the private or public spheres, to protect the interests of those who do not themselves stand formally before the court, for the simple reasons that their interests need protection and it is not feasible or advisable to require them to protect those interests on their own.

Where, in contrast, it is feasible for the individual to employ the system of litigation to protect his own interests, paternalism is usually deemed an insufficient means of assuring procedural due process. For example, it would surely not satisfy due process, in the ordinary course, to appoint a guardian to represent a criminal defendant against that defendant's wishes. This is true, even were we to assume, as an objective matter, that the chosen guardian would be more likely to assure an accurate result and protect the individual's interests than would allowing the individual to protect his own interests through either the selection of his own representative or the conduct of his own defense.[36]

Procedural Autonomy and Liberal Democracy

One can understand this intuitive preference for litigant autonomy by extrapolating the situation to the political system writ large. At its definitional core, democratic theory is grounded in a societal commitment to the notion of self-determination. It is certainly true that absent some form of societal anarchy total individual autonomy cannot exist. But regardless of the manner in which one ultimately balances the competing concerns of societal need and individual will, democracy must, at some level, be deemed to rest on a commitment to the value of self-determination. Normally, this interest in self-determination focuses on a form of collective, or societal autonomy: The electorate decides for itself who is to represent it, and has the power to hold those chosen accountable. However, commitment to collective self-determination is also appropriately seen as dictating recognition of a value in individual choice, for at its most basic level a democratic society is composed of individuals who exercise their power of self-government in the voting booth. Even civic republican theorists have acknowledged that for communitarian democracy to function properly, individuals must possess a zone of individual autonomy.[37] At the very least the individual must have autonomy in his efforts to participate in the processes of government, where democracy operates.

In a democratic society, government may not impose on the populace leaders who are unwanted by the electorate on the grounds that the electorate does not know what is good for it. At the very least, at some point in the process the electorate must retain the ultimate political power to replace those policy makers with governors whose views are more in line with those of the electorate. As democratic theorist Alexander Meiklejohn reasoned, in a democratic system the true governors are the citizens; elected officials are merely their agents.[38]

While a societal commitment to democracy is a necessary condition for attainment of the goals of liberal theory, it is not a sufficient one. In addition, to be complete a democratic system grounded—even in part—in notions of individual integrity must respect and value some level of individual freedom. The United States Constitution legally embodies and enforces these normative theoretical precepts. Thus, in addition to protections against tyrannical government, the Constitution seeks to assure individual dignity and a zone of individual autonomy through the guarantees of the Bill of Rights (Amendments I–VIII) and the Fourteenth Amendment. In particular it is the First Amendment's guarantee of free expression that synthesizes the self-determination and autonomy values of liberal democracy. Consistent with the premises of both autonomy and self-determination, government may not control the minds of its citizens. The First Amendment prohibits government from suppressing private expression on the grounds that it would lead society to make unwise policy choices.[39] These are decisions we leave to the individual citizens to make for themselves. They are not to be made for the individual by external forces, ultimately unaccountable to the electorate, who have paternalistically decided what is and is not good for both the individual and the populace. Nor, under the First Amendment, may government require that individuals utter political messages with which they disagree.[40]

The procedural due process guarantee is appropriately viewed as a constitutional outgrowth of democracy's normative commitment to such process-based political autonomy.[41] Just as a commitment to democracy is normatively inconsistent with externally imposed and unwelcome paternalism in the areas of free expression and political choice, so too should such paternalism be deemed to be in tension with the values of procedural due process found in the litigation context, at least in situations where the individual is realistically in a position to make her own choices. Thus, the reason why we intuitively recoil at the notion that government could paternalistically control a criminal defendant's strategic choices in fashioning his defense or his choice of attorney is, for the most part,[42] that the dignity and process-based power of self-determination that the individual must be afforded in a liberal democratic system is undermined by such a course of action.[43]

It might be argued that the concern with the need to preserve litigant autonomy is greatly overdone, because as a practical matter a litigant will influence day-to-day strategic litigation choices, at most, only rarely. Instead, it is the litigant's chosen representative, far more than the litigant herself, who makes such decisions. Thus, the argument might proceed, to take those choices away from the litigant would actually undermine litigant autonomy very little. While of course there is much practical truth in the insight, it would be a serious mistake, from the perspective of liberal democratic thought, to glean from the absence of such direct litigant involvement in strategic decision making a finding that the values of individual autonomy embodied in the due process clause are therefore irrelevant in the context of litigation control.

By way of analogy, the individual may often choose others to speak on her behalf. It surely does not follow that the individual lacks an important—and constitutionally protected—interest in making the choice of speaker. Indeed, the less likely the individual's ability or opportunity to speak for herself, the greater the constitutional value in assuring autonomy in making her choice of representative speaker, since it is only through exercising this choice that the individual's constitutional right is exercised. The same analysis should be deemed equally applicable to the individual litigant's constitutionally significant interest in choosing who will stand on her behalf as the litigant resorts to the judicial process to protect her property and liberty interests. Surely, government could not forcibly impose legal counsel on a criminal defendant. While the stakes may not be as high in a civil case, the same constitutional value in litigant choice should be deemed present.

The Paternalism-Autonomy Dichotomy and the Mathews-Doehr *Test*

As the prior discussion demonstrated, though it will arise in only limited circumstances the paternalism-autonomy dichotomy in procedural due process implicates many of the basic premises of American liberal democratic theory. One may search the Supreme Court's current procedural due process doctrine in vain, however, for any reference, explicit or implicit, to any recognition of the tension's existence, much less an attempt at its resolution.

The factors to be considered by the reviewing court as part of the balancing process under the *Mathews-Doehr* line of cases, it should be recalled, are (1) the extent to which the private parties' interests will be affected by the case's outcome, (2) the extent to which an accurate decision is threatened by use of the challenged procedures, (3) the extent to which an accurate resolution would be promoted by the use of the procedures urged by a private party but rejected by the government, and (4) the burdens and administrative costs that use of the procedure in question would impose upon the government.[44] How would this test resolve a constitutional dispute over whether either compelled litigation on behalf of an unwilling private individual or forced external control of a private individual's litigation violates the procedural due process guarantee? The answer is likely that, given the presumptive constitutional validity of majoritarian branch action, such activity would have to be deemed constitutional, since there is nothing in the *Mathews-Doehr* test that could possibly dictate a finding of unconstitutionality. More importantly, however, there is nothing in the test's terms that would even permit a reviewing court to ask the question; none of the factors even arguably implicates an inquiry into the constitutional interest in litigant autonomy. On this question, from the autonomy perspective the *Mathews-*

Doehr critics clearly have the edge, since they urge consideration of individual "dignitary" interests that arguably include pursuit of the autonomy goal in litigation control and decision making. But if so, one would have to reach that conclusion by inference. Nothing in the anti-*Mathews-Doehr* dignitary model directly focuses on these foundational considerations.

The position adopted here is that the value in litigant autonomy derives from the basic liberal democratic commitment to the values of political pluralism, self-determination, and individual integrity, embodied in the synthesis of a commitment to representative government and the extensive guarantees of individual rights embodied in the Constitution. Moreover, recognition of the interest in litigant autonomy is consistent with the values derived from use of a process of reverse engineering applied to our nation's long-standing commitment to the adversary system.[45] It is both puzzling and distressing, then, that nothing in the Court's controlling due process jurisprudence even touches on, much less values, the interest in litigant autonomy.

Concededly, purely as a practical matter the interest in litigant autonomy will be threatened only rarely, since it is not often that government will authorize external forces to preempt litigant discretion or control. Moreover, the obvious—albeit indirect—impact of the denial of certain procedural rights will inevitably be some sort of limitation on litigant discretion. The autonomy interest is implicated not by such indirect or incidental restraints on litigant discretion, however, but rather by direct and compelled transfer of control over the conduct of a litigation in which individual property rights are at stake to forces external to, and beyond the control of, the individual litigant.[46] Such forces may include an agency of the government itself, or other private individuals, groups or entities. But the fact that the autonomy value is impacted only rarely is beside the point. When that interest is, in fact, directly affected, it should be of great constitutional concern, as both a pragmatic and theoretical matter.

The Role of a Utilitarian Calculus in the Autonomy Model of Procedural Due Process

The fact that a proper due process analysis must take account of the foundational concern with litigant autonomy does not automatically imply that the autonomy interest will always prevail. Just as the procedural due process measurement has traditionally been thought to require a balancing process in which competing interests are weighed against each other, so too must the autonomy value be weighed against competing concerns. These concerns may involve purely pragmatic interests of cost or efficiency, or competing interests of procedural or substantive fairness on the part of other litigants or non-litigant third parties. Indeed, that our system does not deem the litigant autonomy value to be universally supreme is demonstrated by the provision for compulsory counterclaims[47] and the existence of declaratory judgments.[48] In both situations, a potential plaintiff may be forced to litigate her claim at a time and in a forum not of her choice. In both instances, however, the potential plaintiff's autonomy interest in exercising total control over the litigation of her claim is deemed to be outbalanced by the competing interests in either avoiding wasteful or repetitive litigation, or enabling a party to avoid committing itself to a course of behavior that may prove irretrievably harmful at a later point in time.[49]

In the modern class action, the interest in litigant autonomy is potentially affected more invidiously than in either the compulsory counterclaim or declaratory judgment contexts. Not only is the litigant's choice of timing and forum controlled by external forces, but his control of the actual conduct of the litigation is also severely restricted. In the class action, absent parties traditionally remain passive, ceding the control of litigation strategy to those who serve as named parties. Even if an absent class member wishes to intervene in the action, his ability to make strategic choices concerning the control of the litigation is usually so diluted by the influence and control of other named parties as to be almost non-existent. Moreover, in the context of so-called "mandatory" class actions, the litigant does not even have the choice of whether or not to pursue his claim in the first place.

Thus, the class action illustrates a situation in which the valuable constitutional interest in litigant autonomy is seriously threatened. Yet at no point has the Court either understood the relevance of the foundational value in litigant autonomy to the modern class action or sought to include it in any sort of due process calculus. In the one instance in which the Supreme Court has even expressed unease concerning the constitutionality of mandatory class actions, it completely misunderstood the true nature of the constitutional concern.[50] The reason for this failure, one may reasonably surmise, is the widespread but unstated assumption that the procedural due process concern in the class action context is fully exhausted by invocation of what amounts to a purely paternalistic form of procedural due process analysis.[51] The following section explores the scholarly and judicial failure to consider the role that litigant autonomy should properly play in measuring the constitutionality of the class action procedure, and what the nature of that role should be.

THE AUTONOMY MODEL OF PROCEDURAL DUE PROCESS AND THE MODERN CLASS ACTION

Rule 23 and the Framework of the Modern Class Action[52]

The class action involves a proceeding in which a few named parties litigate on behalf of a large group of absent, and largely passive, class members. As explained at the outset of this book, paradoxically the "absent" class members in one sense are absent and in another sense are present before the court. While they are passive participants who remain uninvolved in the day-to-day conduct of the litigation, they are deemed "parties," whose rights are bound through doctrines of res judicata and collateral estoppel, much as are fully active parties in any litigation.[53]

Under modern federal standards, established largely by the 1966 revision of Rule 23 of the Federal Rules of Civil Procedure, in order to be certified a class must meet all of the four requirements of Rule 23(a) and at least one of the requirements of Rule 23(b). Rule 23(a)'s requirements have been labeled, respectively, "numerosity" (the class is sufficiently large as to make joinder impractical), "commonality" (the named parties and absent class members share at least one common issue of law or fact), "typicality" (the claims of the named parties are typical of those of the absent class members), and "adequacy" (the named parties adequately represent the interests of the absent class members).[54]

These four requirements stand as necessary but not sufficient conditions for class certification. If and only if these four requirements are satisfied, the certifying court will determine whether the class falls within one of the four categories of Rule 23(b): (b)(1)(A) (where the prosecution of separate actions by or against individual members of the class would create a risk of "inconsistent or varying adjudications with respect to individual members of the class which would establish incompatible standards of conduct for the party opposing the class"), (b)(1)(B) (where separate suits would create a risk of adjudications that "would as a practical matter be dispositive of the interests of the other members not parties to the adjudications or substantially impair or impede their ability to protect their interests"), (b)(2) (where final injunctive or declaratory relief on behalf of the class against the party opposing the class is appropriate), or (b)(3) (where common questions of law or fact "predominate over any questions affecting only individual members," and "a class action is superior to other available methods for the fair and efficient adjudication of the controversy").[55]

Especially relevant to the due process analysis is the procedural treatment afforded by the rule to the different forms of Rule 23(b) class actions. If a class is deemed a (b)(1)(A), (b)(1)(B), or (b)(2) class, it is "mandatory," which means that if the class is certified, absent class members are not permitted to withdraw from the action. Their claims must be litigated as part of the class proceeding, with full res judicata consequences, even if the class members would prefer to litigate their claims separately, or not to litigate their claims at all.[56] In contrast, members of a (b)(3) class may opt out of the proceeding, though their failure to act will lead to their inclusion in the class.[57] Moreover, while Rule 23 requires that absent class members in a (b)(3) class action receive the best notice practicable under the circumstances,[58] notice to absent class members in the other categories falls entirely within judicial discretion.[59] In the context of mandatory classes, then, the trial court has authority to decline to require notice of the proceeding to absent class members.

Both the mandatory nature of the (b)(1) and (b)(2) classes and the opt-out procedure for (b)(3) classes give rise to serious constitutional problems under the autonomy model of procedural due process—problems which have, for the most part, been ignored by both courts and scholars.[60] First, however, it is necessary to explore the due process structure that scholars and courts have deemed applicable to the class action. Both have misperceived the true nature and scope of the due process limitation.

The Current Due Process Framework for Class Actions

Due Process and the Entity Theory of Class Actions

In two earlier chapters, I explored the various ramifications of the so-called "entity" model of the class action for different aspects of political theory.[61] Here I re-examine that model from a distinct analytical perspective: its implications for the *constitutional* theory of the modern class action procedure. As will be seen, not only is the entity model severely problematic for the foundations of American political theory, it also invidiously undermines the appropriate constitutional structure established by the due process clauses.

The protections of procedural due process are, of course, triggered only when the individual's property or liberty rights are affected. Hence if absent class members have no individually held property rights that could be extinguished by the class action proceeding, then the requirements of procedural due process are rendered irrelevant as a protection of those absent class members. This is exactly the position that has been taken by some leading commentators who have argued that, at least in certain contexts, the individual claims of absent class members are transformed by the existence of the class proceeding into nothing more than an element of the newly created entity that is the class claim. As such, the argument goes, they do not trigger the due process guarantees as protection of the absent class members as separate individuals.

In order to provide a proper legal and conceptual backdrop for my critique of and response to this position, however, it is first necessary to describe the traditional understanding of the individual's constitutionally protected property right in her claim. With that foundational understanding serving as an anchor, we will be able to see that the use of a procedural device, such as the class action, cannot legally transform those individual claims into a qualitatively distinct, amalgamated entity for purposes of due process.

A "Chose in Action" as Property Protected by Procedural Due Process

Due process provides a floor of protection to the individual that government procedures must meet, in order to ensure that one is not unconstitutionally deprived of life, liberty, or property. A legal claim has long been recognized as a form of property, albeit an intangible form. As such, a person's legal claim may not be extinguished by a state or the federal government without due process of law.[62] The notion that a legal claim, or "chose in action," is a form of protected property is deeply rooted in Anglo-American jurisprudence.[63] For example, it is settled that rights in a chose of action are in many cases assignable.[64] With the status of a chose in action as protected property settled, one might expect a consensus to have developed that deprivation of the rights associated with that property, through class action or otherwise, would have to survive meaningful due process analysis in order to be deemed constitutionally valid under the due process clause. Not everyone agrees with this position, however.

The Entity Theory

Despite the historically uncontroversial status of a chose in action as protected property, Professor Samuel Issacharoff believes that many of the individual legal claims that comprise modern class actions should not be thought of as individual property for purposes of the due process clause.[65] Issacharoff believes that under certain circumstances class action procedures transform or fuse individual causes of action into a cohesive group cause of action, thereby destroying the status of the chose as an individually possessed property right. By defining away the individually held property right in class litigation under Rule 23, we free class action procedures from the strictures of due process, at least as they relate to the individual class member.[66] Thus untethered by any limits imposed by due process, class actions are stretched with more permissible uses, many of which would likely be problematic under traditional conceptualizations of due process.

In support of his view, Issacharoff argues that many class actions take on the form of an entity, rather than an aggregation of individual claims.[67] Issacharoff suggests that, under certain circumstances, an action under Rule 23 is no longer "simply an unaltered aggregation of individual claims."[68] It is, rather, an entity, conceptually distinct from the individual claims that together comprise the class, and something far different from a simple aggregation of those individual claims. The newly created entity may be entitled to due process protections, but since a substantive individually held chose no longer exists, due process does not protect what were formerly individual causes of action. Issacharoff derives this notion of the class as an entity from the earlier writing of Professor David Shapiro.[69] To Issacharoff and Shapiro, a plaintiff class generally constitutes a coherent entity, similar to private voluntary associations such as trade unions and partnerships, where the collectivity is a "litigant in [its] own right."[70] The legal consequence of this view is that the class action plaintiffs, like the individual members of private voluntary associations, are seen as parts of "entities whose members may have at best only a limited say in what is litigated, in who represents the organization, and on what terms the controversy is ultimately resolved."[71]

The constitutional implications of the entity perspective are both striking and troubling. Likening class actions to private voluntary associations permits Shapiro and Issacharoff largely to circumvent the due process inquiry, because where class actions are legally similar to voluntary private organizations, it is not the individual plaintiffs but rather the collectivity which seeks redress for the violation of its substantive rights and is thus afforded due process protection. Issacharoff and Shapiro believe that their reconceptualization of the rights at stake in a class action defines away the tension between individual property rights and coercive collective action.

Under the entity theory, individual rights are not present in the context of a class action and, therefore, the due process guarantee does not present a significant obstacle to class action procedures. To Issacharoff, class actions seeking injunctions against institutional conduct, those seeking recompense from a limited fund that will be exceeded by the total amount of the claims, and those for small individually held claims, appropriately receive such entity treatment.[72] From his perspective, in these cases it is "difficult to identify an individual chose" and thus "difficult to conceptualize an individual right of autonomy" to which due process protections attach.[73]

One type of class action that Issacharoff believes deserves entity treatment involves claims for injunctive relief against institutional conduct. In such cases, he believes, it would be nonsensical to claim that any plaintiff would have an autonomous right to an independent outcome of the litigation, since as a practical matter an injunction on behalf of one is an injunction for all.[74] A suit seeking an injunction against institutional conduct usually involves individuals suing a private corporation or government agency in an effort to stop the institution from engaging in some type of allegedly unlawful, generally applicable conduct. A historic example is a suit brought by African American students against a school board, seeking an injunction ordering school desegregation.[75] Issacharoff points to a school desegregation case as an example of a class action without an individual chose, since it is "nonsensical to claim that any one child has an autonomous right to an independent outcome of the litigation."

Problems with the Entity View

A closer look at Issacharoff's paradigm illustrates the fundamental defect in his analysis from a due process perspective. He confuses the reality of externally imposed practical limitations on the individual's ability to control his chose with the abstract, pristine nature of the chose itself. For purposes of the due process clause, there is all the difference in the world between these two conceptualizations. The point may be illustrated by use of Issacharoff's own example of school desegregation. First, let us assume that there is only one African-American child in the school system. The substantive law creates a cause of action under which that child, acting alone, can sue for an injunction against the school's allegedly unconstitutional conduct. Because, in this hypothetical, there is only one plaintiff, and therefore of course no basis on which to find existence of an entity, one must assume Issacharoff would agree that in this case there exists an individual chose created and conferred by the substantive law, to which due process rights attach. Now assume that there are two African-American students in the school system. If child 1 brings a desegregation challenge, the rights of child 2 will, as a practical matter, likely be affected by the outcome of the litigation, even though child 2 has filed no claim. In such a case, intervention under Rule 24 of the Federal Rules of Civil Procedure is likely to be available to child 2 since the "disposition of the action may as a practical matter impair or impede the applicant's ability to protect" his or her interest in the outcome of the litigation.[76] Intervention under Rule 24, however, does not transform the two individual claims into some type of pre-litigation entity or extinguish the pristine substantive rights of the parties to bring suit on an individual basis. It is simply a procedural device which permits child 2 to protect his substantive rights that may well be impacted by adjudication of child 1's claim. It is not likely that Issacharoff would argue that the individual causes of action that make up this suit are denied due process protection as a result of the intervention.

Now assume that there are one hundred African-American children in the school system. In this situation it is likely that certification under Rule 23(b)(2) would be appropriate.[77] In such a scenario, Issacharoff asserts that it is "difficult to identify an individual chose," and therefore the pre-condition to invocation of the due process right—the existence of a property right—has not been satisfied. But from the perspective of procedural due process, why is certification under Rule 23(b)(2) any different from intervention under Rule 24? Even though it is perhaps convenient to describe the children's rights as collective rather than individual when more than fifty or a hundred are involved, it is simply incorrect, *as a conceptual matter,* to define away the individually held chose. Certification under Rule 23 allows all one hundred children to protect their individually held substantive rights in a unified fashion. However, that does not change the fact that the class action is still nothing more than an aggregation of what are unambiguously pre-existing individually held substantive claims. These pristine underlying rights constitute individual causes of action invested in the individual by the substantive law. In its pristine form, the substantive right is individual and exists whether there is one African American child or many African American children.

The same holds true if there are fifty children but only one decides to sue. It does not necessarily follow, of course, that due process will always require that substantively pristine rights be enforced free from procedural limitation, because due process usually requires at some level a form of utilitarian calculus. However, when a due process inquiry is triggered, a compelling interest must be established to justify impairment of the individual's rights. By somehow recharacterizing what are unambiguously individually held rights as entity-held rights, Issacharoff apparently believes he is able to circumvent this inquiry.

A second type of class action that Issacharoff believes to be deserving of entity treatment involves a class of individual claimants seeking a portion of a so-called limited pie of available funds. In such a case, Issacharoff believes that the individual claimants do not possess an individual chose to which due process protections attach.[78] A limited pie action is one in which the aggregate of all the potential plaintiffs' claims exceeds the maximum amount of funds available to satisfy the judgment.[79] In such a situation, a plaintiff will not receive full compensation for her damages. She will instead receive only a predetermined portion of the available resources. According to Issacharoff, in such a situation the plaintiff's legal right is not simply an abstract independent right against a defendant; rather, it necessarily exists only in relation and comparison to the claims of the other claimants.[80] For this reason, he contends, the plaintiffs should not be deemed to possess an individually held chose. Instead, the inherent intertwining of the plaintiffs' legal rights and the resulting limitation on their ability to collect full damages implies that the individual plaintiffs should be viewed as a collectivity or entity whose members, as a constitutional matter, are guaranteed at best only a limited say in how the controversy is to be adjudicated.

A typical form of limited pie action arises when an accident has occurred in which a number of individuals have been harmed, yet the available insurance funds are insufficient to pay all the claimants.[81] If one posits this same scenario with one claimant, the individual chose is, of course, easily identifiable. Assume that a car accident has taken place and that the injuries to the victim exceed the maximum insurance coverage of the wrongdoer. Depending on the facts of the case and the law of the jurisdiction, the victim will most likely sue for common law negligence, seeking compensatory damages. Substantive common law is the source of the victim's individual cause of action. Under these circumstances, there can of course be no question that the victim's claim constitutes a chose, thereby qualifying as a constitutionally protected property interest. Now let us assume that two parties are harmed, rather than just one. Although each party's injuries are for less than the total liability coverage, their combined injuries exceed the policy's cap. If victim 1 sues and recovers, the ability of victim 2 to sue later and receive full compensation for his injuries will necessarily be compromised. Therefore, Rule 24 intervention is available to victim 2 so that he can protect his interests in court. But the claim of victim 2 does not *arise under* Rule 24; rather, he has standing to sue solely because he possesses an individual chose—a claim for common law negligence. Rule 24 does nothing more than allow him to intervene in the ongoing action and thus protect his legally recognized interest.

If numerous parties are injured in the accident and the insurance coverage is not sufficient to compensate them fully for their injuries, a Rule 23(b)(1)(B) class action would most likely be appropriate.[82] In a manner reminiscent of the intervention process provided for in Rule 24, Rule 23(b)(1)(B) permits class certification, when as a practical matter, the individual interests of those not a party to the suit would be decided by disposition of the current lawsuit.[83] Again, the individual causes of action that comprise the class do not "arise under" Rule 23(b)(1)(B). Rather, their substantive source remains the common law of negligence. Rule 23(b)(1)(B) is simply a joinder device for the aggregation of multiple pre-existing claims. Its purpose is to allow multiple parties to protect their financial interests, not to create a distinct cause of action that alters the underlying DNA of the existing claims, or somehow to modify the underlying substantive law. Therefore, contrary to Issacharoff's assertion, class certification under a limited fund theory does not destroy or obscure the individual claimants' underlying pristine causes of action.

Issacharoff's third category of entity-based class actions includes those comprised wholly of so-called "negative" value claims, or what earlier was referred to as "Type B" claims.[84] These are claims which are so small as not to rationally justify individual litigation. For what he calls "strategic" reasons, whenever claims have a "negative value,"[85] Issacharoff believes they are not a chose in the functional sense, since as a practical matter they are so small that they would never have been brought individually. A plaintiff class made up of negative value claims is appropriately characterized as an entity, he argues, because only the collectivity possesses the requisite incentives to pursue legal redress.

Consider the following example of a negative value class. In 1998, a class action was filed on behalf of all purchasers of a certain type of zipdrive, manufactured by the Iomega Corporation.[86] The complaint alleged that the product was defective because the zipdrive would sometime cause a disk to be unreadable.[87] No one consumer was damaged beyond the relatively small cost of the portable disk. Since product liability suits are usually discovery-intensive and expensive to litigate, it is irrational to expect any one consumer, or even a small group of consumers, to bring suit. Such a suit is rational if brought as a class action, however, since, if successful, the total damages for all consumers would far exceed the cost of litigating the claims. Because the claims would not have been brought individually, Issacharoff argues that "negative value" class actions should not be thought of as an aggregation of individual choses but rather as a distinct, class-based entity.

Issacharoff's characterization of these claims as entity-based is unsatisfying because his analysis is predicated on a fundamental misconception. In *all* types of cases, the class action can inherently be nothing more or less than an aggregation device for pre-existing individual claims. The class action device itself creates no causes of action—nor could it, without unambiguously violating the express dictates of the Rules Enabling Act.[88] Instead, the class action is a procedural device which serves as a tool to aggregate *pre-existing* individual private rights created by substantive law. For example, while a class action permits plaintiffs injured in a mass accident to aggregate their claims, the legal basis for the class's claim is the substantive law of negligence. The right of action that grows out of and enforces that substantive directive is vested by the substantive law *in the individual victim*. If one were to accept the entity theory suggested by Shapiro and Issacharoff, then the class actions device would effectively transform pristine pre-existing individually held private rights into a kind of collective right, *never conferred by the underlying substantive law*. Therefore, the entity theory not only erodes the concept of individually created rights, but also works a serious harm to our democratic political system by transforming the nature of substantive law through resort to the procedural fig leaf of the Federal Rules.[89]

It is certainly true that practical or procedural realities could conceivably develop following the substantive creation of the pristine individual rights, thereby giving rise to procedural difficulties in the individual's autonomous enforcement of those substantive rights. But that does not mean that those rights are not, in their pre-procedural form, anything other than individually held claims that qualify as property rights protected by the due process clause.

Under any form of procedural due process that counterbalances the individuals' interests with competing utilitarian concerns, protected property rights may, on occasion, be forced to give way to competing practical or generalized fairness concerns. But while under a utilitarian balancing framework practical difficulties may factor into the due process calculus, such difficulties do not prevent the triggering of the due process inquiry itself. Issacharoff's mistake, then, is to assume that the class action procedure somehow transforms an autonomous substantive right, which may under certain circumstances be forced to give way to other considerations, into a substantively fused right that is not held individually. As a result, he has confused factors that may on occasion constitutionally justify restriction of the enforcement of otherwise pristine substantive rights on the one hand with the total absence of any due process protection for the individual claim, on the other. This position ignores both structural and substantive realities and, as a result, mistakenly circumvents the need to engage in the procedural due process analysis that is constitutionally required to assure vindication of those pristine pre-procedural substantive rights.

Issacharoff could conceivably respond to this argument in the following manner: Because, by hypothesis, negative value claims are so small that they could not, as a practical matter, survive as individual claims, when these claims are combined in a class action their very essence has been transformed into entity form. The whole, then, is greater than the sum of its parts, because none of the individual claims, standing alone, would have led to a suit. Even in a negative value class, however, the relative size of the claims does not alter the fact that the action arises under the substantive law that confers an individual cause of action *on each victim*. But for the substantive law's creation of an individual chose in each claimant, even if it supposedly has a negative value, there could never have been a class action in the first place. If we assume that negative value claims satisfy standing requirements, the mystical transformation of these claims into entity-like group-wide claims fails, purely as a foundational matter. Any other conclusion would lawlessly transform a procedural aggregation device into its own source of substantive right.[90]

Due Process and Class Actions in the Courts

The "entity" theory has never been expressly adopted by the courts.[91] To the contrary, judicial decisions appear to proceed on the implicit assumption that in all cases absent class members possess individual property rights that are fully protected by the due process clause. On occasion, they have invalidated class action judgments on the grounds that they violate due process. While all of these cases probably fall in the category of "positive" claim damage class actions in that the individual claims were of such a nature as likely to have been able to stand on their own, at no point have the courts suggested a dichotomy for due process purposes between positive and negative claim class actions.[92] Nor have they ever suggested that due process protection turns on any of the factors focused on by Issacharoff.

On occasion, the courts have been quite vigorous in their enforcement of due process limitations on class actions.[93] For example, in the famed decision of *Hansberry v. Lee*,[94] a state court class action not subject to the strictures of the Federal Rules, the Supreme Court held that while "members of a class not present as parties to the litigation may be bound by the judgment where they are in fact adequately represented by parties who are present," due process prohibits those with "dual and potentially conflicting interests" to represent and bind absent class members.

The 1966 revision of Rule 23 inserted the requirement that the named parties adequately represent absent class members[95] for the express purpose of assuring compliance with due process protections, as set out in *Hansberry*.[96] In all of these situations, however, the nature of the due process limit was purely paternalistic, rather than autonomy-based. In other words, the decisions have focused on the concern that those representing the interests of absent class members had failed to do so adequately, or possessed interests that were in conflict with those of absent class members, thereby threatening the adequacy of the representation. However, the courts' implicit assumption appears to have been that satisfaction of the paternalistic element of the due process guarantee exhausts the constitutional concern (an issue that, admittedly, the courts need never have resolved in those cases). As a general matter these decisions have not involved the autonomy-based concern of due process that focuses on the individual litigant's interest in choosing whether to pursue his claim and if so how best to prosecute it. Hence as long as those formally representing the interests of the absent parties are doing so adequately and in good faith, nothing in the Court's class action-due process jurisprudence that has evolved to this point halts the usurpation of litigation control that, for reasons already explained, should be deemed to lie at the theoretical foundations of procedural due process.[97]

Mandatory Class Actions and the Autonomy Model

It is not entirely clear why the revisers of Rule 23 chose to make some class actions mandatory and others not. Commentators have suggested that in those classes that the rule makes mandatory, the interests of the class members are somehow more closely intertwined than in the (b)(3) category of classes, where opt-out by absent class members is possible.[98] However, there is absolutely no basis on which to support this conclusion. Indeed, in (b)(1)(B) classes, where the claims of absent class members may exceed the total amount of a fund into which the claims are made, it would seem that the interests of the class members are inherently antagonistic to each other. Even if the asserted rationale were true, at most it would mean that the *paternalistic* branch of procedural due process was satisfied in those classes designated mandatory; it would in no way imply satisfaction of the autonomy interest in litigant control.

In two cases, the Supreme Court made at least some reference to the constitutionality of mandatory classes. In neither decision, however, did the Court either comprehend or deal with the threat to litigant autonomy to which mandatory classes give rise. In *Phillips Petroleum Co. v. Shutts*,[99] the Court considered a challenge to a Kansas class action in which many of the absent plaintiffs allegedly lacked minimum contacts with the forum. In upholding Kansas's assertion of jurisdiction over absent plaintiffs who had no contacts with the forum, the Court found that the state's provision of an opt-out option satisfied the due process requirements of personal jurisdiction.[100] For absent plaintiffs, upon whom the Court assumed fewer burdens were placed than on defendants, consent to the forum's jurisdiction could come through the absent class member's wholly passive failure to exclude oneself from the case. In a subsequent decision, the Ninth Circuit relied upon *Shutts* for the conclusion that all mandatory damage class actions violate due process.[101] But such a reading of *Shutts* is surely too broad. The case was concerned exclusively with a narrow and unique form of due process, involving established constitutional limitations on a state's assertion of personal jurisdiction. The Court merely held that any constitutional objection to personal jurisdiction is subject to waiver, a well established precept of personal jurisdiction jurisprudence.[102] The only arguably controversial aspect of the *Shutts* Court's holding was its conclusion that passive behavior on the part of absent class members could serve as the equivalent of an affirmative expression of consent, at least for absent class member plaintiffs who lack the requisite minimum contacts with the forum state. The decision tells us nothing about the constitutionality of mandatory class actions in cases in which minimum contacts are present and personal jurisdiction is therefore not an issue.

The second decision is *Ortiz v. Fibreboard Corporation*.[103] In that case the Court invalidated a settlement class action under Rule 23(b)(1)(B) on the grounds that it did not satisfy the requirements of that provision, as narrowly construed. In so holding, the Court expressed unease over the mandatory nature of the proceeding, suggesting that it might undermine the so-called "day in court" ideal traditionally associated with procedural due process.[104] Thus, while the Court's holding was ultimately grounded in construction of the rule, the Court made clear that its narrow interpretation of the provision was influenced, at least in part, by concern over potential constitutional problems to which a broader construction might give rise.[105] But while it is true that the Court in *Ortiz* expressed unease over the constitutionality of mandatory class actions, it is apparent that the Court did not have a clue as to what the nature of that constitutional problem actually was. Surely it cannot be the threat to the "day in court" dictate of procedural due process—at least if one accepts the paternalistic model inherent in the modern class action concept itself. It is true that procedural due process is generally thought to require that before an individual's liberty or property may be taken away or abridged by government, he must receive the opportunity to present his side of the case to a neutral and objective adjudicator.[106] The underlying theory of the class action device is that the absent class member does, in fact, receive his "day in court" in the class proceeding, as long as the named parties adequately represent his interests.[107] Otherwise, neither res judicata nor collateral estoppel could be invoked in later suits brought by or against absent class members, since it is well established that—with extremely limited exceptions—neither res judicata nor collateral estoppel may be imposed on any litigant who has been denied her day in court. That the absent class member is denied the opportunity to withdraw from the proceeding, then, logically in no way undermines the day-in-court ideal, as viewed through the lens of class action theory. Yet the Court in *Ortiz* intimated that just such a constitutional non sequitur underlay its narrow construction of Rule 23(b)(1)(B). At no point in *Ortiz* did the Court ever suggest a recognition of the *true* constitutional difficulty with mandatory class actions: their necessary interference with a litigant's unfettered ability to control the nature, course, and very existence of his own suit.

Litigant Autonomy, Mandatory Class Actions, and the Right of Non-Association

In addition to the traditional litigant autonomy concern that is threatened by any forced inclusion in a class proceeding, there exists an alternative form of procedural autonomy concern that, under certain circumstances, could be implicated by the use of mandatory classes. Potentially problematic is not only the usurpation of strategic control of one's litigation choices, but also the very decision of whether to pursue one's individual claim in the first place. Of course, control of the decision to sue is, to a certain extent, grounded in the very notion of litigant autonomy, purely as a definitional matter. However, in certain instances, forced association with those who seek to pursue courses of action that the litigant finds economically, morally, or politically offensive also threatens fundamental First Amendment dictates that can similarly be discerned from the values appropriately found to explain the procedural due process guarantee.

The Supreme Court has recognized, in other contexts, that the pursuit of litigation may well have political and associational implications, thereby triggering the First Amendment's protection of freedom of expression and association.[108] Since the Supreme Court has wisely recognized a corresponding First Amendment right not to associate,[109] it logically follows that there should also be recognized a corresponding First Amendment-like right not to be forced to litigate when to do so would be deemed politically or morally offensive by the litigant. This is not to suggest, it should be emphasized, that a potential plaintiff necessarily possesses a constitutional right to control all aspects of the timing or choice of forum for suit. The point, rather, is that at the very least a litigant should be recognized to possess a constitutional right to decide not to pursue his claim at all—a right inescapably denied by a mandatory class action.

The relevance of this First Amendment concern to the modern class action is potentially significant. While concededly the majority of class actions are brought solely for the purpose of seeking compensation, rather than to pursue socio-political ends, the two goals are not necessarily mutually exclusive. In fact, the very existence of class action suits is today a controversial political issue. The so-called tort reform movement has focused much of its political fire on the "bounty hunter" class action, in which greedy plaintiffs' lawyers engage in legalized blackmail against large corporations, thereby leading to economic waste, unfair wealth redistribution, and generally higher prices for products and services.[110] It could hardly be controverted that many private citizens find such lawsuits to be politically unwise, economically reckless, and morally offensive. Yet when those citizens are made members of a mandatory class they are made, against their will, to be part of a legal mechanism whose very purpose is to employ the litigation process to achieve political and economic ends that they ideologically abhor. In many ways, this result contravenes the fundamental constitutional prohibition against forced political association.[111]

There are, concededly, a number of potential problems with this argument. First, it is true that the large majority of compensatory class actions found politically, economically, and morally offensive by many are of the (b)(3) variety, where those who find the process offensive are given the option of removing themselves from the class. However, for reasons to be subsequently explored, even the provision of an opt-out procedure raises serious constitutional problems, because it authorizes waiver of basic constitutional rights through an extraordinary and unprecedented form of litigant passivity.[112] Moreover, not all damage class actions are classified as (b)(3) classes. Though in *Ortiz* the Court gave the (b)(1)(B) mandatory class category a limiting construction,[113] it is still conceivable that a damage class action could fall into this category, where—unlike *Ortiz*—class members' claims are made into an identifiable and truly limited fund. Indeed, that mandatory (b)(1)(B) classes continue to exist is supported by examination of recent case law.[114] Finally, the non-associational concern is also present in numerous (b)(2) injunctive class actions, which are usually brought to pursue civil rights claims.[115] It is certainly conceivable that members of a (b)(2) class could be deeply opposed, on moral or political grounds, to the goals sought to be achieved by the class action. Yet because (b)(2) classes are mandatory, these class members are forced to be a part of the proceeding, regardless of their wishes or their ideological preferences.

It might further be responded that in most situations the unwilling class member's presence in the class will have little or no discernible concrete impact on the actual outcome. This is especially true in the case of injunctive class actions, since if successful the action will invariably bring about class-wide relief, whether a particular individual remains a member of the class or not. But the point of the First Amendment right of non-association is not to protect the individual from bringing about concrete effects that he finds offensive, but rather to avoid the ideologically and emotively demoralizing impact on the individual that the very fact of the forced offensive association may cause.[116]

Finally, it might be responded that the First Amendment right of free expression is not itself directly implicated by forced inclusion in a class, because the conduct of litigation constitutes unprotected *action,* rather than protected *expression.* Thus, the argument proceeds, forced participation in the litigation process is not a form of forced expression. But even if this is true, the relevant constitutional prohibition that we are invoking is not against forced *expression,* but rather forced *association,* which inherently possesses both expressive and non-expressive elements. In any event, the issue need not be whether forced participation in a morally or politically offensive class action violates the First Amendment, but rather whether it contravenes the autonomy model of procedural due process. That concept may appropriately be deemed to subsume the values sought to be furthered by recognition of the First Amendment right of non-association, even when the protected activity cannot be properly characterized as pure expression.

Mandatory Class Actions, Due Process, and the Utilitarian Calculus

The Autonomy Model and the Utilitarian Calculus

Although on one level the autonomy value described here could perhaps be characterized as morally foundational in nature,[117] there is no inherent reason why even this morally foundational interest, once recognized, must be deemed a constitutional absolute. To the contrary, as the *Mathews-Doehr* test demonstrates, procedural due process has traditionally involved some form of balancing process, in which a variety of potentially competing interests are measured against one another. I have here urged recognition of the constitutionally grounded autonomy model of procedural due process as a logical outgrowth of our nation's moral and political commitment to a system of liberal democracy. I have further suggested that there exists an inherent tension between this model and the entire notion of mandatory class actions. It does not necessarily follow, however, that as a result all mandatory class actions must automatically be deemed unconstitutional. It means only that one needs to begin the process of conducting a due process calculus in which competing interests are weighed. To date, no one has even begun this process, much less concluded it. It is to the shaping of this calculus that I now turn.

Before one can explore the competing interests to be included in the due process calculus, it is important to consider the weight that the autonomy value should receive as part of that balancing process. For reasons already explained, the autonomy value should be recognized as a central element in that due process calculus. An individual should not be forced to cede to others control over his choice whether or not to resort to the judicial process except for truly compelling justifications. The same is true of a litigant's authority to choose the strategy for litigation of his claims, or to select who will conduct that litigation. For this reason, the autonomy value, in the abstract, should be given a level of protection equivalent to that given fully protected free speech interests.

It could be argued that the weight given to the autonomy value in shaping the due process calculus should be gradated on the basis of the size of the individual litigant's interest at stake in the class proceeding. For example, if the litigant possesses only a minimal interest at stake, like what Issacharoff refers to as a negative value claim,[118] one might reasonably suggest that a less powerful justification should be accepted for overriding the litigant autonomy interest. This result would be consistent with the *Mathews-Doehr* framework, which focuses on the level of competing private and governmental interests at stake.[119] Whether this "interest gradation" approach should be accepted may depend on the extent to which one views the autonomy value as theoretically foundational, rather than merely as a utilitarian value. If one deems the interest in litigant autonomy to be foundational, the amount of the individual's claim should logically be deemed irrelevant. If the individual wishes to forego her right to control the conduct of her litigation because her claim is of only minimal value, the argument proceeds, then it is up to the individual to make that choice; for government to make the decision as to whether the autonomy value is significant is itself a violation of the autonomy value. On the other hand, virtually never does there exist a private interest in the due process calculus deemed so powerful that it supercedes all competing pragmatic interests, no matter how compelling. While the abstract theoretical interest in litigant choice is surely important in and of itself, it is worth considering whether there exist any potentially competing interests that could be deemed overriding.

Exploring the Justifications for Mandatory Class Actions

As already explained,[120] under the existing framework of Rule 23 there are three categories of mandatory class actions: (1) Rule 23(b)(1)(A) classes, where individual actions might result in imposing inconsistent obligations on the party opposing the class; (2) Rule 23(b)(1)(B) classes, where permitting individual actions might prejudice the interests of the absent class members; and (3) Rule 23(b)(2) classes, where the party opposing the class has acted in a manner generally applicable to the class, thereby justifying injunctive or declaratory relief against that party. The Advisory Committee that revised Rule 23 in 1966 never explained why these categories were made mandatory, so one must resort to a form of speculation or reverse engineering in order to hypothesize possible rationales for such treatment.

Least difficult to understand is perhaps the decision to make (b)(1)(A) classes mandatory. That provision reaches situations in which the party opposing the class can act only indivisibly toward the class members. For example, in the famed case of *Supreme Tribe of Ben-Hur v. Cauble*,[121] the substantive legal issue was whether a fraternal benefit organization which had issued insurance policies to members could financially reorganize, a course of action which many policyholders opposed. Though the case was decided long before the 1966 revisions of Rule 23, the Advisory Committee that year expressly pointed to the decision as an illustration of a situation justifying a (b)(1)(A) class action.[122] By the very nature of the organization's proposed action, it would have been impossible to act differently toward different policyholders; either the organization financially reorganized, or it did not. Unlike in the case of aggregated damage actions, the organization could not provide relief to some class members but deny it to others. Thus, absent a class action, the fraternal benefit organization could potentially be subject to a form of inconsistent liability: It could be victorious in litigation against certain policyholders challenging the reorganization, but, because collateral estoppel may not constitutionally bind a party who did not have his day in court, those victories could not stop other policyholders from seeking to enjoin the reorganization. The result might be that according to one holding, the benefit organization could financially reorganize, while according to a separate holding, it could not.

Of course, these holdings would not inexorably impose inconsistent liability on the party opposing the class in the traditional sense: There would be no holdings imposing inconsistent standards of behavior on that party so that no matter what it did it would be found liable to someone. Imposition of such inconsistent judgments has been found to violate due process.[123] By contrast, in the *Ben-Hur* situation the party opposing the class could have avoided such a danger, simply by adhering to the holding denying it the right to reorganize. But then the party would lose the benefit of its victory in the litigation that upheld its right to reorganize. This should not be deemed an acceptable result.

It is easy to understand why the revisers of Rule 23 would authorize a class action under these circumstances. What is not as immediately clear, however, is whether that class action must be mandatory. The argument supporting the mandatory nature of a (b)(1)(A) class, presumably, is that if class members may choose not to participate in the proceeding and instead separately pursue their claims against the party opposing the class, the very danger sought to be avoided by use of the class action device in the first place might well occur. For then the party opposing the class might be subject to opposite findings in separate proceedings despite the continued existence of the class proceeding. Because of the inherent indivisibility of that party's behavior toward the opposing litigants, it could once again be subject to inconsistent behavioral standards growing out of different litigations.

It is at least arguable that the interest in avoiding such inconsistent liability satisfies the compelling interest standard required to justify the loss of litigant autonomy necessarily associated with mandatory class actions. To completely deny a litigant the benefit of its successful litigation imposes severe harm that should be avoided if at all possible. Unless the class proceeding is made mandatory, it is impossible to avoid this danger.

Not nearly as compelling are the likely justifications for the mandatory nature of the other class action categories. Though at no point has anyone satisfactorily explained why *any* class was made mandatory, the Advisory Committee suggested two rationales for existence of the (b)(1)(B) category, untied—at least explicitly—to the class's mandatory nature. The first is the so-called "limited pie" concern—the fear that the sum of the claimants' claims will exceed the amount available to pay those claims. In *Ortiz,* the Supreme Court gave an extremely narrow construction to this "limited pie" category of (b)(1)(B) classes.[124] At the very least, all of the assets of the defendant would need to be included in the measurement of available funds for the purpose of determining whether the total amount of the claims exceed those funds. Moreover, it is arguable that the Court confined the category to "res"-like cases, where the claims were themselves made into an identifiable fund, rather than merely into the composite of defendant's assets.[125] The second rationale mentioned by the Advisory Committee for the use of (b)(1)(B) class actions—though nowhere expressly referred to by the *Ortiz* Court—was what can be appropriately referred to as a "same situation stare decisis" concern. Under these circumstances, the absent claimants are so situated that while their claims will not be formally extinguished by an unsuccessful outcome in the initial action,[126] as a practical matter the situations are so overlapping that it is all but inconceivable that the outcome in the initial action will not be dispositive of the subsequent actions.[127]

It seems perfectly appropriate, as a matter of judicial administration policy, to authorize class proceedings in both situations. In both, there exists a danger that claimants could suffer prejudice unless permitted to participate in the initial action. It is not nearly as clear, however, that those proceedings must be made mandatory, thereby effectively gutting the fundamental due process interest in litigation autonomy. Particularly weak is the "same situation stare decisis" concern. If a member of the class wishes to exclude himself from the class in order to pursue the action on his own, any risk of same situation stare decisis flowing from the class adjudication is purely self-imposed. Moreover, when the class member wishes not to pursue his claim at all, there is of course no stare decisis danger to him whatsoever from the litigation proceeding without his inclusion.

The "limited pie" rationale is somewhat more complex. In this context, unlike the same-situation stare decisis instance, the harm suffered by the absent class member, were there to be no class action, is not self-imposed. That harm is that on a "first come, first served" basis the available funds will be consumed by the claimants who bring their claims to completion first, leaving the remaining claimants with little or nothing to show for their presumably valid claims. By forcing all of the claimants into a single proceeding, the (b)(1)(B) class action prevents this form of litigation Darwinism. Instead, it imposes what can be described as litigation socialism, in which winner does not take all. Instead, available funds are to be evenly divided among claimants, in a manner reminiscent of the bankruptcy system, without permitting the claimants to engage in a race to the courthouse to see which of them can consume the limited pie first.

All other things being equal, reasonable minds could probably differ over whether the Darwinist or socialist model of litigation is more appropriate. In support of the socialist model it can be argued that we should not allow the strong to prevail over the weak, when both claims are equally deserving. On the other hand, litigation often rewards the more aggressive litigant who possesses greater resources, and perhaps there is no reason why the limited pie situation should be any different. If certain claimants are quicker, faster, more resourceful, and more effective and therefore able to bring their claims to judgment first, then so be it. That result is simply the foreseeable consequence of a litigation system that tolerates discrepancies in litigant abilities and resources. When the litigation autonomy factor is included in the analysis the situation takes on an entirely different look. It may be perfectly appropriate to *allow* claimants to band together in a single proceeding in order to ensure equal distribution of the defendant's limited assets. It is quite another to prohibit a litigant from choosing to control his own litigation in the manner he deems wisest and, indeed, to decide whether to pursue his claim at all. Because the use of the litigation socialism model necessarily leads to a rejection of the foundational due process precept of litigation autonomy, it should be deemed unconstitutional.

Even if one were to assume, for purposes of argument, that the goals of the litigation socialism model should be found to prevail, it is possible to achieve those goals without undermining the value of litigant autonomy in the manner caused by the mandatory class action. In the context of interpleader, for example, the Supreme Court has recognized that individual actions may proceed separately, with enforcement of any judgment enjoined until all individual claims have been litigated.[128] In this manner, individual claimants are protected against preemptive judgments by other claimants, yet each litigant is permitted to exercise full control over her own litigation. There is no reason that a similar (though not identical)[129] procedure could not be employed in place of a mandatory class action. It is conceivable that the delay in receipt of judgments in these circumstances would be unreasonable, arguably making this alternative impractical. Even so, at least it would provide the individual litigant with the choice whether or not to participate in the class proceeding or instead pursue his action separately and then await payment for a successful judgment until completion of the class proceeding. The important point is that no one, to this point, has even considered this possibly less invasive alternative, because no one has even recognized the harms to due process values caused by the loss of litigant autonomy resulting from use of mandatory class actions in the first place.

The mandatory nature of (b)(2) injunctive/declaratory class actions gives rise to a somewhat different set of constitutional concerns. To the extent the injunctive action seeks to challenge behavior on the part of the defendant that is indivisible among the class members, then the issue appears to be identical to the one that arises in the context of Rule 23(b)(1)(A) mandatory class actions, previously discussed, and should likewise be deemed constitutional.[130] However, not all (b)(2) class actions necessarily concern such indivisible behavior. For example, a class may complain that a defendant employer is engaging in racial discrimination in hiring and therefore seek injunctive relief requiring the use of remedial and promotion standards designed to rectify those discriminatory practices. While the defendant's behavior may well satisfy the (b)(2) requirement that the party opposing the class have acted in a manner generally applicable to the class, thereby justifying injunctive or declaratory relief, it does not necessarily follow that the defendant will be incapable in all cases of treating different class members differently. For example, if a class member were to choose to remove herself from the class, any injunction requiring the use of remedial hiring or promotion measures need not apply to her; there is no reason, legally or physically, why such different treatment could not be given. On the other hand, were the class to be unsuccessful, a class member who had removed herself would not be bound by res judicata or collateral estoppel principles and could subsequently pursue her own individual action for injunctive relief, at least as a theoretical matter.[131]

Perhaps more of a concern in the (b)(2) context would be the forced ideological association that would push together members of a group who share the goals and values of the named plaintiffs with those who may vehemently oppose them. For example, in a civil rights action brought on behalf of African Americans to enforce affirmative action, such famed African American opponents of affirmative action as sociologist Harry Edwards and conservative Republican politician Alan Keyes would necessarily be forced to be included in the class. It is quite conceivable that all of the harms of forced association, transposed into an element in the litigant autonomy model of procedural due process, would result. Whatever are the due process harms that flow from the mandatory nature of a (b)(2) class, it is difficult to perceive any need for such mandatory treatment that is specific to the (b)(2) category. There is simply no reason that a class must include every injured party in order to achieve the aims of the (b)(2) class.

There are several non-specific procedural harms that are arguably avoided by use of mandatory class actions. For example, if class members are permitted to withdraw from a class,[132] presumably they would have to receive notice of the class action's existence, along with some administrative means for determining who ultimately ends up in the class and who does not. Both would inevitably result in imposition of serious additional costs and delays. But when a class is mandatory, no procedure for withdrawal need be provided, and, in the exercise of the trial judge's discretion, no notice need be required.[133] However, it is dubious whether due process is satisfied by *any* class proceeding where at least some form of reasonable notice is not provided to class members.[134] Even if the class member is not allowed to remove himself from the class, he should be permitted to monitor the actions of those who represent his interests. Indeed, this is an even more compelling interest when he has had effectively little or no say in the selection of who does pursue his interests on his behalf. Whatever additional administrative costs may result from the need to make a record of who is and who is not ultimately a member of the class would seem to be nothing more than a "cost of doing business" of our constitutional commitment to a system of procedural due process.

One commentator has suggested that mandatory class actions are required to prevent disruption of settlements that are valuable to the majority of claimants.[135] But this argument puts the cart before the horse: A class that is constitutionally defective from its inception is incapable of settlement. To argue on the basis of the importance of the settlement is logically to beg the question of the class proceeding's validity in the first place. Another commentator asserts that the absence of mandatory class proceedings can be antithetical to the foundational purposes of a class action, namely to achieve a socially desirable level of deterrence of defendant misconduct.[136] But this argument perversely transforms a procedural aggregation device that may have the incidental benefit of deterring future illegal conduct into a dictate of pre-litigation substantive law. This conclusion is inconsistent not only with the express directives of the Rules Enabling Act[137] but with the essence of democratic theory, which requires that substantive policy choices are not made in a manner that fundamentally deceives the electorate.[138]

On balance, then, there appears to be only one existing category of mandatory class action that likely satisfies a compelling interest standard: the (b)(1)(A) category. Absent a class proceeding in these situations, the party opposing the class could conceivably be placed in an untenable position due to inconsistent judgments in separate suits brought by different class members combined with the indivisibility of his behavior in relation to all class members. In no other context, however, should competing interests be deemed to override the fundamental due process interest in litigant autonomy.

The saddest and most puzzling element of the mandatory class situation is not that the courts have upheld the use of mandatory classes against a due process challenge grounded in considerations of litigant autonomy. It is, rather, that they have never even recognized the possibility that such a challenge could be made.

Litigant Autonomy and the Opt-Out Procedure

Classes brought pursuant to Rule 23(b)(3) are not mandatory; under Rule 23(c), absent class members must receive notice and the opportunity to opt out of the action. If one accepts the conclusion that the autonomy value lies at the normative core of procedural due process, obviously this opt-out procedure is constitutionally preferable to the mandatory procedure imposed by Rule 23(b)(1) and (2). Indeed, respected scholars have pointed to its centrality to the preservation of litigant choice.[139] It does not necessarily follow, however, that the provision of an opportunity to opt out of the class proceeding satisfies procedural due process.

As explained earlier in this book, a process that requires absent claimants to affirmatively opt into a class proceeding is preferable to an opt-out procedure, purely as a matter of democratic theory. Adopting an inference of inclusion in the class on the basis of purely passive behavior on the part of the absent class member has the effect of creating a "faux" class, which does not truly represent aggregation of willing plaintiffs as much as a comatose grouping of absent class members who know little or nothing of the proceeding and are unlikely to pursue whatever relief the proceeding makes available to them on an individual basis. As a result, the class proceeding is often transformed into a bounty hunter action in which the only interested parties are the class attorneys, thus effectively transforming the underlying substantive law into something other than what it purports to be—namely, a compensatory remedial action.[140] The point here, however, is that the opt-out procedure in addition raises potentially serious constitutional problems as a matter of procedural due process.

At first this conclusion may seem puzzling since, as previously noted, purely as a technical matter an opt-out procedure does not violate a constitutional prohibition on mandatory class proceedings: Any party who wishes to remove herself from the class proceeding is free to do so. However, when one recognizes that opt-out effectively amounts to a form of waiver of the constitutional right not to be included in a class proceeding against the individual's will, the inherent passivity of the opt-out procedure becomes problematic. It is well accepted that individuals may waive their personal constitutional rights. However, in both civil and criminal contexts the Supreme Court has unequivocally held that "the courts indulge in every reasonable presumption against waiver of constitutional rights."[141] On a number of occasions, the Court has rejected implied waiver in the civil context. In *Fuentes v. Shevin,* the Court stated that "the waiver of constitutional rights in any context must, at the very least, be clear."[142] In another context, the Court wrote that "constructive consent is not a doctrine commonly associated with the surrender of constitutional rights."[143]

It is true that the Court has not always adhered to its own highly protective standard. On occasion, waiver may be effected unintentionally, through a failure to act. For example, the Seventh Amendment right to jury trial in civil cases may be waived by failure to raise it at the correct point in the litigation.[144] A due process right to individual notice may be waived by means of the signing of a boilerplate contract,[145] as may a constitutional objection to lack of personal jurisdiction.[146] In a federal judicial proceeding, a party may waive the personal jurisdiction defense by failure to raise it within the proper time frame or in conjunction with other motions.[147] In certain state proceedings, traditionally the constitutional objection to personal jurisdiction is waived, simply by the litigant's discussion of the case's merits. But generally an individual *who has not previously been made a litigant* is not deemed to have waived her constitutional right by total and utter passivity.

The one possible exception concerns default judgment: A defendant may be subjected to a default judgment, thereby waiving her constitutional right to have her day in court, simply by failing to respond to service of a complaint. In this one situation, then, total failure to take action of any sort is effectively treated as a waiver of one's constitutional right to a day in court. However, under any sensible version of a due process balancing test, such a conclusion makes perfect sense; a party of course may not be permitted to avoid a lawsuit, merely by failing to respond. A lawsuit is not an RSVP. It is by no means clear, however, that in any other context a constitutional right should be deemed waivable by nothing more than total passivity on the part of the rightholder when the rightholder has not himself filed suit or been made a defendant in an ongoing suit.[148] It is doubtful that we would accept such a constitutional loophole when other significant rights are involved—for example, the free speech right or the right to counsel. If, as argued here, the value of litigant autonomy embodied in the due process clause, is of great importance to the foundations of American constitutional and political theory,[149] then it should not be so easily lost.

One other possible example of totally passive waiver that arguably complicates the argument is the statute of limitations. In a certain sense, the statute of limitations is the mirror image of the default judgment: a plaintiff who fails to take action by a certain date has waived whatever property right he possessed in his cause of action. In two ways, however, the statute of limitations fundamentally differs from the waiver-through-total passivity that characterizes opt out. First, statute of limitations are inherently non-transsubstantive. They are always tied to a specific substantive cause of action, and thus effectively a part of that cause of action. By contrast, both the opt-out and default judgment rules are fully transsubstantive; they are both agnostic to the specific substantive claim being waived. In this important sense, the statute of limitations is, at the outset, an inherent part of the plaintiff's substantive claim. Viewed in this manner, the statute of limitations does not act as a waiver of a pristine substantive claim, but rather as an ex ante element of that substantive claim. Loss of a claim through violation of the statute of limitations, then, does not operate as a procedural waiver of an otherwise unencumbered substantive claim; it *is* part of the claim, and therefore operates as an inherent qualifier of the property right that is protected by due process in the first place.

Secondly, even were one to view the statute of limitations—incorrectly, I believe—as a form of procedural waiver, there can be no doubt that the strong interests protected by the statute of limitations outweigh even an extremely strong interest in avoiding totally passive waiver. The primary point, however, is that at the very least, opt-out must be tested by means of such a due process utilitarian calculus, a test that to date has never been performed. Were a court, following application of a careful, detailed, and thoughtful utilitarian calculus, to determine waiver-through-opt-out to be constitutional, the very conduct of such a traditional due process analysis would be a significant moral victory.

It might be suggested that the concern over passive waiver of a constitutional right is overblown. Under an opt-out procedure a potential class member who does not wish to be part of the class, the argument might proceed, need only take the relatively minimal time and effort required to send in the form indicating her choice not to be a class member. But the enormous impact of inertia will inevitably cloud any inference that might reasonably be drawn from a class member's failure to take such affirmative action. Imagine, for example, a process whereby a notice is sent to voters, clearly indicating that if they neither go to the polls on election day nor send in a form indicating their desire to vote for the Republican candidate they will be deemed to have voted for the Democrat. Presumably, no one would assume the constitutionality of such a law, even though any burden imposed on the voter by the opt-out procedure is no less minimal than the burden imposed on the absent class members. The same is true of opt-out.

It may be that when absent class members' rights are relatively minimal—as in Issacharoff's "negative value" claims[150]—the constitutional interest in litigant autonomy is de minimis, and, at the very least, should be deemed waivable through use of an opt-out procedure that is triggered by the claimant's simple failure to act. The strongest defense of this position would be that, as long as the individual claims are sufficiently large to justify claimant effort to file a claim in any settlement fund or damage award, it is reasonable to assume, ex ante, that a self-interested claimant would, more likely than not, wish to be a member of the class. In light of this reasonable presumption, in this narrow category of cases only, inertia should lie in favor of inclusion, though this presumption may be rebutted in the individual case through a potential class member's affirmative act of opt-out.[151] In all other contexts, however, the presumption of inclusion that inheres in the opt-out rule is inconsistent with both the autonomy model of procedural due process and the traditional precepts of constitutional waiver. Thus, at the very least a due process right to litigant autonomy should be recognized in so-called positive value class actions, and such a right should not be deemed waivable by utter passivity on the part of claimants. Because Rule 23(c) currently draws no distinction between positive and negative value classes for purposes of opt-out, the provision should be deemed unconstitutional.

There has long existed debate and controversy over the wisdom of opt-out rights.[152] Most of that controversy, however, has focused on the choice between opt-out and mandatory class actions.[153] Rarely has it concerned the choice between opt-*out* and opt-*in* procedures. The position taken here is that while of course opt-out is constitutionally preferable to mandatory participation, in many situations the inertia brought about by the opt-out procedure must be reversed: absent expression of an affirmative choice to participate in a class proceeding, the potential absent class member must be deemed not to have waived his right to control the litigation of his claim. This conclusion flows logically from recognition that litigant autonomy constitutes a core element of the procedural due process right. Because neither court nor scholar to date has focused on the litigant autonomy factor,[154] no one has previously viewed the opt-out procedure for Rule 23(b)(3) class actions through the lens of the waiver of constitutional rights. Recognition of the relevance of the jurisprudence of constitutional waiver dictates a rejection of opt-out procedure, in favor of one requiring opt-in.

CONCLUSION

In writing this chapter, I have sought to achieve two goals. First, I have sought to demonstrate that the ability of a litigant to control the conduct of his litigation and to make the choice whether or not to litigate—what has been labeled here "litigant autonomy"—grows out of liberal democratic theory's commitment to the principles of self-determination and individual integrity.[155] It should therefore be recognized as a foundational element in the theory and structure of procedural due process, a constitutional protection that itself grows out of those very same principles of liberal democratic thought. By completely ignoring this concern in the shaping of its modern procedural due process calculus, the Supreme Court has failed to provide procedural due process of the depth and scope required for it to perform its function within American constitutional and political theory.[156]

Second, while it is probably true that litigant autonomy will be implicated by governmental procedural restrictions only relatively rarely, it is also probably true that the increasingly important area of class actions illustrates all too well the harms that flow to this fundamental constitutional value when the applicable due process analysis ignores the litigant's autonomy interest in control of the judicial process for the adjudication of his legal rights. Although both Rule 23 and Supreme Court doctrine seek to protect the due process rights of absent class members, at no point have either the Rule's drafters, the justices, or procedural scholars recognized that what has been implemented is purely a *paternalistic* form of due process—that is, the concern that those who represent the interests of the absent litigants enforce and protect those litigants' rights enthusiastically and in good faith.[157] Under certain circumstances—for example, where, for legal or practical reasons, the absent party is unable to involve herself in decision making concerning the enforcement of her rights—this paternalistic concern constitutes an appropriate element of the due process analysis. It is important, however, not to confuse this *necessary* condition with one that, standing alone, is *sufficient* to satisfy due process. Where it is feasible, under the circumstances, to allow the individual party to make her own decisions about the protection of her own rights through resort to the judicial process, the values of procedural due process cannot be satisfied merely by paternalistically assuring "adequate" representation by some external force not chosen by the litigant herself. Surely our constitutional system would not accept such governmentally imposed paternalism in the political process; it is, according to basic tenets of liberal democratic thought, the individual who is to determine how to exercise her self-governing function when participating in the political process. No less should be demanded when a private individual seeks to enforce her rights in the judicial process. Thus, where class actions are deemed mandatory, as specified categories of Rule 23 are, there exists at least a prima facie conflict between the class action rule and the litigant autonomy value.

Where a truly compelling need can be established, a due process calculus may appropriately require that the litigant autonomy interest give way. Unfortunately, neither Court nor scholar has even recognized the collectivist-individual tension that inheres in the mandatory class action concept, much less undertaken a due process inquiry that takes concerns about that tension into account. In preparing such a calculus, it should be clear that only one of the three existing categories of mandatory class actions even arguably justifies requiring inclusion in the class: Rule 23(b)(1)(A) classes, where, absent the class action, the party opposing the class risks inconsistent judicial directives from individual actions where the party's behavior vis-à-vis all class members is indivisible.[158] While the rationales for the remaining mandatory class actions may reasonably be thought to justify class treatment when absent class members are willing, they cannot overcome the strong constitutional interest in preserving litigant autonomy. Therefore they do not thereby justify mandatory treatment, as a constitutional matter.

This constitutional concern does not directly reach the most widely employed category of class actions, the (b)(3) category, because litigants are, by rule, provided the opportunity to opt out of such classes. However, if one deems the right not to be forced to be included in a litigation in which one does not have full control over the conduct of one's own action to be a significant constitutional right, then the opt-out procedure must be seen as a form of waiver of that right. In virtually no other context may constitutional rights be formally waived by such total passivity on the part of the rightholder when the rightholder has himself neither brought an action nor been made a defendant in an action. For this reason, an opt-in procedure should, in many cases, be deemed constitutionally required to assure some basic level of knowing waiver on the part of absent class members. However, when the individual plaintiffs' claims are sufficiently large to justify active efforts to pursue the claim in a settlement fund or damage award, but insufficiently large to justify individual suit, it may be reasonable to presume, ex ante, an interest in participating in the class, rebuttable by exercise of opt-out.[159] At the very least, however, affirmative opt-in should be constitutionally required when the plaintiffs' individual claims are "positive"—that is, sufficiently large to justify individual suit.

It is likely that acceptance of the constitutional arguments fashioned here would have a dramatic impact on the class action process. There can be little doubt that the class procedure could not operate in the manner it does currently under the framework suggested here. However, in *Ortiz* the Supreme Court gave a relatively narrow construction to the primary category of mandatory class actions, those brought under Rule 23(b)(1)(B), so its current reach is likely to be fairly limited. It is true that other class actions would undoubtedly be impacted by a transformation from an opt-out to an opt-in procedure. However, it begs the question to assume, conclusorily, that this would necessarily be an unwise or morally unacceptable development. Where valuable constitutional interests are recognized and protected, on balance the proposals advocated here are properly deemed an advance, rather than a retreat, in procedural jurisprudence.

CHAPTER SIX

Settlement Class Actions, the Case-or-Controversy Requirement, and the Nature of the Adjudicatory Process

INTRODUCTION

It would hardly be an understatement to suggest that the nature of the litigation process has changed dramatically over the past forty years. Modern procedure has been altered in order to keep up with the significant changes over the same period in governing substantive law, which has significantly expanded the scope of private responsibility and liability through the rapid expansion of both statutory and common law bases for suit. This is particularly true in the areas of civil rights, consumer protection, and products liability. While experts may reasonably debate whether the socio-economic and political effects of these changes in substantive law are beneficial or harmful, few would doubt the troubled state in which modern litigation procedure finds itself as a result, at least in large part, of the dramatic expansion of the scope of substantive liability. The class action is the procedural device routinely employed as the means of resolving the countless individual claims that may now be made against economically powerful defendants. Though the device finds its origins in ancient practice[1] and received codification in the original Federal Rules of Civil Procedure in 1938,[2] the practice assumed its modern form—dramatically different from its earlier structure—in the amendments of 1966.[3] While that alteration was designed to make the class action device capable of resolving the disputes to which the dramatic expansion in substantive liability was to give rise, the difficulties inherent in any attempt to resolve thousands of parallel, but not necessarily identical, claims in one proceeding could not have been foreseen. The sometimes overwhelming complications that inevitably accompany an attempt to litigate countless claims in one proceeding have proven to be more than the device is capable of handling.

Because of these seemingly insurmountable problems in litigating complex claims through the class action device, attorneys and courts have developed a new method of disposing of these thousands of potential suits in one fell swoop. That method is known as the settlement class action. While the name explicitly references the class action device and requires satisfaction of many of Rule 23's requirements,[4] in important ways the practice alters the very essence of the litigation process. It does so, by having as its defining characteristic, from the proceeding's inception, the absence of any dispute to be litigated. Instead, both parties come to the court with a conditional request for certification of a class: The "suit" is to be certified as a class if and only if the court approves the settlement that has been reached by the defendant and attorneys for certain individual plaintiffs who seek to represent all of those similarly injured. The court may approve or disapprove that settlement, but either way there will never be any litigation of the class members' claims against the defendant. If the court approves, then the entire matter will have been resolved through non-litigation means. If, on the other hand, the court disapproves, the parties are returned to the same position they were in prior to the institution of the proceeding. Thus, the so-called settlement class action is a good deal more settlement than action. When the dust settles, the device is nothing more than a non-litigation means of resolving potential disputes. Yet the practice is approved and enforced through the federal courts.

Many courts and commentators have applauded the development of the settlement class action as a welcome means of resolving gigantic disputes without incurring the burdens of extended litigation—if, indeed, such mass litigation was even feasible in the first place.[5] Not surprisingly, then, the growth of settlement class actions as a means of disposing of modern complex claims has been meteoric.[6] The Supreme Court itself has eased the way for use of the practice in the lower courts by holding that it need not satisfy what is often the most difficult hurdle to class action certification: the requirement of Rule 23(b)(3) that litigation of the class be manageable.[7]

A number of respected courts and scholars, however, have sounded cautionary notes about the practice, suggesting that the settlement class action brings with it serious risks of collusion and unfairness that ultimately disadvantage absent class members.[8] Scholars have therefore proposed a number of reforms, designed to reduce the potential harms to which the settlement class action gives rise.[9] Indeed, congressional concern over the use of the settlement class action has resulted in Congress's commission of a study by the Federal Judicial Conference to investigate the problems it poses.[10] Neither those who approve nor those who disapprove the settlement class action device, however, have fully recognized the most serious—and fatal—problem with the settlement class action: Because by its nature it does not involve any live dispute between the parties that a federal court is being asked to resolve through litigation, and because from the outset of the proceeding the parties are in full accord as to how the claims should be disposed of, there is missing the adverseness between the parties that is a central element of Article III's case-or-controversy requirement. The settlement class action, in short, is inherently unconstitutional. Because class action scholars have mistakenly viewed the device—both positively and negatively—in a constitutional vacuum, however, they have uniformly failed to recognize the problematic impact of the settlement class action when it is placed within the broader framework of the nation's constitutional structure.

On the most basic analytical level, the unconstitutionality of the settlement class action should be obvious, purely as a matter of textual construction. There is simply no rational means of defining the terms "case" or "controversy" to include a proceeding in which, from the outset, nothing is disputed and the parties are in complete agreement.[11] Moreover, from both historical and doctrinal perspectives, Supreme Court decisions could not be more certain that Article III is satisfied only when the parties are truly "adverse" to one another,[12] which, at the time the relevant proceeding is undertaken, they are not in the case of the settlement class action.

In light of the dispositive textual and doctrinal problems to which the settlement class action is subject, one might reasonably wonder why neither courts nor scholars have given the Article III concerns anything more than passing attention.[13] One possible answer is that modern constitutional analysis has often refused to focus primarily on matters of textual interpretation. In the area of separation of powers in particular, the Supreme Court has at times openly employed a counter-textual functionalist balancing test to resolve constitutional challenges.[14] One may question the legitimacy of such an approach as a matter of constitutional interpretation.[15] In any event, in-depth theoretical analysis reveals that the adverseness requirement imposed by Article III is justified by far more than merely a textualist rationale. Instead, it is dictated by the foundations of American political theory and an understanding of the judiciary's proper role within that framework.[16]

If one were to search for an explanation of what socio-political purposes are served by Article III's imposition on the federal judiciary of the prerequisite that the parties to litigation be adverse, one would likely be surprised to discover that neither courts nor scholars have devoted significant attention to the question. This is so, despite the requirement's unambiguous recognition in Supreme Court doctrine.[17] This chapter therefore has two intersecting purposes: first, to provide textual, doctrinal, and theoretical analyses of the adverseness requirement of Article III, and then to test the settlement class action in terms of those three criteria. The ensuing conclusions tell us much about both Article III and the settlement class action. In addition to the conclusion that the text, history, and doctrine of Article III clearly demand that the parties to litigation be truly adverse, the analysis reveals that the adverseness requirement is dictated both by precepts of liberal democratic theory and separation of powers.

On what can be described as a "private" level, the litigant adverseness requirement is designed to ensure that those who litigate will adequately protect those absent individuals who will be significantly affected, either legally or practically, by the outcome of the litigation. I describe this as a private concern because it focuses on the private interests of individual litigants.[18] The need to allow individuals to protect and advance their own personal interests through litigation grows out of foundational precepts of autonomy grounded in principles of liberal democracy from which the adversary system has evolved.[19] Absent the assurance of litigant seriousness of purpose which the adverseness requirement seeks to guarantee, the results of litigation could significantly undermine the ability of future litigants to protect their personal interests due to the controlling impact of the resolution of the initial litigation on their subsequent legal actions. Where the future litigants are legally bound through res judicata by the results of the initial litigation, as where subsequent litigants are in privity with litigants in the first case or are members of a class action brought in the initial suit, the impact will be legally imposed. Even where subsequent litigants are not formally bound, however, in numerous situations—for example, stare decisis or claims to limited funds—they may be bound as a practical matter by the outcome of the initial suit.

On what is appropriately described as a "public" level, absence of the adverseness requirement could seriously disrupt the federal judiciary's place in the delicately structured system of separated governmental powers. As the one branch not representative of or accountable to the populace, the judiciary may threaten core democratic values unless its actions are tied to performance of the traditional judicial function of dispute resolution. To allow the judiciary to act in any other manner would threaten to usurp the lawmaking and law-enforcing powers of the other two branches of the federal government.[20] Moreover, given the judiciary's inherently passive role in the adversary system, absent the incentives to compile and present evidence and argument created by the adverseness requirement one could not be assured that a court would have sufficient information to enforce the laws fashioned by the other branches.[21] As a result of this judicial under-enforcement, the federal courts would undermine attainment of the substantive legislative goals set by Congress.[22] Thus, Article III's adverseness requirement serves as a fulcrum of performance of the judiciary's proper role within our governmental framework.

Application of these constitutional insights to the settlement class action reveals that device to be the poster child for the dangers to which violation of the adverseness requirement gives rise. First, on a purely textual level, there is no means by which the settlement class action may be deemed a truly adverse litigation. At the time the class action proceeding is begun, there exists absolutely no dispute between the parties before the court; rather, they both seek the same outcome. Neither the word *case* nor the word *controversy* may—either definitionally or historically—be deemed to include such a proceeding.[23] Moreover, the practice is inconsistent with controlling Supreme Court doctrine. Indeed, the only difference is that the unconstitutional collusion is considerably more open in the case of the settlement class action than in the case of practices invalidated in some of the Court's earlier decisions.

Far beyond the textual and doctrinal difficulties to which the settlement class action is subject, the practice's inherent lack of litigant adverseness contravenes the foundational precepts of American political and constitutional theory that underlie the adverseness requirement. Initially, the practice undermines the private goals fostered by the requirement of adverseness, by threatening the seriousness with which either side takes the litigation. Absent true adverseness between named class plaintiffs and the party opposing the class, it is impossible to ensure that the question of the class's certifiability will be fully explored by the parties. From the outset the party opposing the class, after all, is in complete accord with the named plaintiffs about the appropriateness of certification, because that party's interests will be furthered by class-wide settlement in accord with the terms of the pre-litigation agreement. The court, as a purely passive adjudicator, will therefore have at best limited ability to assure itself of the appropriateness of class certification.[24] As a result, absent class members will be bound by the terms of the settlement, regardless of whether a truly adversary adjudication of the certification issue would have resulted in a different conclusion.

Because of the fear of secret collusion between the named plaintiffs and the party opposing the class, several scholars have suggested reforms of the settlement class action procedure designed to reduce this danger.[25] While such reforms are surely commendable purely as a matter of class action policy, they fail to satisfy the constitutionally dictated adverseness requirement, because they confuse two very different types of collusion. In the class action context, the term *collusion* is used to refer to a secret, unethical agreement between the named plaintiffs and the party opposing the class.[26] For purposes of Article III's adverseness requirement, however, the term has a far broader meaning. It includes *any* suit in which, from the outset, the parties are in agreement as to the outcome. It includes fully open pre-litigation agreements between the parties, and those that are not, on their face, deemed to be unethical or unfair. Rather, Article III proceeds on the assumption that a showing of a lack of adverseness at the outset of a suit *automatically* establishes the improperly collusive nature of the suit. Article III adopts lack of adverseness as an ex ante, categorical basis on which to find inadequate representation of the interests of future litigants who are similarly situated. This is to be contrasted with the more flexible, case-by-case approach to the finding of unfair collusion advocated by would-be reformers of the settlement class action.

To be sure, use of the rigid approach adopted by Article III will, on occasion, result in overprotection. But resort to such objective standards, untied to the specifics of individual litigation, reflects a choice in favor of overprotection of absent and future litigants, rather than the assumption of the risks of under-protection inherent in any case-by-case approach. Even adoption of the reforms proposed by class action scholars designed to avoid secret and unethical collusion in the individual case would not equal Article III's ex ante categorical protection of litigant seriousness of purpose.

At the same time, the settlement class action gives rise to the systemic—or "public level"—dangers designed to be avoided by Article III's adverseness requirement. The class action, it should be recalled, is a procedural device designed to implement and enforce pre-existing substantive legal rights. To the extent that lack of adverseness leads to a lack of seriousness or good faith on the part of one or both of the litigants (and, it should be recalled, Article III categorically equates lack of adverseness with the unacceptable danger of such a risk), then use of the settlement class action gives rise to an unacceptable danger of under-enforcement of the social and economic goals embodied in the underlying substantive law. In this way, the practice threatens to disrupt attainment of legislative goals and policies.[27] Moreover, by authorizing a federal court to redistribute resources as a means of enforcing legislative directives absent an adversary adjudication, the settlement class action effectively transforms the court into an administrative body, which is more appropriately located in the executive branch. In this manner, the device improperly transfers powers reserved to the executive branch to the federal judiciary, in clear contravention of separation-of-powers dictates.[28]

The only seriously arguable defense of the settlement class action's constitutionality is a resort to naked functionalism—the argument that the settlement class action should be deemed constitutional, despite its departure from the textual dictates of Article III and its negative impact on the social and political purposes served by the adverseness required by Article III, simply because it serves a valuable social function. Absent the settlement class action, the nation would be left with a Hobson's choice between burdening the judiciary with countless individual lawsuits and denying a remedy to numerous injured victims. But while on occasion the Supreme Court has resorted to functionalist analysis in separation of powers matters,[29] the approach's use in interpretation of Article III's case-or-controversy requirement is generally not to be found. Acceptance of a functionalist justification for ignoring separation-of-powers dictates would effectively destroy the prophylactic function that such categorically framed protections are designed to establish. Moreover, even if one were to assume the validity of a functionalist analysis, there appears to be no reason that Congress could not remedy the problem by establishing a form of administrative remedial structure in the case of particular categories of suit, as has been done in the contexts of worker's compensation and black lung disease.[30] The fact that it might be more convenient for Congress to ignore the unambiguous constitutional dictates surely cannot satisfy the requirements of a reasonable functionalist approach.

The next section of this chapter explains the concept and practice of the settlement class action. In the course of this exploration, I consider judicial reaction to the device, as well as scholarly criticisms and proposals for reform.[31] In the section that follows, I explore the textual and theoretical foundations of the adverseness requirement—an inquiry that, surprisingly, has never before been undertaken by jurist or scholar, despite the undoubted recognition of the requirement in Supreme Court doctrine.[32] Finally, I apply the constitutional framework I have developed to the settlement class, concluding that the practice is, at its core, constitutionally invalid because it contravenes both the text and purposes served by Article III's case-or-controversy requirement.[33]

The chapter is designed to serve two important functions, neither of which has yet been attempted in the scholarly literature or judicial decisions. First, it provides a detailed examination of the textual and normative groundings of the adverseness requirement that the Supreme Court has regularly gleaned from the case-or-controversy requirement. Second, it explores the fatal constitutional difficulties to which the settlement class action device gives rise. It is time for commentators on class actions to move beyond the constitutional vacuum in which they traditionally view the procedure and instead to consider it within the much broader constitutional and political framework of which it is only a small part.

THE SETTLEMENT CLASS ACTION: CONCEPT AND PRACTICE

Judicial Recognition of the Settlement Class Action

In a settlement class action, the would-be class representatives and the parties opposing the class jointly seek certification of a class, on the condition that the district court approve a proposed settlement between them.[34] For purposes of the settlement class, it does not matter whether the requested settlement/certification occurs when the initial complaint is filed or subsequent to the filing. For purposes of the commencement of the class action proceeding, the two are identical: in both situations, certification of the class proceeding is requested simultaneously with the request for approval of the settlement, and in both, judicial approval of the settlement is a necessary condition for the requested certification. Although Rule 23 on its face neither authorizes nor prohibits the practice, courts that have employed the device assume that the rule at the very least authorizes use of the settlement class. While numerous cases in the lower federal courts consider the nature of the settlement class, by far the most important case on the issue was the Supreme Court's decision in *Amchem v. Windsor*.[35] *Amchem* involved an asbestos class action that, prior to certification, requested certification for settlement only under Rule 23.[36] The circuits were split on whether a settlement class had to fulfill the Rule 23(a) and (b) requirements applicable to a litigated class.[37] The Court in *Amchem* resolved their disagreement, holding that Rule 23 requirements apply equally to all certification decisions, although the suit need not satisfy the 23(b)(3) manageability prerequisite since a settlement class will never be litigated.

The plaintiffs in *Amchem* included "hundreds of thousands, perhaps millions" of persons with past exposure to asbestos products.[38] The defendants were twenty large asbestos manufacturers. The complaint, answer, stipulation of settlement, and request for class certification for the purposes of settlement-only were filed on January 15, 1993. In these documents, the class was defined to include all persons who had been "exposed—occupationally or through the occupational exposure of a spouse or household member—to asbestos . . . for which one or more of the defendants may bear legal liability," but who had not yet filed a complaint in federal or state court.[39] The agreement would have compensated those class members suffering from malignant conditions, albeit subject to caps on the number of claims payable in any given year.[40]

Two weeks later, the District Court for the Eastern District of Pennsylvania conditionally certified the class for settlement. Objectors intervened, arguing, among other things, that the settlement violated Article III's case-or-controversy requirement.[41] The district court ultimately rejected the objectors' claims, but the Third Circuit reversed. Judge Becker, speaking for the court, refused to address the constitutionality of the settlement class, holding that the appropriateness of class certification should be considered prior to jurisdictional challenges under Article III.[42] On the certification question, he concluded that the district court erred in holding that the fairness of the settlement determined its suitability for certification: Rule 23's requirements "must be satisfied without taking into account the settlement."[43] The asbestos class, as defined, did not meet Rule 23(b)(3)'s prerequisites, given the existence of individualized questions. Additionally, "intra-class conflicts precluded the class from meeting the adequacy of representation requirement" of Rule 23(a)(4).[44] The Supreme Court affirmed the dismissal, albeit on subconstitutional grounds. The Court initially held that Rule 23 requirements—including predominance, typicality, and commonality[45]—"demand undiluted, even heightened, attention in the settlement context."[46] However, "a district court need not inquire whether the case, if tried, would present intractable management problems,"[47] given that there will be no trial.

Even though it rejected the *Amchem* class for its failure to satisfy the predominance requirement, the Court implicitly approved the concept of the settlement class as an alternative form of dispute resolution. The Court, in dictum, effectively fashioned a new category of class actions: non-adjudicated classes in which the underlying substantive claims, as well as the procedural issue of the suitability of class treatment, are fully resolved by the parties prior to coming to court. Implicitly relying on the canon of constitutional avoidance, under which courts will dispose of a suit on subconstitutional grounds whenever possible, the Court reserved for a later date the question of whether the settlement class presents a justiciable case or controversy.[48] Because the Court found that the class did not satisfy Rule 23 requirements, there was no need to address the constitutionality of settlement-only certification. The Court's avoidance of the constitutional issue effectively authorized lower courts to continue using the device despite its possible constitutional infirmities.

DEALING WITH THE PROBLEMS OF THE SETTLEMENT CLASS

Existing scholarly criticisms of the settlement class are generally of the subconstitutional, or purely policy, variety, falling primarily under three headings. First, a number of scholars have argued that the negotiations that precede the development of a settlement class improperly serve as a vehicle for opportunistic behavior. A second group has argued that the average amount of damages distributed to absent class members in a typical settlement class is insufficient, as shown by the prevalence of inadequate compensation strategies up to this point. A third area of scholarship has attacked the judiciary's ability to properly assess the fairness of a settlement agreement.[49]

The Settlement Class and Opportunistic Behavior

In a traditional class action, courts are on watch for "a kind of legalized blackmail: a greedy and unscrupulous plaintiff [who] might use the threat of a large class action, which can be costly to the defendant, to extract a settlement far in excess of the individual claims' actual worth."[50] The opposite is true of the settlement class. Stephen Yeazell has summarized the defendant's motivations underlying the creation of a settlement class:

> As a rational economic actor, the defendant wants a single, comprehensive, predictable settlement, one that will enable it to pay out claims in the knowledge that it has paid all claims and can move on with its institutional life. Above all, it wants to avoid multiple rounds of escalating claims. Yet . . . it would have no way—outside bankruptcy—to control the amount of those damages . . . Enter the settlement class . . . From the defendant's standpoint, it is a business planner's dream. . . . [T]he plaintiff class has, in effect, become a defendants class.[51]

In light of these motivations, the most dominant criticism of the settlement class is that "[it] is a vehicle for . . . settlements that primarily serve the interests of defendants—by granting expansive protection from lawsuits—and of plaintiffs' counsel—by generating large fees gladly paid by defendants as a quid pro quo for finally disposing of many troublesome claims."[52] Numerous scholars have noted that in settlement class actions opportunistic behavior prevails, all too frequently "advanc[ing] only the interests of plaintiffs' attorneys, not those of the class members."[53]

John Coffee has explained the bargaining process that precedes the creation of a settlement class, focusing on what he labels "structural collusion": "suspect settlements" that stem from "the defendants' ability to shop for favorable settlement terms."[54] He argues that the settlement class practice was once dominated by fee-shopping, whereby the class attorney bargained for a lump sum and, with the defendant's consent, divided it unequally between herself and the class, resulting in disproportionately high attorneys' fees and low class recovery.[55] This technique no longer dominates the market.[56] Instead, Coffee has identified a number of "new" forms of opportunistic behavior plaguing the settlement class, two of which are relevant to my analysis: (a) the reverse auction; and (b) the inventory settlement.[57]

A reverse auction is a technique by which the defendant solicits a settlement—ordinarily in the large-claim mass tort context where, in the absence of a class, individual litigation would likely devastate the defendant financially[58]—by organizing individual settlement negotiations with various plaintiffs' attorneys.[59] Pursuant to these negotiations, plaintiffs' counsel compete against one another to secure the position as class counsel, motivated by the attorney's fees that will accompany settlement.[60] The lowest bid for the value of the class's claims wins. This practice has been widely thought to deprive the class of the fair value of their claims.[61] An inventory settlement, in contrast, involves a plaintiffs' attorney who represents a large number of individual plaintiffs with claims pending against a single defendant. For the purpose of gaining leverage in the settlement of these individual claims, plaintiffs' counsel offers to independently file, request certification of, and settle the claims of a class of future plaintiffs.[62] The class is then drawn to exclude currently pending claims. In this scenario, class counsel has little or no incentive to haggle over the price of settlement for the class. Rather, she uses the class as a bargaining chip to secure a separate, more favorable settlement for her current inventory of clients. This technique seriously threatens the right of future plaintiffs to adequate representation and their interest in the fair value of their claims.[63]

Scholarly Proposals for Reform of the Settlement Class Device

In response to the numerous problems posed by the settlement class practice, a number of scholars have recommended changes to the operation of Rule 23's procedural safeguards. The proposals for reform fall into three general categories: (1) heightening of standards governing selection of class counsel; (2) enhanced monitoring of attorney conduct, for the purpose of identifying and regulating conflicts of interest; and (3) creation of criteria to identify signs of opportunistic behavior.[64]

Professor Coffee has identified three needed reforms. First, to prevent the defendant from hand-picking plaintiffs' counsel, he would "require the court to oversee the selection of the plaintiffs' counsel, after adequate notice was first given to the specialized bar handling the specific mass tort that certification of a settlement class was contemplated."[65] Second, he proposes using "broad and representative steering committees, deliberately chosen to mirror the composition of the plaintiffs' bar," which would ratify the settlement before it could be submitted to the court for approval.[66] Third, he recommends banning classes "defined exclusively in terms of future claimants," noting they are "silent and passive, and thus . . . cannot monitor their attorneys."[67]

Professor Yeazell, "reflecting on the medieval experience with representative litigation," has suggested that, when the interests of absent class members are at stake, the Court should prohibit the defendant from "approach[ing] . . . a lawyer (and certainly not a lawyer already representing a plaintiff with interests adverse to those of defendant)."[68] Instead, the defendant, if she wishes to initiate class-wide settlement negotiations, must approach "unrepresented parties and offer them terms on behalf of the class, notifying them that they would have to obtain representation."[69] According to Yeazell, this scheme would create a market in "plaintiffs' claims," "precipitat[ing] a frenzy of lawyer's bidding for the representative rights,"[70] which, in turn, would produce settlement terms "better [for the class members] than that originally proposed."[71]

The Unexplored Link Between Unconstitutional Non-Adverseness and Opportunistic Behavior

As demonstrated by this brief survey of the literature, there are numerous changes that could be made to the settlement class device, as well as to the procedures that govern settlement-only certification and settlement approval, to make it more fair or effective. Class action scholars writing in the field have generally done an excellent job of pinpointing the problems with the settlement class, as well as offering suggestions for internal reform. Nevertheless, the purpose and intended scope of these suggestions are far too narrow to rectify the fundamental problems posed by the settlement class.

As previously noted, current proposals for reform have been of the subconstitutional variety, focusing on the rules and regulations that govern the settlement class. As a result, they fail to address the root cause of the problems to which they have pointed: the non-adverseness of the parties. The lack of disagreement between defendant and class counsel as to the desired outcome of the suit ultimately renders ineffective or inadequate all proposed reforms, which rely on hit-or-miss individualized inquiries to assess the legitimacy of the settlement class in the specific case. When the plaintiffs and defendant agree on settlement terms and the desirability of certification prior to coming to court, neither party has the incentive to challenge such important questions as whether class representation is "adequate" or the claims are "typical" of the class as a whole.[72] This inherently deprives the court of the benefit of adversarial litigation concerning the satisfaction of Rule 23's requirements, thereby seriously limiting its ability to protect absent class members.[73] Imposing additional burdens on the parties—over which there will also be no disagreement between them, given that both seek the same outcome—is likely to be no more effective than are current requirements in preventing or remedying opportunistic behavior, because of the inherent lack of adverseness between the parties.

Moreover, even if the proposed reforms were to prove successful in remedying the settlement class's subconstitutional defects, they nevertheless fail to address the practice's inherent unconstitutionality. This failure is reflected in the scholarly approach toward "collusion," or the opportunistic behavior that so often accompanies the development of a settlement class.[74] As noted previously, settlement class action courts have defined "collusion" narrowly, to require a secret, unethical agreement between two parties to a suit.[75] Civil procedure scholars have echoed this approach. A review of the literature indicates that most, if not all, scholars currently writing in this area assume that in order to be illegitimate, the settlement class must involve secret criminal or unethical cooperation between plaintiff and defendant, designed to defraud absent class members, in the individual case.[76]

In contrast to the case-by-case focus employed by class action scholars, Article III employs a far more categorical and prophylactic conception of "collusion." Article III makes an ex ante categorical judgment that a non-adversarial suit is inherently collusive and therefore in violation of constitutional norms. As the Court in *Poe v. Ullman*, construing Article III, explained:

> [The case] may not be "collusive" . . . in the sense of merely colorable disputes got up to secure an advantageous ruling from the Court. [But] [t]he Court has found unfit for adjudication any cause that "is not in any real sense adversary," that "does not assume the "honest and actual antagonistic assertion of rights" to be adjudicated—a safeguard essential to the integrity of the judicial process, and one which we have held to be indispensable to adjudication of constitutional questions by this Court.[77]

This distinction underscores the fundamental inadequacy of reforms proposed by such eminent class action scholars as Coffee and Yeazell. To be sure, these reforms may assist the court in identifying, on a case-by-case basis, conspiracies or attempts to criminally defraud absent class members (behavior that is likely to be present in only a handful of settlement classes). However, they are incapable of addressing the settlement class's fundamental constitutional defect, given that *all* settlement classes—not merely those involving unethical attorney behavior—are, by definition, non-adversarial. An adversarial dispute, according to the text, jurisprudence, and purposes of Article III, cannot be said to exist at the time the class action proceeding begins. At that point, the litigants differ over absolutely nothing. They have agreed on the terms of both certification and settlement prior to the filing of the class proceeding. In fact, the only conceivable reason that class counsel in this position files a complaint and request for certification with the court, rather than simply embodying the terms of their private agreement in an enforceable contract, is to bind absent class members to a settlement negotiated in their absence.

My analysis begins where current courts and scholars have left off: with the constitutional implications of Article III and the adverseness requirement. This analysis demonstrates that the settlement class action is, at its core, inconsistent with the text, history, and purposes of Article III's case-or-controversy requirement.

ADVERSENESS AND THE CASE-OR-CONTROVERSY REQUIREMENT

Adverseness and Constitutional Text

To understand the constitutional implications that flow from the settlement class's lack of adverseness, one must engage in an analysis of the foundations of Article III's adverseness requirement. Article III, §2 extends federal judicial power solely to the adjudication of "cases" or "controversies." Certain categories of suits, particularly those falling within the diversity jurisdiction, must involve a "controversy." The remainder, primarily concerning federal question suits, must qualify as "cases."

The definition of the term *controversy* is straightforward, having been construed consistently throughout the centuries. A current-day legal dictionary defines the word as a "disagreement or a dispute."[78] A non-legal dictionary offers a similar definition: a "controversy" is "a dispute, especially a public one, between sides holding opposing views."[79] This modern interpretation is consistent with the meaning given the term by dictionaries at the time of the framing.[80] For example, "controversy" was defined by a 1755 English dictionary as a "debate" or "dispute,"[81] a definition that mirrors the word's etymology. The root of "controversy" is Latin, from *controversus*, which means "disputed."[82] From these definitions, one can fairly conclude that the word *controversy* plainly requires a substantial disagreement between parties as to the suit's preferred outcome.[83]

The term *case* is arguably more ambiguous. For example, a current-day dictionary includes eleven different definitions of the word, including the broad description of "case" as "an instance of something."[84] However, when one takes into account textual context and circumstance, the term's meaning when used in Article III becomes readily apparent. For example, current-day legal dictionaries define "case" as a justiciable "action or suit,"[85] or an "argument."[86] Eighteenth-century dictionaries suggest a similarly narrow reading of the word in the legal context. A legal dictionary from 1773 contains no entry for "case."[87] Nevertheless, it references—seven times—the phrase, "adverse party" in the course of defining related legal terms such as *demurrer, duces tecum,* and *interrogatory,* suggesting a strong focus on adverseness at the time of the framing.[88]

Even if a textualist analysis were not, standing alone, unambiguously to establish the outer perimeters of a constitutionally permissible "case," more than three hundred years of legal practice and tradition establish a presumption that the word *case,* like the word *controversy,* requires an adversarial suit.[89] Initially, the early English common law system mandated an adversarial relationship between litigants, with few exceptions.[90] While not conclusive evidence of the Framers' intent, this history indicates that in adopting a legal system based largely on the English common law system, the Constitution's drafters likely sought to incorporate a focus on litigant adverseness. Second, nothing in the Framers' records supports a substantive distinction between the words *case* and *controversy* for purposes of adverseness.[91] Indeed, the framers' deliberations indicate that they were committed to the proposition that "jurisdiction given [to the judiciary] was constructively limited to cases of a Judiciary Nature."[92] A "case of a Judiciary Nature," in turn, was defined by early American practice and tradition as excluding feigned, non-adversarial suits.[93] Third, since the late nineteenth century, the Court has conflated the terms *case* and *controversy,*[94] holding that any difference in their meaning is neither supported by historical practice nor the Framers' intent.[95] In light of such history, there is a heavy burden on anyone who suggests that the word *case* was designed to have a far broader reach than the word *controversy.*[96]

The Adverseness Requirement in Supreme Court Doctrine

The Court has widely held that the case-or-controversy language of Article III mandates litigant adverseness.[97] For a suit to be justiciable, according to the Court, the parties must maintain "adverse legal interests" throughout, and their dispute must be "definite and concrete."[98] The leading decision on the subject is *Muskrat v. United States,*[99] where the Court considered two suits by Cherokee citizens to determine the constitutionality of the Act of Congress of April 26, 1906. That Act accomplished two things. First, it increased the number of persons, primarily children whose parents had enrolled as members of the Cherokee tribe post-1902, entitled to share in the distribution of Cherokee lands. Second, it limited the ability of Cherokees, post-distribution, to dispose of their lands. Both suits were initiated under an Act of Congress, passed in 1907, which provided that the specific individuals involved could litigate the constitutionality of the 1906 Act in the Court of Claims.[100]

The Court concluded that federal jurisdiction could not constitutionally extend to the case, despite the express grant of jurisdiction by Congress. The suit constituted "neither more nor less . . . than an attempt to provide for a judicial determination, final in this court, of the constitutional validity of an act of Congress," rather than an actionable, adversarial dispute.[101] While the Cherokees did possess a legal interest in the lands and were allegedly injured by the 1906 Act, the defendant in the case—the government—had "no interest adverse to the claimants."[102] Even if the government does have an abstract interest in establishing the constitutionality of a federal statute, the Court held that this interest was nothing more than de minimis and was insufficient to establish federal jurisdiction.[103]

The Court's conclusion that the United States government was not truly adverse has been questioned.[104] Nevertheless, its constitutional reasoning, as an abstract matter, has never been seriously doubted. The Court relied on the existence of an adverseness requirement, embodied by Article III's case-or-controversy language:

> The exercise of the judicial power is limited to "cases" and "controversies" . . . By cases and controversies are intended the claims of litigants brought before the courts for determination by such regular proceedings as are established by law or custom . . . [and] the existence of present or possible adverse parties whose contentions are submitted to the court for adjudication.[105]

According to the *Muskrat* Court's logic, in any suit where no adverse legal interests are at stake the judiciary has no authority to reach the merits of the underlying issues.

The Court has consistently cited *Muskrat* for the proposition that adverseness plays an essential role in an adversary system, and in appropriately restraining judicial power, has applied its logic to a variety of fact patterns.[106] For example, in *United States v. Johnson*,[107] the Court dismissed a non-adversarial suit, finding it to be in violation of the dictates of Article III. Unlike *Muskrat*, where the parties' non-adverseness flowed from a lack of disagreement as to the desired outcome, the parties in *Johnson* explicitly arranged to bring a non-adversarial case to the court, to further the defendant's economic interests.[108] The plaintiff, a friend of the defendant, had no role in the proceedings. He did not pay the lawyer who appeared in his name, never saw the complaint, and did not learn of the lower court's decision until reading about it in the newspaper.[109] The Court refused to reach the merits of the plaintiff's claims. There was no "genuine adversary issue between the parties" as required by Article III, it held, given that the parties agreed on desired outcome, as well on the underlying facts of the case.[110]

One arguable aberration is the Court's decision in *Swift v. United States*,[111] where the government simultaneously filed a complaint, citing violations of the Sherman Antitrust and Clayton Acts, and a pre-negotiated consent decree enjoining the violations. The district court approved the decree and held that it would retain jurisdiction to take all action "necessary or appropriate for the carrying out and enforcement of this decree."[112] Four years later, two motions to vacate the decree were filed by two separate defendants in the case. Among other things, they alleged that the Court lacked jurisdiction because "there was no case-or-controversy within the meaning of . . . Article III."[113] The Court rejected this argument, holding that, despite the concurrent filing of the complaint and decree, the district court had Article III authority to approve the decree.

The Court in *Swift* did not believe its conclusion was inconsistent with the Court's earlier holdings requiring litigant adverseness. It is difficult, however, to understand the Court's logic. First, the *Swift* Court distinguished the consent decree from precedents in which the Court had held a non-adversarial dispute to be non-justiciable, such as *Lord v. Veazie*. A consent decree, unlike the private contract involved in *Veazie*, "deals primarily with past violations, but with threatened future ones."[114] Under this rule, the *Swift* case was justiciable because of the credible threat of impending adverseness, stemming from future statutory violations.[115] The settlement class does not present a comparable threat: the conflicting interests of the parties to the suit are resolved at the time of settlement.[116] Except for execution of the agreement, there is no remaining area of potential disagreement.

Under precedent such as *Muskrat* and *Johnson*, the facts in *Swift* constitute a paradigmatically unconstitutional scenario: The parties are non-adversarial at the time that they decide to involve the court, having mooted the critical issues in dispute between them. The only reason they seek judicial involvement is to codify their private agreement in a court-sanctioned contract. Under the prophylactic adverseness rule adopted in cases such as *Johnson* and *Muskrat*, which requires litigant adverseness as a preemptive protection against the judicial exercise of non-judicial functions, the pre-negotiated consent decree falls far beyond the scope of a court's Article III powers. Because the *Swift* Court purported to adhere to the Court's earlier holdings adopting adverseness, and because *Swift* is inherently inconsistent with the logic of those decisions, it is *Swift*, rather than the earlier decisions, that should be deemed invalid.

GOING BEYOND THE TEXT:
THE SOCIO-POLITICAL PURPOSES SERVED
BY THE ADVERSENESS REQUIREMENT

The Two Levels of Constitutional Purpose

According to both textual and doctrinal interpretations of Article III, the case-or-controversy requirement unambiguously mandates the existence of an adversarial relationship between opposing litigants. However, neither constitutional text nor case law offers anything approaching an adequate explanation of the purposes served by this restriction on judicial authority. Thus, one must now face a more difficult question: Why, purely as a normative matter, is adverseness an important element in the nation's constitutional democratic structure? This is a particularly pressing inquiry, given the lack of scholarly attention to the issue.[117] A thorough search of the literature indicates that no scholar has yet even attempted to comprehensively evaluate either the individual or systemic interests served by adverseness. In light of this silence, exploration of this issue is an extremely important undertaking. Many scholars of separation of powers reject what they deem the overly formalistic emphasis on textual interpretation, even where text appears unambiguous.[118] At the very least, the argument proceeds, textual directives may be overcome by social needs.[119] It is only if we are able to articulate truly compelling normative rationales underlying the adverseness requirement, then, that we can comprehend the vitally important role that it serves. It is possible, however, to employ a form of reverse engineering to infer the normative goals to be fostered by the requirement.

Initially, litigant adverseness serves as an essential ingredient in the protections and incentives upon which the adversary system depends, including the creation of a well-balanced, well-developed record to facilitate informed judicial decision making. These incentives, in turn, function as a necessary part of the liberal democratic model, which posits that an individual can be bound—legally or practically—by a judgment only when she has had the opportunity to advance her own interests in litigation, employ an advocate to do so, or, at the very least, have her interests represented by one possessing a strong incentive to advance the position.

The adverseness requirement also serves a larger, systemic purpose, that of limiting the judiciary's role in relation to its two co-equal branches. First, the lack of adverseness disrupts Congress's underlying assumptions in choosing a private remedy as the appropriate method by which to punish and deter statutory violations, including that statutory rights will be litigated in a traditional adversary proceeding. When Congress creates a private compensatory remedy for violation of a statutorily dictated behavioral standard, it is seeking simultaneously to accomplish two goals: To compensate the victim, and to deter future violations. Thus, a private compensatory remedy is appropriately viewed as a hybrid of both private and public goals. Were the judiciary to permit a non-adverse litigant to under-enforce the substantive public goals embodied in federal law, legislative goals in creating a private remedy in the first place would be undermined. Second, with respect to judicial-executive relations, the judicial distribution of private resources absent litigant adverseness constitutes the judicial exercise of an inherently non-judicial, administrative function, threatening the separation of powers. Each of these three values will be further explored below.

Private Concerns: The Litigant-Oriented Interest in Adverseness

The requirement that litigants on opposite sides have "adverse" legal interests for a suit to be justiciable is appropriately viewed as a logical outgrowth of the nation's commitment to an adversary system. Both the adverseness requirement and the adversary system of which it is a part, in the Supreme Court's words, derive from a recognition that the "adjudicatory process is most securely founded when it is exercised under the impact of a lively conflict between antagonistic demands, actively pressed, which make resolution of the controverted issue a practical necessity."[120] Indeed, adverseness and the adversary system depend on one another: In the absence of litigant adverseness, the very DNA of the adversary system, which relies on the parties' competitive incentives to investigate the facts and to research and analyze the governing law that grows out of the party's adverseness to her opponent, is transformed. That transformation, in turn, threatens the core assumptions and values on which our legal system depends, primarily the protection of the interests of individuals who may be bound, legally or practically, by the court's judgment. Particularly in group litigation, where individual participation in court proceedings is impractical and the outcome will have formal res judicata impact on absent litigants, the required adverseness between litigants serves as an essential safeguard. It ensures that the group representative has the necessary incentive to seek an outcome that embodies the legal interests of absent but bound individuals. By contrast, when, from the outset of the litigation, the in-court representative seeks the same outcome as the opposing party, she lacks incentive to disclose information to the court that may reflect negatively on the joint, non-adversarial agreement, thereby hindering the court's ability to protect individuals who will—practically, if not legally— be bound by its judgment.

The Adversary System: A Brief Examination

The adversary system can be characterized by its two main features: party control over evidence production and argumentation[121] and a passive adjudicator who acts on the basis of the information presented by the parties.[122] The former, according to Lon Fuller, is the adversary system's "distinguishing characteristic."[123] "[I]t confers on the affected party a peculiar form of participation in the decision, that of presenting proofs and reasoned arguments for a decision in his favor."[124] With regard to the latter, Judge Marvin Frankel has explained: "[t]he plainest thing about the advocate is that he is indeed partisan, and thus exercises a function sharply divergent from that of the judge . . . It is [the judge's] assigned task to be nonpartisan and to promote through the trial [procedures] an objective search for the truth."[125]

The adversary system may be contrasted with the civil law or "inquisitorial" systems in place in various Latin American and European nations.[126] The two systems vary in both ends and means. First, the inquisitorial system is unqualifiedly focused on "ascertain[ing] the truth of the contested matter for itself," a goal that justifies active court involvement in the development of a case's factual and legal foundations.[127] This obligation "has no counterpart in American courts," which are instead focused on party-oriented procedural guarantees.[128] In fact, "[e]mployed by interested parties, the [adversarial system] often achieves truth only as a convenience, a byproduct, or an accidental approximation."[129]

On a procedural level, the two systems also differ in important ways. As a general matter, the inquisitorial court "has primary responsibility for investigating the facts, a load borne primarily by litigants in the United States through both the formal discovery process and informal investigation."[130] This affects the roles performed by both the litigant and the court. While litigants in an inquisitorial system play a minimal role in the substantive development and disposition of the case, the adversary system is far more democratic,[131] placing responsibility over the substantive disposition of the case in the hands of the parties. Moreover, while "inquisitorial trials are conducted by the state's representative"—the judge—"[i]n the adversary system, the judge is a relatively passive party who essentially referees investigations carried out by attorneys."[132] As a result, the American legal system depends heavily on an adversarial relationship between litigants for the resolution of difficult factual and legal questions.[133] The federal courts were constitutionally constructed as passive entities, and thus "need help to adjudicate properly," including a proper, adversarial "context in which to consider the principles they are called upon to expound."[134]

A comparative analysis of the benefits and disadvantages of these two systems is beyond the scope of my inquiry.[135] Suffice it to say that American judges, trained in and accustomed to an adversary structure, are "ill-equipped for effective inquisitorial judging."[136] Not only is an investigatory or managerial judicial role incompatible with the highly entrenched adversary norms and customs in the U.S. legal system,[137] but American judges lack the investigatory resources available to judges in an inquisitorial system. The federal judiciary operates on a limited budget and with restricted fact-finding powers, limiting its capabilities outside the context of an adversarial dispute.[138] Moreover, even if inquisitorial judging techniques were technically compatible with current legal structures, as I subsequently demonstrate, they are not desirable given the democratic premises on which the nation's adversary system is based.

Liberal Democratic Theory and the Foundations of the Adversary System

As noted by one scholar, the "system of adjudication we choose . . . speaks volumes about our more general philosophy of government."[139] The adversary system finds its roots in liberal democratic theory. It flows logically from our societal commitment to self-determination and, to the extent feasible, individual autonomy. At the heart of liberal democratic theory are two visions of adversary theory. One is "self-protective" and conceptualizes the right to sue as a mechanism by which each individual can, as I have put it, " 'watch his back' because someone inevitably will attempt to insert a knife into it."[140] The second views individual consent as a vital part of all political activity, positing that " 'without an opportunity to participate in the regulation of affairs in which one has an interest, it is hard to discover one's own needs and wants.' "[141] These views are jointly premised on the theory that the best way to resolve conflict is "through the use of democratic [legal] processes."[142] A participatory form of adjudication "shifts power to those best equipped to use it: the individuals who will be affected by the decisions."[143]

While the concerns of liberal adversary theory are of course most intense when the private party's legal interests are formally impacted—for example, through the doctrines of claim or issue preclusion—it is important to recognize that the interests of non-litigants will often be affected significantly on a purely practical level by the results of litigation. This impact may derive from a variety of sources. First, while not as legally binding as claim or issue preclusion, the doctrine of stare decisis deriving from a case will often have as virtually a dispositive impact on subsequent suits. This is particularly true in what might be described as "same situation stare decisis"—in other words, cases that give rise to an identical legal issue and that involve the same set of factual circumstances as the initial case. Here, neither issue nor claim preclusion apply because of a lack of privity among the parties in the initial suit and those in the subsequent suits.[144] Nevertheless, as a practical matter it is highly unlikely, in such a situation, that a court in subsequent suits will reach a conclusion that differs dramatically from its decision in the initial case. Second, a decision in an initial suit could indirectly impact future litigants, by so altering circumstances or controlling resources that they are effectively—though not legally—precluded. In these situations, it would be infeasible to require that future litigants have been formally represented in the initial suit. Indeed, in certain situations—for example, in product liability suits, where future plaintiffs have not, at the time of the initial suit, suffered any injury—such formal representation would be impossible. Nevertheless, the basic concern for the individual that characterizes both liberal democratic theory and the adversary system which flows from it dictates the need for the litigant in the initial suit to represent fully the position that similarly situated litigants would take in subsequent suits.

The adverseness requirement may appropriately be seen as a device designed to protect the interests of future litigants when those interests may in some sense be impacted by resolution of the initial action. Indeed, a lack of adverseness in the initial suit automatically gives rise to suspicions about the motivations of the litigants. After all, to the extent that all the parties wish to do is to legally codify their agreement or the already-reached resolution of a prior dispute, they need merely embody their agreement in a legally enforceable private contract. There is absolutely no need to proceed to litigation—unless, of course, they wish to impact the legal interests of others. The very fact that both sides to a litigation are in agreement from the outset, then, renders the action inherently suspect.

It is perhaps conceivable that, in certain instances, the absence of adverseness will not actually imply suspiciousness of motivation. However, commitment to a prerequisite of litigant adverseness represents a choice in favor of an ex ante categorical approach, rather than a case-by-case inquiry into litigant seriousness of purpose. The choice of a categorically applied rule represents a decision in favor of possible over-protection, rather than the risk of under-protection normally associated with a more elusive case-by-case inquiry, where there always exists the danger that a court will mistakenly fail to recognize the improper motivation of non-adverse parties. Because an absence of adversity will, in the large majority of cases, signal the failure of one litigant to protect the interests of future litigants whose legal rights will be affected (if only as a practical matter), Article III is properly construed to employ the absence of adverseness at the outset of a suit as a rule of thumb by which to measure a litigant's lack of seriousness or good faith.

A similar approach to a different aspect of Article III's case-or-controversy requirement was suggested a number of years ago by Professor Lea Brilmayer.[145] She focused on the "unfairness of holding later litigants to an adverse judgment in which they may not have been properly represented,"[146] arguing that Article III's case-or-controversy requirement—particularly the injury-in-fact inquiry—functions to ensure that the interests of those litigants are taken into consideration by the court issuing judgment.

Specifically, Brilmayer identified ideological litigation, where the plaintiff challenges legislation "without the traditional personal stake" in the outcome, as a serious threat to future litigants.[147] If courts were permitted to hear suits by uninjured plaintiffs, two negative effects would flow, she argued. First, the court's judgment in that case may—as a practical matter, if not a legal one—bar future litigation by individuals actually harmed by the operation of the challenged statute. At the very least, it will create persuasive precedent that a future court may follow when the two situations are "indistinguishable."[148] Second, she asserted that the ideological litigant, because he is uninjured, lacks the incentive to serve as a champion for the cause. Absent the self-interest that flows from concrete injury, the plaintiff cannot effectively represent the interests of third parties not currently before the courts, who nevertheless will be affected by the court's judgment. The injured individual, Brilmayer argued, is more likely to fight for the rights of all individuals similarly situated, now or in the future, as well as possess the incentive to invest both time and resources in the suit—not necessarily because of an altruistic desire to assist others, but because of the desire to protect or advance his own interests. Recognizing the role that such incentives play in the proper functioning of an adversary system,[149]

Brilmayer advocated strict adherence to the injury-in-fact requirement of Article III for standing.[150] These limitations "ensure the accountability of representatives" by guaranteeing that "the individuals most affected by the challenged activity will have a role in the challenge."[151]

One may reasonably question the accuracy of Brilmayer's unsupported assumption that it is only injured plaintiffs who will fully and enthusiastically assert their interests. A plaintiff who has been injured only minimally will naturally lack incentive to argue her case to the fullest. In contrast, an uninjured plaintiff driven by ideological considerations who possesses substantial resources may well develop her case to the fullest.[152] For present purposes, however, that issue is beside the point. Like Professor Brilmeyer, I glean from both Article III's case-or-controversy requirement and the political principles of liberal theory that underlie the adversary system a concern for protection of the interests of future litigants, and urge the shaping of the requirement's interpretation to protect those interests. This concern, in turn, leads to the conclusion that the case-or-controversy requirement demands true adverseness between opposing litigants at the outset of a suit, because absent such adverseness we cannot be assured that the litigants will effectively protect the interests of affected individuals not currently before the court.

There are several conceivable problems with the argument that the adverseness requirement protects future similarly situated litigants by assuring litigant enthusiasm and good faith. While there is a certain degree of truth to each of them, I believe that on balance, they do not undermine the essential elements of my analysis. First, it might be argued that my theory proves too much, because litigants may always settle a suit at any point. Even certified class actions may be settled, subject to judicial approval.[153] If, as I assert, the absence of adverseness at the outset of a suit undermines the protection of future similarly situated litigants and therefore a rigid rule demanding adverseness must be imposed, then should not an absence of adverseness that necessarily comes with settlement at *any point* in the litigation process be prohibited?[154] Since prohibition of all settlement would be absurd, the argument proceeds, the absence of adverseness at the outset of a suit should logically also be acceptable. It is not true, however, that the dangers to the interests of future litigants will always be as great from a lack of adverseness due to settlement in the midst of litigation as they will from a lack of adverseness at the outset of a suit. For one thing, when a suit that is adverse at the outset settles during the course of litigation, we can be reasonably assured that the suit was not brought solely for the purpose of legally or practically binding future litigants. When a non-adverse suit is brought, in contrast, it is difficult to understand why the case has been brought to court in the first place, save for an attempt to bind future litigants.[155] The inherent existence of this suspicious motivation automatically distinguishes the two situations. Moreover, when an ongoing suit is settled, it is highly unlikely that any binding legal precedent that might negatively impact similarly situated parties will be promulgated as a result. In contrast, when a non-adverse suit is brought, for reasons already discussed, it is likely that it is filed for the very reason of obtaining some form of binding declaration as to the state of the law; again, why else file a suit in the first place?

A second argument that might be fashioned against my argument is that the constitutional guarantee of due process[156] already assures protection of absent parties whose interests will be affected by the outcome of the suit, rendering the adverseness requirement unnecessary for this purpose. But while due process is, in fact, designed to protect the interests of affected parties to a limited extent, by no means does it adequately perform the protective function designed to be achieved by Article III's adverseness requirement. Initially, due process protects only those who are *legally bound* by the decision in the initial suit. The adverseness requirement, on the other hand, should be deemed to protect those *practically* affected by resolution of the initial action, whose interests do not fall within the protective umbrella of due process. Moreover, the due process protection of absent parties involves a case-by-case determination of the adequacy of the representation of absent parties by a litigant to an ongoing suit. It is certainly conceivable that the litigant could be found to satisfy the objective indicia of adequacy—for example, interests identical to those of absent but affected parties or possession of adequate resources—yet still not possess the incentive or intent to advocate his position to the fullest.[157] Because it will be all but impossible to ascertain existence of this intent in the individual case, the adverseness requirement imposes an ex ante categorical approach, in lieu of such an individualized inquiry.

Of course, it is conceivable that a litigant may outwardly present all the indicia of adverseness, yet in reality be secretly acting in consort with his opponent. In such a situation, it is up to the court in the individual case to attempt to ascertain the validity of the asserted adverseness, and it is certainly conceivable that it will fail in that endeavor. But recognition of this possibility in no way logically leads to a lack of concern for the absence of adverseness when it is recognized from the outset.

Finally, one might argue that adverseness does not necessarily guarantee that an in-court representative will protect the interests of those who may be impacted, legally or practically, by the court's judgment, because there are a number of other factors that might affect the quality of representation. However, adverseness is only the first of many categorical hurdles in establishing Article III jurisdiction. If the parties are adverse, they will still need to satisfy other constitutional requirements flowing from Article III's case-or-controversy dictate, including standing, ripeness, and mootness. Additionally, in most suits, where the in-court litigant seeks the same outcome as the group who will be affected by the court's judgment, and an outcome different from that sought by the adverse party, their interests *will* be one and the same: to secure maximum recovery, monetary or otherwise, from either the same or a similar wrongdoer. In that situation, the representative has an incentive, rooted in her own self-interest, to utilize all available tools to advocate for the interests of the affected individuals. While adverseness may not always be a sufficient condition of adequate representation, then, it is always a necessary condition.

Public Concerns: The Systemic Interests in Adverseness

Not only does the adverseness requirement function to protect the interests of absent parties, but it also plays an indispensable political role within our system of separated powers. The structural concerns implicated by the adverseness requirement are twofold. First, Congress, in setting forth a private remedy as a statutory enforcement mechanism, legislates against an "adversarial backdrop."[158] It assumes that a private remedy simultaneously serves as an effective tool for the punishment of civil wrongdoing *and* the deterrence of future statutory violations, primarily because the private right will be litigated in the traditional adversary form, with all of its attendant incentives and protections. In asserting jurisdiction of a suit seeking a private remedy in the absence of adverseness, the judiciary risks the undercompensation of victims and the transformation of the underlying substantive law.

Adverseness also serves a critical function in distinguishing between the roles constitutionally intended for the judiciary and those to be exercised by the executive branch. In addition to adjudicating cases or controversies, administrative agencies that perform executive functions are solely responsible for distributing private resources in the absence of an adversarial dispute. These agencies, when legislatively empowered to do so, may function as administrators, deciding in the individual situation whether claimants are entitled to compensation for their claims, even in the absence of a formal adversary proceeding. When a federal court, from the outset of a suit, does nothing more than supervise and administer the redistribution of assets dictated by an agreement previously reached by the parties, it is effectively operating as an administrative entity, appropriately found within the executive branch. When an Article III court takes cognizance of a non-adversarial suit, then, it steps into a sphere expressly committed by the Constitution to the discretion of the executive department, threatening the separation of powers.

The Hybrid Model: The Intersection of Private Adversarial Litigation and Public Goals

The legislative decision to make available a private remedy assumes that the statutory provision of monetary damages will motivate the initiation of private litigation in the event of civil wrongdoing, incidentally advancing the statute's social goals. An injured individual, given her interest in compensation, is assumed to have the natural incentive to identify and prosecute wrongdoing, for the purposes of making herself "financially whole."[159] While compensatory awards are first and foremost intended to reimburse the victim for injury, they are, as I have previously argued, "simultaneously and incidentally [designed to] punish and deter lawless, harm-inducing conduct by requiring the defendant to bear the financial burden of providing that compensation."[160] Adoption of a private damage remedy, then, is premised on the assumption that the private individual will functionally assume the role of a quasi-private attorney general, especially in the context of the class action where the private remedy enables one person to bring suit on behalf of a large portion of the general population.[161] Though both the victim and her attorney may be primarily or even exclusively motivated by considerations of personal economic gain, this view deems private litigation to be integrally intertwined with attainment of the statute's social goals. The empowerment of private individuals as quasi-private attorneys general protects the public interest by enforcing the public policies embodied in applicable statutes.[162]

By assuming jurisdiction of a non-adverse suit, the court runs the risk of under-enforcing legislative schemes. Specifically, litigant non-adverseness disrupts the incentives and protections upon which the legislative choice of a private remedy is founded, thereby threatening achievement of the underlying goals of the legislation. It is conceivable, of course, that private litigants will choose not to enforce private compensatory rights vested in them by Congress. Alternatively, they may seek to enforce those remedies, yet ultimately agree to settle their claims for far less than they are objectively worth. In this sense, resort to a private compensatory remedy as a means of enforcing substantive social policies is likely not to be as reliable as, for example, administrative or criminal enforcement. Nevertheless, for reasons already discussed, these dangers are far less than those presented by non-adverse litigation. Initially, at least where the economic and physical harm is sufficiently great to justify resort to litigation, the likelihood that a large percentage of victims will choose not to sue should be small. Additionally, where truly adverse litigation is brought, the legal impact of settlement on similarly situated victims is likely to be limited due to the absence of legally controlling conclusions by the court.[163] Finally, because of the inherent suspiciousness of non-adverse litigation in the first place,[164] there is greater reason to trust the incentive structure in operation when truly adverse litigation is settled.

THE ADMINISTRATIVE COMPENSATION MODEL

The Role of Adverseness in Defining Judicial and Executive Tasks

Article II, §3 of the Constitution defines the executive role in part by means of the so-called Take Care Clause, which provides that the Executive ensure "that the Laws be faithfully executed."[165] Typically, this responsibility consists of the "alteration of social relations or individual status in a specific fact situation, . . . divorced from an adversarial adjudication."[166] In contrast, the jurisdiction of Article III courts "is limited to cases and controversies in such form that the judicial power is capable of acting on them" and does not extend to "administrative or legislative issues or controversies."[167] For example, among other things, the executive branch is responsible for initiating public litigation and creating executive agencies that regulate private behavior. In the narrow instance where a dispute arises over the application of the underlying substantive law to a particular state of affairs, the court takes over enforcement responsibility from the executive branch. For those parties, the judiciary controls the decision of how to best "execute" the law.

The point at which responsibility shifts from the executive to the judiciary is defined by the case-or-controversy element of Article III, including the adverseness requirement. This bright line was first introduced in *United States v. Todd,*[168] in which the Court addressed the Article III implications of the congressional revision of the Act struck down two years earlier in *Hayburn's Case.*[169] An individual had applied for pension benefits in New York Circuit Court. That court held that Article III judges could legitimately act as administrative commissioners in their individual capacities—as opposed to "as a Circuit Court"—and issued an opinion that "Todd ought to be placed on the pension list."[170] The Supreme Court reversed. It held that the Act "could not be construed to give [authority] to the judges out of court as commissioners."[171] Addressing whether pension administration was a proper function for the Circuit Court sitting in its Article III capacity, the Court answered in the negative: The decision of whether individuals are entitled to pension benefits is not the exercise of "judicial power within the meaning of the Constitution," but rather is the type of power typically exercised by administrative "commissioners," such as the Secretary of the Treasury.[172]

There do exist two prominent instances in which the Supreme Court has upheld legislative schemes that seemingly contravened the case-or-controversy requirement by vesting in the hands of Article III judges certain functions that do not directly involve the adjudication of adversarial suits. In *Mistretta v. United States,*[173] the Court approved the required participation of Article III judges on the federal Sentencing Commission, whose function was to promulgate sentencing guidelines for federal crimes. In *Morrison v. Olson,*[174] the Court upheld the performance of what appeared to be non-adjudicatory functions of a special Article III court in the appointment and supervision of independent counsel. One may question the wisdom of one or both of these decisions.[175] Nevertheless, both involved obviously unique situations, and therefore may be distinguished from the vesting of non-adjudicatory jurisdiction, as a general matter, in the federal courts. *Mistretta* concerned not the vesting of non-adjudicatory jurisdiction in an Article III federal court, but rather the use of individual Article III judges for executive purposes, a fact expressly noted by the Court.[176] *Morrison,* too, involved rather unique circumstances. While, unlike *Mistretta,* the case did involve the use of a special Article III court, its administrative functions were tied to a truly unique process that could well lead to subsequent adversarial litigation.

That these cases are, rightly or wrongly, viewed by the Court as presenting very special, and therefore limited, circumstances is made clear by its continued unwavering adherence to the adjudicatory requirements of

Article III in all other contexts. At no point have subsequent decisions construed these cases as in any way affecting the constitutional requirements of standing, ripeness, mootness, or adverseness. Indeed, in reaching its conclusions in these decisions the Court expressly adhered to its venerable precedents prohibiting the Article III judiciary from performing non-adjudicatory executive functions.[177]

The Implications of the Judicial Exercise of Functions Constitutionally Reserved for Executive Agencies

A number of policy-based arguments support construing Article III to prohibit judicial cognizance of all non-adversarial compensation schemes. First, while the judiciary is constitutionally constrained by the case-or-controversy requirement, the executive branch is instead constrained by electoral accountability.[178] When the unelected judiciary exercises executive power by taking cognizance of a non-adversarial suit, it operates without either the adverseness limit imposed by the case-or-controversy requirement or electoral restraint, contrary to the fundamental checks and balances of our constitutional system.

VIEWING THE SETTLEMENT CLASS THROUGH THE LENS OF ARTICLE III

Textualism: The Non-Adverseness of the Settlement Class

To the extent that one believes that the Constitution should be interpreted in accordance with its plain text, one should be able to conclude without much difficulty that the settlement class violates the case-or-controversy requirement of Article III. In order for the court to have jurisdiction under Article III, a settlement class that alleges violation of state law must definitionally constitute a "controversy"; a settlement class that alleges violation of federal law must fulfill the definition of a "case." This section begins the discussion of the settlement class's unconstitutionality by drawing on the plain-meaning analysis of the terms "case" and "controversy" presented earlier[179] to argue that the inherent non-adverseness of the settlement class—whether the underlying claims involve state or federal law—renders it non-justiciable.

Insofar as the word *controversy* mandates an adversarial dispute between two or more parties, as I have argued that it does,[180] any settlement class alleging only violation of state law contravenes the plain meaning of Article III.[181] The only conceivable jurisdictional basis for such suits is the diversity clause, which extends federal judicial power solely to such "controversies." Parties to the settlement class are definitionally non-adverse.[182] At the time of class certification—the point at which the class action proceeding commences as a distinct suit—they do not seek diverse outcomes, and thus do not present a live "dispute" to the court.[183] Instead, prior to seeking certification and often even before filing a complaint with the court,[184] the parties have agreed on terms of settlement, which usually consists of a privately ordered quasi-administrative distribution scheme that distinguishes among claimants based on type and severity of injury. They then agree to seek—or at least not oppose—class certification, which, if granted, will have the effect of binding all absent class members to the private contract between named plaintiffs and defendant. The district court is asked to certify the class if and only if it approves settlement; in other words, if the settlement agreement were to be rejected by the court, the class is not eligible to be litigated. By way of analogy, imagine a case in which, prior to the filing of litigation, opposing parties negotiate a contractual agreement. At that point, they file suit, seeking a judicial declaration that their agreement is valid. In such a situation, it is inconceivable that a federal court would deem this a constitutionally valid adversarial suit. Yet the situation is directly analogous to the settlement class action.

The definition of "case" is arguably broader than that of "controversy,"[185] and one might contend that, where jurisdiction is premised on a federal question, because such adjudications are textually confined to "cases" the non-adverseness of the parties to a settlement class, at least from the textualist perspective, is immaterial. However, even if it were true that the word *case* permits non-adversarial adjudication, it would only mean that settlement classes arising under federal law—which are relatively limited—are constitutional. Settlement classes premised on diversity jurisdiction—the large majority of settlement classes heard in federal court— would still fall beyond the court's Article III authority. In any event, no federal court has ever suggested that the "case" requirement permits non-adversarial suits, nor would such a position be defensible. History, the Framers' intent, and the Court's jurisprudence all support reading the terms *case* and *controversy* synonymously,[186] to require adverseness in diversity and federal question suits alike.

One might argue that if the settlement class's non-adverseness violates Article III's textual dictates, the same must also be true of both the traditional non-class settlement and the post-certification class settlement. There are, however, critical distinctions between these three types of settlements based on the timing and nature of their pre-trial resolution. In *U.S. Bancorp Mortgage Co. v. Bonner Mall Partnership*,[187] the Supreme Court addressed the scope of federal jurisdiction after a suit is rendered non-justiciable by a consensual settlement. There, after bankruptcy and district court proceedings disputing the terms of a reorganization plan and after the Supreme Court had granted certiorari, the parties reached agreement on the key elements of the plan. The Court noted that, as a general matter, parties to a case are free to settle at any time before or after they file a complaint with the court. However, freedom to settle does not mean that there still exists a justiciable, adversarial dispute post-settlement. For example, this case, given the resolution of all underlying claims on appeal, lacked a requisite dispute, barring Article III consideration of the suit's merits. Nevertheless, the Court could "make such disposition of the whole case as justice may require," including any judicial practices "'reasonably ancillary to the primary, dispute-deciding function' of the federal courts."[188]

In traditional non-class litigation, the *Bancorp* rule provides the court the requisite authority to dismiss the suit with or without prejudice when the parties settle. While the act of dismissal is, per se, an exercise of the court's Article III authority in the absence of a continuing adversarial dispute, it is appropriately viewed, in a commonsense manner, as incidental to the underlying adversarial pre-settlement proceedings. Similarly, a court's ability to enter a consent decree that resolves a previously adversarial litigation is appropriately viewed as inherently ancillary to the adjudicatory process. In contrast, the settlement class requires the court to act beyond the scope of its *Bancorp* authority. Where the settlement, request for certification, and complaint are all filed at the same time, there is no in-court adversary proceeding to which the settlement can be deemed ancillary. From the minute the parties file with the court, they seek the same outcome. The court is never privy to competitive adversarial proceedings, distinguishing settlement-only certification from the court's "primary, dispute-deciding" responsibilities discussed in *Bancorp*.

A settlement class in which the request for settlement is filed after the original complaint but at the same time as the request for certification is similarly illegitimate. The court's decision of whether to certify a class cannot be considered "reasonably ancillary" to an underlying adversarial case. The certification request marks a "new case" with new parties who were not previously before the court. When the complaint is filed, and up until the point of certification, the court has legal authority over only the named parties to the suit—the individuals named in the complaint itself. All pre-certification proceedings bind only those individuals.[189] Certification, on the other hand, marks the exercise of a broader judicial authority; the court for the first time gains jurisdiction over all absent class members, who were never privy to the original adversarial proceeding.

In comparison, the class settlement, where settlement is reached after the court grants class certification, is a constitutionally legitimate exercise of judicial authority.[190] First, the suit is adversarial both when filed and certified, and therefore constitutes a valid "case" or "controversy." The same reasoning would seem to apply to a court's required approval of a post-certification settlement of an adversarial class action. Even though the court must conduct a Rule 23(e) fairness hearing after the parties have agreed on the desired outcome of the case,[191] this fairness inquiry—and the accompanying dismissal of the case—can reasonably be viewed as ancillary to the resolution of the adverse dispute.

The Fifth Circuit Court of Appeals has reasoned that because the parties occupied "adversarial positions. . . . before settlement negotiations" concluded, and would return to such positions "if the settlement is not approved," the use of the settlement class device in the case did not violate the textual dictate of Article III, but rather resolved a "truly" adversarial dispute.[192] This argument misinterprets the limits on judicial authority set forth by the case-or-controversy requirement. The text of Article III imposes a categorical limit on the court's jurisdiction, mandating that there be a live, adversarial dispute between plaintiff and defendant at the time they request judicial intervention,[193] as well as at all times during the suit.[194] This line is rooted in the Court's application of Article III's mootness doctrine in the context of the adverseness requirement. There are a number of cases in which the Court has dismissed a suit as non-adversarial due to settlement while appeal was pending.[195] Thus, it matters not at all that, at some point in the proceeding, the parties may have been adverse. The minute the parties no longer have a live dispute, the case is rendered moot and adjudication would be unconstitutional. This well established dictate is completely ignored in the Fifth Circuit's analysis. Moreover, if the Fifth Circuit were correct, it would be impossible to determine at exactly what point prior to the suit the parties would need to be adverse. One year? Five years? One need only recall my hypothetical about the parties who have settled their differences prior to the suit by entering into a contract, and then sue in federal court for a declaration of the contract's validity.

Clearly, there would be no Article III jurisdiction, because the parties are not adverse—at the very least—*at the time of suit*. It makes no difference that, at some point prior to the suit, the parties may have been adverse. The settlement class action is no different.

THE SETTLEMENT CLASS AND THE PURPOSE
OF THE ADVERSENESS REQUIREMENT

The plain meaning of Article III, strongly supported by the Court's case-or-controversy jurisprudence, conclusively establishes the inherent unconstitutionality of the settlement class. One need look no further than these sources to demonstrate the fatal constitutional flaw in certification of a class for settlement only, given that at the point of suit the parties no longer seek diverse outcomes. However, to shed light on the values underlying the adverseness requirement, as well as to demonstrate the harm in permitting the settlement class to operate unobstructed within an adversary system, it is necessary to move beyond these arguments. The settlement class practice undermines the social and political values fostered by the adverseness requirement, including the private interest in protecting the individual litigant and the public interest in maintaining constitutional constraints on the federal judiciary.

An exploration of the effect of the settlement class on the purposes served by adverseness yields three specific conclusions. First, on a private level, the settlement class threatens the interests of absent class members by binding absent class members to a judgment rendered without the protections and incentives that traditionally accompany an adversarial suit. Second, on a public level, the settlement class seriously threatens achievement of legislative goals in choosing a private remedy as an enforcement mechanism. The legislative selection of a private remedy is premised on the assumption that the availability of private damages will incentivize the private individual to act as a quasi-private attorney general, who, in the course of obtaining compensation for her injuries, simultaneously furthers the law's public goals by punishing and deterring civil wrongdoing. The settlement class, given its non-adverseness, disrupts the background assumptions against which this selection was made, including the supposition that private plaintiffs who seek to enforce the law will be driven by the natural competition-driven incentives that accompany an adversary system. Third, due to its quasi-administrative nature, the settlement class involves the federal court in the performance of the tasks of an executive commissioner—that of distributing private resources in the absence of a live adversarial dispute between two parties. Judicial exercise of this exclusively executive power not only threatens the constitutional separation of powers, but demeans the judiciary by jeopardizing its integrity.

Private Concerns: The Settlement Class and the Litigant-Oriented Interest in Adverseness

A typical class action is legitimate because the interests of the plaintiffs and defendant are adverse. In that scenario, the monetary interests of class counsel, which are contingent on class recovery, are aligned with the absent class members' interest in maximum redress, incentivizing a presentation of the issues that benefits both equally. These incentives break down in the context of the non-adversarial settlement class. Because class counsel seeks the same outcome as the defendant, she has no reason to formulate her clients' arguments or destroy her opponent's case. Particularly, she lacks incentive to present to the court evidence that may shed unfavorable light upon the non-adversarial agreement, even though that evidence may reveal critical details about the effect of the settlement on absent class members.

Most courts and commentators have viewed this breakdown in incentives as solely a sub-constitutional problem, looking at it through the lens of the Rule 23(a)(4) adequacy of representation requirement. I take the argument one step further, conceptualizing the link between the settlement class, the constitutional requirements of Article III, and the broader goals of the adversary system. Specifically, I employ the settlement class to demonstrate the importance of the prophylactic nature of Article III's ban on non-adversarial litigation. While the adequacy of representation inquiry, as well as other Rule 23 requirements, offers protection to litigants on a case-by-case basis, it is far more vulnerable to mistakes than is a categorical, ex ante prophylactic rule that non-adversarial suits are non-justiciable.

The Settlement Class, Adversary Protections, and Evidence Production

The parties to a settlement class agree, before requesting class certification, on the desired outcome of the suit. They no longer seek diverse outcomes, and thus do not—and in fact, have a disincentive to—dispute the satisfaction of Rule 23 certification requirements or the fairness of settlement and compensation terms. Two interrelated factors explain the disincentive to create a concrete record for the court's appraisal: the jointly held intent to bind absent class members, and the resultant lack of an economic or structural incentive to present the court with information that would jeopardize court approval of the pre-certification settlement. First, the sole motive of class and defense counsel in bringing to the court their settlement agreement, negotiated prior to class suit, is to bind the interests of absent class members.[196] If this were not so, counsel would presumably draft a private contract, enforceable under state law, embodying the terms of their agreement. By instead filing a request for certification with the court, these parties have decided that their private agreement, standing alone, is insufficient to meet their needs. Instead, the negotiating parties, by seeking class certification for settlement only, have sought the court's assistance in affecting the rights of third parties, over whom the negotiating parties otherwise have no control. The rationales are twofold. For the defendant, binding absent class members to the settlement is necessary to protect it against the threat of future individual litigation, which is likely to be costly in terms of both time and money. For class counsel, the circumstances surrounding the creation of a settlement class is full of temptations that conflict with the interests of absent class members. Because of market competition for position as class counsel and other countervailing interests such as the settlement of her pending non-class suits against the defendant, class counsel has a pressing interest in certification, as well as in excluding the voice of other participants—objectors and absent class members alike—who may discourage settlement approval.[197]

Accompanying the incentive to bind the rights of absent class members is a disincentive to protect their interests—a fact that holds particular import where the judiciary is structurally passive.[198] In a traditional case the parties have a natural incentive to produce evidence in favor of their adverse positions, thus providing the court with a well-balanced view of the issues in the case. In the settlement class, not only do the named plaintiffs and defendants lack motivation to produce a well-balanced record to assist judicial decision making, they actually have a *disincentive* to produce such evidence, given that it would disrupt the accomplishment of their jointly sought goal: to effectuate the terms of the settlement agreement by way of class certification. Instead, they only present to the court information supporting approval of the desired outcome, resulting in an acute information deficit.[199]

It may be true that, in any given case, some absent class members would support the terms of settlement. However, there is no way to make this determination in the individual case. Non-adverseness is a structural deficiency that affects the inner working of representative litigation in an adversary system: When they are non-adverse, the in-court representatives lack any motivation to determine whether it is, in fact, the case that the suit satisfies the requirements of Rule 23. The implications are twofold. First, an incomplete record can have a detrimental effect on the class certification process. In *General Motors*, the Third Circuit explained that in the settlement class, "the issue of certification is never actively contested."[200] As a result, "the judge never receives the benefit of the adversarial process that provides the information needed to review propriety of the class and the adequacy of settlement."[201] Second, the information deficit can influence settlement approval. Because there is not a "fully developed evidentiary record," the court is incapable of "making an independent assessment of the facts and law required in an adjudicatory context,"[202] including whether the settlement fairly reflects the value of class claims.

One could argue that the litigant-oriented harms that flow from the settlement class also plague the *post*-certification class settlement, given that in both scenarios, the parties are non-adverse at the time that the court conducts the Rule 23(e) fairness hearing. Post-certification non-adverseness, the argument might proceed, limits the court's access to necessary information about the fairness of settlement, in much the same way that pre-certification non-adverseness affects the certification and settlement approval process. The class settlement, however, is far less susceptible to the problems recognized by the Brilmayer representation model. First, unlike the settlement class, the interests of class counsel in a post-certification settlement are not dependant on binding the rights of third parties to a private agreement negotiated in their absence. Class counsel in a post-certification settlement need not compete with other attorneys for the right to file the class,[203] and the definition of the class has been already drawn so that she cannot trade the class's claims for those of her inventory clients.[204] Thus, class counsel's interests closely resemble those of the traditional attorney—for example, maximum attorney's fees. These fees are contingent on class recovery, producing an incidental incentive to advance the interest of absent class members in securing a favorable judgment and maximum redress.

Second, post-certification settlement terms are more likely to reflect a fair value of the class's claims than are pre-certification settlement terms. Due to the ubiquitous risk that she will lose her bid as class counsel, the plaintiffs' attorney in pre-certification negotiations enjoys minimal bargaining power, therefore making it unlikely that she will be able to secure for the class a fair value for their claims.[205] In contrast, in settlement negotiations involving a class that has already been certified for litigation, power is distributed relatively equally among the parties. Because the class has already been approved for trial, class counsel will always have the option to walk away from negotiations and threaten to litigate. This option increases the probability that settlement terms are the result of fair negotiation and economics,[206] rather than a one-sided power struggle.

Third, the post-certification settlement is consistent with the prophylactic rule that only when structural adversarial incentives are present is a suit justiciable. Not only does class counsel enjoy an adversarial relationship with the defendant at the time that she files the class complaint, but adverseness defines the relationship between plaintiff and defendant throughout the process of certification. Specifically, in a post-certification settlement, by the time the suit becomes non-adversarial, the court will have already held full hearings on whether the class definition and the quality of class representation satisfies applicable Rule 23(a) and (b) requirements. Because the parties have not yet consented to settle, and the defendant has no guarantee that settlement will be reached before trial, it is in the defendant's best interests to challenge fulfillment of certification requirements.[207] This adversarial dispute gives the court in a post-certification class the benefit of the parties' time and resources on the question of whether the class and its representatives will fulfill the needs of absent class members,[208] a benefit that the settlement class court does not enjoy.[209]

One could argue that the court can counteract the information deficit that flows from pre-certification settlement by encouraging objectors.[210] However, as one recent study found, "[a]ttempts to intervene in cases filed as class actions occurred relatively infrequently."[211] This may be because conditions unique to the settlement class discourage objectors, by making it difficult to file and defend opposition motions. "Objectors are often required to file their opposition motions before class counsel and defendants file their motions in support of settlement. This timing, combined with the limits on objector discovery, leaves objectors at a disadvantage because they must develop their objections without the information possessed by class counsel and defendants."[212]

The Settlement Class and the Passive Judiciary

The lack of litigant adverseness has a significant impact on the court's traditional role in resolving private disputes. In light of the party disincentive to produce evidence challenging the accuracy of certification, the court has two options. First, it could engage in independent factual investigation, without the benefit of an adversarial presentation of the issues, to inform itself of the correctness of certification. Second, the court could approve the settlement class despite the information deficit, absent independent investigation. Under this alternative, fairness hearings often last less than a day, without either expert testimony or the opportunity for cross-examination.[213] This presumption, and judicial passivity in the context of the non-adversarial settlement class generally, threaten the very core of a liberal democratic system. In representative litigation, the absent class member depends on three actors to guard her interests: class counsel, the named plaintiff, and the court, as a type of guardian ad litem. The protection offered by the first two actors is neutralized by the suit's non-adverseness. Class counsel, in deciding to seek the same outcome as the opposing party, loses the natural incentive to advance the interests of absent parties once the action is filed. And the named plaintiff has no real influence in a settlement class, given that he is usually, if not always, named at the time of filing, after settlement agreement is reached.[214] The only actor remaining is the district judge, who, if satisfied to clear the court's dockets and approve the settlement regardless of its impact on the interests of absent class members and its legitimacy under the certification requirements, breaches his obligation to persons bound by the court's judgment.

THE SETTLEMENT CLASS, THE PROPHYLACTIC ADVERSENESS REQUIREMENT, AND ALTERNATIVE SAFEGUARDS

Both courts and scholars have argued that a number of individualized safeguards—including Rule 23 requirements governing class certification and settlement approval—are capable of protecting the interests of absent class members in a settlement class. While this may be true in the typical class action, the lack of adversarial litigation on the fulfillment of governing requirements neutralizes the effectiveness of Rule 23's safeguards in the context of the settlement class.

Rule 23(a)(4): Adequacy of Representation

A number of courts have held that the Rule 23(a)(4) adequacy of representation inquiry effectively protects the interests of absent class members.[215] This view is misguided in the context of the non-adversarial settlement class. Even if Rule 23's requirement were, in the abstract, sufficient to protect the interests of absent class members, the settlement class threatens the conditions upon which those procedural safeguards rely. In contrast to the post-certification settlement, where the court enjoys the benefit of adversarial litigation on the satisfaction of Rule 23 certification requirements,[216] the settlement class removes the adversarial context of Rule 23's operation. Given that they seek the same outcome—class certification and settlement approval—neither plaintiff nor defendant has incentive to provide the court with evidence challenging the adequacy finding or revealing a conflict of interest between the class and their attorney. Additionally, without the benefit of an adversarial presentation of the issues, the court is ill-equipped to engage in independent factual investigation of (a)(4) issues, hindering its ability to protect the interests of absent class members.[217]

Moreover, what exactly Rule 23(a)(4) requires of the class representative is unclear, making impossible a conclusion concerning the abstract effectiveness of the adequacy inquiry. There are currently three distinct approaches to (a)(4) adequacy in the context of the settlement class.[218] A first group of courts employs the "collusion approach," looking at whether the representative "failed to prosecute the class action with due diligence and reasonable prudence" and the "opposing party was on notice of facts making that failure apparent."[219] A second group uses the "fairness" of settlement as a proxy to assess adequacy of representation.[220] A third group analyzes typicality, asking whether "the named representative has common interests with the unnamed members of the class."[221] In contrast to (a)(4), the adverseness required by Article III constitutes an ex ante categorical determination that the absence of adverseness, *in and of itself*, constitutes unconstitutional collusion. In this context, it matters not at all whether the collusion is secret, as it was in most of the Supreme Court decisions applying the adverseness requirement,[222] or totally open, as it is in the settlement class action. Nor does it matter whether the court has been able to find anything improper in the specific case before it. As is the case for all ex ante categorical rules, Article III's adverseness requirement is designed to turn not on whether a showing of impropriety has been made in the specific case, but rather automatically equates failure to satisfy the requirement of the categorical rule with a finding of impropriety. This is due to the fact that the Constitution employs categorical rules *in a prophylactic manner*: Because our system is not willing to take the risk that a more individualized inquiry will fail to unearth hidden impropriety in a specific litigation, it makes the ex ante choice to risk overprotection, rather than underprotection. Thus, a categorical rule necessarily assumes the possibility that cases will arise in which no real danger to absent parties exists, even in the absence of litigant adverseness, but we are willing to take that risk, rather than risk the under-protection danger inherent in a case-by-case inquiry.

The difference between the operation of a categorical rule and an individualized inquiry is similar in many respects to the difference between a "stop" sign and a "yield" sign. While the latter requires a driver to come to a full stop only if traffic requires, the former demands a full stop, no matter what traffic conditions are. Thus, it will be little defense to a ticket for failing to stop at a stop sign to argue that there was, at the time, no need to stop because there was no cross traffic. Stop signs are, presumably, placed in locations where authorities have concluded that the dangers of undetection in the individual case are so great as to justify overprotection—that is, coming to a full stop when in reality there is no need to do so—rather than risk the disaster of underprotection.

Much like the stop sign, Article III's adverseness prerequisite imposes a rigid requirement that the parties to a federal litigation be truly adverse at all times, until the case is resolved one way or another. This is so, regardless of whether any showing of harm to absent litigants can be made in the particular case. Both due process and Rule 23(a)(4)'s adequacy requirement, in contrast, involve exclusively a far more individualized inquiry. This does not mean that either due process or (a)(4) is superfluous. Both may perform an extremely important individualized inquiry to protect absent class members, *once a finding of adverseness has been made*. But surely, neither inquiry can—even in the abstract—perform the salutary protective function performed by Article III's adverseness requirement.

Rule 23(e): The Fairness Inquiry

It has been suggested that the Rule 23(e) fairness hearing sufficiently protects absent class members from unfair preclusion.[223] Under that provision, the court is intended to function as a type of fiduciary, conducting discovery on the terms of settlement and the content of settlement negotiations.[224] The information deficit that inherently plagues this process, however, renders it a questionable means of policing the settlement class. First, at the point of settlement the parties themselves lack any incentive to produce information supporting a finding that the settlement is inadequate. Second, the court lacks the requisite resources or training to unearth such information on its own, especially in a scenario where the parties have an active incentive to shield this information from discovery.[225] Without access to information about the class, the formation of the settlement, and the conditions that may have led to a reverse auction or inventory settlement, the judge cannot "effectively monitor for collusion, individual settlements, buy-offs . . . and other abuses."[226] Finally, while there always exists the possibility that members of the absent class will object to the fairness of the settlement, the inertia and transaction costs inherent in this process render this, too, an unreliable means of policing.

It is true that, at least to a certain extent, the very same problems plague the Rule 23(e) fairness hearing held following settlement of a traditionally litigated class. But, once again, for a number of reasons the dangers of abuse are far greater in the settlement class. First, as previously noted, the settlement of a litigated class occurs only after the court has had the benefit of an adversarial dispute concerning the merits of certification. This is by no means merely a technical difference. When the defendants have an incentive to challenge certification, an affirmative judicial finding assumes that the class representatives who participate in the settlement process are truly adequate champions on behalf of absent class members. This is by no means true of the settlement class, where the defendant has no incentive to challenge any of the asserted bases for certification. Second, where settlement occurs following certification, class representatives are necessarily in a far better bargaining position than in the case of the settlement class, where the threat of actual litigation if the settlement process proves to be unsuccessful is far more theoretical than real. Finally, because many plaintiffs' attorneys enter into settlement class actions with the incentive of disposing of inventory claims and the process is often plagued by the problem of the reverse auction,[227] the dangers of a court approving an unfair settlement are far greater in the case of a settlement class than in approval of a settlement of a litigated class action.

The Opt-Out Right

In recognition of the potential problems posed by class-wide resolution of an individual's claims, Rule 23(c)(2)(B) provides absent class members in a (b)(3) class the right to "opt out" of, or exclude themselves from, the class. One could argue that the availability of this opportunity ensures that no individual will be bound to a settlement agreement, whether pre- or post-certification, absent her consent. If the absent class member removes herself from the class, the argument goes, she will be bound neither by res judicata because she is not part of the class, nor by stare decisis because the settlement has no precedential effect. In contrast, the failure to opt out constitutes assent to be represented by a third party in a non-adversarial setting.[228]

There are a number of problems with reliance on opt-out to remedy the litigant-based harms of the settlement class. First and foremost, even if the failure to opt-out does constitute consent to inadequate recovery, it does not constitute consent to non-adversarial dispute resolution. The decision to opt out is made against the background assumption of an adversary system, which includes the presupposition that the claim was resolved in a traditional adversary context and that the class representative had the incentive to advance the rights of absent class members. The absent class member faced with the decision of whether to opt out of a settlement class is not told that her advocate did not act within the confines of the traditional adversary system and had no incentive to present the court with sufficient information from which to assess whether the compensation promised each class member under the settlement was fair. These factors render the opt-out decision in a settlement class inherently uninformed.

Second, the opt-out device suffers from numerous procedural flaws. As a general matter, "inertia, the complexity of class notices, and the widespread fear of any entanglement with legal proceedings" renders notice and opt-out ineffective in many cases.[229] While these problems plague both the settlement class and the class settlement, the latter contains a structural safeguard absent in the former scenario—the recently amended Rule 23(e)(3).[230] The amendment provides that when settlement occurs *after* certification, the court must issue two separate notices: one at the time of certification; one at the time of settlement. This additional opt-out opportunity significantly increases the effectiveness of the right to opt-out. The amended Rule 23(e)(3), according to the Advisory Committee, "reflects concern that inertia and a lack of understanding may cause many class members to ignore the original exclusion opportunity," while the second notice, "identify[ying] proposed binding settlement terms[,] may encourage a more thoughtful response."[231]

Third, simultaneous notice of certification and settlement to absent class members often skews the opt-out calculus. The settlement offer holds significant persuasive power, regardless of whether it represents a fair value of the class claims, therefore deterring opt-out. In the words of the Third Circuit, "even if [absent class members] have enough information to conclude the settlement is insufficient . . . the mere presentation of the settlement notice with the class notice may pressure even skeptical class members to accept the settlement out of the belief that, unless they are willing to litigate their claims individually—often economically infeasible—they really have no choice."[232]

Public Concerns: The Settlement Class and the Systemic Interest in Adverseness

Most cases involving judicial interference with one of its co-equal branches consist of situations in which the court makes law or declares a statute unconstitutional absent a justiciable controversy.[233] The settlement class does neither of these things. Unlike *Muskrat*, where the parties asked the Court to find a legislative compensation scheme unconstitutional in the absence of an adversarial dispute, and *Johnson*, where the parties sought an advisory opinion on the constitutionality of portions of the Emergency Price Control Act, the parties to a settlement class do not request that the court assess either the constitutionality or legitimacy of congressional action. In fact, from a legal perspective the settlement class is inherently non-substantive. It is concerned not at all with the interpretation of underlying substantive law; the rights of absent class members are resolved without legal exposition. Instead, the settlement class court oversteps its Article III authority far more subtly: first, by altering the adversarial context in which the legislature assumed the underlying substantive law was to be enforced; second, by effectively assuming the role of an executive commissioner, who is responsible for the distribution of funds in the absence of an adversarial case or controversy.

The Hybrid Model: The Settlement Class, Non-Adverse Litigation, and Underlying Public Goals

Even though the settlement class does not require the court to issue an advisory opinion or expound upon the state of the law, it nevertheless represents a substantial intrusion into the inner workings of the state or federal legislative branches that fashion underlying substantive law. In a damage suit, where substantive law specifies enforcement by way of a private remedy, the underlying goal is to provide a mechanism by which to simultaneously compensate victims and punish wrongdoers. The decision to place responsibility for statutory enforcement in the hands of victims and their private attorneys is wholly dependent on the assumption that these individuals will have the necessary tools and incentives to prosecute their claims vigorously. When two parties seek divergent outcomes, the individual plaintiff is presumed to possess a competitive interest in developing her own case, and presenting facts to the court that shed favorable light on her position. Congress must be deemed to presume the existence and effectiveness of this typical adversarial arrangement when empowering the victim to make use of the legal system to enforce the proscriptions contained in the underlying statute.[234]

The conditions upon which the legislative selection of a private remedy is based break down in the context of the settlement class. In a non-adverse suit, the plaintiffs' attorney lacks the incentive to be a champion for the victims' cause or to facilitate accurate judicial decision making through the creation of a balanced record. By altering the context in which the statute was intended to be enforced, the settlement class, as I have previously argued, functionally "transforms that [underlying] private remedial model into a qualitatively different form of remedy that was never part of that substantive law."[235]

It might be argued that the settlement class action actually furthers underlying legislative policies. Absent the settlement class, the argument proceeds, it would often be impossible to attain legislative goals. In many instances, it might be thought, the class could not satisfy traditional Rule 23 certification criteria, and individual claims are often so small as to make individual suit infeasible. Thus, without the settlement class action there would be no enforcement at all of substantive policies.

Though perhaps superficially appealing, this reasoning must ultimately be rejected. Initially, to the extent that resort to the settlement class device effectively circumvents the certification criteria of Rule 23, it is nothing more than a cynical and lawless perversion of the rule. Moreover, it is by no means clear that a truly adversary class could not, in many instances, satisfy accepted certification criteria, yet use of the settlement class precludes the bringing of such an action by attorneys and named plaintiffs who are actually adverse to the defendants. Nor will it always be clear—particularly in mass tort contexts—that individual suits would be financially infeasible. Finally, to the extent private enforcement of legislative policies is infeasible, the legislature should be made aware of that fact so that it may consider alternative enforcement mechanisms, such as the use of criminal penalties or administrative regulation.

The Administrative Compensation Model: The Non-Adversarial Settlement Class as an Exercise of Executive Authority

The distinction between the activities of the judicial and executive branches has become increasingly blurry in recent decades, given the overlapping responsibilities of the judiciary and non-Article III agencies which exercise adjudicatory power. Nevertheless, one model comprehensively explains the constitutional division between the tasks performed by an

Article III court and those reserved for administrative agencies within the executive branch: the Article III adverseness requirement. While existence of an adverse dispute between litigants may not constitute a sufficient condition for the exercise of judicial authority over an issue, since legislative courts can assume jurisdiction over such cases as well, it is always a necessary condition. The judiciary has no authority, under any circumstance, over the distribution of resources in a purely non-adverse context. Thus, if and when the court assumes jurisdiction over such claims, it performs a function expressly reserved for executive agencies, in violation of separation of powers dictates.[236]

The settlement class is a paradigmatic example of such a scenario. The settlement class court functions as a type of administrative "commissioner," under the guise of Article III adjudication. Insofar as the settlement class court assumes an active or supervisory role in the post-certification, post-settlement formulation of distribution and compensation procedures,[237] it performs the executive tasks of "adjust[ing] [private] claims," in the absence of an adversarial relationship between two parties. [238] The non-adverseness of the parties to the settlement class thus strips the Article III court of its traditionally umpireal role. It is true that the court in the settlement class neither makes substantive policy decisions nor issues binding legal holdings, but instead merely serves as a legal conduit for private ordering by self-interested parties. This fact, however, makes the settlement class court function more, rather than less, like an executive commissioner. The settlement class court neither receives evidence, engages in legal exposition, nor supervises adversarial litigation on the substantive requirements of the underlying law. Rather, it is left to perform nothing more than a wholly non-judicial, administrative function—that of making distributive arrangements, and in some circumstances, actually issuing individual compensation decisions pursuant to the non-adversarial scheme.

The same is not true of the post-certification class settlement, despite the fact that the parties are nonadversarial at the time that the Rule 23(e) fairness hearing is conducted. In a settlement of a traditional class action, the suit is adversarial up to the point of settlement. When the suit settles, it does so after certification, such that the court already has jurisdiction over all absent class members. Given the underlying legitimacy of the class proceedings pre-settlement, judicial approval of the settlement is merely ancillary to resolution of an adversarial proceeding,[239] and thus falls on the judicial side of the judicial-executive divide.[240]

Judicial exercise of this type of executive function has a number of implications. First and foremost, it invades a sphere constitutionally reserved for the executive branch. Performance of executive tasks and utilization of executive weapons is textually reserved for the executive branch, regardless of whether those tools currently lay dormant. First, insofar as "the Article II Vesting Clause designates, identifies, and describes the President as the *only* proper recipient of executive power,"[241] judicial cognizance of a settlement class violates the constitutionally mandated separation of powers. Moreover, the case-or-controversy requirement of Article III expressly limits the scope of the judiciary's adjudicatory function, implicitly leaving suits that do not qualify as "cases" or "controversies"—including non-adversarial dispute resolution—for the court's co-equal branches.[242]

On a normative level, judicial exercise of an executive function is similarly unacceptable. Unlike an executive agency, which is subject to both congressional and executive supervision, judicial distribution of resources absent an adversarial case-or-controversy suffers from a lack of oversight or accountability—checks that are necessary to control the unfettered exercise of administrative authority.[243] Additionally, given the judiciary's lack of inquisitorial resources or training,[244] judicial exercise of an executive function is likely to be inefficient and ineffective.[245]

To aggravate matters, the settlement class action gives to the federal court the worst of both worlds. Unlike a court adjudicating an adversarial dispute, the settlement class action court receives no adversarial argument or evidence from the parties. But unlike an executive agency, the court lacks both formal tools to unilaterally seek out relevant argument and evidence and executive or legislative oversight.

THE INCOMPATIBILITY BETWEEN
PRAGMATIC BALANCING AND
ARTICLE III'S ADVERSENESS REQUIREMENT

The preceding discussions demonstrate that the settlement class is unambiguously inconsistent with both the textual directive of Article III and the protective functions performed by Article III's adverseness requirement. Several scholars and members of the judiciary, however, have advocated use of a utilitarian balancing approach to reconcile the settlement class with Article III. This approach contrasts the litigant-oriented benefits of the settlement class to its detrimental effects in order to determine the practice's constitutionality. This balancing test could assume one of two forms. First, one could argue that the court should weigh the benefits of imposing the Article III adverseness requirement, including the private values served by adverseness under the Brilmayer representation model, against a competing social concern, such as the public value in clearing crowded court dockets of mass tort claims and assuring that individual claimants receive *some* compensation for their injuries. Second, with re-spect to the public purposes of the adverseness requirement, one could argue that the court should invalidate judicial exercises of non-judicial authority only when as a result the court unduly aggrandizes its power, at the expense of another branch.

These two versions of the balancing test have in common resort to a case-by-case, entirely pragmatic approach to the question of adverseness. Instead of viewing adverseness as a categorical qualification on the judicial power, it would provide the court the authority, in the individual case, to assess the costs and benefits of assuming jurisdiction of a settlement class. Such an approach is not only contrary to the textual dictate of Article III, but also seriously frustrates achievement of the purposes served by litigant adverseness in the first place, including the protection of absent but bound individuals and the preservation of a constitutional constraint on the judiciary, in relation to its co-equal branches.

Balancing of Private Harms

Several courts and scholars have noted that the settlement class provides a unique method by which to compensate victims en masse and clear court dockets of millions of individual suits. For example, Justice Breyer, dissenting in *Amchem*, deemed it relevant that:

> [t]he District Court, when approving the settlement, concluded that it improved the plaintiffs' chances of compensation and reduced total legal fees and other transaction costs by a significant amount . . . The court believed the settlement would create a compensation system that would make more money available for plaintiffs who later develop serious illnesses . . . [I]t suggests that the settlement before us is unusual in terms of its importance, both to many potential plaintiffs and to defendants, and with respect to the time, effort, and expenditure that it reflects.[246]

Justice Breyer would require that, in each case, the court analyze whether the pragmatic interests served by the settlement class—whether those benefits flow to the plaintiff, the defendant, or the court—are sufficient to waive the limits imposed by Article III on the court's authority.

Not only is such an analysis entirely subjective and therefore hopelessly unpredictable,[247] but purely as a textual matter, it fails to comport with Article III's case-or-controversy requirement. The plain meaning of the terms *case* and *controversy* in Article III permits no compromise based on the costs and benefits of requiring litigant adverseness.[248] The Court has long held that the constitutional requirements embodied in Article III, including the adverseness requirement, in the words of one scholar, "state a limitation on judicial power, not merely a factor to be balanced."[249] This choice between the case-or-controversy requirement as a prophylactic versus individualized rule has been made long since in favor of the former. As the Court has explained:

> Article III . . . is not merely a troublesome hurdle to be overcome . . . it is a part of the basic charter promulgated by the Framers . . . Implicit in the [respondent's position] is the philosophy that . . . cases and controversies are at best merely convenient vehicles . . . and at worst nuisances that may be dispensed with when they become obstacles to that transcendent endeavor. That philosophy has no place in our constitutional scheme.[250]

Even if a balancing test were assumed to be a proper means by which to approach Article III, Justice Breyer's praise of the settlement class's ability to "make more money available for plaintiffs" and reduce transaction costs appears short-sighted, when the practice is viewed in light of the litigant-oriented goals of the adverseness requirement.[251] The pragmatic harms that are likely to result to the individual litigant from a non-adversarial case far outweigh its benefits. No litigant in a settlement class, given the class counsel's lack of adversarial incentives to advance the interests of absent class members, can be guaranteed that his recovery will be fair or adequate. In fact, in some cases, class members may receive far below market rate—if anything—for their claims, calling into question the accuracy of Breyer's analysis.[252] If it is truly the case that, absent a settlement class, victims will be unable to recover for cognizable harm, there is open to the relevant legislative body the option of replacing adjudication with an alternative scheme of administrative resolution.

Balancing of Public Harms

Justice Breyer's discussion of the settlement class parallels the "functionalist" approach taken by the Court in a number of recent separation of powers cases. For example, in *Morrison*,[253] *CFTC v. Schor*,[254] and *Mistretta*,[255] the Court "winked at task commingling between institutions not

because task divisions do not constitutionally exist, or do not constitutionally matter, but because [it] concluded that commingling serves the goal
of good government more than it undermines the goal of precise task-
assignment."[256] Under these precedents,[257] even though the judicial activity in question—like the settlement class—violated Article III, it was found
not sufficiently to threaten the essential functions of its co-equal branches.
Instead, the court will "invalidate only those overlaps of authority which
either undermine one branch's successful performance of its essential function or accrete too much power to one of the branches."[258] In the context
of the settlement class, the argument might go, neither the hybrid nor the
administrative compensation model poses a sufficient threat to the inner
workings of the legislative or executive branches, as to outweigh the benefits promised by settlement-only certification.

Use of a functionalist approach in dealing with the public harms posed
by the settlement class is seriously flawed. First, it undermines the Constitution's fundamental goal in imposing a system of separation of powers. As
I have previously argued, "Madison described the very accumulation of all
power in the hands of one body or individual as the essence of tyranny."[259]
In his view, "'tyranny' is not limited to the misuse of [another branch's]
power, or even to its exercise . . . [I]t is the very fact of its accumulation
that [he] equated with tyranny."[260] As a result, the Framers chose not to
define "case" or "controversy" by the functional impact of judicial activity
on the operations of other departments or by reference to a balancing test.
Rather, the case-or-controversy language itself *was* their determination of
how far the judicial branch could insert itself into the actions and policies
of the other branches. On their view, as evidenced by their definition of
"judicial power" in Article III, the vesting of *any* legislative or executive
authority in the judicial branch unduly accretes power to the judiciary.

Second, a functionalist approach to Article III neglects the importance
of viewing the adverseness requirement, as an element of the proper separation of powers, as a prophylactic tool. As a general matter, the division of
responsibility among branches is designed to "prevent a situation in which
one branch . . . acquire[s] a level of power sufficient to allow it to subvert
popular sovereignty and individual liberty."[261] It is functionally impossible
to determine precisely when the judicial exercise of a legislative or executive function has reached a "danger" point.[262]

Turning to the specific justifications for a prophylactic rule in the
context of adverseness, the adverseness requirement creates the necessary
conditions for accurate, passive judicial decision making, in a context that

gives proper respect for the assumptions of the legislature in enacting a private remedy to be enforced within an adversary system. One cannot evaluate the accomplishment of this twofold purpose on a case-by-case, ex post facto basis, looking solely to whether the non-adversarial settlement class accretes undue legislative or executive power. The risks posed by the settlement class are incremental. Over time, the harms of the non-adversarial suit will accumulate, such that the court will be permitted to openly perform the executive function of distributing private resources outside the context of an adversarial case-or-controversy, and in direct contravention of legislative purpose in empowering the court to grant private relief. The adverseness requirement is necessarily devised to prevent such "damage to the political framework before the truly serious harm intended to be avoided can occur."[263]

CONCLUSION

The lower federal courts have willingly embraced the settlement class action practice for its ability to offer victims compensation and clear dockets en masse. In assuming jurisdiction over such suits, however, these courts have neglected their fundamental Article III obligation to hear only adversarial cases or controversies—an obligation rooted in the text, jurisprudence, and values served by the adverseness requirement. I have sought here to critique current practice, by viewing it through the lens of a new articulation of the values underlying Article III's adverseness requirement. While a number of scholars have called for revisions in settlement class practice, none seems to have recognized that the settlement class is based on fundamentally flawed constitutional foundations, a fact that becomes all too clear once one acknowledges the practice's inherent non-adverseness. This recognition should, in turn, move us toward recognition of the constitutional invalidity of pre-certification class settlement.

CHAPTER SEVEN

Conclusion: The Role of Liberal Theory in the Class Action Debate

Throughout this book, I have argued that the modern class action debate needs to be dramatically restructured to take account of the procedure's impact on the nation's political and constitutional foundations. In a variety of ways, that impact on our liberal democratic system may be substantial and often severely negative. Initially, it is important to recognize that, as presently structured, the class action can be employed to undermine democracy on what I have called a macro level, by the indirect manipulation of underlying substantive law under the guise of a procedural mechanism. In this manner, the class action contravenes basic dictates of legislative transparency and electoral accountability that are essential to the operation of a successful democratic system.[1]

Paradoxically, even if the class action were to be confined to its appropriate procedural context, it would be unwise to ignore its inescapable and often substantial (albeit indirect) impact on matters of substantive policy that extend beyond the four walls of the courthouse. The paradox results from the fact that those who shape the class action device need simultaneously to acknowledge the procedure's primarily procedural function *and* its inescapable substantive impact. This seeming inconsistency, however, is in reality merely part and parcel of the complexities of the American democratic system. To view the purpose of a procedural rule as primarily to impact the fairness or efficiency of the truth-finding process is not necessarily to deny its incidental, yet often inevitable and important, substantive impact. While it is impermissible for a guiding directive expressly labeled as a rule of procedure to be promulgated primarily for the purpose of altering controlling substantive law, it is also important to recognize that substance and procedure will often inescapably intertwine. This insight has significant relevance for the method by which the modern class action rule[2] is shaped. Under the system established by the Rules Enabling Act,[3] the current class action rule is legislatively promulgated by the one branch of the federal government that is unrepresentative of and unaccountable to the electorate. Yet no one could seriously doubt that even when viewed exclusively as a rule of procedure, the class action rule inevitably and dramatically implicates the substantive values of economic redistribution and enforcement of governmental checks on the modern corporate world. Given its substantial impact on the manner in which private claims are adjudicated, there realistically could be no other result. For the modern class action rule to possess both constitutional and democratic legitimacy, it must be promulgated, in the first instance, through legislative enactment in accord with the constitutional dictates of bicameralism and presentment.[4]

The Constitution's system of separation of powers is also undermined by so-called settlement class actions, where the class action court is asked not to resolve a real dispute between a litigant class and a party opposing that class, but rather merely to approve and implement a prearranged legal arrangement between the parties that was reached prior to the seeking of class certification. By allowing the unrepresentative and unaccountable federal judiciary to do more than resole live disputes between adverse litigants, the procedure seriously erodes the case-or-controversy requirement of Article III of the Constitution.[5]

In addition to the problems it poses for the operation of representative government, the modern class action also threatens core notions of liberal democracy on a micro level, by restricting the individual's autonomous ability to employ the judicial process as a means of protecting her substantive legal rights. In this sense, the procedure contravenes both constitutional and political values, by simultaneously violating procedural due process rights[6] and fundamental precepts of process-based liberal individualism that are central to attainment of the liberal values of individual worth, integrity, and development.[7] Moreover, as problematic as is the current legal framework of the class action embodied in Rule 23 of the Federal Rules of Civil Procedure, even more troublesome are the normative class action models proposed in recent years by leading procedural scholars. In one way or another, each of these models substantially increases the systemic and individualist difficulties to which the current class action framework gives rise.[8]

The backdrop to all of the problems of constitutional and political theory plaguing the modern class action is the fact that the class action, in either its existing form or as currently proposed by legal scholars, has no clear historical analogue. On the one hand, while early English practice did authorize certain forms of purely collective adjudication, it appears that in none of those contexts were individuals forced to adjudicate substantive rights that, in their pristine pre-litigation form, were individually held. Rather, collective adjudication was permitted only when the individual's substantive rights were held as part of a pre-existing entity.[9] On the other hand, although as a historical matter individually held substantive rights could on occasion be adjudicated collectively, as in the bill of peace or interpleader contexts, in none of those instances could individuals be forced to adjudicate their claims passively—in other words, where other litigants would conduct the litigation of their claims on their behalf. Instead, the individual in these contexts was able to represent his or her own interests fully as a litigant before the court.[10] Thus, in a number of ways the modern form of the class action, as established by the 1966 amendments to Rule 23 of the Federal Rules of Civil Procedure, is unprecedented in the manner in which it collectivizes the adjudication of individual rights.

It surely does not follow that the class action should be abandoned as a procedural means of collectively litigating individually held claims. Under certain circumstances, both macro and micro aspects of liberal democratic theory are actually fostered, rather than undermined, by use of the class action. Initially, to the extent individual claimants voluntarily join together to facilitate adjudicatory enforcement of their rights, the process is fully consistent with liberal democratic values. By way of analogy, the First Amendment right of free expression, which is undoubtedly held and exercised individually, may be facilitated by exercise of the right of individuals to associate for purposes of making their expression more effective. Similarly, the class action may be employed to facilitate individuals' ability to resort to the judicial process to enforce their legal rights and interests. Of course, it is not always clear how one should measure claimant voluntariness. To the extent the current version of the rule incorporates a principle of litigant voluntariness, as it does under Rule 23(b)(3) in the form of the provision for the ability of class members to opt out of the class, it is far preferable to the mandatory alternative. As a matter of procedural due process, coercive collectivization of individually held rights through use of the class action mechanism should be allowed only in the presence of a truly compelling interest.[11]

Now that I have summarized my theoretical and structural problems with the modern class action, it is appropriate briefly to summarize my more concrete recommendations for changes in the ways that the modern class action should be viewed from a constitutional perspective and for alterations in the structure of Rule 23 to take account of my broader concerns. The major constitutionally dictated changes would be (1) the settlement class action (i.e., a proceeding in which certification has been sought solely on the condition that the court approve a prearranged settlement) would be held to contravene the case-or-controversy requirement of Article III; (2) all mandatory classes, with the possible exception of the (b)(1)(A) category involving situations in which inconsistent behavior on the part of the party opposing the class toward individual class members would be either impossible or unduly oppressive, would be deemed violations of the Due Process Clause; and (3) the existing opt-out structure for (b)(3) classes would be found both to violate due process and to depart from key notions of democratic theory, except in situations in which the individual claims, though sufficiently large to reasonably justify the filing of a claim form as part of a settlement or judicial award, would be insufficiently large to justify individual suit.

In addition, while it is my firm belief that the Rules Enabling Act under which Rule 23 was promulgated contravenes the separation of powers directives of the Constitution by delegating legislative policy-making power to the judicial branch in a non-adjudicatory setting, I fully recognize the practical unlikelihood that such a conclusion would ever be accepted by the Court. Nevertheless, I believe that in light of these structural concerns the substantive-procedural dichotomy contained in the Act should be construed in a manner that reserves to Congress the exclusive power to fashion rules of procedure that significantly impact issues of policy beyond the four walls of the courthouse. I consider Rule 23, concerning class actions, to be the poster child of such rules.

Finally, in order to prevent what I describe as "faux" class actions, Rule 23 needs to be amended to require the court, as part of the certification process, to consider whether success in the class proceeding is likely to result in real relief for class members. In this way, the class action process would be prevented from being transformed into a major alteration in the remedial structure of the substantive laws being enforced—a result authorized neither by the nation's commitment to lawmaking through democratic accountability, nor by the terms of the Rules Enabling Act itself.

A substantial portion of the class action scholarly community may well react negatively to my overall analytical methodology, specific applications of that methodology, or both. Acceptance of my constitutional and political analyses would inevitably result in the significant retrenchment of the modern class action in a number of important ways. As a result, the class action could likely no longer serve as the convenient dispute resolution mechanism and corporate policeman that it has become. Even with my proposed alterations, the modern class action could still facilitate litigants' ability to enforce their individually held claims. Moreover, at least some of the problematic implications of the modern class action for precepts of democratic theory can be resolved through federal legislative action.[12] But to the extent that the convenience of the modern class action would be undermined as a result of my proposals, my simple response is that neither the American democratic system nor its constitutional structure has as its primary purpose the achievement of convenience. Our complex intersecting structure of majoritarian and countermajoritarian directives was clearly designed to attain and protect goals of individual liberty and governmental accountability, and to avoid the dangerous and erosive growth of authoritarianism. Attainment of these underlying goals requires incurring a certain amount of inconvenience. It is time to restructure our examination of the class action by focusing on its inherently limited role within our constitutional and political framework. It is only then that we will be able to reduce its dangers and accentuate its benefits to American constitutional democracy.

Reference Matter

Notes

I. INTRODUCTION: CLASS ACTIONS, LEGAL HISTORY, AND LIBERAL DEMOCRACY

1. Students usually learn that class actions may be restricted by the protections of procedural due process as dictated by the Supreme Court in its well-known decision in Hansberry v. Lee, 311 U.S. 32 (1940). *See generally* Chapter 5, *infra*. However, it is probably safe to assume that only rarely would the inquiry go much beyond this largely superficial doctrinal examination.

2. *See, e.g.,* David Rosenberg, *The Causal Connection in Mass Exposure Cases: A "Public Law" Vision of the Tort System,* 97 Harv. L. Rev. 849 (1984); Owen Fiss, *The Political Theory of the Class Action, in* THE LAW AS IT COULD BE 122 (2003); David Shapiro, *Class Actions: The Class as Party and Client,* 73 Notre Dame L. Rev. 913 (1998). For a detailed examination of the impact of each of these theoretical approaches on the modern class action, see generally Chapter 4, *infra*. Professor Shapiro's theory is also examined, from different intellectual perspectives, in both Chapters 2 and 5, *infra*.

3. I recognize that of course cases will arise in which the individual's claim is so insignificant that as a practical matter his or her interest in controlling its adjudication is likely to be all but non-existent. However, that will not always be the case, especially in mass tort suits or suits brought pursuant to statutes authorizing punitive damages. Moreover, when the individual claim is so small that the claimant would lack incentive even to file a claim to a settlement fund, other significant difficulties arise. *See* discussions in Chapters 2, 4, and 5, *infra*.

4. The point is explained in detail in Chapter 2, *infra*.

5. For a more detailed explanation see Chapter 5, *infra*.

6. I have explained my understanding of liberal democratic theory in my scholarship on the subject of free expression. *See* Martin H. Redish, FREEDOM OF EXPRESSION: A CRITICAL ANALYSIS 9-86 (1984); Martin H. Redish, *The Value of Free Speech,* 130 U. Pa. L. Rev. 591 (1982). See also the exploration of liberal theory included in Chapters 4 and 5, *infra*.

7. *See* Ian Shapiro, THE EVOLUTION OF RIGHTS IN LIBERAL THEORY 275 (1986) (asserting that liberal theory "assumes that individual will is the cause of all actions" and that "individual consent . . . [is] vital to the whole idea of political activity."). *See generally* Chapters 4 and 5 *infra*, for more detailed discussion. *See also* David Held, MODELS OF DEMOCRACY 89 (1987) (rationalizing liberal democracy on the grounds that "without an opportunity to participate in the regulation of affairs in which one has an interest, it is hard to discover one's own needs and wants, arrive at tried-and-tested judgments and develop mental excellence of an intellectual, practical and moral kind.").

8. For more detailed explications of this dichotomy see the analyses contained in Chapters 4 and 5, *infra*.

9. This point is developed more fully in Martin H. Redish, *The Adversary System, Democratic Theory, and the Constitutional Role of Self-Interest: The Tobacco Wars, 1953–1971,* 51 DePaul L. Rev. 359 (2001).

10. U.S. Const. Amend. V, cl. 4; Amend. XIV, § 1, cl. 3 (respectively prohibiting Congress and the states from depriving anyone of life, liberty, or property without due process of law).

11. *See* Chapter 5, *infra* at 144–45.

12. *See, e.g.,* Shapiro, *supra* note 2. *See* Chapter 2, *infra* at 37–38; Chapter 4, *infra* at 115–20; Chapter 5, *infra* at 149–56.

13. *See* Fed. R. Civ. P. 23.1 (concerning class actions involving shareholder derivative actions); 23.2 (class actions involving unincorporated associations).

14. Stephen Yeazell, FROM MEDIEVAL GROUP LITIGATION TO THE MODERN CLASS ACTION 41 (1987).

15. *Id.*

16. *Id.* at 44.

17. West v. Randall, 2 Mason 181, 193 (Story, J., on circuit).

18. 1 How. Lvi.

19. Fed. R. Civ. P. 23 (1938).

20. Fed. R. Civ. P. 23, Advisory Committee Notes (1966). *See also* ZECHARIAH CHAFEE, SOME PROBLEMS OF EQUITY 245–46; 256–57 (1950).

21. Fed. R. Civ. P. 19, Advisory Committee Notes (1966).

22. According to one commentator, "the terms 'joint,' 'common,' and 'several' . . . have confused the courts, perhaps because these terms have not had much historical application to class actions and the learning which accompanies them in other contexts cannot readily be carried over to this area." Note, *Developments in the Law: Multiparty Litigation in the Federal Courts,* 71 Harv. L. Rev. 874, 931 (1958) (footnotes omitted).

23. State Farm Fire & Gas Co. v. Tashire, 386 U.S. 523, 536 (1967) (describing "bill of peace" as a device "capable of sweeping dozens of lawsuits out of the various state and federal courts in which they were brought and into a single interpleader proceeding."). In interpleader proceedings—in contrast to the modern class action—each claimant actively represented his own interest. *See also* Zechariah Chafe, *Bills of Peace with Multiple Parties,* 45 Harv. L. Rev. 1297, 1311 (1932).

24. *See* Fuentes v. Shevin, 407 U.S. 67 (1972) (fact that possessions seized without due process were of relatively minimal value deemed irrelevant).

25. *See* the discussion in Chapter 5, *infra* at 135.

26. See the discussions in Chapters 4 and 5, *infra.*

27. *See* Rule 23, Advisory Committee Notes (1966) (*"The amended rule* describes in more practical terms the occasions for maintaining class action . . .").

28. Fed. R. Civ. P. 23(a) (requiring that class be sufficiently large that joinder would be impractical and that the named class representatives have claims that are typical of those of the entire class and are able to provide adequate representation to absent class members).

29. *See* Chapters 4 and 5, *infra,* for detailed development of the argument.

30. *See* discussion *supra* at 6–9.

31. Fed. R. Civ. P. 23(a)(3), 23(a)(4).

32. Fed. R. Civ. P. 23(c)(2).

33. *See* Chapter 5, *infra.*

34. *See* Chapter 4, *infra.*

35. *See* Chapter 5, *infra* at 169–73.

36. For a detailed exploration of the constitutional implications of such practices, see Martin H. Redish and Christopher Pudelski, *Legislative Deception, Separation of Powers, and the Democratic Process: Harnessing the Political Theory of United States v. Klein,* 100 Nw. U. L. Rev. 437 (2006).

37. *See* Chapter 2, *infra* at 52.

38. 28 U.S.C. § 1332.

39. 304 U.S. 64 (1938).

40. 28 U.S.C. § 2072(a).

41. This approach is developed more fully in Chapter 2, *infra.*

42. In re Rhone-Poulenc Rorer, Inc., 51 F.3d 1293 (7th Cir. 1995) (Posner, J.)

43. Byrd v. Blue Ridge Rural Elec. Co-op., Inc., 356 U.S. 525 (1958).

44. Under Article III, section 1, of the Constitution, federal judges (including Supreme Court justices) are appointed by the president, with Senate confirmation, and sit for life during good behavior. Moreover, during their tenure their salaries may not be reduced.

45. This is the upshot of the "private rights" model of adjudication recognized by Chief Justice John Marshall in Marbury v. Madison, 5 U.S. (1 Cranch) 137 (1803). For a detailed discussion of the private rights model, see MARTIN H. REDISH, THE FEDERAL COURTS IN THE POLITICAL ORDER 87–109 (1991).

46. Immigration & Naturalization Service v. Chadha, 462 U.S. 919 (1983).

47. *See* discussion *supra* at 13–15; Chapter 2, *infra.*

48. Fed. R. Civ. P. 23(e).

49. *See generally* Chapter 6, *infra.*

50. See *id.*

2. CLASS ACTIONS AND THE DEMOCRATIC DIFFICULTY

1. In re Rhone-Poulenc Rohrer Inc, 51 F3d 1293, 1298 (7th Cir 1995).

2. Richard L. Marcus, Martin H. Redish & Edward F. Sherman, CIVIL PRO-CEDURE: A MODERN APPROACH 309 (West 3d ed 2000).

3. See, for example, Jack B. Weinstein, INDIVIDUAL JUSTICE IN MASS TORT LITI-GATION 1–14, 163–71 (1995) (emphasizing the need for the tort system to compensate

harmed plaintiffs and to provide an indirect deterrent effect as well); David Rosenberg, *Class Actions for Mass Tort: Doing Individual Justice By Collective Means*, 62 Ind.
L.J. 561, 567 (1987) (arguing that "bureaucratic justice implemented through class
actions provides better opportunities for achieving individual justice than does the
tort system's private law, disaggregative processes").

4. Pre-existing scholarly critiques of the class action differ substantially from
my own. Professor Coffee has pointed to "three distinct themes" of academic criticism that have been leveled at class actions: first, "that the legal rules governing
the private attorney general have created misincentives that unnecessarily frustrate
the utility of private enforcement;" second, "that the incentive to litigate may be
inherently excessive, in large part because the parties to an action do not bear its
public costs," leading to a "failure to internalize the full cost of litigation, including the costs of the judicial systems," resulting in an artificial inflation in the demand for litigation as a "public subsidy equal to these costs, and the private incentive to litigate exceeds the social incentive," causing "an excessive reliance on law
and lawyers"; and finally, that "the social benefits of litigation brought by private
attorneys general" should be discounted because "rational, well-informed plaintiffs might bring an action that has no chance of success at trial in order to extort
a recovery from the defendants." John C. Coffee, Jr., *Understanding the Plaintiff's
Attorney: The Implications of Economic Theory for Private Enforcement of Law Through
Class and Derivative Actions*, 86 Colum. L. Rev. 669, 671–72 (1986).

In contrast to these economic critiques, my analysis focuses exclusively on
criticisms derived from the perspective of American political theory. Nor is my
critique based on concerns about agency problems growing out of plaintiffs' attorneys' alleged failure to satisfy their attorney-client obligations to the class members. Finally, I am not arguing, as Judge Friendly did many years ago, that "the
benefits to the individual class members are usually minimal" while lawyer compensation "seems inordinate." Henry Friendly, FEDERAL JURISDICTION: A GEN-
ERAL VIEW 119–20 (1976). See also Edward J. Ross, *Rule 23(b) Class Actions—A
Matter of "Practice and Procedure" or "Substantive Right?,"* 27 Emory L.J. 247, 249
(1978) (commenting that "recovery from the settlement of a class action does not
necessarily inure to the allegedly damaged class members; the real reward is often
to their lawyers"). My concern, rather, is with the all-too-frequent situation in
which, for all practical purposes, the class is simply irrelevant to the suit because
class members effectively receive no meaningful relief.

5. *See* Martin H. Redish, THE CONSTITUTION AS POLITICAL STRUCTURE 135–65
(1995).

6. *See* Jerry L. Mashaw, *Prodelegation: Why Administrators Should Make Political
Decisions*, 1 J.L. Econ. & Org. 81, 95–99 (1985).

7. It should be noted that in 1995, Congress did deal with class action representation issues (in the narrow context of securities litigation) when it enacted
the Private Securities Litigation Reform Act Pub. L. No. 104-67 101, 109 Stat 737
(1995), codified at 15 U.S.C. § 78u-4. However, enactment of this legislation in no
way moots the democratic concern to which this chapter points. Initially, the Act
focuses exclusively on aspects of securities class actions, and thus has no relevance
to any other area in which class actions are brought. Second, by imposing a variety

of criteria that named plaintiffs in securities class actions must satisfy, Congress actually evinced its desire to preserve the private rights nature of this category of class actions. Thus, it is only by means of the misleading argument that congressional action in the securities area necessarily implies congressional satisfaction with all other areas that one can conclude that Congress has "spoken." Even if this assertion were true as a matter of congressional understanding (a highly unlikely scenario in any event), it completely ignores the constitutional requirements of bicameralism and presentment for the enactment of legislation.

8. I refer to such a mode of thinking as "the fallacy of the free-standing class action."

9. "The transsubstantive philosophy dictates that procedural rules are to be interpreted and applied in the same manner, regardless of the substantive nature of the claim at issue." Edward J. Brunet, Martin H. Redish, & Michael A. Reiter, SUMMARY JUDGMENT: FEDERAL LAW AND PRACTICE 222 (2d ed. 2000). See also Robert Cover, *For James Wm. Moore: Some Reflections on a Reading of the Rules,* 84 Yale L.J. 718, 718 (1975) (referring to procedural rules "generalized across substantive lines" and noting the "trans-substantive achievement of the Federal Rules of Civil Procedure"); Paul Carrington, *"Substance" and "Procedure" in the Rules Enabling Act,* 1989 Duke L.J. 281, 303 (noting that general sets of rules unrelated to substance put courts in the desirable position of "avoiding 'interest group' politics").

10. 15 U.S.C. §§ 1, 2, 15.

11. See, for example, Truth in Lending Act, 15 U.S.C. §§ 1601–93 and Cable Television Consumer Protection and Competition Act, 47 U.S.C. § 521.

12. 15 U.S.C. § 78j.

13. 28 U.S.C. § 1332.

14. *See* Henry Hart, *The Relations Between State and Federal Law,* 54 Colum. L. Rev. 489, 489 (1954); Hanna v. Plumer, 380 U.S. 460, (1965) (Harlan concurring) (commenting that federal and state tort systems control the "primary activity of citizens").

15. In certain substantive laws the legislature chooses to enforce proscriptions on primary behavior by resort to a synthesis of a variety of remedial models, including, among others, criminal enforcement, civil penalties, or administrative enforcement, in addition to private compensation. *See* discussion *infra* at 44–45.

16. 15 U.S.C. § 15.

17. Under limited circumstances, the Supreme Court has been willing to infer a private damage remedy when Congress has not expressly provided for one. *See* J. I. Case Co. v. Borak, 377 U.S. 426, 431–34 (1964) (inferring an "implied" damage remedy from the Securities Exchange Act of 1934, 15 U.S.C. § 78n(a), based upon Congressional purpose). More recently, however, the Court has severely restricted this practice. See, for example, Thompson v. Thompson, 484 U.S. 174 (1988) (holding that the Parental Kidnapping Prevention Act of 1980 was intended for use in adjudicating custody disputes and not to create an entirely new cause of action). For a criticism of the practice of implied remedies, see MARTIN H. REDISH, THE FEDERAL COURTS IN THE POLITICAL ORDER 39 (1991) ("The facts that the damage remedy may be thought to foster the beneficial purposes served by the statute or that the legislature may not have foreseen the severity of the problem matter

little because the damage remedy was not subjected to the formal requirements of the legislative process. . . .") (internal citations omitted). *But see* Richard Stewart and Cass Sunstein, *Public Programs and Private Rights,* 95 Harv. L. Rev. 1193, 1229 (1982) (rejecting criticism of implied remedies as unduly formalistic).

18. Not all modern 23(b)(3) class actions are properly described as "faux" class actions in the sense described here. In a number of cases, attorneys may obtain meaningful relief on behalf of the class members. See DEBORAH R. HENSLER, ET AL, CLASS ACTION DILEMMAS: PURSUING PUBLIC GOALS FOR PRIVATE GAIN 427–39 (Rand Institute for Civil Justice 2000) (noting that average payments in the mass tort cases studied ranged from $1,400 to $100,000 and that some actions resulted in meaningful nonmonetary relief such as changes in laws or removal of harmful products from the market). But see Chapter 5, *infra* A (questioning validity of opt-out procedure).

19. Note that substantive statutes providing for private damage remedies generally do not distinguish between individual and group rights. Invariably, such statutes create only a damage remedy vested in the individual. Thus, any class action brought to enforce those rights must properly be viewed as nothing more than a procedural conglomeration of individually granted rights. See text accompanying note 151.

20. *See* Fed. R. Civ. P. 23(c)(2); discussion *infra* at 36–42.

21. *See* discussion *infra* at 36–42.

22. *See* discussion *infra* at 35–36.

23. Purely as an empirical matter, however, this question appears to be an open one. Evidence exists to support the proposition that many private class action lawyers do not actually ferret out previously unknown corporate law violations, but merely "tag along" after successful government criminal or civil proceedings. *See* discussion *infra* at 32.

24. It appears that Professor Coffee was the first commentator to employ the term *bounty hunter* in describing class action plaintiffs' lawyers. See John C. Coffee, Jr., *Rescuing the Private Attorney General: Why the Model of the Lawyer As Bounty Hunter Is Not Working,* 42 Md. L. Rev. 215, 218 (1983). However, as subsequent discussion will make clear, Professor Coffee's use of the term was overbroad. *See* discussion *infra* at 33–35.

25. The use of bounty hunters as an auxiliary to law enforcement continues to this very day through the use of the private bail bondsman system. See, for example, State v. Covington, 2002 WL 1592704, *1 (Tenn Crim App); People v. Brewton, 2002 WL 1486572 (Cal App).

26. In the mid-twentieth century, actor Steve McQueen broke onto the national scene as a bounty hunter in the Old West in a half-hour black-and-white prime time network television series titled "Wanted, Dead Or Alive." *See* http://en.wikipedia.org/wiki/Wanted:_Dead_or_Alive.

27. It should be noted that I do not purport to make psychological judgments about plaintiffs' lawyers' personal motivations. The desires to pursue personal gain and serve the public interest are not mutually exclusive, and it is at least conceivable that certain plaintiffs' lawyers are motivated simultaneously by both considerations.

My point is, simply, that even a bounty hunter motivated by nothing more than personal gain may well advance the public interest in her pursuit of personal gain.

28. *See* discussion *infra* at 35–40.

29. *See* Vermont Agency of Natural Resources v. Stevens, 529 U.S. 765, 774 (2000) (pointing to "the long tradition of qui tam actions in England and the American colonies").

30. I take no position here as to whether such bounty hunter suits would satisfy Article III's requirement of injury-in-fact.

31. 28 U.S.C. § 2072(b) (prescribing that Federal Rules may not abridge, enlarge, or modify a substantive right). *See generally* Chapter 3.

32. In class actions in which individual claims are sufficiently large both to concern the individual class member and to justify even the minimal effort required to affirmatively become a class member, it is quite conceivable that the class action procedure would remain viable. Thus, as a practical matter, adoption of my proposed amendments would at most cause a substantial reduction in class actions in which individual claims are relatively minimal. *See* discussion *infra* at 40.

33. I should note at the outset that I do not plan here to reinvent the wheel by providing a normative basis to support the nation's historically established commitment to the basic framework of a democratic system. Perhaps, at the most abstract level, one could fashion persuasive normative arguments to prefer a benevolent dictatorship, a monarchy, or even anarchy in lieu of constitutional democracy. But those arguments are for another day. In this chapter, I assume the positive and normative value of at least some basic level of societal self-determination through resort to the representative process.

34. *See* Jane J. Mansbridge, ed., BEYOND SELF-INTEREST (1990).

35. Cass Sunstein, *Beyond the Republican Revival,* 97 Yale L.J. 1539, 1540 (1988). See also Richard Fallon, *What Is Republicanism, and Is It Worth Reviving?,* 102 Harv. L. Rev. 1695, 1698 (1989) (noting that modern civic republicanism reflects the classical version of the theory in positing "that there exists an objective public good apart from individual goods") (internal citation omitted).

36. Joseph H. Carens, *Possessive Individualism and Democratic Theory: Macpherson's Legacy,* in Joseph H. Carens, ed., DEMOCRACY AND POSSESSIVE INDIVIDUALISM: THE INTELLECTUAL LEGACY OF C.B. MACPHERSON 2 (1993).

37. For a more detailed discussion of these questions, see Martin H. Redish, *The Adversary System, Democratic Theory, and the Constitutional Role of Self-Interest: The Tobacco Wars, 1953–1971,* 51 DePaul L. Rev. 359 (2001) (examining the role of adversary theory as an essential part of modern liberal democratic theory and the way in which it interacts with the civic-republicanism (progressive individualism debate).

38. Cass Sunstein, *Interest Groups in American Public Law,* 38 Stan. L. Rev. 29, 31 (1985).

39. See, for example, Sierra Club v. Morton, 405 U.S. 727 (1972).

40. See, for example, *id.* (noting that an ideological plaintiff lacks the injury in fact required for standing).

41. *See id.*

42. Coffee, *supra* note 3, at 669.

43. *Id.*

44. *Id. See also* Michael L. Rustad, *Smoke Signals From Private Attorneys General in Mega Social Policy Cases,* 51 DePaul L. Rev. 511, 511 (2001) (encapsulating the articles written for a symposium on tort law and social policy that "reflect the reality that tort law has been transformed from compensating private individuals to private law that empowers often disadvantaged individuals with a public purpose"). The term was coined by Judge Jerome Frank in Associated Industries of New York State, Inc. v. Ickes, 134 F.2d 694, 704 (2d Cir. 1943) ("Such persons, so authorized, are, so to speak, private Attorney Generals."), vacd as moot, 320 U.S. 707 (1943). See also Coffee, *supra* note 24, at 215 n.1. Professor Coffee notes, however, that "[t]he issue in Associated Industries was one of standing in an administrative law dispute, and no question of private damages was involved." *Id.* Nevertheless, it is quite clear that today the label is employed for private damage actions. Consider *id.*

45. Deborah R. Hensler and Thomas D. Rowe, Jr., *Beyond "It Just Ain't Worth It": Alternative Strategies for Damage Class Action Reform,* 64 L. & Contemp. Probs. 137, 137 (2001).

46. Stephen C. Yeazell, FROM MEDIEVAL GROUP LITIGATION TO THE MODERN CLASS ACTION 232 (1987) (referencing Harry Kalven, Jr. and Maurice Rosenfeld, *The Contemporary Function of the Class Suit,* 8 U. Chi. L. Rev. 684, 721 (1941)).

47. Yeazell, *supra* note 46, at 232.

48. See Howard M. Erichson, *Coattail Class Actions: Reflections On Microsoft, Tobacco, and the Mixing of Public and Private Lawyering in Mass Litigation,* 34 U.C. Davis L. Rev. 1, 5 (2000) (defining "coattail class action" as "a class action that follows government litigation, seeking to benefit from the government's work"). See also Bryant Garth, Ilene H. Nagel, and S. Jay Plager, *The Institution of the Private Attorney General: Perspectives From an Empirical Study of Class Action Litigation,* 61 S. Cal. L. Rev. 353, 376 (1988) (explaining an empirical study demonstrating that in modern class actions, "private attorneys tended to 'piggyback' their cases on governmental investigations, even to the extent of copying the government's complaint") (internal citation omitted); Coffee, *supra* note 24, at 220–23 ("[T]he available empirical evidence does not provide much support for the thesis that the private attorney general significantly supplements public law enforcement by increasing the probability of detection . . . . [A] recurring pattern is evident under which the private attorney general simply piggybacks on the efforts of public agencies . . . in order to reap the gains from the investigative work undertaken by these agencies. As a result, the private attorney general does not seem to broaden the scope of law enforcement, but rather only intensifies the penalty.") (internal citations omitted).

49. Professor Erichson notes that "[t]he chance of successful private litigation rises dramatically when government litigation paves the way." Erichson, *supra* note 48, at 5 (internal citation omitted).

50. *See id.* at 3 ("[S]ome observers object to the easy ride that plaintiffs and their lawyers get by piggybacking on government actions."). Professor Erichson points to an editorial in the Wall Street Journal labeling class counsel in the Microsoft class actions as "tort parasites" and a reference in the Washington Post to class action lawyers as "predatory" and the class actions, themselves, as "simple buzzardry." *Id.* (internal citations omitted).

51. *See id.* (noting that coattail class actions "offer a relatively fair and efficient mechanism for extending the benefits of government legal work to provide redress to injured citizens").

52. *See also* Coffee, *supra* note 24 at 224 ("This phenomenon of 'free riding' by the private plaintiff on governmental enforcement efforts is by no means without social utility.").

53. *But see* Erichson, *supra* note 48, at 5 ("Coattail class actions are a common feature of mass litigation.").

54. Garth, Nagel, and Plager, *supra* note 48, at 353–54 (noting that sometimes the private attorney general is considered a "Lone Ranger" and at other times, a "bounty hunter").

55. *See* discussion *supra* at 30–31.

56. *See* discussion *supra* at 31.

57. Professor Coffee, for example, has written that "the private attorney general is someone who sues 'to vindicate the public interest' by representing collectively those who individually could not afford the costs of litigation; and as every law student knows, our society places extensive reliance upon such private attorneys general to enforce the federal antitrust and securities laws, to challenge corporate self-dealing in derivative actions, and to protect a host of other statutory policies." Coffee, *supra* note 24, at 216 (internal citation omitted). As I will demonstrate, however, this description of the private attorney general concept improperly mixes compensatory suits and those brought solely due to governmentally created economic incentives.

58. *See* discussion *supra* at 26.

59. 31 U.S.C. §§ 3729, 3730(b).

60. The size of the percentage depends on whether the government intervenes in the action. 31 U.S.C. § 3730(d). The Act gives the government sixty days from the filing date of the suit to investigate the relator's claim and decide whether or not to intervene and assume primary responsibility. 31 U.S.C. § 3730(c)(1).

61. Gretchen L. Forney, Note, *Qui tam Suits: Defining the Rights and Roles of the Government and the Relator Under the False Claims Act,* 82 Minn. L. Rev. 1357, 1364 (1998) (internal citation omitted). The same commentator points out that "Congress amended the (False Claims Act) in 1986 with the stated intent of generating more private suits. The 1986 Amendments strengthened the position of the qui tam plaintiff in three ways: (1) qui tam plaintiffs were given more power to initiate and prosecute claims, (2) financial incentives were enhanced, and (3) protections against employer retaliation reduced the risks inherent in exposing one's employer." *Id.* at 1366–67 (internal citations omitted).

62. Marc S. Raspanti and David M. Laigaie, *Current Practice and Procedure Under the Whistleblower Provisions of the Federal False Claims Act,* 71 Temple L. Rev. 23, 43 (1998) (charting the increasing number of qui tam filings from 1987 to 1997 according to Justice Department figures).

63. Once again, I should emphasize that I am making no judgments about the personal motivations of individual relators. It is, of course, conceivable that a particular relator is motivated as much or more by personal concern about fraud against the government as by the percentage of the proceeds that he expects to

obtain as a result of the qui tam action. As a rough rule of thumb, however, it is fair to predict that the financial incentive is, at the very least, a significant element in the relator's motivation. Apparently the government, in offering the reward, is proceeding on such an assumption.

64. The qui tam analogy may not be a perfect one, since the qui tam relator does more then simply expose private illegality. In addition, she seeks to obtain restitution on behalf of the government. However, the relator is not seeking compensatory damages for private victims, and, unlike the plaintiff class action lawyers, the relator is considered to be a real party in interest.

65. *See* discussion *supra* at 30–32 (describing commentators' overbroad definition of "bounty hunter" concept to include both private compensatory and true bounty hunter actions).

66. Fed. R. Civ. P. 23(b)(2) (authorizing class actions where the party opposing the class has acted in a manner generally applicable to the class, thereby justifying injunctive relief). The Advisory Committee Notes to the 1966 Amendments indicate that the modern civil rights class action served as the inspiration for this category, though by its terms the category is not substantively confined to civil rights claims. See Fed. R. Civ. P. 23; Amendments to Rules of Civil Procedure, 39 F.R.D. 69, 102 (1966). Rule 23(b)(2) class actions may be brought even if damages are sought, as long as injunctive relief remains the primary relief sought. Charles Alan Wright, et al, FEDERAL PRACTICE & PROCEDURE § 1775, at 463–70 (West 2d ed 1986).

67. Compensatory class actions may fall either within the (b)(1) or (b)(3) categories. The former category, which does not necessarily require individual notice to class members and in which class members do not have the option of removing themselves from the class, exists when either the individual class members or the party opposing the class would be placed in a legally or practically precarious position absent the existence of the class action. *See* Fed. R. Civ. P. 23(b)(1)(A)-(B). The latter category, which requires individual notice and provides class members with the right to opt out of the class, includes cases in which the rationale for class treatment is confined largely to the closely parallel nature of the facts and claims. FRCP 23(b)(3). For the most part, my analysis applies to cases falling within the (b)(3) category.

68. It is important not to confuse "idealistic" with "altruistic," or to assume that an action is not motivated by self-interest merely because one finds that self-interest to be ideologically appealing. Even seemingly idealistic class actions often are motivated by self-interest, as where African Americans seek to enjoin continued discrimination. Indeed, in light of our system's injury-in-fact requirement, such actions cannot be brought absent at least some level of self-interest. *See* discussion *supra* at 30–31.

69. Fed. R. Civ. P. 23(c)(2).

70. See Robert Mauk, *Lawsuit Abuse: Public's Welfare Hurt When Lawyers Help Themselves,* CHARLESTON GAZETTE 5A (Apr 28, 1997) ("Many people probably aren't aware of this but, under current rules, you may already be part of a class-action lawsuit and not even know it. . . . [S]uch suits are like those record and book clubs your parents warned you about—until you say stop, you are automatically included as a member.").

71. The term *entity* appears to have been coined by Professor Cooper. See Edward H. Cooper, *Rule 23: Challenges to the Rulemaking Process,* 71 N.Y.U. L. Rev. 12, 26 (1996).

72. David L. Shapiro, *Class Actions: The Class As Party and Client,* 73 Notre Dame L. Rev. 913, 916 (1998) (internal citation omitted).

73. *Id.* at 917. See also *id.* at 921 (finding the entity model "the more appropriate in the class action setting"). Professor Shapiro acknowledges, however, that "substantial institutional problems remain when it comes to implementation." *Id.* at 917.

74. Shapiro, *supra* note 72, at 917.

75. *Id.* at 921.

76. *Id.*

77. *Id.* at 921–22. In particular, Professor Shapiro notes that trade union members may not be free to withdraw from litigation pursued by the union—which represents all workers, whether they voted for the union or not—without leaving the job entirely. Similarly, residents of a municipality cannot freely withdraw from it without the extreme action of moving home and family.

78. For a detailed response to the entity theory on the basis of autonomy concerns, see Chapters 4 and 5, *infra.*

79. *See* discussion *supra* at 36–42.

80. Perhaps a stronger argument can be fashioned that the drafters did, in fact, intend classes certified pursuant to either 23(b)(1) or 23(b)(2) to constitute entity-based classes, since no provision for the right of opt-out, or even of required notification, was made for these classes. See Shapiro, *supra* note 72, at 925–26 (arguing that "the knowledge that these actions generally involve the group as an entity may well have led the rulemakers in 1966 to make such classes 'mandatory' "). On the other hand, arguably the lack of opt-out rights in these classes could be justified by the pragmatically based compelling need to resolve the entire matter in a single proceeding, because of the harmful impact on either absent class members or the party opposing the class in the absence of class treatment. Such reasoning, however, does not respond to my critique grounded in the undermining of the substantive-procedural balance brought about by the denial of opt-out when the underlying substantive law creates only individual rights. The Supreme Court has cast doubt on mandatory classes under certain circumstances, because of their negative impact on litigants' procedural autonomy and therefore construed the scope of the mandatory categories narrowly. *See* Ortiz v. Fibreboard Corp., 527 U.S. 815, 842–43 (1999) (stating that a limiting construction of the Rule 23(b)(1)(B) mandatory class "avoids serious constitutional concerns raised by the mandatory class resolution of individual legal claims"). *See also* Chapter 5, *infra* at 158–59.

81. *See* discussion *supra* at 26–28.

82. Jonathan R. Macey and Geoffrey P. Miller, *The Plaintiffs' Attorney's Role In Class Action and Derivative Litigation: Economic Analysis and Recommendations for Reform,* 58 U. Chi. L. Rev. 1, 28 (1991) (internal citations omitted).

83. Professors Macey and Miller, it should be noted, developed the argument in support of the position that individualized notice in small claim class actions should not be required. *See id.* They were not specifically focusing upon the opt-out question. *See generally id.*

84. See John C. Coffee, Jr., *The Regulation of Entrepreneurial Litigation: Balancing Fairness and Efficiency in the Large Class Action,* 54 U. Chi. L. Rev. 877, 906 (1987) ("Consider the position of a plaintiff whose claim faces either serious problems of factual proof or legal adequacy or who has suffered relatively minor damages. Rationally, such a plaintiff should gravitate to the class action because she has no alternative.").

85. But see discussion in Chapters 4 and 5, *infra* at 131–33, 169–73 (recognizing more refined distinctions on the basis of autonomy concerns). *See also* note 70, *supra.*

86. Coffee, *supra* note 84, at 905. See also Shapiro, *supra* note 72, at 923–24 (defining small claim class actions as "those cases in which the claim of any individual class member for harm done is too small to provide any rational justification to the individual for incurring the costs of litigation"). Professor Shapiro points, as an example, to "a claim on behalf of many purchasers that defendants have engaged in a price-fixing conspiracy to violate the federal antitrust laws. The case would easily fit the small claims category if, even after damages are trebled, the amount due any single purchaser would not exceed, say, $100." *Id.* at 924.

87. Coffee, *supra* note 84, at 904.

88. See Marcus, Redish, & Sherman, *supra* note 2, at 174. ("The concept of privity is rooted in due process, as a non-party should not be found by a judgment unless he had an opportunity to be heard.")

89. *Compare* Edelman v. Jordan, 415 U.S. 651, 673 (1974) (pointing out that "constructive consent is not a doctrine commonly associated with the surrender of constitutional rights"). The one exception that comes to mind is a default judgment, where a judgment is entered against a defendant who has taken absolutely no action. However, such a result may be justified on the grounds that any other treatment of a defendant's failure to respond would effectively transform a notice of suit into an R.S.V.P.

90. Professor Coffee also describes "Type C" class actions, "in which there are both marketable and unmarketable claims." *Id.* at 905–06. He notes that "[a]lthough Type B suits correspond most closely to the traditional rationale for class actions, Type C actions are probably much more common." *Id.* at 906 (internal citation omitted). However, my version of Type C classes is quite different. For more detailed development, see Chapter 4, *infra* at 132.

91. Hensler, et al., *supra* note 18, at 476. They describe this result as "a worrisome possibility." *Id.* This concern provided at least a partial motivation for the 1966 Advisory Committee's decision to use opt-out. See Amendments to Rules of Civil Procedure, 39 F.R.D. at 102–04.

92. See, for example, United Food and Commercial Workers Union Local 751 v. Brown Group, Inc., 517 U.S. 544, 557 (1996) (referring to representative litigation, brought by state governments in their capacity as parens patriae).

93. It should be noted that the modern class action does not constitute a classic parens patriae action, since it is private attorneys, not chosen by or representative of the electorate, who both make the decision to sue on behalf of individuals in need of special protection and conduct the suit.

94. David F. Levi, *Memorandum to the Civil Rules Advisory Committee: Perspectives on Rule 23 Including the Problem of Overlapping Classes 2–3* (Apr. 4, 2002).

95. Benjamin Kaplan, *Continuing Work of the Civil Committee: 1966 Amendments of the Federal Rules of Civil Procedure I,* 81 Harv. L. Rev. 356, 398 (1967).

96. See Gail Hillebrand and Daniel Torrence, *Claims Procedures In Large Consumer Class Actions and Equitable Distribution of Benefits,* 28 Santa Clara L. Rev. 747, 747 (1988) ("Settlements and judgments in class action cases have often required class members to submit claims in order to share in the proceeds of the recovery. Recent cases suggest that claims procedures are ill-suited to consumer class actions in which the class size is very large and the amount of damages per class member is relatively small. These cases are characterized by very low claims rates.").

97. It is thus not surprising that in her empirical study of class actions, Professor Hensler found that "class members do not always come forward to claim the full amount defendants make available for compensation." Hensler, et al, *supra* note 18, at 459 (noting that in cases where settlement required class members to come forward to claim modest amounts of compensation, the fraction of compensation funds actually disbursed was modest to negligible).

98. In a subsequent chapter, I refer to as "Type C" classes small claim classes in which the claims are so small that it is unlikely individual class members would ever bother to file a claim into a settlement fund or a damage fund. *See* Chapter 4, *infra* at 131–32. Professor Hensler, discussing her empirical study of class actions, notes that "[t]he wide range of outcomes that we found in the lawsuits contradicts the view that damage class actions invariably produce little for class members, and that class action attorneys routinely garner the lion's share of settlements." Hensler, et al, *supra* note 18, at 427. She points out, however, that "class counsel were sometimes simply interested in finding a settlement price that the defendants would agree to—rather than in finding out what class members had lost, what defendants had gained, and how likely it was that defendants would actually be held liable if the suit were to go to trial." *Id.*

99. *Id.*

100. *See* discussion *supra* at 30–31.

101. For more detailed exploration of the issue, see Chapter 4, *infra.*

102. Compare Benjamin Barber, STRONG DEMOCRACY (1984) (favoring heavy involvement of the citizenry in the democratic process) with Joseph A. Schumpeter, CAPITALISM, SOCIALISM, AND DEMOCRACY (1942) (urging an extremely limited role for the electorate in the democratic process). Note that I am avoiding here the theoretical debate over *direct* democracy versus *indirect* (or representative) democracy. *See* Nadia Urbinati, *Representation as Advocacy,* 28 Political Theory 758, 760 (2000). I believe that ship sailed long ago.

103. Alexander Meiklejohn, POLITICAL FREEDOM 9 (1960). See also Henry Mayo, AN INTRODUCTION TO DEMOCRATIC THEORY 103 (1960). ("[E]verything necessary to [democratic] theory may be put in terms of (a) legislators (or decision-makers) who are (b) legitimated or authorized to enact public policies, and who are (c) subject or responsible to popular control at free elections."); J. Roland Pennock, DEMOCRATIC POLITICAL THEORY 310 (1979) ("Elections are thought to constitute the great sanction for assuring representative behavior, by showing what the voters consider to be their interests by giving them the incentive to pursue those objectives.").

104. See Randy E. Barnett, *Constitutional Legitimacy,* 103 Colum. L. Rev. 111, 128 (2003) ("Despite their rhetorical commitment to 'popular sovereignty,' by the time the Constitution was written its framers were pretty well convinced that pure majority rule or democracy was a bad idea."); Jack N. Rakove, ORIGINAL MEANINGS: POLITICS AND IDEAS IN THE MAKING OF THE CONSTITUTION 203–43 (1997).

105. U.S. Const. Art. II, § 1, cl. 2; Amend. XII (establishing the manner in which the electoral college representatives will be selected and the procedure that the electors will use to elect the president).

106. U.S. Const. Art. I, § 3, cl. 1. This process of Senatorial election was subsequently changed to a direct electoral process by amendment. See U.S. Const. Amend. XVII.

107. See U.S. Const. Art. I, § 7, cls. 2, 3 (presentment clauses); Art. I, §§ 1 and 7, cl. 2 (bicameralism requirement). See also INS v. Chadha, 462 U.S. 919 (1983) (holding that a federal immigration statute allowing the House to overrule the Attorney General on a deportation decision failed to meet the constitutional requirements for legislative actions of bicameralism and presentment).

108. See Robert W. Bennett, *Counter-Conversationalism and the Sense of Difficulty,* 95 Nw. U. L. Rev. 845, 847–48, 854–71 (2001) (emphasizing that separation of powers and interest group power complicate the majoritarian assumption).

109. See James A. Morone, THE DEMOCRATIC WISH 33 (2d ed. 1998) ("Americans broke from England expressing a democratic wish."). *See also id.* at 39 ("When Parliament imposed taxes on the colonies . . . the Americans charged that their own assemblies had not approved the levies—taxation without representation.").

110. Schumpeter, *supra* note 102, at 285. See also id. at 246 (proposing "government approved by the people"); *id.* at 285 (suggesting that a criterion for "identifying the democratic method" is "competition among would-be leaders for the vote of the electorate"). According to democratic theorist Peter Bachrach, Schumpeter thought "it is absurd to believe that 'the people' have rational views on every issue and that the function of their representatives is to carry out their views in the legislative chamber." Peter Bachrach, THE THEORY OF DEMOCRATIC ELITISM: A CRITIQUE 20 (1967). Thus, according to Schumpeter, "the people must understand that they cannot take political action between elections. Even 'bombarding' representatives with letters and telegrams, Schumpeter argued, ought to be banned." *Id.* at 21 (internal citation omitted). For a rejection of a "vote-centered" model of democracy, consider Bennett, *supra* note 108.

111. Even the Constitution, it should be recalled, is not completely insulated from control of the people, since it is subject to amendment, albeit through resort to a complex and difficult process. See U.S. Const. Art. V.

112. Morone, *supra* note 109, at 1.

113. *Id.* at 2.

114. *See* Alexander Meiklejohn, *The First Amendment Is an Absolute,* 1961 S. Ct. Rev. 245, 255 (arguing that the electorate is the true governor, and that those selected to govern are merely agents of that true governor).

115. See David Held, MODELS OF DEMOCRACY 93 (2d ed. 1996) (pointing out that Madison "conceived of the federal representative state as the key mechanism to aggregate individuals' interests and to protect their rights").

116. For an earlier response to what I have described as "democracy bashing" by a number of modern legal scholars, see Martin H. Redish, *Judge-Made Abstention and the Fashionable Art of "Democracy Bashing,"* 40 Case Western L. Rev. 997 (1990).

117. Bennett, *supra* note 108.

118. *Id.* at 871–76.

119. Sunstein, *supra* note 35 (describing the four central principles of liberal republicanism).

120. *Id.* at 1554. See also Sunstein, *supra* note 38, at 31–32 (positing that "through discussion people can, in their capacities as citizens, escape private interests and engage in pursuit of the public good . . . . [T]his conception reflects a belief that debate and discussion help to reveal that some values are superior to others. Denying that decisions about values are merely matters of taste, the republican view assumes that 'practical reason' can be used to settle social issues.").

121. For a more detailed discussion of this view, see Redish, *supra* note 116 at 135–61.

122. *See* Mashaw, *supra* note 6, at 87 (finding "it difficult to understand why we do not presently have exactly the 'clowns . . . we deserve.' The dynamics of accountability apparently involve voters willing to vote upon the basis of their representative's record in the legislature. Assuming that our current representatives in the legislature vote for laws that contain vague delegations of authority, we are presumably holding them accountable for that at the polls. How is it that we are not being represented?").

123. For the application of this point specifically to the context of class actions and the surreptitious adoption of a bounty hunter remedial model, see discussion *infra* at 51–52.

124. Consider Abner J. Mikva, *Symposium on the Theory of Public Choice: Foreword,* 74 Va. L. Rev. 167 (1988); Mark Kelman, *"Public Choice" and Public Spirit,* 87 Pub. Int. 80 (1987).

125. Levi, *supra* note 94, at 2.

126. George L. Priest, *Procedural versus Substantive Controls of Mass Tort Class Actions,* 6 J. Legal Stud. 521, 525 (1997).

127. *Id.*

128. *Id.*

129. See, for example, Michael Allen and Amy Goldstein, *Bush Urges Malpractice Damage Limits; Plan Includes Goals Sought by Business,* WASHINGTON POST A4 (July 26, 2002).

130. *See* Hensler, et al., *supra* note 18, at 21 ("The 'aroma of gross profiteering' that many perceive rising from damage class actions troubles even those who support continuance of damage class actions and fuels the controversy over them."). See also Coffee, *supra* note 4, at 724 ("[T]he plaintiff's attorney in class and derivative actions has long been a controversial figure."). A Third Circuit task force has noted that "there is a perception among a significant part of the non-lawyer population and even among lawyers and judges . . . that class action plaintiffs' lawyers are overcompensated for the work they do." Chief Judge Edward R. Becker, *Third Circuit Task Force Report on Selection of Class Counsel,* 74 Temple L. Rev. 689,

692 (2001). For an example from the popular press, see Mauk, *Lawsuit Abuse,* CHARLESTON GAZETTE at 5A (cited in note 70).

131. *See* Nicholas Lemann, *The Newcomer: Senator John Edwards is this season's Democratic rising star,* NEW YORKER 58, 82 (May 6, 2002) ("Within the Republican Party, it is axiomatic that trial lawyers are bad guys. The idea is that the old, unsavory ambulance-chaser type has now figured out how to get really rich, in a way that drives businesses into bankruptcy and makes worthwhile activities uninsurable. Talk to Republicans in politics, and you'll get a lurid picture of top trial lawyers riding around in private planes and giving lots of money to Democratic politicians, in order to insure that there won't be any legislative limits placed on their sky-high damage awards . . . It would therefore be natural for Republicans to assume that the way to beat [North Carolina Senator] John Edwards is simply to point out that he is a trial lawyer."). See also Morton Kondracke, *Trial Lawyers As a Political Issue,* SAN DIEGO UNION & TRIBUNE G2 (July 28, 2002) ("Democrats often accuse Republicans of being the 'party of special interests' but the Democrats rarely get tagged as 'the party of trial lawyers,' which they are.").

132. See, for example, Coffee, *supra* note 4, at 670, n. 3 (noting "the frequency with which judicial opinions favoring new restrictions on the availability of class actions or other remedies criticize the plaintiff's attorney").

133. John C. Coffee, Jr., *Class Action Accountability: Reconciling Exit, Voice, and Loyalty in Representative Litigation,* 100 Colum. L. Rev. 370, 371–72 (2000) (internal citation omitted). Professor Coffee further notes the "standard depiction (of the plaintiff class attorney) as a profit-seeking entrepreneur, capable of opportunistic actions." *Id.*

134. Hensler, et al, *supra* note 18, at 21.

135. Note the arguable inconsistency between this view and the alternative criticism of my democratic critique that the furtive transformation underlying substantive law matters not at all, because the electorate is wholly ignorant about current legislation. One would think that critics of my democratic critique cannot have it both ways.

136. *See* discussion *supra* at 31.

137. *See* discussion *supra* at 36–42. For far more detailed discussions of my proposed revision of the current opt-out system, see Chapter 4, *infra* at 130–33.

138. *See* Chapter 4, *infra* at 128–30; Chapter 5, *infra* at 162–69.

139. Fed. R. Civ. P. 23(b)(2).

140. Fed. R. Civ. P. 23(e).

141. A 2000 RAND study on class action suits recommended that "judges require settling parties to detail plans for disbursing benefits to eligible claimants and suggested that preference be given to automatic disbursement schemes, such as crediting accounts of eligible class members." Hensler and Rowe, *supra* note 45, at 150. While this proposal would no doubt represent an improvement, my recommendation is to include the inquiry at the certification stage, rather than solely the settlement stage. Of course, in the context of settlement class actions, whose frequency is increasing, the difference is moot.

142. Fed. R. Civ. P. 23(b)(3) (listing as one of the factors pertinent to the court's findings as to the maintainability of the action as a class action, "the difficulties likely to be encountered in the management of a class action").

143. Note that the dichotomy between the initial certification decision and subsequent approval of settlement assumes the classic form of the class action. In light of the dramatic development in recent years of the so called settlement class action, in many cases the two stages have been collapsed into one stage. *See generally* Chapter 6, *infra*. However, the only impact of this change on my suggested reforms would be that both would necessarily take place simultaneously.

144. Such a proposal was made in Professor Hensler's RAND study, which suggested that "if judges approve coupon settlements . . . they (should) base fee awards on the monetary value of coupons redeemed, not offered." Hensler and Rowe, *supra* note 45, at 151 (emphasis in original).

145. See, for example, William N. Eskridge, Jr., *Dynamic Statutory Interpretation*, 135 U. Pa. L. Rev. 1479, 1497–98 (1987) (arguing that statutory interpretation need not conform to the intent of Congress (and therefore, presumably the intent of the electorate) and recommending a dynamic approach to meet changing societal circumstances).

146. *See* discussion *supra* at 44–50.

147. *See* discussion *supra* at 26.

148. *See* discussion *supra* at 56–60.

149. Note that in subsequent chapters, I explore in more detail the specific contexts in which opt-in should be required. I also explore the grounding in constitutional and the political theory of individualism to support such a requirement. See Chapters 4, 5 *infra*. For present purposes, however, I need not explore those questions. Suffice it to say, at this point, that democratic theory, in certain situations, dictates the need for an opt-in, rather than an opt-out, procedure.

150. *See* discussion *supra* at 43.

3. THE SUPREME COURT, THE RULES ENABLING ACT, AND THE POLITICIZATION OF THE CLASS ACTION

1. In re Rhone-Poulenc Rorer, Inc. 51 F.3d 1293 (7th Cir. 1995).

2. *See generally* Chapter 2, *supra*.

3. *See* 28 U.S.C. § 2072(a) ("The Supreme Court shall have the power to prescribe general rules of practice and procedure").

4. *See* 356 U.S. 525, 549 (1958) (Whittaker, J., concurring in part and dissenting in part) ("The words 'substantive' and 'procedural' are mere conceptual labels and in no sense talismanic.").

5. *See* 304 U.S. 64, 91–92 (1938) (Reed, J., concurring) ("The line between procedural and substantive law is hazy").

6. See, *e.g.*, Stephen B. Burbank, *Procedure, Politics and Power: The Role of Congress*, 79 Notre Dame L. Rev. 1677, 1705 (2004); Paul D. Carrington, *"Substance" and "Procedure" in the Rules Enabling Act*, 1989 Duke L.J. 281, 290 (1989).

7. *See* U.S. Const. Art. III (providing federal judges with protections of tenure and salary).

8. U.S. Const. Art. III, § 2, cl. 1 (granting federal judicial power to adjudication of cases and controversies).

9. *See* 28 U.S.C. § 2072(b) ("Such rules shall not abridge, enlarge or modify any substantive right.").

10. *See* Mistretta v. United States, 488 U.S. 361, 387 (1989) (discussing Sibbach v. Wilson & Co., 312 U.S. 1 (1941), and various other cases); Sibbach v. Wilson & Co., 312 U.S. 1, 9–10 (1941) ("Congress has undoubted power to regulate the practice and procedure of federal courts, and may exercise that power by delegating to this or other federal courts authority to make rules not inconsistent with the statutes or [C]onstitution of the United States").

11. 28 U.S.C. § 2072(b).

12. *See, e.g.,* Bus. Guides, Inc. v. Chromatic Commc'ns Enters., Inc., 498 U.S. 533, 552 (1991); Cooter & Gell v. Hartmarx Corp., 496 U.S. 384, 391–93 (1990); Burlington N. R.R. Co. v. Woods, 480 U.S. 1, 8 (1987); Hanna v. Plumer, 380 U.S. 460, 472 (1965); Sibbach, 312 U.S. at 9–10.

13. *Compare* Stephen B. Burbank, *The Rules Enabling Act of 1934,* 130 U. Pa. L. Rev. 1015, 1085–97 (1982) (advocating a historical approach to interpreting the Rules Enabling Act and requiring the allocation of power between the Supreme Court and Congress, not between the federal government and state government), *with* John Hart Ely, *The Irrepressible Myth of Erie,* 87 Harv. L. Rev. 693, 718–38 (1974) (arguing that the Rules Enabling Act subordinates the Federal Rules to state rules based on substantive policy).

14. *See* sources cited in note 13, *supra.*

15. 28 U.S.C. § 2072(a).

16. Under the terms of the Enabling Act, Congress retains power, through legislative action, to reject Federal Rules submitted to it by the Supreme Court. *See id.* § 2074(b).

17. *See* Chapter 1, *supra* at 2–5; Chapter 2, *supra* at 35–53.

18. U.S. Const. Art. I, § 7.

19. Note that when the issue is the interpretation of the counter-majoritarian Constitution, concern about the responsiveness of the decision maker works in exactly the opposite manner. *See* Martin H. Redish, THE FEDERAL COURTS IN THE POLITICAL ORDER 75–85 (1991) (explaining the nature of the counter-majoritarian principle and the role of the unaccountable Supreme Court in enforcing the Constitution). That issue, however, is irrelevant here.

20. Stephen N. Subrin, *How Equity Conquered Common Law: The Federal Rules of Civil Procedure in Historical Perspective,* 135 U. Pa. L. Rev. 909, 944, 947, 964 (1987).

21. *See* Burbank, *supra* note 6, at 1706–08; *see also* Subrin, *supra* note 20, at 944, 946, 1000.

22. Subrin, *supra* note 20, at 917. *See also id.* (citations omitted):

Due to the countless pleading rules, a party could easily lose on technical grounds. Lawyers had to analogize to known writs and use "fictions" because of the rigidity of some forms of action. Lawyers also found other ways around the common law rigidities, such as asserting the common count and general denials, which made a mockery of the common law's attempt to define, classify, and clarify.

23. Charles E. Clark, *Fundamental Changes Effected by the New Federal Rules I,* 15 Tenn. L. Rev. 551, 560 (1939).

24. *See id.* at 551–52.

25. *Id.* at 551.

26. *See id.* at 560–62; see also Subrin, *supra* note 16, at 962–63; cf. *id.* at 922 (stating that the "underlying philosophy of, and procedural choices embodied in, the Federal Rules [of Civil Procedure] were almost universally drawn from equity rather than common law").

27. For a more thorough description of the battle to enact the Rules Enabling Act, *see* Burbank, *supra* note 13, at 1094–98.

28. Subrin, *supra* note 20, at 944–48.

29. *Id.* at 946.

30. 28 U.S.C. § 723(b) (1934) (current version at 28 U.S.C. § 2072(a)-(b)).

31. *See* Clark, *supra* note 23, at 555–56.

32. See *id.* at 557. The current version provides: "(a) The Supreme Court shall have the power to prescribe general rules of practice and procedure and rules of evidence for cases in the United States district courts (including proceedings before magistrate judges thereof) and courts of appeals. (b) Such rules shall not abridge, enlarge or modify any substantive right." 28 U.S.C. § 2072(a)-(b).

33. *See* Clark, *supra* note 23, at 555–56.

34. *See generally* Michael E. Smith, *Judge Charles E. Clark and The Federal Rules of Civil Procedure,* 85 Yale L.J. 914 (1975) (providing a description of Clark's involvement in crafting the Federal Rules).

35. *See* Burbank, *supra* note 13, at 1114. Professor Burbank notes that the "individuals concerned about allocation standards were not primarily animated by constitutional considerations . . . To the extent [they] referred to constitutional limitations, it was to fortify support for statutory limitations independently deemed appropriate, which Congress had the power to impose in the Act." *Id.* at 1114–15.

36. *See, e.g.,* Sibbach v. Wilson, 312 U.S. 1, 6–16 (1941).

37. *See* Burbank, *supra* note 13, at 1063–95. Senator Walsh's opposition ended with his death in 1933, finally allowing the long-awaited passage of the bill in 1934. *Id.* at 1095.

38. *See id.* at 1064.

39. *See* S. Rep. No. 64-892, pt. 2, at 6–9 (1917); *see also* Burbank, *supra* note 13, at 1064 (observing that a majority of the committee signed the "Views of the Minority" section of the Senate report).

40. Burbank, *supra* note 13, at 1064.

41. *See id.* at 1063–65.

42. Senator Thomas J. Walsh, *Reform of Federal Procedure,* Address at a meeting of the Tri-State Bar Association (Apr. 23, 1926), in S. Rep. No. 69-1174, at 20, 33 (1926).

43. *See* Burbank, *supra* note 13, at 1072–73.

44. *See id.* at 1073.

45. *See id.* at 1073 n.260 (quoting the full text of the letter).

46. *See id.* at 1085–89. "The Senate Committee deemed the suggestion that the bill involved an unconstitutional delegation of legislative power to the Supreme Court one that could 'hardly be urged seriously' in light of the history of such delegations and the opinions of the Supreme Court discussing them." *Id.* at 1085

(quoting S. Rep. No. 69-1174, at 8 (report submitted by Mr. Cummins, member of Committee on the Judiciary)).

47. *See* S. Rep. No. 69–1174, at 9-10.

48. *See* Burbank, *supra* note 13, at 1137. In its report, the Senate Committee wrote:

> Any power in the Supreme Court to deal with such matters as those referred to must be rested solely upon the provision authorizing it to make rules relating to "practice and procedure in actions at law." In view of the express provision inhibiting the court from affecting "the substantive rights of any litigant," any court would be astute to avoid an interpretation which would attribute to the words "practice and procedure" an intention on the part of Congress to delegate a power to deal with such substantive rights or remedies. It would rather conclude that in using the words "practice and procedure" Congress only intended to confer the power to make such rules of practice and procedure as the court itself could make without enabling legislation, and they would not include matters of the kind referred to.
>
> Where a doubt exists as to the power of a court to make a rule, the doubt will surely be resolved by construing a statutory provision in such a way that it will not have the effect of an attempt to delegate to the courts what is in reality a legislative function. And it is inconceivable that any court will hold that rules which deprive a man of his liberty, as in the case of an order of arrest, or put an end to a good cause of action, as in the case of a limitation or abatement of an action, or determine what jurors shall try a case and how they shall be selected, are merely filling "up the details," even though they relate to remedial rights. S. Rep. No. 69-1174, at 11.

49. *See* Burbank, *supra* note 13, at 1133 n.530. Clark himself articulated this uncertainty in a letter to Professor Carl Wheaton in 1935, stating:

> I cannot avoid the feeling that much of our procedural discussion gets really quite barren, that it is in effect word play, where we make words mean the definite things which they mean to us but which they have never meant to the code makers; and then, having gotten ourselves all tied up in words and achieved unlovely results, the only way out we can suggest is by remaking the code, a result utterly unrealistic and practically never to be expected.

Letter from Charles E. Clark to Professor Carl Wheaton (Feb. 16, 1935), in JUDGE CHARLES EDWARD CLARK 139, 139 (Peninah Petruck ed., 1991).

50. Burbank, *supra* note 13, at 1132.

51. *See id.* at 1133–35.

52. *Id.* at 1137.

53. Mistretta v. United States, 488 U.S. 361, 392 (1989). "Rule 23 . . . has inspired a controversy over the philosophical, social, and economic merits and demerits of class actions." *Id.* at 392 n.19.

54. Fed. R. Civ. P. 11.

55. Fed. R. Civ. P. 26.

56. *See, e.g.,* Transcript of Public Hearing on Proposed Amendments to the Federal Rules of Civil Procedure, Dallas, Tex. (Jan. 28, 2005), http:// www .uscourts.gov/rules/e-discovery/DallasHearing12805.pdf [hereinafter Dallas Hearing Transcript]. Among the various groups testifying at the Dallas hearing were the Texas Trial Lawyers Association, corporate counsel from Exxon Mobil Corporation, and consumer advocate groups. *See id.* at 3–19, 35–51, 68–101. Similarly, representatives from organizations such as the American Insurance Association, Defense Research Institute, National Association of Consumer Advocates, American Trial Lawyers Association, Lawyers for Civil Justice, and Alliance of American Insurers attended the class action amendment hearings. Other rules scrutinized in the context of tort reform are the notice pleading rule, Fed. R. Civ. P. 8, and the summary judgment rule, Fed. R. Civ. P. 56. *See, e.g.,* Arthur R. Miller, *The Pretrial Rush to Judgment: Are the "Litigation Explosion," "Liability Crisis," and Efficiency Clichés Eroding Our Day in Court and Jury Trial Commitments?,* 78 N.Y.U. L. Rev. 982, 1009–10, 1074–77 (2003).

57. *See* Miller, *supra* note 56 (discussing these contentions and concluding that the drive toward efficiency threatens to undermine the right to a trial by jury); *see also* Carl Hulse, *Bill To Require Sanctions on Lawyers Passes House,* N.Y. Times, Sept. 15, 2004, at A20 (describing legislation to amend the current version of Rule 11 to mandate sanctions for filing baseless lawsuits).

58. *See* Jeffrey W. Stempel, *Not-So-Peaceful Coexistence: Inherent Tensions in Addressing Tort Reform,* 4 Nev. L.J. 337, 363–68 (2003/2004).

59. *See id.* at 340.

60. *See, e.g.,* Hulse, *supra* note 57 (describing the political debate over Rule 11 in the context of tort reform).

61. Fed. R. Civ. P. 11(b)-(c).

62. *See* Fed. R. Civ. P. 11 (1983) (amended 1987, 1993).

63. *See* Stephen N. Subrin, *Teaching Civil Procedure While You Watch It Disintegrate,* 59 Brook. L. Rev. 1155, 1164 (1993) (observing that the two rules are "almost self-contradictory").

64. Fed. R. Civ. P. 8(a) (1938) (amended 1966, 1987); *see also* Fed. R. Civ. P. Form 9 (1938) (amended 1963) (providing a legally sufficient sample pleading).

65. *See* Mary Margaret Penrose & Dace A. Caldwell, *A Short and Plain Solution to the Medical Malpractice Crisis: Why Charles E. Clark Remains Prophetically Correct About Special Pleading and the Big Case,* 39 Ga. L. Rev. 971, 1007 (2005) (quoting Judge Charles Clark).

66. *See* Swierkiewicz v. Sorema N.A., 534 U.S. 506, 514 (2002) (rejecting heightened pleading requirements for employment discrimination claims); Leatherman v. Tarrant County Narcotics Intelligence & Coordination Unit, 507 U.S. 163, 168 (1993) (rejecting heightened pleading requirements for claims under 42 U.S.C. § 1983); Conley v. Gibson, 355 U.S. 41, 47 (1957) ("[T]he Federal Rules of Civil Procedure do not require a claimant to set out in detail the facts upon which he bases his claim. To the contrary, all the Rules require is 'a short and plain statement of the claim' that will give the defendant fair notice of what the plaintiff's claim is and the grounds upon which it rests.") (quoting Fed. R. Civ. P. 8(a)(2)); *see also*

Christopher M. Fairman, *Heightened Pleading,* 81 Tex. L. Rev. 551, 556–57 (2002). *See generally* Fed. R. Civ. P. 8(a) (describing claims for relief).

67. Note that Rule 11's impact on pleading standards came indirectly, since the revisers in 1983 purported to leave the Rule 8(a) burden unchanged.

68. *See* Fed. R. Civ. P. 11. Professor Miller wrote that the "strengthening of Rule 11 [in 1983] created a theoretically significant barrier to entering the judicial system . . . [T]he 1983 Rule was criticized for having a disproportionate impact, particularly in areas of the law considered 'disfavored' by some." Miller, *supra* note 56, at 1007–08. Because of the Rule's sanctioning measure, it could "be used against a party who brings a frivolous pretrial disposition motion, and may serve to deter them." *Id.* at 1009. Professor Miller further noted that "[a]fter several years of extraordinary activity under the [1983] Rule, a comprehensive study by the Federal Judicial Center (FJC) revealed that Rule 11 motions were filed much more frequently by defendants, that defendants' motions were granted with greater frequency, and that Rule 11 motions were filed disproportionately more often in civil rights cases, although the grant rate was not necessarily higher." *Id. See also* Carl Tobias, *The 1993 Revision of Federal Rule 11,* 70 Ind. L.J. 171, 176–78 (1994), for a description of the process of revising the 1983 version of Rule 11.

69. *See* H.R. 4571, 108th Cong. (2004).

70. Hulse, *supra* note 57.

71. *Id.* Democrats also commented that Republicans were "wasting time with frivolous legislation," and said the measure "represented a needless Congressional intrusion into local court matters." *Id.* Representative Sheila Jackson Lee stated that the House should "[g]ive the decision back to the courthouse, and let's have a fair judicial system for all." *Id.*

72. 1275 S. Ct. 1955 (2007).

73. Fed. R. Civ. P. 8(a).

74. *See* cases cited in note 66, *supra.*

75. Rules 26 and 34, which regulate the production of evidence in litigation, are the critical rules governing the discovery of electronic information. *See* Fed. R. Civ. P. 26, 34. On May 17, 2004, the Civil Rules Advisory Committee submitted to the Standing Committee on Rules of Practice and Procedure a comprehensive package of proposed amendments to the Federal Rules of Civil Procedure addressing discovery of electronically stored information, including revisions of Rules 16, 26, 33, 34, 37, and 45. *See* Civ. Rules Advisory Comm., Report to the Committee on Rules of Practice and Procedure of the Judicial Conference of the United States (2004), http:// www.uscourts.gov/rules/comment2005/CVAug04.pdf [hereinafter Advisory Comm. Report].

76. *See, e.g.,* Dallas Hearing Transcript, *supra* note 54, at 3–19, 35–51, 68–101, 136–53. Similarly, the class action amendment hearings were attended by representatives from organizations such as the American Insurance Association, Defense Research Institute, National Association of Consumer Advocates, American Trial Lawyers Association, Lawyers for Civil Justice, and Alliance of American Insurers.

77. *See* Advisory Comm. Report, *supra* note 75, at 20.

78. See Dallas Hearing Transcript, *supra* note 54, at 17–19 (statement of Jim Wren, Counsel, Texas Trial Lawyer's Association); *id.* at 80–81 (statement of Paul

Bland, Counsel, Trial Lawyers for Public Justice); *id.* at 146–49 (statement of Steve Morrison, Past President, Lawyers for Civil Justice).

79. *See id.* at 47 (statement of Charles Beach, Coordinator of Corporate Litigation, Exxon Mobil Corporation); *id.* at 58–61 (statement of Ann Kershaw, Founder of A. Kershaw, PC, Attorneys and Consultants, a litigation management firm that surveyed large companies and compiled findings on the burdens of electronic discovery).

80. *See id.* at 71 ("In the consumer class action world a great deal of litigation can only be proven with respect to financial services companies, HMOs or whatnot, with databases, with documents that are never, ever put onto paper. The documents simply don't exist on paper.") (statement of Paul Bland, Counsel, Trial Lawyers for Public Justice).

81. *See* Chapter 1, *supra* at 10–12. The original rule was complex and confusing and therefore underutilized. *See* Fed. R. Civ. P. 23 (1938) (amended 1966, 1987, 1998, 2003); Benjamin Kaplan, *Continuing Work of the Civil Committee: 1966 Amendments of the Federal Rules of Civil Procedure (I),* 81 Harv. L. Rev. 356, 380–86 (1967). Kaplan rewrote the rule to make it more coherent and easier to use. See *id.* at 386–94.

82. *See* Kaplan, *supra* note 81, at 380–86, 397–98.

83. *See id.* at 386–94.

84. *See, e.g.,* Al Meyerhoff, Op-Ed., *Legal Reform It's Not,* L.A. Times, Jan. 31, 2005, at B9.

85. *See* U.S. Const. Art. III, § 1 (providing members of the federal judiciary with protections of salary and tenure).

86. *See* A.L.A. Schechter Poultry Corp. v. United States, 295 U.S. 495, 529–30 (1935) ("Congress is not permitted to abdicate or to transfer to others the essential legislative functions with which it is thus vested.").

87. *See* U.S. Const. Art. III, § 2.

88. *See* Schechter Poultry, 295 U.S. at 529–30; Pan. Ref. Co. v. Ryan, 293 U.S. 388, 432–33 (1935).

89. *See* Valley Forge Christian Coll. v. Ams. United for Separation of Church & State, 454 U.S. 464, 471 (1982) ("The constitutional power of federal courts cannot be defined, and indeed has no substance, without reference to the necessity 'to adjudge the legal rights of litigants in actual controversies.'" (quoting Liverpool S.S. Co. v. Comm'rs of Emigration, 113 U.S. 33, 39 (1885)). The case-or-controversy requirement is the textual foundation for all of the prudential justiciability doctrines that forbid federal courts from adjudicating purely political questions, issuing advisory opinions, hearing moot issues, or hearing a case when a litigant lacks standing to maintain an action.

90. Mistretta v. United States, 488 U.S. 361, 374 (1989) (holding that "Congress' delegation of authority to the Sentencing Commission is sufficiently specific and detailed to meet constitutional requirements"); *see also* Morrison v. Olson, 487 U.S. 654, 695 (1988).

91. U.S. Const. Art. 1, § 1.

92. *See, e.g.,* Nat'l Broad. Co. v. United States, 319 U.S. 190, 225–26 (1943) (upholding largely standardless delegation of authority to the Federal Communications

Commission pursuant to the Federal Communications Act of 1934, 47 U.S.C. § 305 (2000)).

93. *See* U.S. Const. Art. II, § 2, cl. 2 (stating that the president shall have the power to nominate Supreme Court justices).

94. U.S. Const. Art. III, § 1 (guaranteeing salary and tenure).

95. Jerry L. Mashaw, *Prodelegation: Why Administrators Should Make Political Decisions*, 1 J.L. Econ. & Org. 81, 95 (1985). So-called "independent" agencies are somewhat more problematic, because their members are not subject to total executive control. *See* Humphrey's Ex'r v. United States, 295 U.S. 602, 625 (1935). At the very least, however, members of such agencies do not sit for life, nor do they have constitutionally imposed protections of their salaries. Thus, they are far more responsive than are members of the federal judiciary, who are protected by Article III. *See* U.S. Const. Art. III, § 1 (providing that a judge's compensation may not decrease during his or her tenure).

96. *See* Sherman Act § 1, 15 U.S.C. § 1.

97. *See* Lincoln Mills v. Textile Workers Union of Am., 353 U.S. 448, 448 (1957).

98. *See* U.S. Const. Art. III, § 2.

99. *See* Marbury v. Madison, 5 U.S. 137, 170–72 (1803) (justifying judicial review as a necessary element of the resolution of live disputes).

100. For an argument seeking to distinguish administrative and adjudicatory delegations, *see* Martin H. Redish, THE CONSTITUTION AS POLITICAL STRUCTURE 140–41 (1995).

101. *See* THE FEDERALIST No. 78, at 468–71 (Alexander Hamilton) (Clinton Rossiter ed., 1961) (explaining the need for an independent judiciary); *see also* Martin H. Redish & Lawrence C. Marshall, *Adjudicatory Independence and the Values of Procedural Due Process*, 95 Yale L.J. 455 (1986) (exploring various rationales for judicial independence).

102. *See* U.S. Const. Art. III, § 2.

103. This also appears to have been the early Supreme Court's view. *See* Sibbach v. Wilson & Co., 312 U.S. 1, 9–10 (1941).

104. *See, e.g.*, Fed. R. Civ. P. 8(a) (addressing the level of detail expected from a party in the pleading filed at the outset of the suit); Fed. R. Civ. P. 56 (concerning summary judgment).

105. *See* Kaplan, *supra* note 81, at 398 (explaining how the 1966 revision of Rule 23, expanding class action availability, was designed in part to facilitate enforcement of Great Society social measures of the 1960s).

106. An illustration is the new amendment concerning electronic discovery. *See* Fed. R. Civ. P. 26(a)-(d).

107. *See, e.g.*, Fed. R. Civ. P. 13(a) (establishing a compulsory counterclaim rule having a preclusive effect on subsequent litigation).

108. For example, the level of detail demanded in pleading will inevitably impact the scope of post-pleading discovery.

109. *See, e.g.*, Fed. R. Civ. P. 10 (concerning captioning).

110. I should emphasize, once again, that I do not intend to refer to constitutional questions, though of course the case-or-controversy requirement should logically apply to the judicial resolution of those issues as well. My point here,

however, is merely that for policy choices not even arguably implicating the scope of a constitutional provision, the nation's commitment to foundational normative precepts of democratic theory, embodied in the Constitution, prohibits the unrepresentative judiciary from making them apart from as an incident to the resolution of live disputes.

111. *See* A.L.A. Schechter Poultry Corp. v. United States, 295 U.S. 495, 529–30 (1935).

112. *See* INS v. Chadha, 462 U.S. 919, 954–59 (1983) (characterizing a one-house veto as lawmaking).

113. I have explored this issue of legislative process in a different constitutional context. *See* Martin H. Redish & Shane V. Nugent, *The Dormant Commerce Clause and the Constitutional Balance of Federalism,* 1987 Duke L.J. 569, 592-93 ("The congressional legislative process is an arduous one that may entail a series of compromises from the time the bill is introduced until it is finally voted upon by the members of each house. Further, the process is lengthy, time-consuming, and replete with opportunities for delaying or *killing* a bill."); see also id. (citing sources).

114. U.S. Const. Art. I, § 7, cl. 2. *Cf.* INS v. Chadha, 462 U.S. 919 (1983) (bicameralism and presentment requirements render one-house veto unconstitutional).

115. *Cf.* Martin H. Redish, *Reassessing the Allocation of Judicial Business Between State and Federal Courts: Federal Jurisdiction and "The Martian Chronicles,"* 78 Va. L. Rev. 1769, 1769 (1992) (employing the construct of a Martian observer to test, de novo, the wisdom and logic of long-standing doctrines of federal jurisdiction).

116. *See* 312 U.S. 1, 6 (1941) ("This case calls for decision as to the validity of Rules 35 and 37 of the Rules of Civil Procedure for [d]istrict [c]ourts of the United States.") (citation omitted).

117. *See id.* at 13–14.

118. *Id.* at 9–10 (citation omitted).

119. *See* discussion *supra* at 68–70.

120. *Sibbach,* 312 U.S. at 10. While the Court spoke only of substantive rights created by state law, Professor Burbank has correctly noted that the Act's exemption of substantive rights applies equally to federal- and state-created substantive rights. See Burbank, *supra* note 11, at 1122 (noting that while "Professor Ely has invigorated the second sentence [of the Act] so as more effectively to protect substantive state policy reflected in state law in an area covered by a Federal Rule," history starkly contradicts this notion, as the protection of state law is a probable effect rather than the primary purpose of the allocation scheme established by the Act). Indeed, at the time the Act was passed in 1934, the Supreme Court had not even decided Erie Railroad Co. v. Tompkins, 304 U.S. 64 (1938), invalidating general federal common law, *id.* at 78.

121. *Sibbach,* 312 U.S. at 10.

122. *Id.* at 11.

123. *Id.* at 14.

124. *See id.* at 9–14.

125. *See* discussion *supra* at 75–76.

126. *See* Hanna v. Plumer, 380 U.S. 460, 475 (1965) (Harlan, J., concurring) (referring to "those primary decisions respecting human conduct which our constitutional system leaves to state regulation").

127. 380 U.S. 460, 464–66 (1965).

128. 488 U.S. 361, 387–90 (1989).

129. *Id.* at 362.

130. *Id.* at 385.

131. *Id.* at 386.

132. *Id.* at 387 (quoting Sibbach v. Wilson & Co., 312 U.S. 1, 9–10 (1941)).

133. 312 U.S. at 9–10.

134. *Mistretta,* 488 U.S. at 388.

135. *See id.* at 388–91.

136. *See* U.S. Const. Art. III, § 2.

137. *See, e.g., Mistretta,* 488 U.S. at 422–26 (Scalia, J., dissenting).

138. I am of course not suggesting that at no point does the federal judiciary engage in policy making. The point, rather, is that under the constitutional scheme set out in Article III, such policy making is authorized only to the extent it is incident to the resolution of live disputes. *See* discussion *supra* at 75–76.

139. *See* discussion *supra* at 70–73.

140. *Mistretta,* 488 U.S. at 392.

141. *Id.* at 392 n.19.

142. *See id.* at 385.

143. *See id.* at 386–88.

144. *Id.* at 412.

145. *See* Burbank, *supra* note 13, at 1034–35.

146. Linda S. Mullenix, *The Constitutionality of the Proposed Rule 23 Class Action Amendments,* 39 Ariz. L. Rev. 615, 618 (1997).

147. *See, e.g.,* Bus. Guides, Inc. v. Chromatic Commc'ns Enters., Inc., 498 U.S. 533, 540–64 (1991).

148. *Compare* Carrington, *supra* note 6, at 297–326 (suggesting a functional analysis and interpretation of the Rules Enabling Act), with Ely, *supra* note 13, at 724–28 (proposing alternative interpretations of the "substantive rights" exception to the Rules Enabling Act).

149. *See* discussion *supra* at 68–73.

150. *See* Burbank, *supra* note 13, at 1023–24, 1065–68.

151. Note, however, that such an approach would, in fact, likely result from acceptance of the constitutional attack fashioned here. *See* discussion *supra* at xx.

152. Fed. R. Civ. P. 23.

153. Fed. R. Civ. P. 8, 11.

154. Fed. R. Civ. P. 26(a)-(d). More debatable would be rules such as those dealing with summary judgment, Fed. R. Civ. P. 56, and judgment as a matter of law, Fed. R. Civ. P. 50, where although there has been relatively little political controversy, the scope of the Rules could have a significant impact on the nature of the enforcement of substantive rights. *See* Martin H. Redish, *Summary Judgment and the Vanishing Trial: Implications of the Litigation Matrix,* 57 Stan. L. Rev. 1329, 1340–41 (2005).

155. Burlington N. R.R. Co. v. Woods, 480 U.S. 1, 8 (1986) (holding that procedural rules that incidentally affect substantive rights are permissible under the second sentence of the Rules Enabling Act).

156. *Id.* at 5.

157. *Id.*

158. *See, e.g.,* Carrington, *supra* note 6, at 301–02.

159. *See* Mistretta v. United States, 488 U.S. 361, 419–22 (1989) (Scalia, J., dissenting).

160. It is important to emphasize that for purposes of my critique of the class action grounded in the dictates of American democratic theory, I remain wholly agnostic on the issue of Rule 23's wisdom or advisability. My views on those questions appear throughout the remaining chapters of this book.

161. *See* discussion *supra* at 70–73.

162. *See* discussion *supra* at 68–73; 78–83.

163. *See* Carrington, *supra* note 6, at 284.

164. *See Mistretta,* 488 U.S. at 370–74 (majority opinion).

165. *See id.* at 416–22 (Scalia, J., dissenting).

166. *See* Burbank, *supra* note 13, at 1027–28.

4. THE CLASS ACTION AS POLITICAL THEORY

1. Although the idea of some form of group litigation goes back to medieval England, that form of litigation was in fundamental ways distinct from the modern class action. *See* Stephen C. Yeazell, FROM MEDIEVAL GROUP LITIGATION TO THE MODERN CLASS ACTION 4–7 (1987). *See also* Chapter 1, *supra.*

2. *E.g.* David Rosenberg, *The Causal Connection in Mass Exposure Cases: A "Public Law" Vision of the Tort System,* 97 Harv. L. Rev. 849 (1983–1984); Owen Fiss, *The Political Theory of the Class Action, in* THE LAW AS IT COULD BE 122, 122 (2003).

3. *See, e.g.,* Jonathan R. Macey & Geoffrey P. Miller, *The Plaintiffs' Attorney's Role in Class Action and Derivative Litigation: Economic Analysis and Recommendations for Reform,* 58 U. Chi. L. Rev. 1, 27–61 (1991); Roger H. Trangsrud, *Mass Trials in Mass Tort Cases: A Dissent,* 1989 U. Ill. L. Rev. 69, 82–84; *see also* Mark A. Peterson & Molly Selvin, *Mass Justice: The Limited and Unlimited Power of Courts,* 54 Law & Contemp Probs. 227, (1991) (arguing that aggregative litigation necessarily compromises the ideals of justice).

4. The class action differs from other multi-party joinder devices listed in the Federal Rules of Civil Procedure [see, e.g., Rule 14 (impleader); Rule 19 (compulsory joinder), Rule 20 (permissive joinder), Rule 22 (interpleader), and Rule 24 (intervention)], because it allows for a total lack of participation by affected litigants. Other devices require all parties whose interests are the subject of the litigation to participate in the adjudication.

5. Benjamin Kaplan, *Continuing Work of the Civil Committee: 1966 Amendments of the Federal Rules of Civil Procedure (I),* 81 Harv. L. Rev. 356, 386 (1967).

6. *See* Chapter 1, *supra.*

7. *See* Fed. R. Civ. P. 23(a).

8. *See* Fed. R. Civ. P. 23(b).

9. Rule 23 does, however, provide a judge with discretion to direct some degree of notice to absent class members. *See* Fed. R. Civ. P. 23(c)(2)(A).

10. *E.g.* Robert G. Bone, *Statistical Adjudication: Rights, Justice, and Utility in a World of Process Scarcity,* 46 Vand. L. Rev. 561 (1993); Macey & Miller, *supra* note 3, at 105–16.

11. *See* Chapter 2, *supra* at 22–23.

12. *See, e.g.,* David L. Shapiro, *Class Actions: The Class as Party and Client,* 73 Notre Dame L. Rev. 913 (1998); Rosenberg, *supra* note 2; Fiss, *supra* note 2; discussion *infra* at 107–25.

13. *See* Rules Enabling Act, 28 U.S.C. § 2072. *See* Chapter 3, *supra.*

14. The two arguable exceptions are Owen Fiss, *The Political Theory of the Class Action, supra* note 2, and Rosenberg, *supra* note 2. Neither article, however, recognizes or deals with the foundational competing political theories potentially triggered by use of the modern class action.

15. 15 U.S.C. § 1501(a).

16. *See* discussion *infra* at 94–99.

17. *See infra* discussion at 99–101.

18. *See infra* discussion at 101–05.

19. *See infra* discussion at 105–06.

20. John C. Coffee, Jr., *The Regulation of Entrepreneurial Litigation: Balancing Fairness and Efficiency in the Large Class Action,* 54 U. Chi. L. Rev. 877, 904 (1987).

21. Fed R. Civ. P. 23(a).

22. Fed R. Civ. P. 23(b).

23. Fed R. Civ. P. 23(c)(2).

24. A district court has discretion to require notice even in the cases of mandatory classes based on its discretion. Fed. R. Civ. P. 23(d)(2).

25. Fed. R. Civ. P. 23(b)(1)(A). For a discussion of how the (b)(1)(A) class functions in practice, see In re A. H. Robbins, Inc., 880 F.2d 709 (4th Cir. 1988).

26. Fed. R. Civ. P. 23(b)(1)(B). The classic illustration are what can be called "limited pie" situations, where the total of the individual claims exceeds the amount of an identifiable fund available for compensation.

27. *E.g.* Baker v. Wash. Mut. Fin. Group, Inc., 2006 U.S. App. LEXIS 18551 (5th Cir. 2006).

28. *See* Fed. R. Civ. P. 23(c)(2)(A) (2007).

29. Fed. R. Civ. P. 23(b)(2) (2007).

30. *E.g.* Holland v. Steele, 92 F.R.D. 58 (N.D. Ga. 1981).

31. *See* Fed. R. Civ. P. 23(c)(2)(A) (2007).

32. Fed. R. Civ. P. 23(b)(3) & advisory committee's note (1966).

33. Fed. R. Civ. P. 23(b)(3) (2007).

34. *Id.*

35. *Id.*

36. Fed. R. Civ. P. 23(c)(2)(B) (2007).

37. The significance is not merely theoretical. Few potential class members ever opt-out of a class action. *See* Thomas E. Willging et al., EMPIRICAL STUDY OF CLASS ACTIONS IN FOUR FEDERAL DISTRICT COURTS: FINAL REPORT TO THE ADVISORY COMMITTEE ON CIVIL RULES 10 (1996) ("Across all four districts, the median percentage of members who opted out of a settlement was either 0.1% or 0.2% of the total membership of the class.").

38. Coffee, *supra* note 20, at 904–06.

39. *Id.* at 904.

40. *Id.* at 905. Professor Coffee also describes a third category of class actions, the Type-C class action, which occurs when the class includes absent class members with both Type-A and Type-B claims. *Id.* at 905–06. Specific consideration of this type of class action is unnecessary for the analysis presented in this Article. At a later point, I describe my own version of Type C class actions. *See* discussion *infra* at 131–33.

41. *See e.g., id.* at 904–06.

42. *See* discussion *infra* at 120–25.

43. *E.g.* Rhonda Wasserman, *Tolling: The American Pipe Tolling Rule and Successive Class Actions,* 58 Fla. L. Rev. 803, 819 (2006).

44. *See* Immanuel Kant, FUNDAMENTAL PRINCIPLES OF THE METAPHYSICS OF ETHICS 62 (Thomas Kingsmill Abbott trans., Longmans, Green & Co. 5th ed. 1916) (1873) ("A rational being must always regard himself as giving laws either as member or as sovereign in a kingdom of ends which is rendered possible by the freedom of will.").

45. John Stuart Mill, ON LIBERTY 63 (Elizabeth Rapaport ed. 1978) (1863).

46. *See* John Rawls, A THEORY OF JUSTICE 250 (1971).

47. *Id.* at 515; *see also* Immanuel Kant, FOUNDATIONS OF THE METAPHYSICS OF MORALS 51–52 (Lewis White Beck trans., Bobbs-Merrill 1959) (1785).

48. Ronald Dworkin, for example, has also focused on the conditions surrounding the exercise of decision making in defining autonomy by claiming "[a] person is autonomous if he identifies with his desires, goals, and values, and such identification is not influenced in ways which make the process of identification alien to the individual." Ronald Dworkin, *The Concept of Autonomy, in* THE INNER CITADEL: ESSAYS ON INDIVIDUAL AUTONOMY 61 (1989).

49. Whether these distinctions would impact how a model of the class action derived from liberal theory would be constructed is a subject best left for another day.

50. Many democratic theorists recognize the indispensable role of individual participation in political institutions in a legitimate democratic state. *E.g.* Alexander Meiklejohn, POLITICAL FREEDOM 9 (1960).

51. *Cf.* Joseph Shumpeter, CAPITALISM, SOCIALISM, AND DEMOCRACY 285 (1942) (noting that in a democracy "the people have the opportunity of accepting the men who are to rule them.").

52. Robert Nozick, ANARCHY, STATE, AND UTOPIA ix (1974).

53. Nozick's libertarian philosophy is closely tied to John Stuart Mill's earlier idea of the "Harm Principle," which claims the state may only coerce the will of its citizens to the extent necessary to prevent harm to others. Mill, *supra* note 45, at 61. Mill claimed that "[t]he only purpose for which power can be rightfully exercised over any member of a civilized community, against his will, is to prevent harm to others. His own good, either physical or moral, is not sufficient warrant." *Id.*

54. It is worth noting, however, that Nozick later described some of his views as "seriously inadequate" and appeared to recant aspects of his extreme form of libertarianism. Robert Nozick, THE EXAMINED LIFE 286-96 (1989); *but see, An*

Interview with Robert Nozick, The Robert Nozick Pages (Jul. 26, 2001), http://www
.juliansanchez.com/nozick/jsinterview.html (noting that "[w]hat I was really saying in *The Examined Life* was that I was no longer as hardcore a libertarian as I had
been before. But the rumors of my deviation (or apostasy!) from libertarianism
were much exaggerated.").

55. Rawls, *supra* note 46, at 136–42.

56. Rawls argues that the basis for any such restriction "can be defended only if
it is necessary to raise the level of civilization so that in due course these freedoms
can be enjoyed." *Id.* at 152.

57. *Id.* at 250.

58. *Id.* at 83.

59. *Id.* at 75–78.

60. Even in the "New Liberalism" of L.T. Hobhouse, which has been described as "communitarian liberalism," such a restriction would not appear to be
justifiable. *See* Alan Ryan, *The Liberal Community, in* DEMOCRATIC COMMUNITY:
NOMOS XXXV 95 (John W. Chapman & Ian Shapiro eds., 1993). Under this form
of liberal theory, which arguably justifies a more extensive role for the state in
regulating individual autonomy, the state may limit the decision-making power of
an individual any time where doing so would prevent an individual from exerting
coercion over other members of the community. L.T. HOBHOUSE, LIBERALISM 63
(Batoche Books ed., 1999) (1911). Yet any argument that would use Hobhouse liberal theory to justify the restriction of an individual's procedure-based choices in
the civil justice system would have to show that those decisions have the effect of
constraining another person's ability to make similar decisions. Such an argument
seems tenuous, at best.

61. Girardeau A. Spann, *Expository Justice,* 131 U. Pa. L. Rev. 585, 650 (1983).

62. Lon L. Fuller, *The Forms and Limits of Adjudication,* 92 Harv. L. Rev. 353,
364 (1978).

63. *See* Chapter 6, *infra* at 197–202.

64. Martin H. Redish, *The Adversary System, Democratic Theory, and the Constitutional Role of Self-Interest: The Tobacco Wars, 1953–1971,* 51 DePaul L. Rev. 359,
366 (2002).

65. *Id.*

66. RAWLS, *supra* note 46, at 515. Ronald Dworkin has also focused on the
conditions surrounding the exercise of decision making in defining autonomy by
claiming "[a] person is autonomous if he identifies with his desires, goals, and
values, and such identification is not influenced in ways which make the process of
identification alien to the individual." Ronald Dworkin, *The Concept of Autonomy,
in* THE INNER CITADEL: ESSAYS ON INDIVIDUAL AUTONOMY 61 (1989).

67. *See, e.g.,* 28 U.S.C. § 1335 (statutory interpleader). It should be emphasized,
however, that even in the case of interpleader, the individual litigant is still fully
responsible for the control of his participation in the adjudicatory process. In this
important sense, it is to be distinguished from the class action. See the discussion
in Chapter 1, *supra.*

68. *See* Chapter 6, *infra* at 190–93.

69. Henry Sidgwick, THE METHODS OF ETHICS 413 (1907).

70. Jeremy Bentham, INTRODUCTION TO THE PRINCIPLES OF MORALS AND LEGISLATION. Modern utilitarians appear to be in disagreement as to whether measuring the "total utility" created by an action means increasing the average utility of all the members of society or the sum of all utility among societal members. J. J. C. Smart, *An Outline of a System of Utilitarian Ethics, in* UTILITARIANISM: FOR AND AGAINST 1, 27–28 (J. Smart and B. Williams eds., 1973). As this ambiguity does not impact the analysis of utilitarianism from a liberal individualist perspective, I skip over this problem, noting only that accepting the Utilitarian Model of the class action likely requires an answer to this question.

71. James E. Crimmins, *Contending Interpretations of Bentham's Utilitarianism,* Canadian J. Pol. Sci. 751 (1996). Bentham has been quoted as saying that:

> Liberty . . . not being more fit than other words in some of the instances in which it has been used, and not so fit in others, the less the use that is made of it the better. I would no more use the word liberty in my conversation when I could get another that would answer the purpose, than I would brandy in my diet, if my physician did not order me: both cloud the understanding and inflame the passion.

Id. at 752 (citing Douglas G. Long, BENTHAM ON LIBERTY: JEREMY BENTHAM'S IDEA OF LIBERTY IN RELATION TO HIS UTILITARIANISM 173 (1977)).

72. R. Crawford Pratt, *The Benthamite Theory of Democracy,* 21 Can. J. of Econ. & Pol. Sci. 20, 20 (1955).

73. *Id.*

74. Jeremy Bentham, 1 PRINCIPLES OF THE CIVIL CODE IN WORKS 322 (1830).

75. *See* Richard A. Posner, *Utilitarianism, Economics, and Legal Theory,* 8 J. Legal Stud. 103, 112 (1979) (noting that "this formulation does not exclude the possibility that A may know B's true preferences better than B does—the possibility, that is, of paternalism.").

76. *E.g.* Fred Rosen, *The Origin of Liberal Utilitarianism: Jeremy Bentham and Liberty, in* VICTORIAN LIBERALISM: NINETEENTH-CENTURY POLITICAL THOUGHT AND PRACTICE (Richard Bellamy ed., 1990).

77. A source of disagreement among utilitarian theorists lies with whether that happiness is measured in terms of an aggregate of individual happiness or the general happiness of the entire society. *See* Posner, *supra* note XXX at 113.

78. Lawrence Haworth, *Autonomy and Utility,* 95 Ethics 5, 5 (1984).

79. *See* Mill, *supra* note 45.

80. Posner, *supra* note 75, at 116.

81. A common criticism of utilitarianism is to point to the "parade of horribles" that may emerge from the utilitarian state. The father of utilitarianism, Jeremy Bentham, did little to help his disciples in this regard as he once proposed eliminating begging by enslaving beggars. *Id.* Yet, in this regard, utilitarians frequently point out that, practically speaking, these sorts of horrible consequences are unlikely to ever occur as people typically do not derive sufficient pleasure from the suffering of others to allow such extreme results. *See* Smart, *supra* note 70, at 70–71.

82. Samuel Brittan, *Two Cheers for Utilitarianism,* 35 Oxford Econ. Papers 331, 334 (1983).

83. Christopher T. Wonnell, *Problems in the Application of Political Philosophy to Law,* 86 Mich. L. Rev. 123, 142 (1987–88).

84. Rawls, *supra* note 46, at 26.

85. *See* David A. J. Richards, *Rights and Autonomy,* 92 Ethics 3, 5 (1981) (noting that utilitarianism "fails to treat persons as equals in that it literally dissolves moral personality into utilitarian aggregates.").

86. That is not to suggest, however, that many of the core concepts of communitarian theory only emerged after Rawls. Aspects of communitarian theory date back as far as ancient Athens, and can be seen as a recurring theme in political theory. However, the focus of this chapter is solely on the communitarian political philosophers who have offered distinct approaches over the last twenty years.

87. It is this aspect of democratic communitarianism that has led some commentators to label it as simply a new approach to "majoritarianism." Michael J. Sandel, Liberalism and the Limits of Justice (1998).

88. *See* Charles Taylor, The Ethics of Authenticity (1991); *see also* Robert C. Post, *The Constitutional Concept of Public Discourse: Outrageous Opinion, Democratic Deliberation, and* Hustler Magazine v. Falwell, 103 Harv. L. Rev. 601, 685 (1990).

89. Charles Taylor, *Atomism, in* Philosophy and the Human Sciences: Philosophical Papers 2 (1985). It should be noted that "Atomisim" is primarily a response to rights-based libertarian theorists in the Nozickian tradition, rather than a critique directly aimed at the sort of liberal individualism of Rawls. Rawls in fact does address the role of social organizations in shaping social identity in *A Theory of Justice. See* Rawls, *supra* note 46, at Part III. This does not render Taylor's criticism of liberalism irrelevant, as subsequent communitarians have explained, because the extent to which Rawls incorporates the role of community in shaping identity is relatively minor.

90. Taylor, *supra* note 89, at 189.

91. *Id.* at 191.

92. *Id.* at 204.

93. *Id.*

94. *Id.* at 205.

95. *Id.* at 206.

96. *Id.* at 207.

97. Frank I. Michelman, *Conceptions of Democracy in American Constitutional Argument: The Case of Pornography Regulation,* 56 Tenn. L. Rev. 291 (1989).

98. *See* discussion *supra* at 94–99.

99. Linda Kerber, *Making Republicanism Useful,* 97 Yale L.J. 1663, 1665 (1988).

100. *See generally* Cass Sunstein, *Beyond the Republican Revival,* 97 Yale L.J. 1539 (1988); Frank Michelman, *Law's Republic,* 97 Yale L.J. 1493 (1988).

101. *Id.*

102. Martin H. Redish & Gary Lippman, *Freedom of Expression and the Civic Republican Revival in Constitutional Theory: The Ominous Implications,* 79 Cal. L. Rev. 267 (1991).

103. David Rosenberg, *Mandatory-Litigation Class Action: The Only Option for Mass Tort Cases,* 115 Harv. L. Rev. 831, 831 n.1 (2002) (claiming that his theory of the class action draws on "theories of deterrence, insurance, law enforcement, rational choice analysis, and welfare economics.").

104. *E.g.* Rosenberg, *supra* note 2.

105. *See id.* at 905–908.

106. *Id.* at 907.

107. *Id.* at 908. Professor Rosenberg also discussed the importance of restructuring the nature of remedies as an important element of the "public law" system of tort liability in mass exposure cases. *Id.* at 916–24.

108. *Id.* at 855–56. Professor Rosenberg also noted that the problem is compounded by the prohibition of statistical correlation evidence as the sole basis for liability under the traditional tort system. *Id.* at 857 & n. 37–38.

109. *Id.* at 855–56.

110. Peter Schuck, AGENT ORANGE ON TRIAL 23 (1987).

111. *Id.* at 29.

112. *Id.*

113. *Id.* at 143–67.

114. *Id.* at 270.

115. Rosenberg, *supra* note 103, at 859–60.

116. *Id.*

117. *Id.* at 859.

118. *See generally* David Rosenberg, *Mass Tort Class Actions: What Defendants Have and Plaintiffs Don't,* 37 Harv. J. on Legis. 393 (2000) (discussing the impact of the relative economies of scale between plaintiffs and defendants).

119. Bruce Hay & David Rosenberg, *"Sweetheart" and Blackmail Settlements in Class Actions: Reality and Remedy,* 75 Notre Dame L. Rev. 1377, 1379 (1999–2000). In making this argument, Professor Rosenberg departs from his traditional focus on mass exposure cases alone and speaks more generally about class actions across areas of substantive law.

120. *Id.* at 1379–80.

121. *Id.* at 1380.

122. Rosenberg, *supra* note 103, at 832.

123. *Id.* at 834.

124. *Id.* at 831–32.

125. *Id.* at 831. Professor Rosenberg does qualify this proposal by suggesting that this only applies to the adjudication of mass tort cases. *See id.* ("[m]y prior writings develop the argument for adjudicating *mass tort cases* collectively by mandatory litigation") (emphasis added). This limitation, however, neither alters my analysis nor does it remain consistent with the content-neutral role of procedure envisioned by the Rules Enabling Act.

126. Rosenberg, *supra* note 103, at 838.

127. *See* David Rosenberg, *Individual Justice and Collectivizing Risk-Based Claims in Mass Exposure Cases,* 71 N.Y.U. L. Rev. 210, 214 (1996) (claiming that his "perspective focuses analysis of civil procedure for tort cases on the discrete functions of tort liability in minimizing the costs of accident, most importantly by achieving

appropriate levels of deterrence and compensation consistent with the efficient administration of justice.").

128. "'Proceduralist' refers to the approach that ignores deterrence and compensation objectives and related individual welfare effects of the substantive law in evaluating the operation and potential redesign of the civil liability system." David Rosenberg, *Adding a Second Opt-Out to Rule 23(b)(3) Class Actions: Cost Without Benefit,* 2003 U. Chi. Legal F. 19, 19 n. 2.

129. *Id.* Professor Rosenberg has also been highly critical of the 1966 amendments to Rule 23 claiming that they are "basically flawed," *id.* at 20, and that they reflect an "inexplicable proceduralist disregard of the deterrence and insurance functions of civil liability and general neglect of the relative effects of rule choices on individual welfare." *Id.* at 20 n. 4. Further, "the 1966 revisions also displayed neophytic understanding of substantive law governing mass production risks, operational dynamics of procedure, and economies of practice." *Id.*

130. *Cf.* Rawls, *supra* note 46, at 136–42.

131. As with utilitarians that attempt to quantify the value of individual integrity, Rosenberg claims that his model provides for "appropriate regard for individual rights," rather than any sort of absolute protection in the Kantian tradition. *See* Rosenberg, *supra* note 103, at 860.

132. Rosenberg, *supra* note 103, at 211 n. 3.

133. Rosenberg maintains that from a political theory perspective, his model is consistent with a wide range of philosophies, relying on utilitarian theorists, as well as liberals like Rawls and libertarians like Nozick. *See* Rosenberg, *supra* note 103, at 860; Rosenberg, *supra* note 103, at 840 & n. 23. Yet in presenting his argument that liberal theory supports his model, Rosenberg still notes that his model is "intuitively more compatible with utilitarian premises than with notions of individual rights." Rosenberg, *supra* note 103, at 860.

134. *Id.*

135. In this way, he appears to conflate utilitarianism with law and economics, an approach of debatable merit. *See* Posner, *supra* note 75 (distinguishing economic analysis of the law from Benthamite utilitarianism).

136. Rosenberg, *supra* note 103, at 831.

137. Jeremy Bentham, THE THEORY OF LEGISLATION 1 (Upendra Baxi ed., 1975); *see also* George H. Sabine, A HISTORY OF POLITICAL THEORY 681 (1961) (noting that under Bentham's conception of the law "legislation is to be measured in terms of its effectiveness, the costliness of its enforcement, and in general by its consequences in producing a system of exchanges which on the whole is most advantageous to most members of the community. Utility is the only reasonable ground for making action obligatory.").

138. Rawls, *supra* note 46, at 22 (citing Henry Sidgwick, THE METHODS OF ETHICS (7th ed. 1907)). It should also be noted, given the link between the model proposed by Professor Rosenberg and other law and economics scholars, that Jeremy Bentham is recognized in some circles as "the parent of law and economics." *Animal Welfare and Economic Analysis,* The University of Chicago Legal Blog (April 18, 2006), http://uchicagolaw.typepad.com/faculty/animal_welfare/index.html.

139. *See generally* Rosenberg, *supra* note 103.

140. *Id.*

141. *See* Rosenberg, *supra* note 103, at 877–87.

142. *Id.* at 877 (citing Charles Fried, RIGHT AND WRONG 81–82 (1978); Nozick, *supra* note 54, at 57).

143. *Id.*

144. *Id.*

145. *Id.* at 878–79.

146. *Id.* at 879.

147. Nozick, *supra* note 54, at ix.

148. *Id.*

149. *See* Rosenberg, *supra* note 103, at 840–43; discussion *supra* at 96–97.

150. *Id.* at 840. It should be noted that under Rule 23 as it exists currently, the large majority of mass tort class actions will fall into the (b)(3) category, where both notice and an opt-out option are required. This is quite different from Rosenberg's approach.

151. *Id.*

152. Rawls, *supra* note 46, at 22.

153. *Id.* at 26.

154. *Id.* at 27.

155. *See id.* at 61–63.

156. *C.f.* Rawls, *supra* note 46, at 30–31. Rawls notes that in utilitarian theory,

> if men take a certain pleasure in discriminating against one another, in subjecting others to a lesser liberty as a means of enhancing their self respect, then the satisfaction of these desires must be weighed in our deliberations according to their intensity, or whatever, along with other desires. If society decides to deny them fulfillment, or to suppress them, it is because they tend to be socially destructive and a greater welfare can be achieved in other ways.

Id.

157. *See* discussion *supra* at 94–95. It should be noted that constitutional and normative barriers to such a transformation would be far greater were it to be imposed retroactively, as well as prospectively.

158. *See* discussion *supra* at 96–97.

159. *See generally* Martin H. Redish & Christopher R. Pudelski, *Legislative Deception, Separation of Powers, and the Democratic Process: Harnessing the Political Theory of United States v. Klein*, 100 Nw. U. L. Rev. 437 (2006).

160. The entity model is discussed extensively throughout this book in other legal and theoretical contexts. *See* Chapter 2, *supra* at 36–42; Chapter 5, *infra* at 149–56. However, I summarize the theory at this point in order to make the chapter stand on its own.

161. *See* discussion *supra* at 101–05.

162. Shapiro attributes the notion of a class as an entity to a number of other scholars, and the specific "entity" terminology to Professor Edward H. Cooper. *See* Edward H. Cooper, *The Institute of Judicial Administration Research Conference*

on Class Actions: Class Actions and the Rulemaking Process: Rule 23: Challenges to the Rulemaking Process, 71 N.Y.U. L. Rev. 13, 26–32 (1996). While the language of a class as an entity and many of the ideas associated with that theory do emerge from Professor Cooper's 1996 article, Professor Shapiro's work has helped to provide a more complete portrait of the impact of an entity approach to a class.

163. Shapiro, *supra* note 12, at 917.

164. *Id.* at 917.

165. *Id.* at 919. It is notable that Shapiro is careful to note that the entity theory does not eliminate every element of individualism from a class member. *Id.* (noting that "even this entity model does not deny the class member the opportunity to seek private advice, or to contribute in some way to the progress of the litigation."). Yet he correctly notes that this nominal retention of individual autonomy still "severely limits such aspects of individual autonomy as the range of choice to move in or out of the class or to be represented before the court by counsel entirely of one's own selection." *Id.*

166. *Id.* at 916.

167. *Id.* at 923.

168. *Id.*

169. *Id.*

170. *Id.* at 926. This is a view he attributes to Professor Robert Bone. Robert G. Bone, *Personal and Impersonal Litigative Forms: Reconceiving the History of Adjudicative Representation,* 70 B.U. L. Rev. 213, 234–87 (1990). Such a view of the (b)(2) and (b)(1) classes, it should be noted, is conceptual nonsense. Both (b)(1) and (b)(2) claims, are, in their pristine substantive form, individually held, as proven by the fact that, in the abstract, each could be legally pursued to fruition on an individual basis. They are transformed into class form solely because of procedural considerations or fairness or efficiency. For a more detailed explication of this point, see Chapter 5.

171. *See* discussion *supra* at 92–93.

172. Shapiro, *supra* note 12, at 926.

173. *Id.* at 925.

174. *Id.* at 926. As Shapiro notes, the Advisory Committee Note to the 1966 amendments to rule 23 specifically said that class actions would not be appropriate in mass tort cases because they typically would involve different questions of damages, liability, and defenses for each individual member. PROPOSED AMENDMENTS TO RULES OF CIVIL PROCEDURE FOR THE UNITED STATES DISTRICT COURTS, 39 F.R.D. 69, 103 (1966) (advisory committee's notes on proposed Rule 23).

175. *Id.* at 932.

176. *Id.* at 938.

177. *See* discussion *supra* at 99–101.

178. Given Shapiro's relatively scant analysis of (b)(1) and (b)(2) classes, however, it is difficult to determine which of these two approaches he takes in these contexts. Indeed, he may find the distinction irrelevant in (b)(1) and (b)(2) classes, as, practically speaking, "the class must in essence stand or fall as a unit because of the truly indivisible interests of the class members . . . or because the granting of equitable relief is bound to affect the group as a whole." *Id.* at 925.

179. *See also* Samuel Issacharoff, *Governance and Legitimacy in the Law of Class Actions,* 1999 Sup. Ct. Rev. 337, 357. Professor Issacharoff's work is examined in detail in Chapter 5, *infra.*

180. Shapiro, *supra* note 12, at 923.

181. *See* discussion *infra* at 101–102.

182. *See* discussion *supra* at 101–102.

183. See Shapiro, *supra* note 12. For more detailed discussion of the autonomy-paternalism dichotomy specifically in the context of procedural due process, see Chapter 5, *infra.*

184. Indeed, where appropriate such paternalistic concerns are dictated by due process. See Hansberry v. Lee, 311 U.S. 32 (1940). *See* Chapter 5, *infra.*

185. *See* discussion *supra* at 37–38.

186. *See* discussion *supra* at 101–05.

187. Owen Fiss, *The Allure of Individualism, in* THE LAW AS IT COULD BE, *supra* note 2, at 118; *see also id.,* at 122 ("It is not surprising, therefore, that the class action gained great currency during the civil rights era, when private attorneys generally received their greatest endorsement through the actions of groups such as the NAACP Legal Defense Fund.").

188. John Bronsteen & Owen Fiss, *The Class Action Rule,* 78 Notre Dame L. Rev. 1419, 1419, 1423 (2003).

189. *Id.*

190. Fiss, *supra* note 2, at 125 (noting that "the level of compensation must be high enough to make it worthwhile for the best and brightest to undertake such ventures.").

191. *See id.* at 120.

192. Bronsteen & Fiss, *supra* note 188, at 1423.

193. *Id.* at 1419.

194. *Id.* Fiss also fails to make clear whether a private lawsuit that provided no public benefit or operated against the public interest could be legitimately certified as a class if it still met the formal Rule 23 requirements, although he does seem to suggest that the Rule 23(b)(3) "superiority" factor could be used to preclude class actions where no public goals were achieved through a specific class action. *See id.* at 1424 (discussing the use of "superiority" as a means of limiting the instances where classes are certified).

195. As a general matter, Fiss believes the job of courts is "not to maximize the ends of private parties nor simply to secure the peace by to explicate and give force to the values embodied in authoritative texts such as the Constitution and statutes: Their job is to interpret those values and bring reality into accord with them." Owen Fiss, *Against Settlement, in* THE LAW AS IT COULD BE, *supra* note 2, at 101.

196. *See* Fiss, *supra* note 2, at 121.

197. *Id.* at 116.

198. *Id.*

199. *Id* at 119–120.

200. Bronsteen & Fiss, *supra* note 188, at 1421.

201. Fiss, *supra* note 2, at 118.

202. *Id.* at 120. In drawing this distinction, Fiss is differentiating these types of litigation from structural injunctions that appear in civil rights litigation.

203. *Id.*

204. Bronsteen & Fiss, *supra* note 188, at 1419.

205. Fiss, *supra* note 2, at 120; *see also* Judith Resnick, *From "Cases" to "Litigation,"* 54 Law & Contemp. Probs. 5, 52 (1991) (claiming that "the primacy of the individual in relation to her or his own case has declined.").

206. *See* Fiss, *supra* note 2, at 120.

207. *See* Bronsteen & Fiss, *supra* note 188 at 1419; 1424.

208. *See* Redish & Lippman, *supra* note 102.

209. *See* discussion *supra* at 105–06.

210. *See* discussion *infra* at 125–33.

211. Harry Kalven, Jr. & Maurice Rosenfield, *The Contemporary Function of the Class Suit,* 8 U. Chi. L. Rev. 684, 686–87 (1941) (going on to note that "[Administrative law] is a method of preventing injuries by the injunction, the stop order and the cease and desist order . . . an administrative body does not normally act to remedy wrongs which have occurred.").

212. *Id.* at 687.

213. *Id.* at 688.

214. *Id.* at 717.

215. *See* Kaplan, *supra* note 5, at 394. *See also* Chapter 2, *supra* at 29–35.

216. *Id.* at 386. *See also* Snyder v. Harris, 394 U.S. 332, 342 (1969) (Fortas, J., dissenting).

217. *Id.* at 1422. Interestingly, Professors Fiss and Bronsteen appear to propose changes to the rule in the same breath that they question the obligations of courts to observe the niceties of any procedural rule. *Compare id.* at 1423–50, *with id.* at 1451 ("Rule 23 lacks the force of law as that term is ordinarily understood. The rule is but a guideline or rule of thumb whose force derives only from consistent practice and the wisdom that the rule embodies.").

218. Notably, Kalven and Rosenfield made a similar argument with respect to the elimination of the older distinctions between "true," "hybrid," and "spurious" class actions. *See* Kalven and Rosenfield, *supra* note 211, at 703.

219. *See* discussion *supra* at 120–33.

220. Fiss & Bronsteen, *supra* note 188, at 1419, 1423. They go on to claim that the numerosity requirement should be used to help "limit class actions to circumstances in which they are necessary to uphold a value that is important enough to absent class members inherent in any class action." *Id.* at 1423.

221. *Id.* at 1427.

222. *See id.* at 1434–39.

223. *See* Chapter 2, *supra.*

224. *See generally id.*

225. This does not, I should note, represent a legal construction of the specific provisions of the current version of Rule 23. Rather, it is a normative approach to how the class action should be utilized, grounded in ideas drawn from political theory.

226. *See* discussion *supra* at 94–99.

227. Rawls, *supra* note 46, at 61.

228. *See* discussion *supra* at 94–97.

229. Rawls, *supra* note 46, at 62.

230. *Id.*

231. I recognize, of course, that the analogy to Rawls breaks down when viewed on a purely normative level. While I establish my two principles on the basis of an unwavering normative commitment to the value of process-based individualism, Rawls's Second Principle quite clearly contemplates a significant modification of the seemingly unbending commitment to individual liberty embodied in his First Principle. Still, I do not consider my model to be diametrically and inherently opposed to Rawls's Second Principle, because my focus is exclusively on the value of *process-based* autonomy, while Rawls's modification exclusively concerns the *substantive* version—an issue on which I am here agnostic. *See* discussion *supra* at xx. More importantly, my analogy to Rawls is purely a structural one: Like Rawls, I develop two principles, the second of which restricts the first when and only when to do so would paradoxically further the liberty of all individual claimants.

232. *See, e.g.,* NAACP v. Button, 371 U.S. 415 (1963).

233. 28 U.S.C. § 2072.

234. My analysis here focuses exclusively on issues of normative political theory. I challenge the mandatory class on constitutional grounds in Chapter 5, *infra*.

235. I should emphasize that to say that an individual has the right to refuse to initiate litigation does not necessarily mean that the individual will always possess unfettered autonomy in choosing *the timing of suit*. Thus, I see no problems with compulsory counterclaims [see Fed. R. Civ. P. 13(a)] or declaratory judgment proceedings, in which a potential defendant can effectively require a potential plaintiff to litigate his claim. The key difference is that in both of these contexts, the potential plaintiff always has the option of having res judicata imposed against him due to his refusal to pursue his claim at all. In contrast, a member of a mandatory class has no option to withdraw the legal pursuit of his claim under any circumstances.

236. *See* Shapiro, *supra* note 12, at 925–26.

237. *See* discussion *supra* at 115–19.

238. Richard A. Nagareda, *The Preexistence Principle and the Structure of the Class Action,* 103 Colum. L. Rev. 149, 228–31 (2003).

239. A litigant may seek damages in addition to an injunction or declaratory judgment, but that relief must be the secondary form of relief being sought. Charles Alan Wright, et al., FEDERAL PRACTICE AND PROCEDURE § 1775, at 463–70 (2d ed. 1986).

240. *See* discussion, *supra*, at 91–92.

241. *See* discussion *supra* at 107–15. Note that this is generally not current practice under Rule 23, since most mass exposure cases are likely to fall within the (b)(3) category, where the opt-out right is guaranteed.

242. *See* Coffee, *supra* note 220, at 904–06.

243. *See* Chapter 2, *supra*.

244. *See id.*

245. This is an argument more completely developed in Chapter 2, *supra*.

246. *Id.* at 81–82.

247. As previously discussed, Professors Rosenberg and Fiss appear to be exceptions to this description. However, as explained in prior discussion neither scholar accurately describes the true theoretical implications of their respective class action models. *See* discussion *supra* at 107; 120–25.

5. CLASS ACTIONS, LITIGANT AUTONOMY, AND THE GOALS OF PROCEDURAL DUE PROCESS

1. The thirteenth and fourteenth questions of the October 5, 2004 vice-presidential debate between John Edwards and Dick Cheney regarded the issues of tort reform and Edwards' career as a trial attorney. *See* Nathaniel L. Bach, *Trial Lawyer on the Ticket: Electoral Rhetoric and the Depiction of Lawyers in the 2004 Presidential Campaign,* 19 Geo. J. Legal Ethics 317 (2006).

2. U.S. Const. amend. V, cl. 4; amend. XIV, §1, cl. 3.

3. *See, e.g.,* Hansberry v. Lee, 311 U.S. 32 (1940).

4. *See, e.g.,* Richard A. Nagareda, *Administering Adequacy in Class Representation,* 82 Tex. L. Rev. 287 (2003).

5. Another commentator has also argued that for the most part, mandatory class actions are due process violations. However, at no point does he recognize or explore either the foundational nature of the autonomy factor or its relevance to the due process analysis as applied to class actions. *See* Steven T.O. Cottreau, Note, *The Due Process Right to Opt Out of Class Actions,* 73 N.Y.U. L. Rev. 480 (1998).

6. *See* discussion *infra* at 137–47.

7. *See* discussion *infra* at 138–39.

8. *See generally* Chapter 4, *supra.*

9. In this sense, I seek to distinguish myself from a critique of class actions grounded in a more sweeping form of libertarianism. *See generally* Natural Rights Liberalism From Locke to Nozick (Ellen Frankel Paul, Fred D. Miller, & Jeffrey Paul, eds.) (2004).

10. *See* discussion *infra* at 139–45.

11. *See* discussion *infra* at 142–44.

12. Fed. R. Civ. P. 23(b)(1) (A); (b)(1)(B); (b)(2).

13. It is thought by some that in Phillips Petroleum Co. v. Shutts, 472 U.S. 797 (1985), the Court held all mandatory class actions to violate due process. *See, e.g.,* Brown v. Ticor Title Ins. Co., 982 F.2d 386 (9th Cir. 1992); *cert. granted,* 510 U.S. 810 (1993); *cert. dismissed as improvidently granted,* 511 U.S. 117 (1994). However, this is a clear misreading of *Shutts. See* discussion *infra* at note 43.

14. Fed. R. Civ. P. 23(e).

15. 424 U.S. 319 (1976).

16. *Id.* at 334–35.

17. The Court found that the social security claimant's interest was minimal, because a relatively small amount was involved. *Id.* at 340–41.

18. 501 U.S. 1 (1991).

19. *Id.* at 10–11.

20. *Id.* at 10 (quoting *Mathews,* 424 U.S. at 334 (quoting Cafeteria & Restaurant Workers v. McElroy, 367 U.S. 886, 895 (1961)).

21. *Doehr,* 501 U.S. at 10.

22. *Id.* at 13.

23. *Id.* at 16.

24. *Id.*

25. Jerry Mashaw, *The Supreme Court's Due Process Calculus for Administrative Adjudication in* Mathews v. Eldridge: *Three Factors in Search of a Theory of Value,* 44 U. Chi. L. Rev. 28 (1976); Martin H. Redish & Lawrence C. Marshall, *Adjudicatory Independence and the Values of Procedural Due Process,* 95 Yale L.J. 455 (1986).

26. Mashaw, *supra* note 25, at 899.

27. *Id. See* also Redish & Marshall, *supra* note 25, at 481–83.

28. Mashaw, *supra* note 25, at 899.

29. I refer to this value as the "presumptive" foundation, because I fully acknowledge that, under sufficiently compelling circumstances, this presumption in individual control of the protection of her own interests may be rebutted.

30. *See* Martin H. Redish, *Judicial Parity, Litigant Choice, and Democratic Theory: A Comment on Federal Jurisdiction and Constitutional Rights,* 36 UCLA L. Rev. 329 (1988).

31. Democratic theorists have differed over the role that the individual should play in government, beyond the selection of governing officials. The most extreme of the theorists in support of a narrow role was Joseph Schumpeter. *See generally* Joseph Schumpeter, CAPITALISM, SOCIALISM AND DEMOCRACY (1942).

32. On the general issue of paternalism, see David L. Shapiro, *Courts, Legislatures and Paternalism,* 74 Va. L. Rev. 519 (1988).

33. *See* Lea Brilmeyer, *The Jurisprudence of Article III: Perspectives on the "Case or Controversy" Requirement,* 93 Harv. L. Rev. 297 (1979).

34. *See, e.g.,* Hawaii v. Standard Oil of California, 405 U.S. 251, 258 (1972); Missouri v. Illinois, 180 U.S. 208 (1901).

35. *See, e.g.,* Mullane v. Central Hanover Bank & Trust Co., 339 U.S. 306 (1950) (statutory provision for appointment of guardian to represent interests of beneficiaries of common trust fund).

36. Powell v. Alabama, 287 U.S. 45 (1932) ("It is hardly necessary to say that, the right to counsel being conceded, a defendant should be afforded a fair opportunity to secure counsel of his own choice." *But see* United States v. Walters, 309 F.3d 589, 592 (9th Cir. 2002) ("The Sixth Amendment grants criminal defendants a qualified constitutional right to hire counsel of their own choice but the right is qualified in that it may be abridged to serve some 'compelling purpose,' " (quoting United States v. D'Amore, 56 F.3d 1202, 1204 (9th Cir. 1999)); *See also* United States v. Panzardi-Alvarez, 816 F.2d 813, 816 (1st Cir. 1987) ("A criminal defendant's exercise of this right cannot unduly hinder the fair, efficient and orderly administration of justice.").

The right to defend oneself pro se has also been recognized in the courts. *See, e.g.,* Faretta v. California, 422 U.S. 806, 834 (1975) (citation omitted):

It is undeniable that in most criminal prosecutions defendants could better defend with counsel's guidance than by their own unskilled efforts. . . . The defendant, and not his lawyer or the State, will bear the personal consequences of a conviction. It is the defendant, therefore, who must be free personally to decide whether in his particular case counsel is to his advantage. And although he may conduct his own defense ultimately to his own detriment, his choice must be honored out of "that respect for the individual which is the lifeblood of the law."

37. *See* Frank I. Michelman, *Law's Republic,* 97 Yale L.J. 1493, 1533–36 (1988). For a more detailed exploration of the grounding of the commitment to individual autonomy in liberal political theory, see Chapter 4, *supra*.

38. Alexander Meiklejohn, POLITICAL FREEDOM 9 (1960) ("So far . . . as our own affairs are concerned, we refuse to submit to alien control."). I fully recognize, of course, that in a *constitutional* democracy certain choices are excluded from simple majoritarian choice. Unless the concept of accountable government is to be lost completely, however, the bulk of decisions must be made by those responsive to public will.

39. The Supreme Court has stated that "there is no such thing as a false idea." Gertz v. Robert Welch, Inc., 418 U.S. 323, 339 (1974).

40. *See, e.g.,* Wooley v. Maynard, 430 U.S. 705 (1977) (Jehovah's witnesses may not be required to display state slogan, "Live Free or Die" on their license plate).

41. By "process-based" autonomy I refer to an individual's autonomous right to protect his interests through participation in the governmental process. This is to be contrasted with a right to exercise total control over all aspects of one's life—a power that is infeasible, even in a democracy. The concept may also be described as "meta autonomy," because it refers to the individual's autonomy to make choices as to how he participates in the processes of self-government. *See generally* Chapter 4, *supra*.

42. Of course, if the very same unit of government that was prosecuting the defendant were permitted to choose his representative and/or direct the nature of his defense, additional constitutional problems would develop. However, the intuitive problem with this course of action is present, even if we posit that the branch or level of government making the choices as to defense strategy is wholly distinct from the branch or level involved in the prosecution.

43. In *Phillips Petroleum Co. v. Shutts,* 472 U.S. 797 (1985), the Court assumed that a plaintiff's property rights in her chose in action is somehow more diluted than is a defendant's constitutionally protected interest in avoiding judgment. *Id.* at 812. Like much in the *Shutts* decision, however, this conclusion is wholly unsupported with logic or reason, and is surely not intuitive. Both plaintiffs and defendants have a great deal to lose or gain as the result of litigation. Moreover, this suggestion of a gradation in the relative interests of plaintiffs and defendants is inconsistent with clearly established prior Court doctrine, that the *Shutts* Court in no way purported to affect. *See* Schlagenhauf v. Holder, 379 U.S. 104 (1964). In any event, as a bottom line matter, it is clear that the Court in *Shutts* recognizes in plaintiff claims a constitutionally protected interest, sufficient to trigger the due process guarantee.

44. *See* discussion *supra* at 138–39.

45. *See* discussion *supra* at 142–44. For a more detailed exploration of this reverse engineering process in the context of the adversary system, see generally Chapter 4, *supra*.

46. It is true, of course, that when government seeks, for example, to protect consumer interests through administrative or criminal enforcement of consumer protection laws, protected individuals do not possess a due process right to control the litigation. However, in such cases the individuals do not have constitutionally protected property interests—a necessary trigger to the guarantees of procedural due process—at stake. *See* discussion *infra* at 142–44.

47. *See* Fed. R. Civ. P. 13(a) (providing for compulsory counterclaims where counterclaim arises out of same transaction or occurrence as primary claim).

48. *See* the Declaratory Judgment Act, 28 U.S.C. §§ 2201, 2202.

49. Purists might suggest that attempting to mix utilitarianism, which traditionally cared not at all for the interests of the individual, with a formalistic commitment to individualism is equivalent to incongruously mixing oil and water. However, from a real-world perspective there exists no a priori reason why recognition of the value of individual autonomy cannot be tempered by pragmatic concerns. *See* Chapter 4, *supra*.

50. Ortiz v. Fibreboard, 527 U.S. 815, 845, 847-48 (2001); *see* discussion *infra* at 158–59.

51. *See* discussion *infra* at 144–45.

52. The discussion that follows largely reiterates the description of the modern class action contained in Chapter 1, *supra*. However, it is included at this point in order to allow the reader to treat each chapter as an integral whole, as well as one part of a broader analysis.

53. *See, e.g.,* Cooper v. Fed. Reserve Bank of Richmond, 467 U.S. 867, 874 (1984).

54. Fed. R. Civ. P. 23(a)(1)-(4).

55. Fed. R. Civ. P. 23(b)(1)-(3).

56. Fed. R. Civ. P. 23(c); (d).

57. Fed. R. Civ. P. 23(c)(3).

58. Fed. R. Civ. P. 23(c)(2)(B).

59. Fed. R. Civ. P. 23(d)(2).

60. *See* discussion *infra* at 148–73. It should be noted that while after *Ortiz* the scope of Rule 23(b)(1)(B) class actions has been limited, this category of class actions is still employed. *See, e.g.,* Devlin v. Scardelletti, 536 U.S. 1 (2002).

61. *See* Chapter 2 (democratic theory); Chapter 4 (liberal individualism).

62. *See* U.S. Const. Amend. XIV, § 1; U.S. Const. Amend. V.

63. *See* Logan v. Zimmerman Brush Co., 455 U.S. 422, 429 (1982) ("The Court traditionally has held that the Due Process Clauses protect civil litigants who seek recourse in the courts, either as defendants hoping to protect their property or as plaintiffs attempting to redress grievances."); Standard Oil Co. v. State of N.J., by Parsons, 341 U.S. 428, 439 (1951) ("There is no fiction . . . in the fact that choses in action . . . held by the corporation, are property."); Sentry Ins. v. Sky Management, Inc. 34 F. Supp. 2d 900 (D.N.J. 1999) ("A chose in action is an item of intangible personal property."); Commonwealth v. Kentucky Distilleries & Warehouse Co., 136 S.W. 1032, 1036 (1911) ("The term 'property' . . . include[s] . . . choses

in action."); Gibbes v. National Hospital Service, 24 S.C.2d 513, 515 (1943) ("In *McLemore v. Blocker, Harp.* [5 S.C.] Eq. 272 [(1824)], it said that "the word property, is of very extensive meaning," and includes choses in action."); Hutton v. Autoridad Sobre Hogares De La Capital, 78 F. Supp. 988, 994 (D.P.R. 1948) ("A vested right of action is property in the same 'sense in which tangible things are property, and is equally protected against arbitrary interference, and whether it springs from contract or from the principles of the common law, the legislature may not take it away." Quoting 11 Am.Jur.Sec. 377, p. 1206); Halling v. Industrial Commission of Utah, 263 P. 78, 81 (1927) (To not allow the widow to bring cause of action against her husband's employer for wrongful death, even though the husband had unsuccessfully brought a wrongful death cause of action, would, given Utah's Constitutional scheme, deprive "applicant of property without due process of law."); Mark Weber, *Preclusion and Procedural Due Process in Rule 23(b)(2) Class Actions,* 21 U. Michigan J.L. Reform 347 (1988) (making the argument that there is an individual property right in a cause of action, including those causes of action for injunctive or declaratory relief that the possessor has not personally filed in court).

Issacharoff characterizes the discussion of property rights in a chose as a "return to an older, more formal conception of a legal claim." Samuel Issacharoff, *Preclusion, Due Process, and the Right to Opt Out of Class Actions,* 77 Notre Dame L. Rev. 1057, 1058 (2002). Although this pejorative characterization is probably meant to imply that the notion of a chose as property is outdated, federal and state courts continue to consistently and explicitly recognize a property right in a cause of action. *See* cases cited in note 63, *supra*. It is worth noting that the modern trend has been to recognize new property rights for which due process rights attach, rather than to reject traditional definitions of property. *See, e.g.,* Goldberg v. Kelly, 397 U.S. 254 (1970) (giving procedural due process protections to welfare recipients); *See generally* Charles A. Reich, *The New Property,* 73 Yale L.J. 733 (1964). Similarly, an assertable defense is also a form of property protected by the Due Process Clause. *See* Baltimore & O.S.W. Ry. Co. v. Read, 158 Ind. 25, 62 N.E. 488, 490 (1902) ("The law recognizes that a vested right of defense to an action is, in a sense, property,—as much so as is a vested right of action,—and is equally protected as is the latter against an attempt of the legislature to destroy or take it away"); Logan, 455 U.S. at 429.

64. *Best Practices for Gatekeepers Emerging Communications, Inc. Shareholders Litigation Opinion, in the Court of Chancery of the State of Delaware in and for New Castle County,* 1530 PLI/Corp 167, 249–50 (2006) ("[I]t is established Delaware law that choses in action that survive the death of the victim are validly assignable").

65. Issacharoff, *supra* note 64.

66. Even proponents of such a view probably agree that an individual cannot be bound to a judgment unless he was adequately represented by the class proceeding. *See* discussion *infra* at 156–59.

67. *Id.* at 1060. To a similar effect, *see* David L. Shapiro, *Class Actions: The Class as Party and Client,* 73 Notre Dame L. Rev. 913, 917 (1998) ("[T]he notion of class as entity should prevail over more individually oriented notions of aggregate litigation."). *See* Chapter 2, *supra;* Chapter 4, *supra.*

68. *See also,* Shapiro, *supra* note 67.

69. *Id.*

70. *Id.* at 921.

71. *Id.*

72. *Id.* at 1058–61.

73. *Id.* at 1060.

74. Shapiro, *supra* note 67, at 1058–59. At least as a technical matter of collateral estoppel, however, *rejection* of an injunction does not decide future cases.

75. *See, e.g.,* Brown v. Board of Ed., 347 U.S. 483 (1954).

76. Fed. R. Civ. P. 24(b) (permissive intervention).

77. Certification under Rule 23(b)(2) is appropriate where "the party opposing the class has acted or refused to act on grounds generally applicable to the class, thereby making appropriate final injunctive relief or corresponding declaratory relief with respect to the class as a whole." Fed. R. Civ. P. 23(b)(2). Illustrative of class actions appropriately certified under Rule 23(b)(2) "are various actions in the civil-rights field where a party is charged with discriminating unlawfully against a class, usually one whose members are incapable of specific enumeration." *See* 39 F.R.D. 69, 102 (1966) (listing numerous appellate court decisions finding a proper class action in school desegregation and public accommodation cases).

78. *Id.* at 1059.

79. Such suits typically fall under Rule 23(b)(1)(B), at least when the claims are made into an identifiable fund. Traditional limited fund class actions "include claimants to trust assets, a bank account, insurance proceeds, company assets in a liquidation sale, proceeds of a ship sale in a maritime accident suit, and others." *See* Ortiz v. Fibreboard Corp., 527 U.S. 815, 834 (1999) *quoting* 1 NEWBERG ON CLASS ACTIONS § 4.09, 4–33; *See also* Rule 23 Adv. Comm. Notes 697; *See, e.g.,* Dickinson v. Burnham, 197 F.2d 973 (2nd Cir.), *cert. denied,* 344 U.S. 875 (1952).

80. *Id.*

81. *See* Fed. R. Civ. P. 23(b)(1)(B) and Advisory Committee's Note to the 1966 Amendment.

82. *Id.*

83. *Id.*

84. *See* Chapter 1, *supra;* Chapter 4, *supra.*

85. *See, e.g.,* In re Mexico Money Transfer Litigation, 267 F.3d 743 (7th Cir. 2001) (court approved coupon settlement in case against wire transfer companies alleging RICO and state anti-fraud violations).

86. Rinaldi v. Iomega Corp., Not Reported in A.2d, 1999 WL 1442014, 41 UCC Rep.Serv.2d 1143, Del.Super., Sep 03, 1999. A zipdrive is a portable inexpensive computer disk drive that permits users to save large amounts of electronic information on a relatively small magnetic disk.

87. Rinaldi v. Iomega Corp., 1999 WL 1442014, 41 UCC Rep.Serv.2d 1143, Del.Super., Sep 03, 1999.

88. While the Rules Enabling Act vests in the Supreme Court the power to prescribe procedural rules, the power is limited by the REA's substantive limitation which acts as a prohibition against procedural rules which trammel on existing substantive rights or which otherwise approximate substantive law making. *See* Rules Enabling Act, 28 U.S.C. §§ 2072; *see also* Chapter 3, *supra.*

89. For a more detailed exploration of the effects of this approach on democratic theory, see Chapter 2, *supra*.

90. *See* Rules Enabling Act, 28 U.S.C. § 2072; Chapter 3, *supra*.

91. The theory has nevertheless received so much attention here, because it clearly constitutes the most detailed theoretical argument against litigant autonomy.

92. In one instance, the Supreme Court, in a footnote, cryptically suggested a due process dichotomy between damage and injunctive claims. Phillips Petroleum Co. v. Shutts, 472 U.S. 797 (1985). However, it is my belief that the decision was intended to be confined to the highly limited due process context of constitutional limits on personal jurisdiction. *See* discussion *infra* at 158.

93. *See, e.g.,* Hansberry v. Lee, 311 U.S. 32 (1940); Stephenson v. Dow Chemical Co., 273 F.3d 249 (2nd Cir. 2001), *aff'd by equally divided court,* 539 U.S. 111 (2003). *See also* Amchem Prods., Inc. v. Windsor, 521 U.S. 591, 625–26 (1997) (recognizing importance of avoiding conflict between interests of class representatives and absent class members).

94. 311 U.S. 32 (1940).

95. Fed. R. Civ. P. 23(a)(4).

96. Proposed Amendments to Rules of Civil Procedure of the United States District Courts, 39 F.R.D. 73, 107 (Advisory Committee Note to Rule 23(c)(2)).

97. *See* discussion *supra* at 137–48.

98. 7A Charles Alan Wright, Alan R. Miller, & Mary Kay Kane, FEDERAL PRACTICE AND PROCEDURE §1786 (Civ. 3d ed. 2005).

99. 472 U.S. 797 (1985).

100. *Id.* at 812.

101. Brown v. Ticor Title Ins. Co., 982 F.2d 386, 392 (9th Cir. 1992) *cert. granted,* 510 U.S. 810 (1993); *cert. dismissed as improvidently granted,* 511 U.S. 117 (1994). *See generally* Arthur R. Miller & David Crump, *Jurisdiction and Choice of Law in Multistate Class Actions After Phillips Petroleum Co. v. Shutts,* 96 Yale L.J. 1 (1986).

102. Fed. R. Civ. P. 12(b)(1).

103. 527 U.S. 815 (1999).

104. *Id.* at 846.

105. Note that if *Shutts* had, in fact, found all mandatory damage class actions unconstitutional, the narrow construction given to Rule 23(b)(1)(B) in *Ortiz* for the purpose of reducing the scope of mandatory class actions would have been mooted.

106. *See, e.g.,* National Ass'n for Advancement of Colored People v. Button, 371 U.S. 415 (1963).

107. Hansberry v. Lee, 311 U.S. 32 (1940).

108. *See, e.g.,* National Ass'n for Advancement of Colored People v. Button, 311 U.S. 32 (1940).

109. *See, e.g.,* Abood v. Detroit Bd. of Educ., 431 U.S. 209 (1977); Democratic Party of U.S. v. Wisconsin *ex rel.* La Follette, 450 U.S. 107 (1981).

110. *See* Chapter 2, *supra* at 51–52.

111. For a detailed examination of the First Amendment right of non-association, see generally Martin H. Redish & Christopher McFadden, *HUAC, the Hollywood Ten, and the First Amendment Right of Non-Association,* 85 Minn. L. Rev. 1669 (2001).

112. *See* discussion *infra* at 170–73.

113. 527 U.S. at 838–39; see discussion *supra* at 158–59.

114. *See, e.g.,* In re Enron Sec., Derivative & ERISA Litig., 228 F.R.D. 541 (S.D. Tex. 2005); *In re* Syncor ERISA Litig., 227 F.R.D. 338 (C.D. Cal. 2005); Thomas v. Smithkline Beecham Corp., 201 F.R.D. 386 (E.D. Pa. 2001).

115. Proposed Amendments to Rules of Civil Procedure of the United States District Courts, 39 F.R.D. 73, 102 (Advisory Committee Note to Rule 23(b)(2)).

116. *See* Martin H. Redish, THE LOGIC OF PERSECUTION 147–48 (2005).

117. *See generally* Immanuel Kant, FOUNDATIONS OF THE METAPHYSICS OF MORALS (Lewis White Beck trans., Bobbs-Merrill 1959) (1785). In a similar vein, a respected modern democratic theorist has argued that liberal democracy "assumes that the individual will is the cause of all actions, individual and collective and . . . ascribes decisive epistemic and hence moral authority to the individual over his actions, on the grounds that he has privileged access to the contents of his own mind." Ian Shapiro, THE EVOLUTION OF RIGHTS IN LIBERAL THEORY 275 (1986). Democratic theory, Shapiro asserts, further assumes that "individual consent . . . [is] vital to the whole idea of political activity." *Id.*

118. *See* discussion *supra* at 154–55.

119. *See* discussion *supra* at 138–40.

120. *See* discussion *supra* at 148.

121. 255 U.S. 356 (1921).

122. Proposed Amendments to Rules of Civil Procedure of the United States District Courts, 39 F.R.D. 73, 100 (Advisory Committee Note to Rule 23(b)(1)).

123. Western Union Tel. Co. v. Pennsylvania, 368 U.S. 71 (1961) (state denied due process when it escheated unclaimed property held by Western Union because the state could not guarantee that no other state would make a conflicting and duplicative escheat claim).

124. 527 U.S. at 838–40. *See* discussion *supra* at 158–59.

125. *Id.*

126. This would be due to the fact that parties who have not had their day in court cannot legally be bound by either res judicata or collateral estoppel.

127. Proposed Amendments to Rules of Civil Procedure of the United States District Courts, 39 F.R.D. 73, 100–01 (Advisory Committee Note to Rule 23(b)(1)(B): "This clause takes in situations where the judgment in a nonclass action by or against an individual member of the class, while not technically concluding the other members, might do so as a practical matter.").

128. State Farm Fire & Cas. Co. v. Tashire, 386 U.S. 523 (1967).

129. In the case of a class action, where there are potentially countless claimants, it would be impractical to delay enforcement of judgment until all claims have come to judgment. It would therefore make more sense to set up some type of time limit on awards as a control device.

130. *See* discussion *supra* at 163–66.

131. Even though neither res judicata nor collateral estoppel would apply to the class member who had removed herself from the class, the problem of same situation stare decisis would remain a very significant concern. *See* discussion *supra* at 165. Moreover, given the modern demise of the mutuality of estoppel doctrine, it

is conceivable that an absent class member who chose to opt out of the class could nevertheless invoke collateral estoppel against the party opposing the class in a subsequent individual proceeding. However, the Supreme Court has recognized as a possible limitation on the modern breach of mutuality those situations in which the litigant not participating in the first suit has consciously chosen to "sit on the sidelines." Parklane Hosiery Co., Inc. v. Shore, 439 U.S. 322, 331–32 (1979).

132. At this point, I take no position on the exact manner in which a class member would be permitted to withdraw. *See* discussion *infra* at 169–73.

133. Fed. R. Civ. P. 23(d)(2).

134. *See* Mullane v. Central Hanover Bank & Trust Co., 339 U.S. 306 (1950) (due process requires the best notice practicable under the circumstances). In the case of far-reaching (b)(2) classes, of course, anything approaching individual notice would be impossible. That does not mean, however, that, under *Mullane,* notice reasonably designed to publicize the existence of the class could not be required.

135. Michael A. Perino, *Class Action Chaos? The Theory of the Core and an Analysis of Opt-Out Rights in Mass Tort Class Actions* 46 Emory L.J. 85, 143–44 (1997).

136. David Rosenberg, *Adding a Second Opt-Out to Rule 23(b)(3) Class Actions: Cost Without Benefit,* 2003 U. Chi. Legal F. 19, 23.

137. 28 U.S.C. §2072 (prohibiting Federal Rules from modifying, enlarging, or abridging substantive rights).

138. *See generally* Martin H. Redish & Christopher R. Pudelski, *Legislative Deception, Separation of Powers, and the Democratic Process: Harnessing the Political Theory of United States v. Klein,* 100 Nw. U. L. Rev. 437 (2006).

139. Richard A. Epstein, *Class Actions: Aggregation, Amplification, and Distortion,* 2003 U. Chi. Legal F. 475.

140. *See generally* Chapter 2, *supra.*

141. Ohio Bell Tel. Co. v. Pub. Utilities Comm'n of Ohio, 301 U.S. 292, 307 (1937). ("We do not presume acquiescence in the loss of fundamental rights.")

142. 407 U.S. 67, 95 (1972).

143. Edelman v. Jordan, 415 U.S. 651, 673 (1974).

144. *See, e.g.,* United States v. Moore, 340 U.S. 616 (1951).

145. *See, e.g.,* Nat'l Equip. Rental v. Szukhent, 375 U.S. 311 (1964).

146. *See, e.g.,* Carnival Cruise Line v. Shute, 449 U.S. 585 (1991).

147. Fed. R. Civ. P. 12(h)(1).

148. This is especially true in the context of class action opt-out. Professors Eisenberg and Miller have noted, based on their empirical study, that "[o]pt-outs from class participation and objections to class resolutions are rare: on average, less than 1 percent of class members object to classwide settlements." Theodore Eisenberg & Geoffrey Miller, *The Role of Opt-Outs and Objectors in Class Action Litigation: Theoretical and Empirical Issues,* 57 Vand. L. Rev. 1529, 1532 (2004). These "trivially small percentages" of opt-outs [*Id.* at 1566] arguably demonstrate absent class members' uncertainty or ignorance about their opt-out rights. *See also* Thomas E. Willging et al., *An Empirical Analysis of Rule 23 to Address the Rulemaking Challenges,* 71 N.Y.U. L. Rev. 74, 134 (1996) ("Many, perhaps most, of the notices [in federal court class actions] present technical information in legal jargon. Our impression is that most notices are not comprehensible to the lay reader.").

149. *See* discussion *supra* at 142–44.

150. Issacharoff, *supra* note 64; *see* discussion *supra* at 154–55.

151. For a detailed exploration of the nature and basis of this presumption, see Chapter 4, *supra*.

152. *See* Eisenberg & Miller, *supra* note 148, at 1538–39, for a catalogue of the existing scholarship.

153. *See,* sources cited in *Id.,* at 1538–40, nn.34–48.

154. The only exceptions appear to be Richard A. Epstein, *Class Actions: Aggregation, Amplification, and Distortion,* 2003 U. Chi. Legal F. 475, 510 ("the control of one's own litigation cannot be regarded as a small detail within the overall scheme of civil procedure."), and John E. Kennedy, *Class Actions: The Right to Opt Out,* 25 Ariz. L. Rev. 3, 79 (1983) (recognizing the right to control one's own litigation.). However, neither of these sources provides an extensive theoretical or constitutional analysis of the litigant autonomy right as an outgrowth of the democratic process, and neither recognizes that recognition of this constitutional interest necessarily implies the constitutional inadequacy of opt-out procedures. Instead, both view opt-out as satisfying the constitutional interest in litigant autonomy.

155. See Chapter 4, *supra,* for a detailed examination of the foundations of process-based individual autonomy in political theory.

156. *See* discussion *supra* at 144–45.

157. *See* discussion *supra* at 144–45.

158. *See* discussion *supra* at 163–65.

159. It should be noted, however, that the positive-negative claim dichotomy is incoherent in the context of a (b)(2) class, where injunctive relief is the primary relief sought. In these cases, for reasons previously mentioned, opt-in should be preferred. Whether opt out is permissible as a matter of macro democratic theory is beyond the scope of this chapter. For a discussion of that issue, see generally Chapter 2, *supra;* Chapter 4, *supra*.

6. SETTLEMENT CLASS ACTIONS, THE CASE-OR-CONTROVERSY
REQUIREMENT, AND THE NATURE OF THE ADJUDICATORY PROCESS

1. Stephen C. Yeazell, FROM MEDIEVAL GROUP LITIGATION TO THE MODERN CLASS ACTION 232 (1987) (referencing Harry Kalven, Jr. & Maurice Rosenfeld, *The Contemporary Function of the Class Suit,* 8 U. Chi. L. Rev. 684, 721 (1941)). *See* Chapter 1, *supra*.

2. 28 U.S.C. app. (1934) (original version of Rule 23, effective Sept. 1, 1938).

3. 28 U.S.C. app. (Supp. V 1964) (1966 version of Rule 23, effective July 1, 1966).

4. *See* discussion *infra* at 184–85.

5. *See, e.g.,* 2 Herbert Newberg & Alba Conte, NEWBERG ON CLASS ACTIONS § 11.09, at 11–13 (3d Ed. 1992) (noting that the settlement class offers substantial savings in litigation expenses to both plaintiffs and defendant).

6. Thomas Willging, et al., EMPIRICAL STUDY OF CLASS ACTIONS IN FOUR FEDERAL DISTRICT COURTS: FINAL REPORT TO THE ADVISORY COMMITTEE ON CIVIL RULES 9, 35 (1996) (finding that of the class actions studied, 39% were certified for

settlement purposes only); Howard Erichson, *Mass Tort Litigation and Inquisitorial Justice,* 87 Geo. L.J. 1983, 2000 (1999) (citing cases in which the settlement class was praised as a "viable approach to resolving mass tort litigation," including *Hanlon, Cincinnati Radiation,* and *Prudential Insurance*); Minutes, Advisory Committee on Civil Rules (Nov. 9–10, 1995), *available at* http://www.uscourts.gov/rules/ Minutes/min-cvII.htm (summarizing a Federal Judicial Center study finding that, in four districts studied, 18% of certified classes were "settlement classes" involving "simultaneous certification and settlement").

7. Amchem Prod., Inc. v. Windsor, 521 U.S. 591, 620 (1997).

8. *See, e.g.,* In re General Motors Corp. Pick-Up Truck Fuel Tank Products Liability Litigation, 55 F.3d 768, 778–79 (3d Cir. 1995) (citing the dangers of a "premature, even a collusive, settlement" when settlement is reached pre-certification, and noting that "[e]ven some courts successfully using these devices to achieve settlements apparently recognize these dangers since they certify these actions more cautiously than ordinary classes"); In re Diet Drugs, 2000 U.S. Dist. LEXIS 12275, at *136–37 (E.D. Pa. 2000) (discussing inventory settlements specifically); In re Bronco II Litigation, 1995 U.S. Dist. LEXIS 3507, at *23 (E.D. La. 1995); Bowling v. Pfizer, 143 F.R.D. 141 (S.D. Ohio 1992). *See also* Fed. R. Civ. P. 23(a)(4) (2004) (requiring that the class representatives "fairly and adequately protect the interests of the class").

9. *See* discussion *infra* at 185–89.

10. Class Action Fairness Act, S. 1751 §6 (108th Cong.).

11. Note that most mass tort settlement classes, as diversity suits, are "controversies," while federal question suits are "cases." *See* discussion *infra* at 206–10.

12. United States v. Johnson, 319 U.S. 302 (1943); Muskrat v. United States, 219 U.S. 346 (1911); *See* discussion *infra* at 191–93.

13. *See* discussion *infra* at 183–89.

14. *See* discussion *infra* at 205–06.

15. *See, e.g.,* Martin H. Redish & Elizabeth J. Cisar, *If Angels Were to Govern: The Need For Pragmatic Formalism in Separation of Powers Theory,* 41 Duke L.J. 449 (1991).

16. *See* discussion *infra* at 210–27.

17. *See* discussion *infra* at 191–93.

18. *See* discussion *infra* at 191–93.

19. *See* discussion *infra* at 196–202. 4 and 5, *supra.*

20. *See* discussion *infra* at 221–23.

21. *See* discussion *infra* at 214–15.

22. *See* discussion *infra* at 220–21.

23. *See* discussion *infra* at 190–91.

24. *See* discussion *infra* at 214–15.

25. For examples of proposed reforms that are designed to enhance the effectiveness or fairness of the settlement class, see Stephen C. Yeazell, *The Past and Future of Defendant and Settlement Classes in Collective Litigation,* 39 Ariz. L. Rev. 687, 702 (1997) (proposing a requirement that defendants negotiate with class representatives rather than class attorneys); Susan P. Koniak, *Feasting While the*

Widow Weeps: Georgine v. Amchem Products, Inc., 80 Cornell L. Rev. 1045, 1117, 1120 (1995) (arguing that courts should adopt a presumption against settlement class approval, requiring parties to make an unambiguous showing of the lack of collusive activity); Roger C. Cramton, *Individualized Justice, Mass Torts, and Settlement Class Actions: An Introduction,* 80 Cornell L. Rev. 811 (1995) (proposing limits on futures classes).

26. John C. Coffee, Jr., *Class Wars: The Dilemma of the Mass Tort Class Action,* 95 Colum. L. Rev. 1343, 1367.

27. *See* discussion *infra* at 220–21.

28. *See* discussion *infra* at 221–23.

29. Redish & Cisar, *supra* note 15, at 450 n.4 (citing Morrison v. Olson, 487 U.S. 654 (1988)).

30. *See* discussion *infra* at 225–27.

31. *See* discussion *infra* at 187–89.

32. *See* discussion *infra,* at 190–93.

33. *See* discussion *infra* at 206–19.

34. Under Fed R. Civ. P. 23(e), no certified class action may be settled absent approval of the court.

35. 521 U.S. 591 (1997).

36. Under the current version of Rule 23, for a class to be certified, it must meet all 23(a) requirements—numerosity, commonality, typicality, and adequacy of representation—and fit within one of the three categories under 23(b). Almost all settlement classes request damages and thus, as a matter of practice, seek certification under Rule 23(b)(3). Rule 23(b)(3) requires that common questions of law or fact "predominate" over questions affecting individual class members and that the class is "superior to other available methods" for adjudicating the controversy. Fed. R. Civ. P. 23(b)(3). For more detailed description, see Chapter 1, *supra* at 10–12.

37. *Compare, e.g.,* In re General Motors Corp. Pick-Up Truck Fuel Tank Products Liability Litigation, 55 F.3d 768 (3d Cir. 1995), *cert. denied,* 516 U.S. 824 (1995) ("Settlement classes must satisfy the Rule 23(a) requirements of numerosity, commonality, typicality, and adequacy of representation, as well as the relevant 23(b) requirements."); Georgine v. Amchem Products, Inc., 83 F.3d 610, 617 (3d Cir. 1996) (applying the *General Motors* rule to the 23(b)(3) settlement class) *with* White v. Nat'l Football League, 41 F.3d 402, 408 (8th Cir. 1994) ("[A]dequecy of class representation . . . is ultimately determined by the settlement itself."); In re A.H. Robins Co., 880 F.2d 709, 740 (4th Cir. 1989) (giving Rule 23 a "liberal construction" as applied to the settlement class and holding that "settlement should be a factor" in "determining certification"); In re Absestos Litigation, 90 F.3d 963, 975 (5th Cir. 1996) (same).

38. *Amchem,* 521 U.S. at 597.

39. *Amchem,* 521 U.S. at 602. The stipulation of settlement excluded the claims of persons who had filed suit for "asbestos-related personal injury or damage . . . against the defendants" before January 15, 1995, thus allowing plaintiffs' counsel to separately negotiate "inventory" settlements: non-class settlements of class counsel's pending claims against the defendants. *Id.*

40. *Amchem,* 521 U.S. at 602–03; *see also* Coffee, *supra* note 26, at 1394 (criticizing the "substantive terms of the [*Amchem*] settlement," given that it did not recognize a number of compensable state law claims); Brief for the Respondents George Windsor ("[A]pproximately half the claims that are filed in state and federal court . . . would not [have] qualif[ied] for payment under the exposure and medical criteria contained in the [*Amchem*] settlement.").

41. Objectors included: The Windsor Group, the New Jersey White Lung Group, the Cargile Group, and Margaret Balonis, whose husband had been fatally exposed to asbestos in the workplace. *See also Amchem,* 521 U.S. at 612 (summarizing the objectors' arguments).

42. Georgine v. Amchem Prods., Inc., 83 F.3d 610, 623 (3d Cir. 1996) ("[T]he jurisdictional issues in this case would not exist but for the [class action] certification.").

43. *Id.* at 626.

44. *Id.* at 630 (focusing on conflict between the representative plaintiffs and unnamed class members rather than the question of attorney-class conflicts).

45. The *Amchem* decision primarily affects the 23(b)(3) class. Neither "a limited fund class action under Rule 23(b)(1)(b) nor an equitable class action under Rule 23(b)(2) must satisfy the predominance requirement," the primary obstacle that *Amchem* imposes to settlement-only certification. Sofia Adrogue, *Mass Tort Class Actions in the New Millennium,* 17 Rev. Litig. 427, 438 (1998).

46. *Amchem,* 521 U.S. at 610 (holding that Rule 23(a) and (b)'s class-qualifying criterion function to ensure that all class members receive fair and equal treatment). Ultimately, the Court concurred with the Third Circuit that the application of these factors to the facts of the case required rejection of the request for class certification. The class members' common interest in receiving compensation was insufficient to establish that common questions predominated over disparate individual issues. *Id.* at 611–13.

47. *Id.* at 620. "The manageability inquiry under Rule 23(b)(3)(d) concerns "such matters as the size or contentiousness of the class, the onerousness of complying with the notice requirements, the number of class members that may seek to intervene and participate, or the presence of special individual issues." Christopher J. Willis, *Collision Course or Coexistence? Amchem Products v. Windsor and Proposed Rule 23(b)(4),* 28 Cumb. L. Rev. 13 (quoting 7A Charles A. Wright, et al., Federal Practice and Procedure 1780 (2d ed. 1986)). As such, it overlaps substantially with the predominance inquiry: Individual issues that render a class unmanageable also often mean that common issues do not predominate, suggesting that the scope of the *Amchem* decision is broader than it appears on surface.

48. *Amchem,* 521 U.S. at 612 (although noting that "Rule 23's requirements must be interpreted in keeping with Article III constraints").

49. There are a number of other criticisms of the settlement class that fall beyond the scope of this chapter. For example, Professors Carrington and Apanovitch argue that the settlement class "is replete with substantive consequences" in violation of the Rules Enabling Act, such as the alteration of "the substantive rights of state governments to enact and enforce their own laws governing such matters as standards of care, measures of damages, statutes of limitations, and the

law of judgments," the displacement of "not only the states' laws of torts, but also the states' laws of conflict of laws," and the establishment "of a fictional contract of employment between members of the class and class counsel." Paul D. Carrington and Derek P. Apanovitch, *The Constitutional Limits of Judicial Rulemaking: The Illegitimacy of Mass-Tort Settlements Negotiated under Federal Rule 23*, 39 Ariz. L. Rev. 461 (1997) at 464–73; *see also The Rules Enabling Act and the Limits of Rule 23*, *supra* note 18 (arguing that the settlement class violates the Rules Enabling Act by, among other things, undermining the individual's substantive right to "control [his own] causes of action," as well as the right to "have their causes of action resolved through litigation at all").

50. In re General Motors Corp. Pick-Up Truck Fuel Tank Products Liability Litigation, 55 F.3d 768, 784 (3d Cir. 1995).

51. Stephen C. Yeazell, *The Past and Future of Defendant and Settlement Classes in Collective Litigation*, 39 Ariz. L. Rev. 687, 701 (1997).

52. *General Motors*, 55 F.3d at 778.

53. Coffee, *supra* note 26, at 1348.

54. *Id.* at 1354, 1373–82.

55. *Id.* at 1367.

56. *See also* Willging, *supra* note 6, at 10 (finding that fee-recovery ratios were within a normal range in most class actions studied: "We did not find any patterns of situations where (b)(3) actions produced nominal class benefits in relation to attorneys' fees . . . The fee-recovery rate . . . exceeded 40% in 11% or fewer of settled cases").

57. Coffee, *supra* note 26 at 1371–73 (describing the reverse auction); *id.* at 1373–75 (describing the inventory settlement).

58. Professor Coffee dismisses the potential for a reverse auction in a small-claim class action. *Id.* at 1352 ("In 'small claimant' class actions, defendants tend to resist class certification (because plaintiffs have no realistic alternative), whereas in 'large claimant' classes, defendants increasingly prefer class certification for a variety of reasons"). I disagree. It is true that in a large-claim class, the defendant has significant incentive to settle the claims prior to certification, given the litigation expenses at stake. But a similar level of risk is involved in the small-claim class. Even though absent class members are less likely to bring individual suit, the probability of certification is higher. Because small-claim classes are not mass torts, they involve fewer individualized questions—e.g., differences in severity or timeframe of injury. One could persuasively argue that the defendant's decision to settle precertification is determined not by the likelihood of individual opt-out, but rather by the likelihood of certification, given the litigation expenses that flow from certification hearings and related proceedings. Thus, a defendant confronted with a small-claim class has an equal, if not greater, incentive to solicit pre-certification settlement than a defendant confronted with a large-claim class.

59. Empirical studies confirm the prevalence of this practice. *See* Willging, *supra* note 6 at 8 ("Multiple filings of related class actions might indicate a race by counsel to the courthouse, perhaps to gain appointment as lead counsel . . . At least one form of multiple filing occurred in 20% to 39% of the class actions in the four districts.").

60. *But see* Class Action Fairness Act, S. 1751, Sec. 1713 (108th Cong.) (regulating attorneys' fees by requiring that, for any settlement "under which any class member is obligated to pay sums to class counsel that would result in a net loss to the class member," the court "make a written finding that nonmonetary benefits to the class member substantially outweigh the monetary loss"). It has yet to be determined what effect the Class Action Fairness Act will have on the reverse auction. However, two factors suggest that the effect will be minimal. First, even though absent class members receive only minimal monetary benefit from most settlement classes, it is rare that they actually have to pay attorney's fees out-of-pocket. Instead, the small net recovery distributed to each class member is what remains after the fees have been deducted from the net settlement. This type of distribution arrangement would not fall under the Act's terms. Second, the Act includes a significant loophole, enabling courts to approve a settlement even when absent class members will suffer a net loss. *See also* discussion *infra* at 225–27 (detailing the role that docket burdens have in influencing approval of settlement classes).

61. *See, e.g.,* Coffee, *supra* note 26 at 1372 (explaining that a reverse auction often results in "suboptimal outcome[s]" for class members).

62. *Id.* at 1373–74 (explaining how the inventory settlement benefits both defendant and class counsel).

63. *Id.; see also* Coffee, *supra* note 26 at 1373, 1394 (noting that the "substantive terms of the [*Amchem*] settlement clash sharply with the contemporaneous inventory settlements reached by the same plaintiffs' attorneys"); discussion *supra* at 183–85 (discussing the terms of the *Amchem* settlements). *See generally* Todd Latz, *Who Can Tell The Futures? Protecting Settlement Class Action Members Without Notice,* 85 Va. L. Rev. 531 (1999).

64. For other proposals that fall beyond the scope of this chapter, see Kent A. Lambert, *Class Action Settlements in Louisiana,* 61 La. L. Rev. 89 at 129–33 (suggesting that the court should ban inventory settlements and classes consisting exclusively of future plaintiffs, as well as hold collateral estoppel inapplicable to legal malpractice suits against class counsel for inadequate representation); Nikita Malholtra Pastor, *Equity and Settlement Class Actions: Can There Be Justice for All in Ortiz v. Fibreboard?,* 49 Am. U. L. Rev. 773 (2000) (advocating the reform of ethical standards); Greg Zipes, *After* Amchem *&* Ahearn: *The Rise of Bankruptcy Over the Class Action Option,* 1998 Det. C.L. Rev. 7 (1998) (arguing that the bankruptcy system is a "perfect forum for resolving mass tort issues," because it has inherent structural safeguards not present in the normal federal system—for example, a group-rights model and pre-approval of creditors' counsel). *See also* Joseph F. Rice & Nancy Worth Davis, *The Future of the Mass Tort Claims: Comparison of Settlement Class Action to Bankruptcy Treatment of Mass Tort Claims,* 50 S.C. L. Rev. 405 (1999) (arguing that "preferring chapter 11 over settlement class actions [as a way to solve the problems with the settlement class] this early in the evolution of each method threatens to limit the proper application of both").

Another proposal is that of Professors Macey and Miller. They advocate the adoption of a closed-bid, court-regulated auction of the right to litigate the class's claim. *See* Jonathan R. Macey & Geoffrey P. Miller, *The Plaintiffs' Attorney's Role in Class Action and Derivative Litigation: Economic Analysis and Recommendations for*

Reform, 58 U. Chi. L. Rev. 1 (1991) [herein "Plaintiff's Role"]; Jonathan R. Macey and Geoffrey P. Miller, *Auctioning Class Action and Derivative Suits: A Rejoinder,* 87 Nw. U. L. Rev. 458 (1993): *see also* Randall Thomas & Robert Hansen, *Auctioning Class Action And Derivative Lawsuits: A Critical Analysis,* 87 Nw. U. L. Rev. 423 (outlining criticisms of Macey and Miller's auction model). Macey and Miller describe their proposed solution as follows:

> A lawsuit is filed containing class or derivative allegations, or containing allegations that clearly support class relief. At this point the judge can make an initial investigation of the case to determine whether it would be appropriate for auction treatment . . . The judge would then cause notice to be posted in suitable newspapers and other periodicals announcing that the claim will be auctioned off . . . and setting forth bidding procedures. The most workable bid procedure would seem to be a standard sealed-bid protocol with the claim going to the highest bidder . . . The judge, at her discretion, might state a minimum bid in order to prevent an excessively low sale price . . . [T]he judge would [then] award the claim to the highest bidder. That bidder, not necessarily an attorney or law firm, would then pay the bid amount to the court.

Macey & Miller, *Plaintiffs' Attorney's Role,* at 106–08. The highest bidder would then "succeed to the rights of the plaintiffs who have not opted out" and have the right to either settle or litigate the claim. *Id.* at 108. While Macey and Miller do not directly discuss the settlement class, this procedure would functionally amount to banning the settlement class practice; the auction presumably occurs after certification, which would prohibit settlement prior to the court-regulated auction of the right to control the class's claims. Insofar as this is true, I concur with the result. *See* discussion *infra* at 188–227 (arguing that, given the settlement class's inherent unconstitutionality, it should be prohibited).

65. Coffee, *supra* note 26 at 1454 (although noting that this requirement could be easily abused by a court that wanted to clear its dockets by facilitating settlement: it could merely pick a plaintiffs' attorney willing to negotiate).

66. *Id.* at 1455 (although noting that there is a potential for deadlock on the committee).

67. *Id.* at 1455–56. Coffee also offered a fourth recommendation: that the Court align the standards governing the class action and the settlement class. *See id.* at 1456 (arguing that when a class is certifiable for settlement but not litigation, the plaintiffs' attorney "lack[s] negotiating leverage and may accept recoveries far below what the plaintiffs could receive in individual actions"). The Court has already adopted this suggestion, at least in part. *See Amchem,* 521 U.S. at 620 (requiring the settlement class to meet all 23(a) requirements and applicable 23(b) requirements, with the exception of manageability).

68. Yeazell, *supra* note 25 at 702.

69. *Id.* (also noting the problems with his suggested approach: "How would defendant select these 'class' representatives? How many would it have to notify to rid itself of the suspicion that it had merely substituted gullible parties for hungry lawyers? Moreover . . . the defendant would be notifying previously quiescent

plaintiffs not only that they had claims but that the defendant thought these claims viable").

70. *Id.*

71. *Id.*

72. *See* discussion *infra* at 198–202 (discussing the link between adverseness and adversarial incentives); *infra* at 209 (distinguishing between the settlement class and the post-certification class settlement on this basis).

73. This is especially true given that the court lacks the institutional capacity to investigate such facts on its own. *See* discussion *infra* at 214–15.

74. *See* discussion *supra* at 188–89 (distinguishing between Article III collusion and opportunistic behavior).

75. *See* discussion *supra* at 181.

76. For example, Professor Coffee has defined "collusion" as "essentially . . . an agreement—actual or implicit—by which the defendants receive a 'cheaper' than arm's length settlement and the plaintiffs' attorneys receive in some form an above-market attorneys' fee." Coffee, *supra* note 26 at 1367.

77. Poe v. Ullman, 367 U.S. 497, 505–06 (1961).

78. BLACK'S LAW DICTIONARY (8th ed. 2004).

79. THE AMERICAN HERITAGE DICTIONARY OF THE ENGLISH LANGUAGE (4th ed. 2000).

80. As a result, I need not address the potential dispute between textual meaning and originalism that often arises in other contexts.

81. Nathan Bailey, AN UNIVERSAL ETYMOLOGICAL ENGLISH DICTIONARY 210 (16th ed. 1755); *see also* Thomas Blount, A LAW-DICTIONARY AND GLOSSARY 42 (3d ed. 1717) (in the context of defining the phrase *batable ground,* using the terms *in debate* and *controversy* interchangeably—although not separately defining the word *controversy*).

Early American dictionaries, however, do not contain an entry for the word *controversy. See, e.g.* John Bouvier, 1 LAW DICTIONARY (1st ed. 1839). "Controversy" was not separately defined in an American dictionary, according to my search, until around 1848, at which time it was described as "a dispute arising between two or more persons; it differs from case, which includes all suits criminal as well as civil; whereas controversy is a civil and not a criminal proceeding." John Bouvier, 1 A LAW DICTIONARY 337 (3d ed. 1848); *see also* John Harrison, *The Power of Congress to Limit the Jurisdiction of Federal Courts and the Text of Article III,* 64 U. Chi. L. Rev. 203, 222 n.47 (1997) (summarizing early American definitions, in the context of arguing that "controversies" are limited to civil proceedings, while "cases" include suits of both civil and criminal variant). Despite the absence of entry in American dictionaries, one could argue that an English definition of "controversy" from the pre-Framing era provides persuasive evidence of the Framers' assumptions when using the word to define judicial power in Article III.

82. *See* WEBSTER'S DICTIONARY (1913) (describing the word's history).

83. *See also* In re Asbestos Litigation, 90 F.3d 963, 988–89 (5th Cir. 1996) (noting that Article III plainly "requires that the parties be truly adverse").

84. THE AMERICAN HERITAGE DICTIONARY OF THE ENGLISH LANGUAGE (2000).

85. MERRIAM-WEBSTER DICTIONARY OF LAW (1996).

86. BLACK'S LAW DICTIONARY (8th ed. 2004).

87. Giles Jacob, A NEW LAW-DICTIONARY: CONTAINING THE INTERPRETATION AND DEFINITION OF WORDS AND TERMS USED IN THE LAW (10th ed. 1773).

88. *Id.* A thorough search of early American dictionaries turned up entries for the word, *case* in two different sources. A 1792 publication defined it as a situation where "the party injured is allowed to bring a special action . . . according to the peculiar circumstances of his own particular grievance." Richard Burn, A NEW LAW DICTIONARY: INTENDED FOR GENERAL USE, AS WELL AS FOR GENTLEMEN OF THE PROFESSION (1792). An 1860 publication offered this definition: "[t]hat form of action which is adopted for the purpose of recovering damages for some injury resulting to a party from the wrongful act of another." EDITORS OF THE LAW CHRONICLE, THE MODERN LAW DICTIONARY (1860). While neither of these definitions explicitly mention adverseness, the focus on both injury and causation suggests a strong emphasis on those conditions necessary for a successful suit within a traditional adversary legal system.

89. Additionally, even if I were to concede the ambiguity of the word *case* as a textual matter, settlement classes are invariably diversity suits, controlled by the word *controversy.*

90. *See* Colin Croft, *Reconceptualizing American Legal Professionalism: A Proposal For Deliberative Moral Community,* 67 N.Y.U.L. Rev. 1256, 1298 n. 270 (1992) ("Adverseness has played an influential role in American law and society since its adoption from English common law."); Stephan Landsman, *A Brief Survey of the Development of the Adversary System,* 44 Ohio St. L.J. 713, 717 (1983) (noting that the current adversary system is the "product of the slow evolution of English and American judicial procedure"); *see also* Ellen E. Sward, *Values, Ideology, and the Evolution of the Adversary System,* 64 Ind. L.J 301, 319–26 (1989).

91. The scholarly literature indicates that one can parse numerous distinctions between the terms *case* and *controversy,* although none are immediately relevant to this discussion. For example, it has been suggested that "controversy" is less comprehensive than "case," in that it includes only "suits of a civil nature," whereas "case" is an umbrella, encompassing civil and criminal actions alike. Aetna Life Insurance Co. v. Haworth, 300 U.S. 227 (1937); William A. Fletcher, *Exchange on the Eleventh Amendment,* 57 U. Chi L. Rev. 131, 133 (1990) (tracing this interpretation to St. George Tucker). *But see* Robert J. Pushaw, Jr., *Article III's Case/Controversy Distinction and the Dual Functions of Federal Courts,* 69 Notre Dame L. Rev. 447, 460 (1994) (arguing that had the Framers intended a criminal/civil distinction, they would have used "civil cases" instead of "controversies" and noting the conspicuous lack of eighteenth-century discussion of such a distinction). Additionally, Akhil Reed Amar argues that the use of the word *all* before Article III's reference to the three types of "cases" indicates that the court's jurisdiction over those subject matters is mandatory, whereas the omission of "all" before references to the six party-defined "controversies" proves that the Court's jurisdiction in that context is permissive. Akhil Reed Amar, *A Neo-Federalist View of Article III: Separating the Two Tiers of Federal Jurisdiction,* 65 B.U. L. Rev. 205 (1985). *But see* Martin H. Redish, *Text, Structure, and Common Sense in the Interpretation of Article III,* 138 U. Pa. L. Rev. 1633, 1636 (1990) (criticizing Amar's approach as analyzing a "few selected

words . . . in a vacuum," contrary to "any reasonable textual construction" and Framers' intent). Neither of these distinctions, however, is relevant to the narrow question of whether the definition of "controversy" as an adversarial dispute also extends to the definition of "case."

92. Max Farrand, 2 THE RECORDS OF THE FEDERAL CONVENTION OF 1787, 430 (Madison, August 27) (1911).

93. For nineteenth-century cases where the Court held a non-adversarial suit to be non-justiciable, see, for example, Cleveland v. Chamberlain, 66 U.S. 419 (1862); Wood-Paper Co v. Heft, 75 US 333, 336 (1869); Chicago & Grand Trunk R. Co. v. Wellman, 143 U.S. 339 (1892); *see also* discussion *infra* at 191–93 (describing the Supreme Court's case-or-controversy jurisprudence).

94. *See, e.g.,* Smith v. Adams, 130 U.S. 167, 173 (1889) (jointly defining the "meaning given to the terms 'cases and controversies'"); In re Pacific Railroad Commission, 32 Fed. Rep. 241, 255 (1887) (explaining that the *only* distinction that can be parsed between the terms *case* and *controversy* is that the latter includes only suits of a civil nature; otherwise, the terms are interchangeable); Virginia v. Rives, 100 U.S. 313, 336 (1880) (Field, J., concurring) (using the phrase "case or controversy" to define the judicial power granted by the constitution).

95. *See* New Jersey v. Heldor Ind., 989 F.3d 702 (3d Cir. 1993) (internal citations omitted) (holding that "[a]lthough it is possible to parse distinctions between a 'controversy' and a 'case' . . . , the records of the Framers supports the more common modern practice to merge the terms, as Justice Frankfurter did in *Joint Anti-Facist Refugee Comm. v. McGrath*"). *Cf.* Joint Anti-Facist Refugee Comm. v. McGrath, 341 U.S. 123 (1951) (Frankfurter, J., concurring).

96. Professor Pushaw has attempted to carry this burden. He argues that the Framers intended that a "case" would permit a more expansive judicial role than a "controversy." The "case," he argues, refers to the public, law-espousing function of the courts and thus, unlike a "controversy," does not mandate that the parties claim adverse legal interests. *See, e.g.,* David E. Engdahl, *Intrinsic Limits of Congress' Power Regarding the JudicialBranch,* 1999 B.Y.U.L. L. Rev. 75, 149. In any event, there can be no doubt that the Court has never accepted the argument.

97. *See* Muskrat v. United States, 219 U.S. 346, 356-57 (1911); United States v. Johnson, 319 U.S. 302, 302 (1943) (per curiam); Lord v. Veazie, 49 U.S. 251 (1850) (if the parties' interests are "one and the same," they do not present a "case" capable of judicial resolution); Chicago & Grand Trunk Railroad Co. v. Wellman, 143 U.S. 339, 345 (1892) (articulation of adverse rights must be "real, earnest and vital"); Flast v. Cohen, 392 U.S. 83, 94 (1968) (question must be presented in an "adversary context and in a form historically viewed as capable of resolution through the judicial process"). *But see* Susan Bandes, *The Idea of a Case,* 42 Stan. L. Rev. 227, at 227–28 (arguing that the Court's doctrine reveals no consistent "overarching definition of a case" and that instead, it has treated the case-or-controversy requirement as a receptacle, filling it with specific doctrines as the need arises). Professor Bandes, however, does not address the adverseness requirement specifically, or the Court's treatment of it.

98. Aetna Life Ins. Co. v. Haworth, 300 U.S. 227, 240–41 (1937). See also Lord v. Veazie, 49 U.S. 251 (1850).

99. 219 U.S. 346 (1911).

100. *Id.* at 349–50.

101. *Id.* at 361.

102. *Id.* at 361–62 (explaining that the government alleged no property interest in the case).

103. *Id.* at 361–62 (holding that if it were to accept that the Government always has an "adverse interest" in upholding the constitutionality of the legislation it passes, "the result will be that this court . . . will be required to give opinions in the nature of advice concerning legislative action, a function never conferred upon it by the Constitution, and against the exercise of which this court has steadily set its face from the beginning").

104. *See, e.g.,* Alexander M. Bickel, THE LEAST DANGEROUS BRANCH: THE SUPREME COURT AT THE BAR OF POLITICS at 123 (classifying *Muskrat* as a decision "in which adjudication of the merits was declined despite the presence of an adequately concrete and adversary case"). This portion of the *Muskrat* holding, however, is generally irrelevant to the decision's importance as a general statement of Article III's adverseness requirement. Nor does it undermine the relevance of the adverseness requirement as applied to the settlement class. *See discussion infra* at 200–01 (explaining that the settlement class is completely substantive and involves no constitutional, or even legal, interpretation, unlike the underlying issue in *Muskrat*).

105. *Muskrat*, 219 U.S. at 356–57.

106. *See, e.g.,* United States v. Johnson, 319 U.S. 302 (1943) (per curiam); Moore v. Charlotte-Mecklenberg Board of Education, 402 U.S. 47 (1970). *See also* Congress of Ind. Orgs. v. McAdory, 325 U.S. 472 (1945) (holding that the city's agreement not to enforce the Act in question deprived the suit of a justiciable case or controversy, by rendering the parties non-adversarial).

107. 319 U.S. 302 (1943).

108. 319 U.S. at 302. The plaintiff's complaint alleged that, under the Emergency Price Control Act of 1942, the defendant's rental property was within the statutorily defined "defense rental area" and thus that the rent collected by the defendant "was in excess of the maximum fixed by the regulation." *Id.* In turn, the defendant argued that the Emergency Price Control Act of 1942 was unconstitutional because it delegated authority to the Price Administrator without setting forth comprehensible standards to guide price-setting. *Id.*

109. Also, the parties did not disclose their connection to the court. However, aside from this omission, the pleadings and other documents filed with the court contained no "false or fictitious" facts. *Id.*

110. *Id.* See also Swann v. Charlotte-Mecklengerg Bd. Of Educ., 402 U.S. 1 (1970).

111. Swift & Co. v. United States, 276 U.S. 311 (1928).

112. *Id.* at 320–21. This is easily distinguished from a consent decree that is entered after the government files a complaint with the court. That scenario is analogous to a class settlement, where proceedings are adversarial from their inception and the case later settles. There, an Article III court has the jurisdiction to enter any order—including dismissal or settlement approval—that is incidental

or ancillary to the underlying, justiciable proceedings. *See* discussion *infra* at 208 (discussing the *Bancorp* ruling).

113. 276 U.S. at 325.

114. *Id.* at 316.

115. Richard A. Nagareda, *Turning From Tort To Administration*, 94 Mich. L. Rev. 899, 928 n.115 (1996) (citing the prospective nature of a consent decree as a key element of its Article III justiciability).

116. *See also* Ralph E. Avery, *Article III and Title 11: A Constitutional Collision*, 12 Bankr. Dev. J. 397, 410 (arguing that "*Swift* marks the outer limits of what parties may do to memorialize private agreements by way of court orders. Parties whose negotiations have carried them so far as to give them coincident interests ought not to be permitted to 'record their contract' by way of a consent judgment").

117. *See* U.S. Parole Comm. v. Geraghty, 445 U.S. 388, 402 (1980) (internal citations omitted) (calling for "reference to the purposes of the case-or-controversy requirement," given "Article III's 'uncertain and shifting contours' with respect to nontraditional forms of litigation"); Bandes, *supra* note 97 at 276 (lamenting the lack of cohesive treatment of the case-or-controversy requirement and noting that "[r]easoned application of the case limitation requires interpretation of the case requirement's underlying principles and their implications for the scope of federal judicial power").

118. *See, e.g.,* Redish & Cisar, *supra* note 15, at 454 n.19 (citing scholars who deem formalism an "epistemologically naïve methodology").

119. *See, e.g.,* John M. Breen, *Statutory Interpretation and the Lessons of Llewellyn*, 33 Loy. L. A. L. Rev. 263, 277 (2000) (quoting William N. Eskridge, Jr. & Phillip P. Frickey, *Statutory Interpretation as Practical Reasoning*, 42 Stan. L. Rev. 321, 359 (1990)).

120. Poe v. Ullman, 367 U.S. 497, 503 (1961).

121. This also encompasses control over legal argumentation in the case: "Through vigorous advocacy each party helps the court to perceive and to respond properly to weaknesses in the presentations made by the other parties. In addition, vigorous advocacy can illuminate facets of a case that are not immediately apparent and might not otherwise be considered by the court. These benefits and vigorous advocacy serve as the foundation of the adversarial system." Girardeau Spann, *Expository Justice*, 131 U. Pa. L. Rev. 585, 650 (1983).

122. *Id.* at 588 (explaining that the adversary system understands the court to be "an attentive, unbiased apparatus for the production of just results which the litigants will perceive as legitimate and authoritative").

123. Lon L. Fuller, *The Forms and Limits of Adjudication*, 92 Harv. L. Rev. 353, 364 (1978).

124. *Id.*

125. Marvin E. Frankel, *The Search for Truth: An Umpireal View*, 123 U. Pa. L. Rev. 1031, 1035 (1975). According to Fuller, this objective search depends on three interrelated conditions:

> (i) The adjudicator should attend to what the parties have to say; (ii) The adjudicator should explain his decision in a manner that provides a substantive reply to what the parties have to say; (iii) The decision should be strongly

responsive to the parties' proofs and arguments in the sense that it should proceed from and be congruent with those proofs and arguments.

Melvin Aron Eisenberg, *Participation, Responsiveness, and the Consultative Process:
An Essay for Lon Fuller,* 92 Harv. L. Rev. 410, 411–12 (1978) (paraphrasing Fuller's
list of three conditions that define a proceeding as an adversary adjudication); *see
also* Christopher Peters, *Adjudication as Representation,* 97 Colum. L. Rev. 312, 375
(1997) (discussing Fuller's theories on the relationship between court and litigant).

126. *See generally* Erichson, *supra* note 6 at 2005–10 (making this comparison
in the context of discussing the effect of the settlement class on judicial decision-
making); *see also* Franklin Strier, *What Can the American Adversary System Learn
from an Inquisitorial System of Justice,* 76 Judicature 109, 109 (1993) ("The inquisitorial system generally refers to trial practices developed in Europe and adopted in
other countries.").

127. *Id.*

128. Erichson, *supra* note 6, at 2006; *see also* Frankel, *supra* note 125, at 1032
(arguing that "our adversary system rates truth too low among the values that
institutions of justice are meant to serve.").

129. *Id.* at 1037; Dean Robert Gilbert Johnston & Sara Lufrano, *The Adversary
System as a Means of Seeking Truth and Justice,* 35 J. Marshall L. Rev. 147, 147 (2002)
("The underlying theory [of an adversary system] . . . is that the truth is best served
by placing the responsibility on the parties themselves to formulate their case and
destroy the case of their adversary.").

130. Erichson, *supra* note 6, at 2006.

131. *See* Peters, *supra* note 125, at 347 ("Most judicial decisions are to a very great
extent products . . . of a process of participation and debate among the parties to
the case that greatly restricts the decisional options available to the court. In this
sense, judicial decisions resemble the decisions made by a democratic legislature
after debate and a fair hearing at which all relevant views have been aired.").

132. Strier, *supra* note 126, at 109.

133. Specifically, adverseness "optimize[s] the likelihood that [judicial] exposition will be well-informed and that the power to expound will be exercised pru-
dently." Spann, *supra* note 121, at 632.

134. *Id.* at 647. This principle is reflected in the Court's jurisprudence. The
Court in *Baker v. Carr,* for example, framed the Article III standing question as
follows: "Have the appellants alleged such a personal stake in the outcome of the
controversy as to assure that concrete adverseness which sharpens the presentation
of issues upon which the court so largely depends for illumination of difficult . . .
questions?" 369 U.S. 186, 204 (1962); *see also* Butz v. Economou, 438 U.S. 4768, 413
(1978) (holding that the agency proceedings in question were legitimate because
they enjoyed the adversarial "safeguards" available "in the judicial process": "The
proceedings [were] adversary in nature. They [were] conducted before a trier of
fact insulated from political influence. A party [was] entitled to present his case.");
GTE Sylvania, Inc. v. Consumers Union of the United States, 445 U.S. 375, 382
(1980) ("The purpose of the case-or-controversy requirement is to 'limit the business of federal courts to questions presented in an adversary context and in a form
historically viewed as capable of resolution through the judicial process.'").

135. For scholars who have criticized the adversary system and advocated the American adoption of a system similar to that used in civil law countries, see John Langbein, *The German Advantage in Civil Procedure,* 52 U. Chi. L. Rev. 823 (1985) (arguing that the German civil law system is far more precise and efficient than the American adversary system: the German court "investigates the dispute in the fashion most likely to narrow the inquiry," minimizing the expenses associated with "full pretrial and trial ventilation of the whole of the plaintiff's case"); Hein Kotz, *The Reform of the Adversary System,* 48 U. Chi. L. Rev. 478, 486 (1981); Sward, *supra* note 90, at 302-03. *See also* Allen, Kock, Reichenberg & Rosen, *The German Advantage in Civil Procedure: A Plea for More Details and Fewer Generalities in Comparative Scholarship,* 82 Nw. U. L. Rev. 705 (1988) (critiquing Langbein's arguments).

136. Erichson, *supra* note 6, at 2010-12; *see also* Frankel, *supra* note 125, at 1042 ("Because the parties and counsel control the gathering and presentation of evidence, I have made no fixed, routine, expected place for the judge's contribution.").

137. Erichson, *supra* note 6, at 2011-12 (arguing that "U.S. judges for the most part continue to behave in accordance with deeply ingrained notions concerning the judicial role," a self-image that presents a formidable "barrier to effective inquisitorial judging."). Additionally, countries with inquisitorial systems view the judicial profession as a career path that is entirely distinct from legal practice, and as a result, provide "institutionalized training" for their court officials. In contrast, in the U.S., one typically enters the judiciary after a number of years practicing law, without specialized judicial training. *Id.* at 2014; Strier, *supra* note 125, at 109. The lack of an American "career judiciary" has been criticized as endowing the judicial branch with an intractable adversarial ethic. *See, e.g.,* Frankel, *supra* note 125, at 1033.

138. Sol Wachtler, *Judicial Lawmaking,* 65 N.Y.U. L. Rev. 1, 20–21 (1990); *see also infra* at 220–23 (discussing the difference between judicial tools on the one hand, which are dependant on adversarial presentation by the parties, and executive and legislative tools on the other, which enable independent fact-finding).

139. Peters, *supra* note 125, at 350.

140. Martin H. Redish, *The Adversary System, Democratic Theory, and the Constitutional Role of Self-Interest: The Tobacco Wars, 1953–1971,* 51 DePaul L. Rev. 359, 368 (2001), (discussing Joseph H. Carens, *Possessive Individualism and Democratic Theory: Macpherson's Legacy,* in DEMOCRACY AND POSSESSIVE INDIVIDUALISM: THE INTELLECTUAL LEGACY OF C. B. MACPHERSON 2 (Joseph H. Carens ed., 1993)).

141. Redish, *Adversary System, supra* note 140, at 369–70 (citing David Held, MODELS OF DEMOCRACY 89 (1987)) (associating this theory with John Stuart Mill).

142. *Id.*

143. Peters, *supra* note 125, at 332.

144. RESTATEMENT (SECOND) OF JUDGMENTS ch. 1 (1982) ("[T]he underlying theme is that the interest being represented in the second action was in some sense represented in the original action.").

145. Lea Brilmayer, *The Jurisprudence of Article III: Perspectives on the Case-or Controversy Requirement,* 93 Harv. L. Rev. 297 (1979). For criticism of Professor Brilmayer's thesis, see Mark V. Tushnet, *The Sociology of Article III: A Response to Professor Brilmayer,* 93 Harv. L. Rev. 1698 (1980) (arguing that Brilmayer's distinc-

tion between the ideological and traditional plaintiff is inconsistent with the "sociological realities of litigation"); Bandes, *supra* note 97, at 297–98 (arguing that Brilmayer's approach "sweep[s] too broadly," in that it "exclude[s] nontraditional cases in which sufficient concrete adversity exists," and proposing that the court instead "assess concreteness and adversity in [the] individual case"); Martin H. Redish, *The Passive Virtues, the Countermajoritarian Principle, and the "Judicial-Political" Model of Constitutional Adjudication,* 22 Conn. L. Rev. 647 (1990) (arguing that "imposition of the injury-in-fact prerequisite on litigants," as Brilmayer strongly advocates, "is not an essential element of the judicial aspects of the federal judiciary's function, and may well undermine performance of its important political function," as well as noting that Brilmayer cites no "empirical, psychological or anthropological evidence" in support of her argument that an injured plaintiff is a better advocate than an ideological plaintiff). For scholars making arguments similar to Brilmayer's, see Peters, *supra* note 125, at 426–28 (contending that ideological plaintiffs prevent the court from being able to limit its decisions to "specific facts applied to specific people," and thus require broader decisions, binding more later litigants than necessary); Amy Coney Barrett, *Stare Decisis and Due Process,* 74 U. Colo. L Rev. 1011 (2003) (examining the due process implications of stare decisis, including the preclusive effects that flow from its application).

146. Brilmayer, *supra* note 145, at 302.

147. *Id.* Brilmayer further distinguished the ideological plaintiff from the traditional plaintiff by way of this example:

> [I]magine a citizen in a town that has recently enacted an ordinance prohibiting the posting of campaign signs on residential property. Assume he believes it is unconstitutional to restrict political expression, but has posted no campaign signs himself . . . What can he do? First, he might initiate litigation by alleging his ordinance infringes the first amendment rights of others. His neighbor would put up signs but for the ordinance. Second, he might attempt to show that his own future first amendment rights are threatened. Next year, he may wish to post campaign signs.

Id. at 300. Brilmayer believed that neither the first nor the second option should create a justiciable case under Article III's ripeness and injury-in-fact requirements, which function to prevent merely concerned citizens from "litigat[ing] abstract principles of constitutional law when the precedent established will govern someone else's . . . rights." *Id.* at 308.

148. *Id.* at 307 ("A device somewhat akin to the 'similarity of circumstances' requirement in class actions is at work. [If] the situations are 'indistinguishable,' [the future plaintiff] will be bound.").

149. *See also* discussion *infra* at 211–14. (discussing the role that adversarial incentives play in evidence production).

150. Brilmayer, *supra* note 145, at 298–300.

151. *Id.* at 310. Unlike the position taken here, Brilmayer focused on the "due process problems" created by the preclusive effects that flow from ideological litigation. *But see* discussion *infra* at 201 (explaining that the problem need not rise to

a due process violation in order to constitute an encroachment on the rights upon which a liberal democratic system is founded).

152. Brilmayer, *supra* note 145.

153. Fed. R. Civ. P. 23(e).

154. This may be especially true of adverse class actions that settle. For this reason, one might argue that allowing the settlement class action gives rise to no greater dangers than does allowing settlement of any class action, even those that were adverse at the outset. For reasons I will explain, however, there are significant differences in the degree of danger of absent class members in the two situations. See discussion *infra* at 211–15.

155. See discussion *supra* at 213–14.

156. U.S. Const. Amend. V.

157. The converse is also true. In some instances, due process will not be satisfied, even where the adverseness required by Article III exists, because of inadequate representation in the individual case.

158. In re Fibreboard Corporation, 893 F.2d 706, 710–11 (5th Cir. 1990).

159. Martin H. Redish & Andrew L. Mathews, *Why Punitive Damages Are Unconstitutional*, 53 Emory L.J. 1, 16 (2004).

160. *Id.*

161. The term *private attorney general* is generally used to refer to an attorney in a case where it is clear that " 'the law' should be implemented or enforced—so that we do not need to ask at whose behest or on whose behalf." Jeremy Rabkin, *The Secret Life of the Private Attorney General*, 61 Law & Contemp. Probs. 179, 179, 181 (1998) (also noting that "with sympathetic nurturing from courts and Congress," the private attorney general "form of legal advocacy seemed for a time to be a powerful engine of public policy"); *see also* Trevor W. Morrison, *Private Attorneys General and the First Amendment,* 103 Mich. L. Rev. 589 (2005) (surveying the history of the private attorney general, including the rise of citizen-suit provisions and qui tam suits). *But see* Edward H. Cooper, *The (Cloudy) Future of Class Actions,* 40 Ariz. L. Rev. 923, 944 (1998) (recognizing the argument that "the Enabling Act does not permit adoption of a rule designed to increase deterrence . . . 'It is outside the scope of the Rules Enabling Act for the Advisory Committee to confer upon class counsel the role of a private attorney general.' "). For a different perspective on the private attorney general concept, see Chapter 2, *supra* at 32–35.

One difference between the private individual in the hybrid model and the private attorney general is the relief sought. While this chapter focuses on private damages, most private attorneys general instead tend to seek broad non-monetary relief: "rather than seeking redress for discrete injuries, private attorneys general typically request injunctive or other equitable relief aimed at altering the practices of large institutions." Morrison, *supra* at 590.

162. *See* Chapter 2, *supra* at 26–27 (explaining the history of the bounty hunter, who, "[m]otivated . . . by personal greed," "effectively furthered the public interest by seeking to promote [his] own personal economic interests" by apprehending criminals and wrongdoers). The key difference between the hybrid model and the bounty hunter model is the source of the incentive to litigate. In the hybrid model, the incentive to monitor and punish wrongdoing is natural: it flows from the per-

sonal interest in compensation for one's injuries. In the bounty hunter model, the incentive is artificial: it is the manufactured result of the availability of a reward for apprehending wrongdoers. The bounty hunter, at least in most cases, has suffered no personal injury and thus has no independent interest in the prosecution of wrongdoing. *See also* Morrison, *supra* note 161, at 590 (defining the private attorney general as a "plaintiff who sues to vindicate public interests not directly connected to any special stake of her own").

163. *See* discussion *supra* at 200–01.

164. *See* discussion *supra* at 192–93.

165. U.S. Const. Art. II § 3.

166. Martin H. Redish, *Separation of Powers, Judicial Authority, and the Scope of Article III: The Troubling Cases of Morrison and Mistretta,* 39 DePaul L. Rev. 299, 315 (1990) [herein after *"Morrison & Mistretta"*].

167. Keller v. Potomac Electric Power Co., 261 U.S. 428, 443-44 (1923) (holding that the judicial branch cannot be granted appellate or original jurisdiction over the valuation of public utilities—a function it defined as inherently administrative and noted was best performed by the Public Utilities Commission).

168. United States v. Todd (unpublished case reported in United States v. Ferreira, 54 U.S. 40 (1852)).

169. *Hayburn's Case* arose when the Circuit Courts for the districts of New York, Pennsylvania, and North Carolina all refused to perform the functions delegated to them by the Act of 23d of March, including the examination of soldiers' pension claims. The Court held that pension administration was not a proper judicial function, primarily because the courts' decisions were subject to revision by the executive branch. In response, Congress amended the law, setting forth a nonjudicial mode of taking testimony but nevertheless providing a method through which to obtain "an adjudication of the Supreme Court on the validity of [the pension] rights." *Ferreira,* 54 U.S. at 52 (discussing United States v. Todd).

170. *Id.* at 52.

171. *Id.* at 53.

172. *Id.* at 53.

173. 488 U.S. 361 (1989).

174. 487 U.S. 654 (1988).

175. I have in the past seriously questioned the wisdom of both decisions. *See generally* Redish, *Morrison & Mistretta, supra* note 166.

176. 488 U.S. at 402.

177. *Mistretta,* 488 U.S. at 394, n.20. *Morrison* and *Mistretta* both discussed a number of non-adjudicatory functions traditionally performed by Article III courts, including the issuing of search warrants and the supervision of grand juries. *See* Mistretta v. United States, 488 U.S. 361, 390 (1989); Morrison v. Olson, 487 U.S. 654, 681 n.20 (1988). However, these functions are easily distinguished from the non-adversarial administrative functions rejected in *Todd* and *Ferreira.* The issuing of a search warrant and supervision of a grand jury alike are incidental to underlying adversarial proceedings between the state and criminal defendant, and in furtherance of the adjudication of an adversarial case. The same cannot be said of claim administration. *See also* Redish, *Morrison & Mistretta, supra* note 166;

at 315 (noting that the hiring of law clerks—another non-adjudicatory function discussed by the *Morrison* and *Mistretta* Courts—is a function "ancillary to the effective performance of the adjudicatory function that lead[s] to no direct, legally binding effect on society"); *id.* at 303 (also arguing that *Morrison* and *Mistretta* should be viewed "with considerable concern," given the Court's willingness to disregard the role of separation of powers as "an effective prophylactic tool for assuring the appropriate interaction of the different branches").

It could be argued that a similar situation arises in the context of bankruptcy proceedings, given that, like the claims proceedings in *Ferreira,* most Title 11 actions are uncontroverted. *See* Douglas G. Baird & Thomas H. Jackson, CASES, PROBLEMS & MATERIALS ON BANKRUPTCY 1 (2d Ed. 1990) ("The legal proceeding [in bankruptcy] of the typical individual who asks for a discharge is an uncontested affair . . . There is nothing to fight over."); Robert E. DeMascio, et al., FOURTEEN YEARS OR LIFE: THE BANKRUPTCY COURT DILEMMA 1 (1983) (same); Avery, *supra* note 155, at 400 (arguing that the Bankruptcy Code "frequently give[s] rise to cases that fail to comply with the case or controversy requirement of Article III"); *see also* Kilen v. United States, 129 B.R. 538, 542 (N.D. Ill. Bankr. 1991) (explaining that although bankruptcy judges are not Article III judges, they "are statutorily deemed to be 'unit[s] of the district court' " and thus must meet Article III requirements). Given the complexity of the subject matter and the fact that the Supreme Court has not spoken directly on this question, the constitutionality of bankruptcy proceedings reaches far beyond the scope of this chapter. It suffices to note that the bankruptcy scheme is a narrow exception to the adverseness requirement. Surely no one would argue that this exception consumes the general rule that in order for a suit to be justiciable, the parties must enjoy an adversarial relationship. Similarly, the Court has never suggested that the presence of bankruptcy distribution in the federal courts somehow voids the adverseness requirement in other contexts or affects its adverseness jurisprudence as a whole. The unique nature of bankruptcy, as distinguished from other non-adversarial litigation like the settlement class, has been recognized by courts and scholars alike. In bankruptcy, the presence of adverseness is a case-by-case inquiry. Because the creditor is always a *possible* adverse party, some bankruptcy cases will be adversarial while others will not, rendering any *ex ante* determination as to adverseness impossible. *See* Thomas Galligan, Jr., *Article III and The "Related To" Bankruptcy Jurisdiction: A Case Study in Protective Jurisdiction,* 11 U. Puget Sound L. Rev. 1, 39 n.145 (1987) (analogizing bankruptcy to the fact pattern in *Tutun v. United States,* 270 U.S. 568, 577 (1926), where the Court held naturalization proceedings to be justiciable because the United States is always a "possible adverse party"); Susan Block Lieb, *The Case Against Supplemental Bankruptcy Jurisdiction: A Constitutional, Statutory, and Policy Analysis,* 62 Fordham L. Rev. 721, 773 n. 301 (1994) (same). The same is not true of the settlement class: *all* settlement classes are, by definition, non-adversarial, given that the parties agree on desired outcome before coming to court.

178. Steven Calabresi, *Some Normative Arguments for the Unitary Executive,* 48 Ark. L. Rev. 23, 67 (1995) (explaining that "[b]ad poll ratings, unfavorable results in special or midterm elections, and negative constituent feedback all have a way

of rapidly pulling presidents and their unelected aides and subordinates back onto the majority coalition's electoral bandwagon"); *see also* THE FEDERALIST NO. 70, at 479 (Alexander Hamilton) (discussing these fundamental checks).

179. *See* discussion *supra* at 190–91.

180. *See* discussion *supra at* 190.

181. This is true regardless of whether the settlement class was preceded by a reverse auction or an inventory settlement. While the courts that have addressed the constitutionality of the settlement class have focused on whether settlement negotiations were "collusive," or alternatively, conducted at arms-length, *see* In re Asbestos Litigation, 90 F.3d 963, 988–89 (5th Cir. 1996), this position is inherently flawed. It assumes that Article III bans merely criminal fraud or conspiratorial cooperation between plaintiff and defendant, whereas in reality it is far more broad. By its plain language, Article III bans all suits that—at the time that they are presented to the court—have already been resolved by the parties. Article III, *Poe v. Ullman* reminds us, renders unfit for adjudication "any cause that 'is not in any real sense adversary,' that 'does not assume the 'honest and actual antagonistic assertion of rights' to be adjudicated—a safeguard essential to the integrity of the judicial process.'" 367 U.S. 497, 505–06 (1961); *see* discussion *supra* at 188–89 (discussing the distinction between the term, "collusion" as employed by civil procedure scholars and "collusion" as defined by Article III).

182. *See also* Carrington & Apanovitch, *supra* note 49, at 463 ("[T]he proposed rule [Rule 23(b)(4) [which would have authorized certification of a class for settlement-only] applies only to matters that will never be the subject of litigation in a federal court. It has nothing to do with the Article III mission of deciding cases or controversies, but is instead a means of promoting and endorsing putative private dispositions by lending them the imprimatur of the court, thus garbing contracts in the dress of judgments.").

183. One could argue that the absent class members are still adverse to the defendant, despite the fact that agreement as to the case's desired outcome is reached between class and defense counsel. However, until certification, there *is* no "class"; while absent parties may have *potential* claims against the defendant, prior to certification they have sued no one and are legally not parties to the suit until the class is certified. Yet given the inherently conditional nature of the settlement class, once the class is certified and the absent class members do become parties, the case is automatically settled, thereby precluding any adversity between absent class members and the defendant.

184. *See* discussion *supra* at 177–78 (noting that a "settlement class" encompasses all cases where a request for settlement is filed at the same time as a request for class certification, regardless of when the complaint is filed).

185. *See* discussion *supra* at 190–91 (explaining the inherent ambiguity of the word *case,* although noting that some clarity is achieved when one limits its definition to a legal context).

186. *See* discussion *supra* at 191.

187. 513 U.S. 18 (1994).

188. *Id.* at 18; *see also* Avery, *supra* note 116, at 409 ("[Under *Bancorp,*] [a]s a general rule, all settled issues in a case are moot. Although the court lacks jurisdiction

to decide the merits of any issue which has been settled, it retains jurisdiction to enter a judgment, dismiss or take any other action necessary to dispose of the case.").

189. Glidden v. Chromalloy Am. Corp., 808 F.2d 621, 626–27 (7th Cir. 1986) (explaining that absent class members are not bound by judgments issued prior to certification).

190. Of course, merely because the class settlement is, as a general matter, constitutional under the Article III adverseness requirement does not mean that all class settlements are legitimate. The class settlement may still pose structural difficulties, wholly apart from its adverseness, which are beyond the scope of this chapter.

191. Fed. R. Civ. P. 23(e) (2007) ("The claims, issues, or defenses of a certified class may be settled only with the court's approval.").

192. In re Asbestos Litigation, 90 F.3d 963, 988-89 (5th Cir. 1996); *see also* In re Orthopedic Bone Screw Products, 176 F.R.D. 158 (E.D. Pa. 1997) (finding no violation of Article III because up until the time of certification and settlement, the parties were adverse).

193. Muskrat v. United States, 219 U.S. 346, 357 (1911) ("[Case or controversy] implies the existence of *present* or possible adverse parties."); Brief of Respondents White Lung Association, *Amchem Prods., Inc. v. Windsor,* No. 96–270, 1996 U.S. Briefs 270 (arguing that a "case or controversy cannot be supplied by prior adversity between the same," given that "Article III compels the Court to look beyond the pleadings to the actual state of affairs *when the case is filed* in deciding whether the parties' interests are sufficiently adverse").

194. *See, e.g.,* Lake Coal Co., Inc. v. Roberts & Schaeffer Co., 474 U.S. 120, 120 (1985) (dismissing the case on appeal due to the "complete settlement of the underlying causes of action").

195. See, e.g., Cleveland v. Chamberlain, 66 U.S. 419 (1862).

196. In this way, the settlement class strongly resembles the fact pattern in *Cleveland v. Chamberlain,* 66 U.S. 419 (1862), where the Court rejected as nonjusticiable a suit in which the plaintiff bought out the defendant, such that the interests on both sides of the dispute were one and the same. The Court held that the plaintiff's only remaining interest in the outcome of the suit was to bind the interests of third parties not before the court. "It is plain that this is no adversary proceeding," the Court wrote. "Chamberlain becomes the sole party in interest on both sides, makes up a record, and has a case made to suit himself, in order that he may obtain an opinion of this court, affecting the rights and interests of persons not parties to the pretended controversy." *Id.* at 426 (concluding that this constituted "punishable contempt of court").

197. *See* discussion *supra* at 185–87 (describing the inventory settlement and reverse auction). Moreover, because absent class members are inherently passive in the negotiation and certification process, they do not have a chance to assert their own interests.

198. *See* discussion *supra* at 211–15. (contrasting the active role played by the parties in an adversary system with the passive role played by the judicial decision maker).

199. For courts that have recognized the information deficit that flows from the settlement class's non-adverseness, see, e.g., Plummer v. Chemical Bank, 668 F.2d 654 (2d Cir. 1982) (holding that the trial court record was insufficient to "support a responsible finding that the settlement was fair, reasonable, and adequate" and suggesting that the non-adverseness of the settlement class was to blame for the information deficit); Pettway v. American Cast Iron Pipe Co., 576 F.2d 1157, 1169 (5th Cir. 1978); In re General Motors Corp. Pick-Up Truck Fuel Tank Products Liability Litigation, 55 F.3d 768, 789–90 (3d Cir. 1995).

200. In re General Motors Corp. Pick-Up Truck Fuel Tank Products Liability Litigation, 55 F.3d 768, 789–90 (3d Cir. 1995).

201. *Id.* (explaining that the information deficit is far worse in a settlement class, where the "motion for certification and settlement are presented simultaneously," than in a post-certification class settlement).

202. Pettway v. American Cast Iron Pipe Co., 576 F.2d 1157, 1169 (5th Cir. 1978).

203. *See* discussion *supra* at 286–87. (describing the reverse auction). The reverse auction is unique to negotiations that occur pre-certification. It is the result of competition among plaintiffs' attorneys for position as class counsel and the attendant right to file a complaint on behalf of the class.

204. *See* discussion *supra* at 186–87 (describing the inventory settlement).

205. *Amchem* exacerbated this situation by drawing a distinction between settlement and litigation classes, holding that the former did not need to meet manageability standards to be certified. *See* Amchem Prods., Inc. v. Windsor, 521 U.S. 591, 620 (1997). Because many mass torts actions, given their size and the presence of individualized questions, present a problem of manageability, they are certifiable for settlement only, preventing the plaintiffs' attorney from being able to threaten to litigate the class claim—even when the defendant's settlement offer is well below expected market value.

206. *Cf.* Leandra Lederman, *Precedent Lost: Why Encourage Settlement, and Why Permit Non-Party Involvement in Settlements,* 75 Notre Dame L. Rev. 221, 228–29 (1999) ("Economic models of settlement assume that the parties derive a settlement amount from the likely amount the court will award if the case is tried. In other words, if the two parties to a case were to agree, for example, that after trial the court will definitely award the plaintiff $20,000, but it will cost each side $4,000 to bring the case to trial, then the parties could save time and money by settling for some where between $16,000 (what the plaintiff would net from trial) and $24,000 (what the defendant would spend in damages plus litigation costs).""). *But see* George L. Priest & Benjamin Klein, *The Selection of Disputes for Litigation,* 13 J. Legal Studies 1 (1984) (arguing that economic models of settlement are distorted by party optimism and other estimation errors).

207. In re General Motors Corp. Pick-Up Truck Fuel Tank Products Liability Litigation, 55 F.3d 768, 790 (3d Cir. 1995) ("Because certification so dramatically increases the potential value of the suit to the plaintiffs and their attorneys as well as the potential liability of the defendant, the parties will frequently contest certification vigorously.").

208. *See* discussion *supra* at 211–14 (surveying scholarly work showing that party-controlled evidentiary dispute facilitates truth finding). The same argument

applies equally to other motions and briefs, including but not limited to those that accompany certification. When a suit is adversarial at its inception, the court benefits from the multiple formal filings that precede settlement, which enable it to evaluate the underlying legitimacy of the claims and defenses in the case. This ultimately allows the judge to more accurately assess whether the settlement represent a fair estimation of the worth of the class's claims. *Cf.* Rhonda Wasserman, *Dueling Class Actions,* 80 B.U. L. Rev. 461, 480 (2000) (noting that the information deficit stemming from dueling class actions is "less severe when the parties reach a settlement after having engaged in some adversarial proceedings before the court").

209. Willging, *supra* note 6, at 26 ("Settlement classes are difficult for the court to evaluate because of the lack of an adversarial proceeding on class certification. Complicated issues, such as conflicts between class counsel and counsel or individual plaintiffs or the need to protect future claimants, may challenge the court").

210. Wasserman, *supra* note 208, at 483 (noting that objectors are likely to alleviate some of the "informational deficiencies inherent in class action settlements," although speaking in the context of dueling federal/state classes where there is a disincentive "to take discovery on the facts underlying the federal claims").

211. Willging, *supra* note 6, at 10; *see also id.* at 56 ("[Rates of participation by absent class members were] 11%, 0%, 9%, and 5% of the cases in the four districts . . . In all four districts, a total of six nonmembers of an alleged class attempted to intervene."). This low level of participation pervaded fairness hearings as well. *Id.* at 57 ("[N]onrepresentative parties were recorded as attending the settlement hearing infrequently, with 14% in E.D. Pa. being the high mark and the other three districts showing 7% to 11% rates of participation.").

212. Alexandra Lahav, *Fundamental Principles for Class Action Governance,* 37 Ind. L. Rev. 65, 85 (2003). The availability of objectors is a critical distinction between the settlement class and post-certification class settlement. Insofar as the quick pace of and lack of public information available in most settlement classes discourages objectors, when settlement occurs post-certification, objectors have an opportunity to compile a motion for intervention and to provide the court with critical information on the benefits and disadvantages of the class format.

213. *See, e.g.,* Walker v. Bayer Corp., 1999 U.S. Dist. LEXIS 10060 (N.D. Ill. 1999).

214. *See* In re General Motors Corp. Pick-Up Truck Fuel Tank Products Liability Litigation, 55 F.3d 768, 788 (3d Cir. 1995) (citing In re Joint Eastern & Southern District Asbestos Litig., 129 Bankr. 710, 802 (E. & S.D.N.Y. 1991)) ("[In a settlement class] [t]here is in fact little or no individual client consultation."); *see also* Macey & Miller, *Plaintiffs' Attorney's Role, supra* note 64, at 5 (offering a general criticism of relying on named plaintiffs: "The named plaintiff does little—indeed, usually does nothing—to monitor the attorney in order to ensure that representation is competent or zealous.")

215. Specifically, for courts that have noted that collusive behavior in the settlement class raises (a)(4) adequacy issues, see Amchem v. Windsor, 521 U.S. 591 (1997); In re Diet Drugs, 2000 U.S. Dist. LEXIS 12275 (E.D. Pa. 2000); In re Bronco II Litigation, 1995 U.S. Dist. LEXIS 3507, at *23 (E.D. La. 1995).

216. *See* discussion *supra* at 209–10.

217. *See* discussion *supra* at 214–15.

218. *See* G. Chin Chao, *Securities Class Actions and Due Process,* 1996 Colum. Bus. L. Rev. 547 (1996) (summarizing these approaches and examples of each).

219. *Id.* at 571.

220. *Id.* at 572–74.

221. *Id.* at 566–70.

222. See United States v. Johnson, 319 U.S. 302 (1943).

223. *See, e.g.,* Jean Sternlight, *As Mandatory Binding Arbitration Meets the Class Action, Will the Class Action Survive,* 42 Wm. & Mary L. Rev. 1, 33 (2000) (arguing that due process problems that flow from binding unrepresented absent class members to a class agreement can be remedied through Rule 23 judicial supervision over the formulation and operation of the class action).

224. There are some examples of "active" courts that, because of the absence of information on the terms and fairness of settlement, have rejected the settlement class after a fairness hearing. *See, e.g.,* Plummer v. Chemical Bank, 668 F.2d 654 (2d Cir. 1982) (concluding that the record was insufficient to "support a responsible finding that the settlement was fair, reasonable, and adequate" and remanding for further development of the record). However, even the rejection of a settlement class can be problematic. Specifically, it implicates the hybrid model, under which the decision to address the fairness of the settlement outside the confines of an adversarial dispute works a change in the foundation of underlying substantive law. It also implicates the litigant-oriented interest in being free from unfair preclusion: even when the settlement is rejected, the court's judgment regarding the unacceptability of class certification is binding on class members, evoking concern about the class representative's proper advancement of the interests of absent but bound individuals.

225. *See* discussion *supra* at 214–15 (outlining the limitations on a judge's investigatory abilities in an adversary system).

226. In re General Motors Corp. Pick-Up Truck Fuel Tank Products Liability Litigation, 55 F.3d 768, 786 (3d Cir. 1995).

227. See discussion *supra* at 185–87.

228. *Cf.* Phillips Petroleum v. Shutts, 472 U.S. 797 (1985) (holding that failure to opt-out is consent to jurisdiction in a particular forum). *But see* Brilmayer, *supra* note 145, at 298 (noting that Article III's case-or-controversy requirement is not waivable: if there is no "case-or-controversy, "courts are without power to proceed, regardless of the wishes of the parties"); Commodity Futures Trading Comm. v. Schor, 478 U.S. 833, 849–51 (1986) (holding that while the individual interest in impartial adjudication can be waived, the structural guarantees of Article III cannot).

229. Cooper, *supra* note 161, at 936; *see also* Chapter 2 (arguing that inertia warrants a rule requiring affirmative "opt-in" instead of "opt-out"). For example, opt-out requires the class member to take a number of affirmative steps: she must open her mail; fill out a form; and then send it back. Each required step lessens the probability that the individual will actually seize the opportunity to exclude herself from the class.

230. Rule 23(e)(3) is inapplicable to the settlement class, given that certification and settlement approval occur simultaneously. *See* The Report of the Judicial Conference Committee on the Rules of Practice and Procedure to the Chief Justice of the United States and Members of the Judicial Conference of the United States, Proposed Amendments to the Federal Rules of Civil Procedure, Advisory Committee Notes to Proposed Amendment Rule 23(e)(3) (effective Dec. 2003) (noting that Rule 23(e)(3) does not apply when the "class is certified and settlement is reached in circumstances that lead to simultaneous notice of certification and notice of settlement. In these cases, the basic opportunity to elect exclusion applies without further complication.").

231. *Id.*

232. In re General Motors Corp. Pick-Up Truck Fuel Tank Products Liability Litigation, 55 F.3d 768, 789 (3d Cir. 1995). This is especially true in small claim classes, where maximum possible recovery on the claim is often less than the cost of bringing individual suit, rendering the right to opt-out futile.

233. *See, e.g.,* Muskrat v. United States, 219 U.S. 346 (1911); United States v. Johnson, 319 U.S. 302 (1943).

234. In re Fibreboard Corporation, 893 F.2d 706, 710–11 (5th Cir. 1990) (explaining that the "adversarial backdrop," against which Congress legislates, is a "way of proceeding [that] reflect[s] far more than habit": "[It] reflect[s] the very culture of the jury trial and the case-or-controversy requirement of Article III").

235. *See* Chapter 2, *supra* (discussing the bounty hunter model of class actions).

236. *See* discussion *supra* at 221–22 (describing the "administrative compensation" model and its implications).

237. One could argue that in some settlement classes, the court plays only a minimal role in the creation and implementation of a distribution scheme—tasks that are instead performed by the private parties. For example, in *Amchem,* the parties proposed that the administrative compensation scheme would be run by the conglomeration of defendants, and that this group would, on the basis of information provided by individual claimants, make all final determinations as to the claimant's level of injury and corresponding level of compensation. *Amchem,* 521 U.S. 591. Despite the semi-private nature of this scheme, it nevertheless poses constitutional difficulty. First, the court still supervises the distribution of resources, which constitutes judicial exercise of an executive function. Second, even if this is not true, and instead private parties are actually responsible for all distribution decisions in the absence of court supervision, the settlement class effectively concedes executive authority to private parties. The implementation of a non-adversarial administrative compensation scheme is the exclusive responsibility of the executive branch. Giving government sanction to the settlement agreement and terms of implementation, the court transfers authority that rightfully belongs to another branch to private persons, jeopardizing the liberal democratic system. Specifically, private individuals lack the "objectivity and accountability" necessary to control the exercise of the power of resource allocation, threatening the interests of both absent class members and the public-at-large:

> [In taking on a purely public power,] private actors do not simultaneously assume the constitutional and political restrictions traditionally imposed on

those who exercise pure public power. Instead, the private actors remain free to ground all of their decisionmaking—both strategic and formal—on their assessment of how best to advance their own private interests, free from the ethical, political, and constitutional constraints imposed on public actors.

Redish & Mathews, *supra* note 159, at 4. One could argue that, in this regard, the settlement class is no different from a traditional settlement, where the distribution of resources pursuant to their private agreement would also be left to the private parties, to be carried out as they saw fit. However, the non-class settlement does not receive judicial sanction. Rather, upon settlement, the court merely dismisses the suit; the implementation of the agreement is an exercise of a purely private power, regulated by state contract law. In contrast, the settlement class is a governmental directive. The parties choose to bring their non-adversarial agreement to the court to secure Article III approval of the distribution arrangement. And once the court certifies the class for settlement, the settlement requires government approval to bind the thousands of absent class members whose interests are at stake. The terms of settlement are then embodied in a court order—a judicially mandated administrative compensation scheme.

238. United States v. Ferreira, 54 U.S. 40, 46–47 (1852); *see also id.* at 49 (holding that the lower court proceedings were non-adversarial, given that no party was required to appear on behalf of the United States).

239. *See* discussion *supra* at 208 (summarizing the *Bancorp* rule).

240. *See* discussion *supra* at 213–14 (explaining that adversarial litigation on Rule 23 prerequisites is one manifestation of the parties' adverseness in a post-certification class settlement).

241. Steven Calabresi & Kevin Rhodes, *The Structural Constitution: Unitary Executive, Plural Judiciary,* 105 Harv. L. Rev. 1153, 1189 (1992) (noting that Article II may reserve executive power exclusively for the executive branch, "just as [some argue that] the Article III Vesting Clause designates, identifies, and describes the Supreme and inferior Article III courts as the only proper recipients of federal judicial power"); *see also* Steven Calabresi & Saikrishna B. Prakash, *The President's Power to Execute the Laws,* 104 Yale L.J. 541 (1994) (making a textual case for a unitary executive).

242. Even if one were to conclude—despite clear evidence to the contrary—that the settlement class does not trample on the executive sphere, it nevertheless does not constitute a "judicial function," given its non-adverseness in violation of Article III.

243. *See* Richard J. Pierce, Jr., *Chevron and its Aftermath: Judicial Review of Agency Interpretations of Statutory Provisions,* 41 Vand. L. Rev. 301, 307–08 (1988) ("Because agencies are more accountable to the electorate than courts, agencies should have the dominant role in policy making when the choice is between agencies and courts."); Spann, *supra* note 121, at 636 (explaining that the judiciary is "insulated purposely from immediate political accountability"). *Cf.* Mistretta, 488 U.S. at 393, 394 n.20 (reserving the question of whether non-adjudicatory activities are appropriate for bodies that "enjoy the constitutionally mandated autonomy of courts"—a scenario not encompassed by the terms of the Sentencing Act, given

that "the [Sentencing] Commission is fully accountable to Congress, which can revoke or amend any or all of the Guidelines as it sees fit.").

244. *See* discussion *supra* at 197.

245. *See* Calabresi, *Normative Arguments, supra* note 178, at 65 ("Even leaving aside conflicts of interest, it is inherently difficult for one person to do two jobs. Yet, that is what is demanded if we rely on members of Congress or judges to perform the executive tasks that the Constitution leaves to the President and his agents.").

246. Amchem Prods., Inc. v. Windsor, 521 U.S. 591, 633, 636–39 (1997) (Breyer, J., dissenting) (concluding that any problems with regard to conflicts of interests among class members were endemic to "toxic tort cases," and that the likelihood of *some* type of compensation under the terms of the settlement agreement—compensation that was unlikely in the absence of settlement—rendered the agreement inherently "fair").

247. *See* John A. Siliciano, *Mass Torts And The Rhetoric Of Crisis,* 80 Cornell L. Rev. 990 (1995) (arguing that the threat posed by mass torts to the court system—in terms of docket pressures—is greatly overblown; indeed, the "perception that mass tort cases present 'special' problems . . . may arise not from the cases themselves, but from the threshold decision to [how] view them").

248. *Cf.* In re Fibreboard Corp., 893 F.2d 706 (5th Cir. 1990) (rejecting the argument that statistical sampling is the "only realistic way of trying [the class action]" as irrelevant); In re Joint Eastern and Southern District Asbestos Litigation in Keene Corp., 14 F.3d 726 (2d Cir. 1993) (rejecting the argument that proceeding by way of a 23(b)(1)(B) class was far more efficient than filing in a bankruptcy court, given that the latter was statutorily mandated: "[T]he function of federal courts is not to conduct trials over whether a statutory scheme should be ignored because a more efficient mechanism can be fashioned by judges").

249. Gene Nichol, Jr., *Ripeness and the Constitution,* 54 U. Chi. L. Rev. 153, 160 (1987) (describing the Court's jurisprudence); *see also* Whitmore v. Arkansas, 495 U.S. 149, 161 (1990) ("[P]etitioner argues next that the Court should create an exception to traditional standing doctrine for this case. The uniqueness of the death penalty and society's interest in its proper imposition, he maintains, justify a relaxed application of standing principles. The short answer to this suggestion is that the requirements of an Article III 'case-or-controversy' is not merely a tradition 'rule of practice,' but rather is imposed directly by the Constitution. It is not for this Court to employ untethered notions of what might be good public policy to expand our jurisdiction in an appealing case."); Bickel, *supra* note 104 at 49 (quoting Herbert Weschler, *Toward Neutral Principles of Constitutional Law,* in Wechsler, PRINCIPLES, POLITICS AND FUNDAMENTAL LAW) ("Professor Herbert Weschler . . . offers this formulation: " 'I put it to you that the main constituent of this judicial process is precisely that it must be genuinely principled . . . A choice of competing values is reflected in legislative and executive action, and it is this choice that the Court must consider in light of its own value judgment; but what is critical 'is not the nature of the question, but the nature of the answer that may validity be given by the courts.' For the courts, the answer may not proceed from expediency.").

250. Valley Forge v. Americans United for Separation of Church and State, Inc., 454 U.S. 464, 489 (1982).

251. *See* discussion *supra* at 210–14.

252. *See supra* text accompanying notes 81–87 (describing the effects of the reverse auction and inventory settlement); *see also supra* notes 35–38, 240–41, 334 and accompanying text (explaining that even if in some cases, class counsel may desire to protect the interests of absent class members, there is no way—ex ante—to determine which settlement classes are fair and which are not).

253. Morrison v. Olson, 487 U.S. 654 (1988).

254. Commodity Futures Trading Comm. v. Schor, 478 U.S. 833 (1986).

255. Mistretta v. United States, 488 U.S. 361 (1989).

256. Laura S. Fitzgerald, *Cadenced Power: The Kinetic Constitution,* 46 Duke L.J. 679, 705 (1997). This position reflects a "functionalist" approach towards the separation of powers. *See also Mistretta,* 488 U.S. at 381 (1989) (holding that only when "the whole power of one department is exercised by the same hands which possess the whole power of another department" are "the fundamental principles of a free constitution . . . subverted") (quoting THE FEDERALIST NO. 47 (James Madison)). Functionalism can be contrasted with formalism, which "posits perfect identity between the three categories of power and the Constitution's three decisionmaking institutions," and "tolerates no task-sharing among [them]. *See* Redish & Cisar, *supra* note 15, at 474; *Mistretta,* 488 U.S. at 426 (Scalia, J., dissenting) ("In designing [the constitutional] structure, the Framers *themselves* considered how much commingling was, in the generality of things, acceptable, and set forth their conclusions in the document.").

257. The Court's doctrine in this area, however, reflects a certain amount of eclecticism, given its contemporaneous application of both the formalist and the functionalist approach to separation of powers. For explanations of how to reconcile the Court's jurisprudence in this area, see Matthew Tanielian, Comment, *Separation Of Powers And The Supreme Court: One Doctrine, Two Visions,* 8 Admin. L.J. Am. U. 961 (1995) (noting that when the "challenged action 'encroaches upon a power that the text of the Constitution commits in explicit terms to [another branch],'" the Court applies a formalist approach, but when "the power at issue was not explicitly assigned by the text of the Constitution," the Court applies functionalism); Timothy Hui, Note, *A Tier-ful Revelation,* 34 Wm. & Mary L. Rev. 1403 (1993) (explaining that the Court consistently applies a formalist analysis when Congress is overreaching, and applies functionalism when judicial or executive self-aggrandizement is in question). *But see* Ronald Krotoszynski, *On the Danger of Wearing Two Hats:* Mistretta *and* Morrison *Revisited,* 38 Wm. & Mary L. Rev. 417 (1997) (critiquing the Court's distinction between legislative aggrandizement on the one hand and judicial or executive aggrandizement on the other, arguing that "[t]he Court has it precisely backwards").

258. Redish, *Morrison & Mistretta, supra* note 166, at 306.

259. Redish & Cisar, *supra* note 15, at 463–64.

260. *Id.*

261. *Id.* at 463.

262. *Id.* at 465 ("[I]t is all but impossible to ascertain the concrete likelihood of the danger occurring, until it has actually occurred, and then it will be too late for effective remedial action.").

263. Redish, *Morrison & Mistretta, supra* note 166, at 303.

7. CONCLUSION: THE ROLE OF LIBERAL THEORY IN THE CLASS ACTION DEBATE

1. *See generally* Chapter 2, *supra.*

2. Fed. R. Civ. P. 23.

3. 28 U.S.C. § 2072.

4. U.S. Const. Art. I, § 7. *See generally* Chapter 3, *supra.*

5. *See* Chapter 6, *supra.*

6. U.S. Const. Amend. V. *See* Chapter 5, *supra.*

7. *See* Chapter 6, *supra.*

8. *See* Chapter 4, *supra.*

9. *See* Chapter 1, *supra.*

10. *See id.*

11. *See* Chapter 5, *supra.* Under this compelling interest standard, only mandatory classes authorized by Rule 23 (b)(1)(A) should be found constitutional, because the defining characteristic of this category is the unfairness and untenability that might result to the party opposing the class absent class treatment. *See* Chapter 5, *supra.*

12. *See generally* Chapter 2, Chapter 3, *supra.*

Table of Cases

Index

The authorized representative in the EU for product safety and compliance is:
Mare Nostrum Group
B.V Doelen 72
4831 GR Breda
The Netherlands

www.ingramcontent.com/pod-product-compliance
Lightning Source LLC
Chambersburg PA
CBHW021550210326
41599CB00010B/379